ENGLAND, THEIR ENGLAND

ENGLAND, THEIR ENGLAND

Commentaries on English Language and Literature

DENIS DONOGHUE

University of California Press
Berkeley • Los Angeles • London

University of California Press
Berkeley and Los Angeles
University of California Press, Ltd.
London, England

Owing to limitations of space, all acknowledgements for permission to
reprint previously published material can be found on pages 364–65.

Library of Congress Cataloging-in-Publication Data

Donoghue, Denis.
    England, their England : commentaries on English language and
literature / Denis Donoghue.
        p.   cm.
    Reprint. Originally published: New York : Knopf, 1988.
    ISBN 0-520-06692-8 (alk. paper)
    1. English literature—History and criticism.   I. Title.
PR99.D66   1989
820.9—dc20   89-4962
                                                           CIP

Manufactured in the United States of America
First California Paperback Printing 1989

For Frances

CONTENTS

Contents

INTRODUCTION

England, Their England is a selection of my essays on English literature and criticism. Most of them have been published in journals: *The New York Review of Books, The New York Times Book Review, The London Review of Books, The Sewanee Review, The Times Literary Supplement, Raritan.* Some were written as chapters of books on a particular author: Sterne, Jane Austen, Dickens, D. H. Lawrence, Ford Madox Ford, George Orwell. A few pieces have not been published before. The one on Empson's "Arachne" is distantly related to an early essay, but I have rewritten it. Mostly, I've left the material pretty much as it was published. A few sentences which seemed worthy when I wrote them have been deleted.

The book is a companion to my *We Irish* (1986) and *Reading America* (1987). I had some misgiving about dividing my occasional writings along national lines, but in the end decided that I could not make a disposition that would be much better. There was a time when I felt intimidated by critics who argued for a global sense of literature. Over the years, however, it has become clear that membership in the European Economic Community, the United Nations, and other international bodies has done much to intensify the conviction of national differences among the member states. I see no evidence that nationalism is a diminished sentiment. I am interested in literary relations, especially those between the literatures of Ireland, England, and the United States, but a relation between two entities is pointless if it blurs the differences between them. This is not an argument against Comparative Literature.

Most of my essays are fairly short. Indeed, the review-essay is one of my favourite forms: it seems to me to offer a welcome mixture of freedom and constraint. I don't know what I would do, given complete freedom; and I enjoy coping with what amounts to constraint.

D.D.

ENGLAND, THEIR ENGLAND

THE STORY OF ENGLISH

I

On September 22, 1986, BBC 2 showed the first of a series of programmes called *The Story of English*. The programmes were designed to show how English has developed into an international language and to indicate some of the social consequences which arise from that fact. About 350 million people speak English as their mother tongue, and perhaps 400 million—some scholars in the sociology of English claim that the true figure is 650 million—use English as their second language: that is, they speak something else at home but their jobs require them to communicate in English. The TV programmes offered to explain how this situation has come about and to consider its social and political bearings.

To accompany the programmes, BBC Publications and Faber and Faber published a lavishly illustrated book under the same title, *The Story of English*.[1] It was written by the novelist and publisher Robert McCrum in collaboration with the TV producer William Cran. Robert MacNeil, who narrated the programmes, contributed so much to the Canadian and American aspects of the subject that he shares with McCrum and Cran the credit of authorship. But McCrum was evidently "first among equals," and in the talk on BBC Radio 3 which I gave in some loose and unofficial relation to the series, I referred to the book as if it were entirely McCrum's work. The talk was shorter and smoother than the version here printed.

The story of English is one of diversity and proliferation. The diversity is well illustrated by the front cover of Robert McCrum's book, which takes pleasure in multiplicity of instances: it has photographs of the Union Jack, the Stars and Stripes, Dr. Martin Luther King, Bob Marley, and the landscape of the moon; cameos of Samuel Johnson and Abraham Lincoln; signatures of Virginia Woolf and T. S. Eliot; the logo of IBM, an engraving of Shakespeare, several woodcuts; and a pinup photograph of Betty Grable.

The history of the English language would be easy to tell if it coincided at every point with the activities of one race upon one island. But it didn't even begin with such coherence. The first chapters of McCrum's book describe the several invasions of Britain by the Angles, the Saxons, and the Jutes in the fifth century, the Christian missionaries in the last years of the sixth, the Viking invasions at the end of the eighth, the Norman invasion in 1066, and the two hundred years thereafter in which English might have capitulated to French and Latin. It was only in the thirteenth century that English was finally established as the governing language of Britain, the symbol of its destiny.

Even then, English was not regarded as at all comparable to Latin, French, and Italian for precision and eloquence. If you wanted to say something grave and enduring, you said it in Latin; if you aspired to elegance, you wrote in French. But the interval between Chaucer and Shakespeare—say between *The Canterbury Tales,* about 1387, and *Hamlet,* about 1603—was the period of supreme development and assimilation. Indeed, Sir Philip Sidney felt himself ready to claim, in 1595, that English was now "capable of any excellent exercising of it." It was a mingled language, compounded chiefly of Anglo-Saxon and Latin elements, and all the better for that. "For the uttering sweetly and properly the conceit of the minde, which is the end of speech," Sidney claimed, English "hath it equally with any other tongue in the world."

That was the language which Sir Walter Ralegh brought, along with his broad Devonshire accent, to America in 1584: it marked the first phase of colonization which culminated in the settlement of Jamestown in 1607. If we want a particularly rich occasion to represent the glory of the English language, we may agree upon 1611, the year of Shakespeare's

The Tempest and, even more tellingly, of the King James or Authorized Version of the Bible. When Samuel Johnson came to write his *Plan of a Dictionary of the English Language,* in 1747, he banished all "antiquated or obsolete words" and retained only such words, he said, "as are to be found in authors who wrote since the accession of Elizabeth"—that is, since 1558—"from which we date the golden age of our language." By the end of the eighteenth century there were those—like John Adams and Noah Webster—who felt that the English language as spoken in England had passed into its decadent phase and that a more vigorous future depended upon the English spoken in America. In 1780 Adams prophesied that the increasing population in America, "and their universal connection and correspondence with all nations," would make English— and he meant American English—"the language of the world." In 1785 Ezra Stiles claimed, in *The United States Elevated to Honor and Glory,* that the English language, established in North America, would (like other plants strengthened by transplantation) renew itself:

> The rough, sonorous diction of the English language may here take its Athenian polish, and receive its Attic urbanity; as it will probably become the vernacular tongue of more numerous millions than ever yet spoke one language on earth. It may continue for ages to be the prevailing and general language of North America. The intercommunion of the United States with all the world in travels, trade, and politics, and the infusion of letters into our infancy, will probably preserve us from the provincial dialects risen into inexterminable habit before the invention of printing. The Greek never became the language of the Alexandrine, nor the Turkish of the Ottoman conquests, nor yet the Latin that of the Roman empire. The Saracenic conquests have already lost the pure and elegant Arabic of the Koreish tribe, or the family of Ishmael, in the corrupted dialects of Egypt, Syria, Persia, and Hindostan. Different from these, the English language will grow up with the present American population into great purity and elegance, unmutilated by the foreign dialects of foreign conquests.

It is evident that "the triumph of the English language" was achieved by the same forces which also expressed themselves in worldly versions of translation and assimilation: the voyaging of Ralegh and Drake, imperial settlements, trade, conquest, the grammar of exercised power. Language has never been neutral; its spirituality as breath and voice has always issued from bodies and the space they occupy, and therefore from the political conflicts in which they engage. In some cases there has been a direct relation between the triumph of the English language and the exercise of domination.

In Ireland, for instance, the gradual extinction of the Irish language was the result of the establishment of Dublin and the Pale as the place of English power. That part of the story includes the colonization of Ulster in the early seventeenth century and the imposition of English as the language of such education as was provided. But England had the help of Ireland's weather in destroying the Irish language. After the terrible potato blight and the famines of the 1840s, Irish parents knew that the children who had to emigrate to England and America would have a better chance if they could speak English, even with a brogue.

In Scotland, the defeat of Scots Gaelic was inevitable when Bonnie Prince Charlie's Jacobite rebellion was crushed at Culloden in 1746. Within a generation, the clans had lost themselves and their identity; Edinburgh and the Lowlands had made their peace with English manners. When Johnson made a tour to the Western Islands of Scotland in 1773, he reported, with a degree of sympathy which hardly interrupted the contempt he normally offered Scotsmen, that:

> Of what they had before the late conquest of the country, there remain only their language and their poverty. Their language is attacked on every side. Schools are erected, in which English only is taught, and there were lately some who thought it reasonable to refuse them a version of the holy scriptures, that they might have no monument of their mother-tongue.

Not that Johnson was much concerned with the loss of "the Earse language," of which he knew nothing but what he had been told. "It is the rude speech of a barbarous people," he concluded, "who had few thoughts to express, and were content, as they conceived grossly, to be grossly understood."

Ireland and Scotland are clear instances of the bearing of language upon power, and power upon language. But it is one of the distinctive features in the history of the English language that it continued to extend itself even when the British Empire had contracted. It was as if the language had acquired such momentum, by the middle years of the twentieth century, that it thrived even in the absence of the power it once denoted. McCrum surveys, with something approaching the emotion of awe, the spread of English and the variety of its forms. He has chapters on the English of India, America, Canada, Australia, New Zealand, South Africa, Jamaica, Singapore, Sierra Leone, Gambia, Ghana, and Nigeria; on cockney, the Irish brogue, flash or convict speech, Romany, pidgin English, Caribbean creole, black speech, California and its surfers' jargon.

The cavalcade is immensely interesting. McCrum emphasizes that when English is used as a second language, it becomes a *lingua franca,* especially in African countries where there may be a miscellany of local languages, mutually opaque. English as a second language is also the mark of high breeding, superior education, and polite society, as elegant girls in India, for instance, turn their minds toward marriage. It is the international language of technology, aviation, banking, computers, and popular entertainment.

But English as a second language is mostly American English, not English English. Indian girls refer to the men they hope to marry as guys and otherwise take their information from American films. The English which is everybody's second language doesn't hold Chaucer and Shakespeare in its communal mind: it is animated not by the history it has come through but by the history it thinks it is making. For such an attitude, American English is far more suitable than English English, and not only because it is the instrument of present and future power in the world. The American language, as H. L. Mencken called it, has largely rid itself of density and freight in the interests of mobility: it cultivates a grammar of transit, not of memories and inheritances. To the extent to which it has disengaged itself from the past, it is available to millions of people who plan to do the same. It is a further relief that no institution in American English has the intimidating force of BBC English, the concept of Standard English, or Received Southern Pronunciation.

These factors together suggest that the English which is someone's second language is rented rather than owned: it is picked up whenever it is needed and dropped off somewhere else. So it is associated with advancement, getting on in the modern world, money, and the conditions of power understood or at least sensed as being American.

McCrum's book presents these matters in a form compatible with the television programmes it accompanies: history as a spectacle to be witnessed. Observation is deemed to amount to experience by giving the visual gist of it. The history of a language is to be conveyed as the social history of the countries in which its diverse forms have been produced. If the speech of Texan cowboys includes several Spanish words which arrived with Mexicans, we read of these matters as visually available history, and in the programme we see cowboys and listen to them. Indeed, the visual images are so engrossing that it requires a specific act of goodwill to listen to what is being said. Our minds are crowded by forms, shapes, and landscapes.

It follows from the visual sense of history—of history as an illustrated book or a series of moving pictures—that discrimination is made to seem redundant. McCrum accepts that the English language is now like an extended family in which the children have grown up and gone away and don't write home anymore. It may be a pity, but the narrative doesn't stop to say that it is. Whatever is the case is right. Even when McCrum quotes examples of Jamaican dub poetry which seem dismally impoverished, he presents them as events having a mainly social dignity. And he avoids using, on his own responsibility, the suspect terminology with which questions of linguistic usage are normally discussed, or with which discussion is forestalled. He never resorts to the vocabulary which implies moral rebuke. He doesn't refer to the corruption of language, the need to guard its purity, the infections to which it is liable, or the diseases it has contracted. He quotes Johnson's remark about "the American dialect, a tract of corruption to which every language must always be exposed," but he never allows himself the pleasure of indulging a preference. He doesn't talk of dialects—he thinks the word obnoxious—he talks rather of varieties of English.

We have evidently come a long way, or stepped far aside, from the situation in which Henry James urged the girls of Bryn Mawr College to take care of their pronunciation. Or in which T. S. Eliot worried about "the dialect of the tribe" and the desperate task of purifying it. Or, more invidiously still, from the situation in which F. R. Leavis regarded it as amounting to a disability if not an incapacity that Eliot, Ezra Pound, W. B. Yeats, and James Joyce had not been born in England: they couldn't therefore have taken intimate and creative possession of the English language as a native speaker—a William Blake or a D. H. Lawrence—so richly did: they were tourists at large. Shakespeare was a great writer not chiefly because of his individual talent but because he was born to the possession of a great language at the moment of its supreme development. Leavis thought of the development as simultaneously an expressive and a moral capacity.

Such discriminations ought to be heard in any consideration of the English language; but they are evidently made in the cause of furthering a great literature and the cultural values it testifies to. McCrum's book, and the television programmes, are concerned with the varieties of spoken English, all over the world, rather than with the literatures they have produced. Written language changes far more slowly than speech; its forms have something like the fixity of print. Johnson took pleasure in asserting:

> Much less ought our written language to comply with the corruptions of oral utterance, or copy that which every variation of time or place makes different from itself, and imitate those changes, which will again be changed, while imitation is employed in observing them.

The differences between written English and spoken English certainly belong to the history of the language. But *The Story of English* is told on the assumption that its character is chiefly an acoustic phenomenon, while the circumstances to which it responds are visually presented. Whatever has come into speech, such that it may be heard in airports or on buses and trains, in offices or in slums, has the privilege of having appeared. Many forms of speech haven't survived, like the word "incarnadine," which wasn't saved even by incorporation in one of Shakespeare's most resounding lines, and even though there must be many occasions on which something is painted to the colour of blood. It didn't "take"; no form of speech has received it.

I gather that McCrum's range of attention is defined by this consideration: has the word or the phrase come onto the streets, could we hear it in a disco or a coffee bar? So he is well disposed to phrases which a man of print would like to see enduring for some years before taking much note of them. McCrum cheerfully, it seems, recognizes "the upwardly mobile," talks of "high tech" and "state of the art," mentions that the Chinese are taking "a crash programme" of English, and that at the end of 1983 a nomadic African tribe, the Tuareg, delayed their annual migration by ten days "in order to catch the last episode of *Dallas.*" The Blitz, he says, "dealt a body blow to the London docks."

It is not McCrum's aim to exert any critical pressure on the report from the streets. He discusses Standard English and Received Southern Pronunciation, but without implying that he would be distressed if they were lost. In matters of usage, he is as nearly neutral as it is possible to be. But even to describe the hundreds of varieties of spoken English, he can't avoid positing the Standard English from which they are derived, however circuitously, or from which they deviate. The question he always raises takes this form: has the relation between Standard English and spoken English in, say, Jamaica become so distant that Jamaican English should be accounted a separate language and a dictionary of it consulted? In some cases the answer is clear. In Sierra Leone, the local pidgin has developed into Krio, a mixture of English and Yoruba, with several other elements, mainly Portuguese. Krio is the result not only of the slave trade but of the circumstances of its abolition. There is now a Krio-English dictionary which gives the language the stability of standard spelling.

McCrum describes this development with notable verve, and I assume that, in addition to recognizing it, he approves of it: as well he may. But he's not forthcoming with his criteria. The only evaluative term he uses is "confidence": if people speak with confidence and without pretending that their form of speech is something else, it is enough. The only note of irritation in his book comes when he is describing the English spoken in South Africa under the shadow of the Afrikaans the authorities prefer. The English of the South African Broadcasting Corporation, he says,

> betrays the uneasy, non-official status of the language. To British and American ears, it has the clipped formality of BBC English in the 1950s—in other words, the authorities, unable to deny the presence of English in South Africa, broadcast it as a foreign language. White South Africans who take elocution lessons—"Speech and Drama" is the euphemism—to improve their English are, perhaps unwittingly, reinforcing the foreignness of English in South Africa. There is a distinctive South African English, of course, but it has lacked the confidence of Australian or New Zealand English.

I detect a little prejudice in that passage: in every other case where English is spoken with the nuance of local conditions, McCrum describes it handsomely. But here he imputes bad faith.

The theory of the development of English that McCrum alludes to is the one which Robert Burchfield, chief editor of the *Oxford English Dictionary,* offered several years ago: that just as, upon the decline of the Roman Empire, Latin broke up into mutually unintelligible European languages—French, Spanish, Italian—so over a period of several centuries English will similarly disintegrate into separate languages. Burchfield's idea is that "English, as the second language of many speakers ...is no more likely to survive the inevitable political changes of the future than did Latin, once the second language of the governing classes or regions within the Roman Empire." The theory has often been challenged, if only because in such a long run we are all silent. Besides, even if the British Empire has lapsed, the American one hasn't, and the American sphere of interest is such as to enforce the particular values—ambition, speed, assertiveness—to which American English is especially suited.

But if Burchfield's thesis is pursued, it suggests a plausible destiny for spoken and written English. Standard English is no longer an empire of signs, it is hardly even a commonwealth, or if it is, it doesn't approach London with any particular reverence or defer to the proprieties of the BBC. It is quite conceivable that the proliferations of spoken English—the new Englishes, as McCrum calls them—will one day amount to hundreds of separate languages. Standard English will develop into a kind of Esperanto, the sum of the technical jargons and the trade speeches it contains. The English language will retain a chiefly Platonic existence, as a transcendent idea or recollection, ascribed to an origin on that account mythical. The masterpieces of English literature—which Dr. Leavis fought to maintain against the force he thought well enough described as "Americanization"—will then be read as Virgil and Horace are now read, for the educational value of imagining gone times and archaic perceptions. Or they will have the existence of artifacts in a large modern museum; like the African masks and spears in the Metropolitan Museum in New York, which can be inspected with impunity now that they have been separated from the occasions they once served.

NOTE

1. Robert McCrum, William Cran, and Robert MacNeil, *The Story of English* (London: Faber and Faber and BBC Publications, 1986).

II

In January 1987, Mrs. Thatcher's Secretary of State for Education, Kenneth Baker, set up a "Committee for English," under the chairmanship of Professor Kingman, to recommend "a model of the English language, whether spoken or written, which would serve as the basis of how teachers are trained to understand how the English language works [and] what, in general terms, pupils need to know about how the English language works and in consequence what they should have been taught and be expected to understand on this score at age 7, 11, and 16." The Committee was also requested to define "principles which should guide teachers on how far and in what ways the model should be made explicit to pupils, to make them conscious of how language is used in a range of contexts." Perhaps the instructions to the Committee might have been given in more elegant sentences. But the roughness of the phrasing has the merit of indicating the messy context in which such a committee must do its work: a more urbane tone would be misleading, because the sentiments provoked by questions of linguistic usage are often surprisingly aggressive. Think of the distemper caused, a few years ago, when someone in *The Times Literary Supplement* used or abused the word "hopefully." Or the degree to which one's style of speaking or of writing is taken as a sign of one's taste, breeding, and tone.

It is not surprising that leaders of education and communication in Britain are endlessly worried about the state of the English language. A few years ago the BBC established a small committee to report on the quality of spoken English on BBC programmes. As a member of the committee, I spent an inordinate amount of time listening, notebook in hand, to the Queen's English as spoken by professional broadcasters. My conclusion was that things were bad but could be much worse. Mr. Baker's Committee has been formed, however, to respond to a far more extensive feeling of misgiving.

It is my impression that English politicians have not yet fully acknowledged that the society they administer is an agglomeration of diverse races and cultural formations. When three Bengali children are killed in an English school, the constituents of diversity and conflict are hard to ignore. But there is still an assumption, among administrators and politicians, that one of these days an agglomeration will become a community. The English language is supposed to be the sign of that community. The foreigners will gradually join in speaking English.

But whose English? Since the late years of the seventeenth century there have been intermittent attempts to stabilize English at some supposedly high point of its development. Many English writers have felt envious of the French, who since 1635 have had an Academy to take care of their language. In 1712, Jonathan Swift, a conservative in these matters, published *A Proposal for Correcting, Improving and Ascertaining the English Tongue.* Samuel Johnson's *Plan of a Dictionary of the English Language* (1747) didn't offer to prevent English from changing. Johnson accepted, with whatever regret, that "language is the work of man, of a being from whom permanence and stability cannot be derived." But he hoped that a dictionary would establish meanings and fix pronunciation, "determine the accentuation of all polysyllables by proper authorities."

When the question of English is argued, it is always assumed, by English disputants, that the language is the only remaining form of Empire but that much significance depends upon the character of that remnant. Thereafter, attitudes enter into conflict. According to one view, it is a matter of pride that English in many diverse forms has virtually taken possession of the modern world. Diversity is welcome; it is a sign of the plenitude of the culture from which its forms are derived. Even if reference to the Mother Tongue is disingenuous, there is still a sense in which everyone who speaks English, even in a local dialect or pidgin, belongs to the Queen's extended family. *The Story of English,* as I have remarked, expressed that attitude. But those TV programmes were mainly concerned with spoken English. I assume that McCrum and MacNeil are content to find written English changing at a slower rate than spoken English and splitting into fewer cultural segments.

The other attitude is more conservative. According to this sentiment, Standard English and its oral form, Received Southern Pronunciation — BBC English — should be maintained, if only as a model and even if it is rarely found in its pure state. The fact that the Empire has declined into the Commonwealth and now into a notional sense of such unity makes it a crucial matter to preserve the language as the embodiment of an aesthetic, moral, and political sentiment. For that reason, the "Americanization" of English should be resisted. The spiritual form of Empire should retain its unity.

Peter Levi is the only member of Mr. Baker's Committee who has made any comment on the work in hand. Interviewed by Lorna Sage for *The Times Literary Supplement* (February 13, 1987), Levi seemed to accept that the gap between spoken and written English is wide and may get wider. The Committee, he suggested, will have to take account of looser constructions than those sanctioned by an austere syntax. I presume he means that spoken English is now so various that it would be absurd to try to make it toe any line.

But perhaps he means that no attempt should be made to apply to spoken English the rules of syntax which have dominated the written language. He says that the Committee is likely to concentrate not on syntax but on parataxis; that is, on what the *OED* defines as "the placing of propositions or clauses one after another, without indicating by connecting words the relation (of co-ordination or subordination) between them." Levi says that natural language—I presume he means colloquial speech—isn't syntactically organized. "That was a rhetorical strategy that originated in the law courts in the fourth century B.C." Levi mentions, as an example of parataxis, Mistress Quickly's description of Falstaff's death:

Nay, sure, he's not in hell: he's in Arthur's bosom, if ever man went to Arthur's bosom. A' made a finer end and went away an it had been any christom child; a' parted ev'n just between twelve and one, ev'n at the turning o' th' tide; for after I saw him fumble with the sheets, and play with flowers, and smile upon his fingers' end, I knew there was but one way; for his nose was as sharp as a pen, and a' babbl'd of green fields. "How now, Sir John!" quoth I: "What, man, be o' good cheer." So a' cried out "God, God, God!" three or four times. Now I, to comfort him, bid him a' should not think of God; I hoped there was no need to trouble himself with any such thoughts yet.   [*Henry V,* Act II, Scene 3.]

It is not especially loose. Except for the turning of the tide, the phrases are placed in the order of the actions they report. I don't see that it exemplifies parataxis.

In his *Pelican History of Greek Literature* (1985), Levi quotes a better example of looseness, Homer's "paratactic composition" in Book IX of the *Iliad.* Agamemnon is wandering about, distraught, because Zeus has let him down and decided that the Achaians won't, after all, defeat the Trojans:

> So the Trojans kept watches; but infinite panic held the Achaians, companion of cold fear, with grief unbearable all the best were struck. As two winds arise on the fish-haunted sea, Boreas and Zephyros, and they rush down from Thrace, suddenly they come, and the dark wave is confused together, and it sheds much seaweed out of the salt sea, so was their spirit divided in the breasts of the Achaians.

Levi points out that no one in real life has ever felt two winds at once, "but the slight obscurity adds to the force of these verses." Besides, it compels the reader to imagine an experience which he hasn't had; and so much the worse for real life that it hasn't contained it. If the modern idea of clarity were to predominate, the fish-haunted character of the sea (or "fish-delighting," in E. V. Rieu's translation) would be deleted as an irrelevance. The seaweed, too. These details have nothing to do with the case; they have been produced by a shift of attention from the Achaians to the sea. They exceed the case just as profusely as the comparison of the Myrmidons, in Book XVI, to wolves:

> They fell in like flesh-eating wolves in all their natural savagery, wolves that have killed a great antlered stag in the mountains and rend him till their jowls are red with blood, then go off in a pack to lap the dark water from the surface of a deep spring with their slender tongues, belching gore, and still indomitably fierce though their bellies are distended. Thus the captains and commanders of the Myrmidons . . .

Levi's point is that a clear syntax would remove the small puzzles and contradictions but that Homer's looseness makes the reader imagine the emotion for himself. "The case" is apprehended along with many other imagined details in excess of it. The *Iliad* becomes, as Levi puts it, "a do-it-yourself poem." Still, there must be more to it than that. I find a helpful comment in Erich Auerbach's *Mimesis* (1946), where he says that the basic impulse of the Homeric style is "to represent phenomena in a fully externalized form, visible and palpable in all their parts, and completely fixed in their spatial and temporal relations." When Homer imagines two winds conspiring to assault the sea, he goes on to think of the fish and the seaweed, and gives every phenomenon he imagines the same degree of emphasis. He does not play with light and shade, past and present. As Auerbach says, "the Homeric style knows only a foreground, only a uniformly illuminated, uniformly objective present."

It is evident that the understanding of clarity as involving the subordination of one phenomenon to another is a modern convention, our particular economy. It is not a law of nature, or even of language. But we are bewildered by sentences in which every apprehended detail is treated equally, and six of one type are given no more weight than half a dozen of another. We think of the production of meanings on the analogy of visible objects, disclosed or created, and we want to be assured that some claimants are more compelling than the rest.

It will be interesting to hear what Mr. Baker's Committee recommends on these matters. But the reference to English "whether spoken or written" is odd. Peter Levi is probably right in saying that ordinary speech is paratactic. If so, there is no merit in trying to shame speakers into toeing a strict line. But writing is a different matter, if only because the orthodoxy of sentences is far more demanding there than in speech. A sentence in which no single clause is supposed to be more telling than another is now thought to be absurd: fine if you're Samuel Beckett; if not, not. Or just difficult. John Ashbery's poems are difficult because he doesn't seem to regard any part of their discourse as more crucial than any other part: he avoids reaching a conclusion or making a big start.

The gap between oral and written English is wide and probably getting wider. I'm not sure that it's a regrettable development, or that Mr. Baker's Committee should worry about it. Teachers of literature like to assume that students have an especially intimate relation to the literature of their native language. I think the assumption is false. We would be better teachers and students if we were to read our native literature as a second language. We would maintain a proper distance between our minds and the literature, instead of domesticating it on the supposition that it is, after all, merely an extension of ourselves. A native speaker of English should read Shakespeare, Jane Austen, Hawthorne, and Melville much as he would read Flaubert in French or Rilke in German.

The modern sense of clarity doesn't help these experiences, mainly because it insists upon the forms of subordination which are now virtually one's second nature. It is like reading a novel only for the plot. Sometimes we read on the understanding that the sentences, being reasonably clear, don't need to be pestered. Take, as an example, these sentences from Max Beerbohm's *Zuleika Dobson:*

> Zuleika was not strictly beautiful. Her eyes were a trifle large, and their lashes longer than they need have been.

The joking manner invites intimacy rather than analysis: we are supposed to be initiates. But if we read it from outside, as William Empson did in *Seven Types of Ambiguity,* it may appear like this:

> "Do not suppose that she was anything so commonplace; do not suppose that you can easily imagine what she was like, or that she was not, probably, the rather out-of-the-way type that you particularly admire"; in this way (or rather, in the gambit of which this is a parody) jealousy is placated, imagination is set free, and nothing has been said (what *is* this strict type of beauty, anyway?) which can be used against the author afterwards.

As for her lashes, Empson says:

> Not knowing how *large* the *trifle* may be, the reader has no means of being certain whether he would be charmed or appalled.

I don't claim that this sort of thing depends upon its being written and read and reread: for all I know, people may be able to divine as much in a conversation by means of a lifted eyebrow. Jeremy Irons's performance in *Brideshead Revisited* assumed the possibility. But my guess is that our sense of clarity must be appeased by the conventions of print, and by the subordinations enforced through grammar and punctuation; while parataxis offers more casual pleasures.

III

Sir Herbert Grierson's edition of Donne's poems, published by the Clarendon Press in 1912, was sent to Rupert Brooke for review. Musing upon the book as an indisputably fine thing, Brooke listed other grand institutions, including "Charing Cross Bridge by night, the dancing of Miss Ethel Levey, the Lucretian hexameter, the beer at an inn in Royston, . . . the sausages at another inn above Princes Risborough, and the Clarendon Press editions of the English poets." And among these he made a temporal discrimination. "The beer and the sausages will change," he admitted, "and Miss Levey one day will die, and Charing Cross Bridge will fall; so the Clarendon Press books will be the only thing our evil generation may show to the cursory eyes of posterity, to prove it was not wholly bad." Peter Sutcliffe has quoted this encomium in his informal history of Oxford University Press, partly for its intrinsic interest, and partly to illustrate his assertion that by 1914 OUP had established itself "as a national institution with a responsibility to survive in the interest of civilization as a whole."

The history of OUP is deemed to start in 1478, when a printer named Theodoric Rood came from Cologne to Oxford and published the *Expositio Sancti Hieronymi in Symbolum Apostulorum.* The book had two errors on its title page; one of attribution, one of typography. The true author of the *Expositio* was not St. Jerome but Rufinus of Aquileia, and an X was dropped from the Roman date, making it MCCCCLXVIII rather than 1478. It is universally agreed that OUP has greatly improved its work in both respects. The several books published to mark Oxford's quincentenary are impeccable productions. Nicolas Barker's illustrated history is a gorgeous book, as handsome as the exhibition held in the Pierpont Morgan Library in New York to celebrate the same event. Harry Carter's book is a detailed history of OUP from 1478 to 1780, and it includes as an appendix a list of extant Oxford books published between 1690 and 1780, excluding Bibles, Testaments, and Books of Common Prayer which would be "too numerous to mention." Peter Sutcliffe's book skips through the early years to concentrate on the period from 1860 to now. His pages are too crowded with print to be as beautiful as Barker's or Carter's, and I spotted a misplaced quotation mark as evidence, presumably, of the informality mentioned in his subtitle, but I find no other fault in a notably inexpensive and lively book.

Like Mr. Carter, Mr. Sutcliffe tells the story of the Press mainly through the people who managed its policy and saw that the books were published: his leading characters are Charles Cannan, Lyttelton Gell, Henry Frowde, Alexander Macmillan, Humphrey Milford, Bartholomew

Price, Kenneth Sisam, but he has rich material also on Jowett, Murray, Fowler, and many other men associated with the Press. Carter's men include Rood, Scolar, Barnes, Archbishop Laud, Bishop Fell, and Sir William Blackstone, but he takes enough time and space to give fascinating accounts of the technical problems involved in the early years of the Press, the acquisition of exotic types, and the fortunes of the Press in an age of political and religious quarrels. Mr. Carter is much and properly concerned with charters, "print and privilege," royal constraint, censorship, the paper wars of belief, definitions, theologies. But in one respect the three books I have mentioned leave me in the dark: the relation between the University and the Press is rarely clarified. Did the Press conduct its business, from the beginning, as a virtually autonomous institution under the loosely construed auspices of the University and subject only to the nominal ratification of its activities by the Delegacy? To what extent did (do?) the delegates of the Clarendon Press take into account the curricula of the University, the research of Oxford scholars, the requirements of Oxford undergraduates, in selecting books to be published? The relation between University and Press is still vague to me.

I mention the matter because I have been reading Lawrence Stone's essay "The Size and Composition of the Oxford Student Body 1580–1909"[1] and he has many references to the charges of corruption and Jacobitism directed against Oxford in the first years of the eighteenth century, culminating in the University's open sympathy with the Jacobite rebellion in 1715. I hoped to find these exacerbations treated in Mr. Carter's book, but they are noted only briefly and by implication in references to Thomas Hearne and the difficulties he faced in publishing the truth. Admittedly, the archives of OUP are so extensive that Mr. Carter expects to need three large volumes to deal with them, and even with that allowance he has not promised to say much about the University itself or the social and political pressure exerted from time to time upon the dons who occupied themselves with the Press. But I would like to feel that pressure in his pages.

These books, then, are internal histories of OUP; they are not directly concerned with the social conditions in which the Press worked and works. Or with the impact of print, the theme of *The Coming of the Book,* David Gerard's translation of *L'Apparition du Livre* (1958). Readers of *The Gutenberg Galaxy* will recall that *L'Apparition du Livre* was one of the many books which Marshall McLuhan cited in support of his account of "typographic man." They will also recall that McLuhan ascribed to the printing press the rise of nearly every form of cultural life from the sixteenth to the twentieth century. A short list would include visual perspective, individualism, nationalism, the fixed point of view, the shift from words as performance to words as meaning, visibly observed relations, the separation of meaning from voice and sound. Febvre and Martin ridicule the old notion that "the Reformation was the child of the printing press," but they show that printing, and especially the quick production of posters which could be nailed upon cathedral doors, proved to be important in the development of Protestantism in the sixteenth century.

Luther would not have gone beyond Wittenberg without his handbills and *Flugschriften.* Febvre and Martin also emphasize the relation between vernacular publication and nationalism, and the eventual destruction of "the unified Latin culture of Europe." The Princeton scholar Lawrence Lipking has recently quoted Heine on this theme.[2] In *The Romantic School* Heine made a creative error in confusing Faust with Gutenberg's financier Johann Fust, naming Faust as the inventor of the art of printing, the art which gave Knowledge victory over Faith, *"die dem Wissen einen Sieg über den Glauben verschafft."* Heine thought, of course, that this shared knowledge would result in a social and political brotherhood more beneficial than the purely spiritual brotherhood offered by Catholicism. If we can have all this and Heaven too, so much the better, but meanwhile we should put our money on knowledge.

In an essay on Girolamo Cardano, reprinted in *Abinger Harvest,* E. M. Forster said that for a century or so after the invention of the printing press men were still mistaking it for an engine of immortality and hastening "to commit to it their deeds and passions for the benefit of future ages." Plenitude was increasingly conceived in personal terms; one's own knowledge shared; one's own experience tendered. Shakespeare found it easy to use the terminology of printing to favor another form of reproduction, as in Sonnet 2, where Nature

> ... *carved thee for her seal, and meant thereby*
> *Thou shouldst print more, not let that copy die.*

It seems clear that until the end of the seventeenth century people were pretty thrilled with their new toy, and that the proliferation of books didn't begin to irritate them until the beginning of the eighteenth century, when books started getting on the nerves and under the skin of Pope and Swift. The clue is Latin. Febvre and Martin say that 77 percent of books printed before 1500 were in Latin, mostly religious incunabula, with texts in classical literature and law making up the rest. Latin began to lose out to the vernacular languages about 1530. After that, there is a shift from faith to knowledge, in Heine's version, or from one concept of authority to another, from doctrine to feeling, or from one kind of reader to another, from "clerisy" to "the common reader." Print rendered impossible the continued proximity of the sign to any authenticating Logos. The mass production of books deprived each book of the aura, the sacred quality inherent in any unique object. Even the Bible lost its radiance, opened itself to each reader's interpretation, an experience to be disclosed and shared rather than a statutory revelation, the Word incarnate.

OUP is important in this respect. The prestige of the Press is largely based upon three factors: its Bibles, its dictionaries, and the scholarly works entrusted to the Clarendon Press. The main problem in the Clarendon Press has normally been clear: once you choose the unsalable, now do you sell it? The books by Harry Carter and Peter Sutcliffe are informative on this question. But the three books about OUP treat the Bibles and the dictionaries as separate transactions. I think they are closely related. Is it fanciful to suggest that Bible and Dictionary came together to form not a sacred text, a Book of Revelation, but a domestic morality? The Word of God, for centuries mediated through the doctrines of the Roman Catholic Church, was eventually secularized as the King's English. King replaced Pope, Fowler's *The King's English* (1906) became the new version of authority. *A Little Quincentenary History* 1478–1978, issued by OUP as a guide to its larger enterprises, refers to the opening of offices and branches throughout the world and says that "in O.U.P.'s eyes, education and scholarship would follow Queen Victoria's Empire, no part of which was to be deprived of the benefits of British civilization as evidenced by Oxford books."

Precisely: the history of OUP is an imperial theme because its greatest and most typical books replaced the presence of a speaker by the presence of an institution, not the British Empire but, a more durable thing, the English language. The constituents of that empire are not bureaucrats, soldiers, governors, and gunboats; they are signs, names, sentences, usage, grammar, a White syntax, habits of commentary, interpretation, classical and European texts in English translation, dictionaries which translate foreign tongues into the King's standard English. Simon Gray's new play *The Rear Column,* which I saw in London a few weeks ago, is based upon his understanding that Victorian officers and gentlemen, on service in Africa, felt a direct connection between moral authority and linguistic power. Monsters they might be and often were, but they spoke the Queen's English. They punished recalcitrant natives by imposing sentence, often the whip, but their authority issued from their command of English sentences. The connection between Bible and Dictionary is that the English language was deployed, and continues to be deployed as far as possible, as the secular substitute for the propagation of the Faith.

"Education and scholarship would follow Queen Victoria's Empire": yes, in several senses. Soldiers, civil servants, and businessmen would open up the territory, and the OUP would come later with Bible and Dictionary. But even after Queen Victoria's delegates had departed, and Empire dwindled, the OUP books remained. Presence in personal form was not required. In *De la grammatologie* Jacques Derrida writes of writing as the disappearance of natural presence, *"cette écriture comme disparition de la présence naturelle."* But a book is a pretty good substitute for natural presence, if the presence was imperial and the book is the epitome of moral authority. McLuhan has referred to English as the "P.A. system" for the West: true, and it issues from Westminster or from Oxford, places which, like the Vatican, have moral authority disproportionate to their latitude. English has become the dominant international language among those people whom the English are prepared to regard as civilized or ready to be civilized. English literature provides the poor man's classics. When Dr. Richard Chenevix Trench, Dean of Westminster, described the idea of a new dictionary in 1857, he spoke of "the love of our own language, what is it but the love of our country expressing itself in one particular direction?" And again he said that "language may be regarded as a 'moral barometer,' which indicates and permanently marks the rise or fall of a nation's life."

Trench's sentences are taken from Hans Aarsleff's *The Study of Language in England,* 1780–1860 (1967) and are quoted again in *Caught in the Web of Words,* Elisabeth Murray's biography of her grandfather, James Murray, the great lexicographer, first editor of the *Oxford English Dictionary.* Murray started work on the dictionary in 1877, produced the first volume

(A–Ant) in January and kept the whole thing going until he died in 1915, leaving the enormous task to be completed by Henry Bradley, William Craigie, and Charles Onions: the last volume came out in 1928, with a supplement in 1933. [Further supplements are now (1988) complete.]

On April 21, 1832, according to *Table Talk*, Coleridge said that there had been three silent revolutions in England: "first, when the professions fell off from the church; secondly, when literature fell off from the professions; and thirdly, when the press fell off from literature." Murray knew those falls, and wasted no spirit in regretting them. Perhaps he was content with the degree of stability imposed by the printing presses themselves, by dictionaries, grammar books, which always tend to draw usage toward an authoritative centre. He was interested in dialects, as the author of *The Dialect of the Southern Counties of Scotland* (1873), so he may have felt that the authorized version of the King's English implicit in the great *OED* could well afford to take its examples where it found them.

Ms. Murray does not go into this question, but it seems implicit in her narrative. Ostensibly, the *OED* is neutral, disinterested, it resorts to "historical principles" without proposing to tell history its business. But in fact it is a secular Bible, mediated through reformed doctrines of judgement and taste which are deemed to be uttered in the King's English. The King has ousted the Pope. When Henry Fowler proposed to R. W. Chapman an idea for a book eventually called *Modern English Usage*, Chapman told him that such a book, a Utopian book, would sell very well in Utopia. In the event, *Modern English Usage* has sold triumphantly everywhere, because it amounts to a book of good manners, a courtesy book, a manual of etiquette published in 1926 just when the completed *OED* had demonstrated that linguistic manners have been nearly unmanageably diverse.

Modern English Usage was reprinted four times in the year of its publication, including an impression of 50,000 copies for the United States, where Putnam's issued a special edition. I have no information on the current sales of the book, but it has lost much of its authority. So has the doctrine of Standard English. The great *OED* is still recognized as a masterpiece, but only by those who care for such things. Coleridge called them the clerisy, meaning a nation's learned people, "whether poets or philosophers or scholars," and thought that they were crucial in a society as points of rest: "there could be no order, no harmony of the whole, without them." These are the people who consult the *OED*. But they are in the position of that other clerisy, Latinists in the sixteenth century who resorted to Latin for stability and continuity when the world was resorting to the vernacular languages for other and more immediate reasons. Standard English, the Queen's English, is the Latin of the West: for millions of people, it is their second language, used on formal, diplomatic occasions, or when high financial matters are to be transacted.

But relatively few people speak Standard English as their native or first language: we speak dialects, idiolects, in regional accents. Westminster and Oxford are nominal centers. No other human being speaks as the Queen of England speaks in her Christmas message to her people. It is vulgar to explain this phenomenon by saying that Her Majesty is simply a desiccated, boring speaker. What she speaks is not English but the idea of English, and it falls dead from her lips because the idea, the ideal form of the language, is archaic, its god has disappeared. Idea, spirit, voice, idiom, and meaning have split apart. The Queen's purposes are identical in this context with those of Oxford University Press, a fact appropriately marked by the special copy of the Bible which OUP printed for Her Majesty's coronation in 1953, and the equally distinguished copy of the same text which the Press printed to celebrate her silver jubilee in the present year (1978).

The idea shared by Queen and Press is simply this: Britain. The Queen is its symbol in every respect; the Press in one only, the English language. But the imperial motive, thwarted in the political sphere, is still lively in linguistic and cultural ambitions. Peter Sutcliffe's book begins and ends with a significant image. When I was at school, maps of the world showed the British Empire in bold red. Mr. Sutcliffe's book begins and ends with a map of the world showing only the offices and branches of OUP. There have been some failures: offices in Peking, Shanghai, Lahore, Beirut, Addis Ababa, Lagos, and Belfast are now closed. Russia remains unattempted. But OUP has a trading post in so many places that Mr. Sutcliffe and his publisher are only mildly exaggerating in referring to the world as "the O.U.P. at large."

NOTES

1. In Lawrence Stone (ed.), *The University in Society: Volume I: Oxford and Cambridge from the 14th to the Early 19th Century* (Princeton: Princeton University Press, 1974).
2. *University of Denver Quarterly,* Spring 1977.

Review of *The Oxford University Press and the Spread of Learning: An Illustrated History*, by Nicolas Barker; *A History of the Oxford University Press*—Vol. I: *To the Year 1780*, by Harry Carter; *The Oxford University Press: An Informal History*, by Peter Sutcliffe; *Caught in the Web of Words: James Murray and the Oxford English Dictionary*, by K. M. Elisabeth Murray; and *The Coming of the Book: The Impact of Printing 1450–1800*, by Lucien Febvre and Henri-Jean Martin, translated by David Gerard. From *The New York Review of Books*, June 1, 1978.

IV

In November 1940, the poet Robert Graves and the editor and author Alan Hodge published *The Long Week-End: A Social History of Great Britain 1918–1939*, a book designed "as a reliable record of what took place, of a forgettable sort, during the twenty-one-year interval between two great European wars." The moral of the story was not merely that human activities are mostly of the forgettable sort, but that from November 11, 1918, to September 3, 1939, the British people gave themselves up to distractions, amusements, and sundry follies. When Germany declined to withdraw its troops from Poland, Neville Chamberlain informed his people that they were now at war. The last chapter of *The Long Week-End* is called "Rain Stops Play, 1939."

Graves and Hodge found most of their evidence in newspapers, magazines, parliamentary debates, and radio (then known as the wireless). Their themes included domestic life, politics, religion, the Loch Ness monster, screen and stage, sex, art, literature, pacificism, nudism, hiking, women, a royal abdication, the popularity of the Lambeth Walk, social consciences, reading matter, and the rain. They did not assume that these matters had been reported to the British people in impeccable prose: readers of *The Daily Mail* and *The News Chronicle* did not insist upon style.

But Graves and Hodge found that bad writing was not confined to Grub Street. Defective prose issued from some of the most celebrated writers, including Sir Arthur Eddington, T. S. Eliot, Ernest Hemingway, Aldous Huxley, J. M. Keynes, F. R. Leavis, John Middleton Murry, Eric Partridge, Ezra Pound, J. B. Priestley, I. A. Richards, Bertrand Russell, George Bernard Shaw, Stephen Spender, H. G. Wells, and A. N. Whitehead. Common people were often frivolous, as *The Long Week-End* sufficiently demonstrated, but ostensibly great and serious writers had their own versions of frivolity; carelessness in the use of language, sloppiness, indifference to the decency to be observed between writer and reader. "English has for some time been written with great carelessness," Graves and Hodge reported, "not only among the uneducated and semi-educated but also among the educated classes, who once prided themselves as much on their ability to write and speak well as on their lineage, wealth, or administrative capacities." They decided that the irresponsibility of writers should be disclosed with the same zeal that had been devoted in *The Long Week-End* to the giddiness of the British populace. In May 1943 they published *The Reader Over Your Shoulder.*

The situation of the English language then was indeed critical. Graves and Hodge regard English as a messy, eccentric language, a rascal, undisciplined, often loose, but on its best days wonderfully exuberant. It needs a good domestic life and loving guardians. The years between the wars were largely frivolous, so language was encouraged to play the fool. War made the situation worse, since language was forced to accommodate propaganda, evasion, obfuscation, bureaucracy, and lies.

"We regard the present crisis as acute enough to excuse this book," Graves and Hodge asserted in *The Reader Over Your Shoulder.* "Our book concerns English as it should be written for the large general public always, and for a small special public on any but the most unusual occasions." The title was justified by the suggestion "that whenever anyone sits down to write he should imagine a crowd of his prospective readers (rather than a grammarian in cap and gown) looking over his shoulder." Readers should be expected to ask such questions as: "What does this sentence mean? Why do you trouble to tell me that again? Why have you chosen such a ridiculous metaphor? Must I really read this long, limping sentence? Haven't you got your ideas muddled here?" The authors also remembered that one of Graves's early poems was called "The Reader Over My Shoulder," and that the reader was addressed on that occasion as the poet's other self. The poem ended:

> *Know me, have done: I am a proud spirit*
> *And you for ever clay. Have done!*

In *The Long Week-End* Graves and Hodge told their readers to stop playing the fool. In *The Reader Over Your Shoulder* they told writers to maintain the strength and decency of the English language and thus merit the attention of readers recently converted to gravity.

The Reader Over Your Shoulder has been out of print for several years, and is now available again in an edition revised by its authors; but the revisions are odd. The first edition started with about 200 pages dealing with the peculiar qualities of English, the use and abuse of the language, sources of confusion, the different styles of prose, principles of clear statement, and samples of the language at each recognizable moment of its history from King Alfred to James Joyce. Of these pages, the samples have been deleted, the lessons of history in regard to the language are taken either as read or dead and the different styles are suppressed in favour of one, the plain style. In the first edition, erring prose by 54 authors was quoted, analyzed with extraordinary finesse and rewritten by Graves and Hodge to show in each case the benefits to be gained from care and responsibility. This part of the book was called "Examinations and Fair Copies," and it accounted for much of the fame and nearly all of the delight that the book has given its readers since 1943. The examinations are impeccably urbane, and therefore devastating. The fair copies are nearly always fair.

I append the adverb only because I think two or three of the emended versions unfair. One example, from an essay by J. Wentworth Day: "Queen Elizabeth, that wise woman who saw future truths centuries before their birth, said that London was too big." Graves and Hodge comment that "if Queen Elizabeth's remark was not true until nearly four hundred years later, it was not a wise one." Non sequitur: Elizabeth did not reveal herself as unwise by saying that London was too big. If she thought it too big, she was sensible in speaking her mind, and not to be blamed for the fact that she was not taken seriously. Graves and Hodge say that Mr. Day probably meant: "Queen Elizabeth, in a fit of petulance, anticipated by nearly four centuries the present complaint: 'London is too big.'" I say: "Foul play!" Mr. Day's sentence does not imply that he thought the Queen petulant; he thought she correctly divined the shape of the future.

I think we should read Graves and Hodge just as severely as they have read Eliot, Russell, Whitehead, Leavis, and the rest. More especially now, since they have reduced the erring passages from 54 to 17, for unstated reasons. The snubs addressed to Sir Norman Angell, I. A. Richards, and Whitehead are retained, but many gems have been withdrawn from the exhibition. I am pleased to report that the analysis of H. G. Wells's nonsense is retained; when Wells refers to "the impartial destructiveness of nature," Graves and Hodge reply that "this, as H. G. Wells knew, is offset by Nature's equally impartial constructiveness, e.g. the creation of fertile islands by cooperation between the coral insect, sea-birds, tides and currents."

I have no notion of the reason why the book has been cut from 446 to 290 pages, or why cuts have been made in the passages of offensive prose. Or why the reader's attention is drawn to the exhibits taken from G. D. H. Cole and J. W. N. Sullivan, since these have been deleted from the book in hand. Revised by the authors? Both of them? I can easily believe that Graves is not passionately exercised by the revision of his umpteenth book, but Hodge might be expected to show more interest in the matter than merely deleting 156 pages. Not a word is uttered about the present situation of English, which was already deemed "acute" in 1943.

Maybe the authors have been reduced to silence by the fact that the eminent writers whose prose was examined so thoroughly have preserved the defects as devoutly as if they were virtues. T. S. Eliot did not change a word in the first paragraph of his essay on the dramatist Philip Massinger, reprinted several times since 1943, despite the demonstration here that nearly any change would be an improvement. Some of the 54 writers may have taken their scolding to heart, but I doubt it.

The Reader Over Your Shoulder is subtitled *A Handbook for Writers of English Prose,* but it is also an inspiration for readers. I don't know any other book in which expository prose is read so seriously, carefully, helpfully. For this reason, the book is just as important as I. A. Richards's *Practical Criticism,* in which the attempts of Cambridge undergraduate students of English literature to read certain passages of English verse were produced and examined. That book transformed the teaching of literature in the universities by showing that the governing assumptions about reading and interpretation were mostly wrong. If our educational systems were sound, *The Reader Over Your Shoulder* could have the same effect on the teaching of expository writing by showing what the reading of such prose entails. The questions Graves and Hodge ask, the objections they raise to the particular sentences exhibited, are never pedantic; they arise from a decision to take the prose seriously. The exhibited prose is bad because it does not live up to the seriousness that it expects of its reader. If the reader attends to the prose as seriously as its tone appears to require, he finds that the sentences are wretchedly composed, culpably vague.

Of course Graves and Hodge take the reader's side, and assume that he is a far more serious person than the eminent writer he is reading. With such a virtue, he is not to be pestered by difficult syntax, obscurity of reference, laxity in phrasing. The principles of clear statement that Graves and Hodge announce are concerned "partly with the secure conveyance of information and partly with its decent, or graceful, conveyance, and have been suggested by our recent examination of a great mass of miscellaneous writing."

Some of the principles are debatable; that is, I hope they will be debated. And the debate should start at the beginning, with the page on which Graves and Hodge assert that "every writer should envisage his potential public—which may be twenty people, two hundred, twenty thousand, or the whole wide world—and should write nothing either above or below its supposed capacity." My own view is that a writer is likely to fall into grave error, and perhaps into sin, by taking that principle to heart. Since I constantly address the whole wide world, I keep my soul pure by attending to the theme and letting the millions of readers behind my shoulder do whatever they like. I am a proud spirit, and they for ever clay.

One merit of *The Reader Over Your Shoulder* is particularly telling. Graves and Hodge evidently thought in 1943 that English was in a bad way. What they now think, there is no knowing; but they can hardly believe that the situation has been miraculously transfigured. Their book finds many famous writers guilty of bad writing. But it does not apply to the linguistic or cultural situation the apocalyptic metaphors of disease, corruption, pollution, and vice that have been applied by George Steiner. In *Language and Silence,* Mr. Steiner treats the German language as if it were a victim of cholera or some Black Death caused by Nazi rhetoric. The trouble with that argument is that its metaphors make the whole subject lurid rather than lucid. The reader is involved in a monstrous drama, a morality play transposed into the idiom of horror cinema. A German sentence begins to appear suspect in principle: the reader approaches it as if it contained a deadly nerve gas.

In 1943 Graves and Hodge probably thought that English and German were in the same mess, and that strategic lies on both sides would only make the situation worse. But their reaction was to write a book showing not only that famous writers were careless but that a writer who went to the trouble of setting one clear sentence beside another could still produce good sense and decency. Eliot, Russell, and the other writers are rebuked, but not browbeaten; and, more important, they are shown how to do better. So the whole subject of language, style, vocabulary, sense, truth, and grace is kept within the range of discourse: nobody is to be scared out of his residual wits.

If the book had been genuinely revised and brought up to date, Graves and Hodge would have found it necessary to expound a basic assumption: that there is a decent, privileged norm in the use of English, whether it is called civilized speech or Standard English. They say they do not want to produce stereotypes of English, but their emendations of the defective paragraphs are invariably in styles associated with the ancient British universities. I have no objection to this procedure, although my university is neither ancient nor British. It seems to me that there is indeed an official form of English and that it is reasonable to call it Standard English. If such a style is alien to a particular person's experience and tradition, he can regard it as a foreign language and learn it in that spirit, as if it were French, German, or Italian.

I am aware that there is more to be said on this subject. It is not my intention to out-Simon Simon or out-Safire Safire, but merely to say that there is no point in being scandalized by the assumption in *The Reader Over Your Shoulder* that good English is the sort of English written by Graves and Hodge. In my opinion, that claim is justified.

Review of *The Reader Over Your Shoulder: A Handbook for Writers of English Prose,* by Robert Graves and Alan Hodge. From *The New York Times Book Review,* April 29, 1979.

V

I should not have ended a review of *The Reader Over Your Shoulder* with such a limp sentence, or with one which simply said that the English written by Graves and Hodge is good English. Good for what? Such a style wouldn't be good for every occasion. I should have said that when Graves and Hodge undertook to correct, say, one of Stephen Spender's discursive paragraphs, having accepted that Spender's genre in that passage was properly discursive and expository, they improved it. Here is Spender's paragraph:

> Political beliefs and events play a part in the lives of contemporaries which religious and spectacular warnings of the working out of doom amongst the great used to play in the past. Problems of social organization are so crucially important that any religious mind which ignores them, instead of providing an example to the world, like the teaching of Christ, has shrunk into a shelter from the world. The destruction which one nation can inflict on another has dwarfed even terrible natural events and examples of happiness or unhappiness in private life made public.

Graves and Hodge analyzed the paragraph, according to criteria which they established in an earlier section of *The Reader Over Your Shoulder,* and replaced it by this fair copy:

> Since political creeds have largely superseded religious ones, popular dramatic interest is no longer concentrated on natural catastrophes or on the supernatural doom which overtakes the ambitious Great. It has turned instead to the prolonged conflict between the working-classes and their exploiters, which is now complicated by the hideous destructiveness of international warfare. How the conflict can best be resolved is a question of such crucial importance that to make formal Christianity an excuse for ignoring it would be more than cowardice: it would be a rejection of the example set by Jesus Christ, who actively championed the poor against oppression in an age not yet consciously committed to the class-struggle.

The considerations which Graves and Hodge brought to bear upon Spender's paragraph are too numerous to paraphrase: they amount to an impressive critical analysis, and may be consulted with profit.

Maybe the point is obvious, but I shouldn't have supported the common notion that every form of style is defective if it isn't clear. Clarity is merely one quality; not every occasion has need of it.

The reason for this is that what most people mean by clarity of expression is the delivery of a sentiment or an idea as if the linguistic character of the delivery were neutral; or as if the reader were enabled to see the delivered object as if through impeccably clear glass.

But this desire is not self-evident or "natural"; it is a consequence of a specific historical and cultural development. Only a socially achieved consensus has given clarity its current privilege. I should say a little about this.

On November 22, 1956, Hugh Kenner gave a lecture, under the title "Words in the Dark," to the Royal Society of Literature. The aim of the lecture was to explain how a certain development of the English language has issued in an American poetry alien to English ears: the poetry of William Carlos Williams and Marianne Moore, for instance. Kenner argued that the English language, in what we may call its central tradition, developed in particular relation to the Elizabethan theatre. Shakespeare and Marlowe, though they greatly enriched the language, suppressed certain qualities which may be found in Chaucer, qualities of precision, translucence, the immediacy of a relation to objects and percepts. The language might have developed on Chaucerian lines, but it didn't, mainly because the requirements of the Elizabethan theatre gave it a decisive character: it became a language not of transcribed sensation but of "auditory effects whose impact was incumbent on the actor." What Marlowe's audience saw, when a vision of Helen was to be evoked, was merely a graceful painted boy: the vision was accomplished by words which didn't encourage the audience to examine what might be seen on the stage but to "dream away from the visible":

> O, thou art fairer than the evening air
> Clad in the beauty of a thousand stars;

—the evening air, whose character could only be divined, not the sky, which might be seen.

Such a development of the language proceeded not by denoting sensibilia which might be verified, but by incantation, to which one could only offer one's ears; a style of majestic imprecision:

> O noble weakness!
> If they had swallow'd poison, 'twould appear
> By external swelling; but she looks like sleep,
> As she would catch another Antony
> In her strong toil of grace.

The "bright halo of imprecision" which surrounds the crucial words, crucial because they are those which dominate the auditor's mind, is created by a quality of language which removes the mind from mere appearances. Grace, as Kenner says, "is neither the theologian's grace nor the hostess's nor the dancer's but mingles the prestige of all three."[1] With toil, meaning a snare, it has the further prestige, I might say, of something that so catches the victim that he wouldn't wish himself uncaught. But none of these effects depends upon anything seen, or held in the state of being seen. Cleopatra looks like sleep, but once we look at her in that glimpsing phrase our minds are directed away from her appearance to what, in her life, she has chiefly signified. We are not allowed to see her as a personified Sleep, or even as a Grace, long enough to let her meaning coincide with her appearance. Plenitude of association, not lucidity, is the value the words enforce.

Kenner's argument is that majestic imprecision was the character the English language settled upon, Shakespeare and the Elizabethan theatre being decisive. But the language transplanted to New England had to forget Shakespeare, having no theatre worth mentioning, and to serve more quotidian purposes. I presume Kenner means the pamphlet, the letter, the delivered and often printed sermon, a language going about its ordinary business with ambitions American and no longer English.

That is another story. In England, indeed, there were several attempts to revise the histrionic character of the language. After the Restoration, there was a clear determination to remove the conflicts which had issued in the Civil War, by putting forward for emulation the true-born Englishman, a type of person ideally unaffected even by such local conflicts as those of Whig and Tory. One of the marks of such unity was an agreed style, predicated not upon theatrical conflict or Elizabethan fluidity but upon the sobriety of natural science. There were of course mavericks like Burton and Browne, upon whose amateur exertions no typology of the Englishman could be constructed. But the Royal Society was not alone in urging a style of consent, in which anything that one would judiciously want to say could be said. The production of a visible object, standing clearly apart from its surroundings, was the analogy regularly proposed. This is what a famous passage in Sprat's *History of the Royal Society* (1667) comes to:

> They have . . . a constant Resolution, to reject all the amplifications, digressions, and swellings of style: to return back to the primitive

purity, and shortness, when men deliver'd so many things, almost in an equal number of words. They have exacted from all their members, a close, naked, natural way of speaking; positive expressions; clear senses; a native easiness: bringing all things as near the Mathematical plainness, as they can: and preferring the language of Artizans, Countrymen, and Merchants, before that, of Wits, or Scholars.

Defoe, as I'll suggest, capitalized on this sentiment, and evidently thought himself a patriot for showing what an Englishman in such a relation to the English language could do.

It would be absurd to say that the Royal Society and the other forces for mathematical plainness didn't succeed. The fact that George Orwell is still regularly praised for linking political decency to a plain English style shows that it did. It would be truer to say that the general English understanding of prose has agreed upon lucidity as a chief virtue, and that it has taken pleasure in poetry as the place of acoustic splendour. But this isn't quite true. Arnold and other writers have complained that English prose is, in its way, dishevelled, impatient with ideas because of the precision the expression of an idea requires.

In "Words in the Dark" Kenner quotes a passage from Ford Madox Ford's *Joseph Conrad: A Personal Remembrance* (1924). Ford is recalling that Conrad, especially when he was working on *Nostromo* (1904), was always complaining "that English was a language in which it was impossible to write a direct statement." Ford agreed with him, and thought that French was as superior to English for prose as it was inferior to English for poetry:

> Conrad's indictment of the English language was this, that no English word is a word; that all English words are instruments for exciting blurred emotions. "Oaken" in French means "made of oak wood" —nothing more. "Oaken" in English connotes innumerable moral attributes: it will connote stolidity, resolution, honesty, blond features, relative unbreakableness, absolute unbendableness—also, made of oak. The consequence is that no English word has clean edges: a reader is always, for a fraction of a second, uncertain as to which meaning of the word the writer intends. Thus, all English prose is blurred. Conrad desired to write prose of extreme limpidity.

Ford thought that Conrad achieved limpidity in later years: "he then regretted that for him all the romance of writing was gone—the result being *The Rover,* which strikes the writer as being a very severe and beautiful work."[2]

But Conrad's position is curious. If he thought that English went in for grand and blurred effects, he might have worked against its dissipations. Like Ford, he might have made his English as French as possible. Instead, he conspired with English to produce effects so blurred that F. R. Leavis, the most resolutely English critic, felt impelled to protest. In *The Great Tradition,* Leavis quotes a passage from *Heart of Darkness* and comments on it:

> Conrad must here stand convicted of borrowing the arts of the magazine-writer (who has borrowed his, shall we say, from Kipling and Poe) in order to impose on his readers and on himself, for thrilled response, a "significance" that is merely an emotional insistence on the presence of what he can't produce. The insistence betrays the absence, the willed "intensity" the nullity. He is intent on making a virtue out of not knowing what he means. The vague and unrealizable, he asserts with a strained impressiveness, is the profoundly and tremendously significant.[3]

Conrad would have claimed, I imagine, that he was swaying with the language, according to the character of it which he found in using it. We know that he veered; much as he complained of English, he asserted that if he hadn't written in it he wouldn't have written at all. But Leavis's insistence on "produce" and "unrealizable" shows that, at least for the moment, he is bringing to bear upon Conrad's English in *Heart of Darkness* a criterion which his own English tradition achieved only by working against the grain of the language exemplified by Shakespeare and Marlowe. No wonder he praised the un-Tennysonian Keats of "moss'd cottage-trees" as against the Keats of "perilous seas, in faery lands forlorn."

Read in this context, *The Reader Over Your Shoulder* now seems to me Graves and Hodge's contribution to the war effort. If Englishmen could be shamed into writing clear prose, they might learn by the same means to think straight, and to win the war.

NOTES

  1. Hugh Kenner, "Words in the Dark," in E. V. Rieu (ed.), *Essays by Divers Hands, Being the Transactions of the Royal Society of Literature,* New Series, Vol. XXIX (London: Oxford University Press, 1958), pp. 113–23.

  2. Ford Madox Ford, *Joseph Conrad: A Personal Remembrance* (Boston: Little, Brown, 1924), pp. 217–30.

  3. F. R. Leavis, *The Great Tradition* (London: Chatto & Windus, 1948), p. 199.

SHAKESPEARE'S RHETORIC

Hamlet to the Mob

Now that our play is over I would tell you how you have been persuaded—or deceived—into acquiescence; into a kind of joy, perhaps. You were transported, of course, by my death; struck by the "sublime," the awe-ful. In your inarticulate way you felt that my death was somehow "right," not just because it was inevitable but because it was in keeping with the "inner logic" of my life. It was as fitting, in its own way, as the death of Claudius; and of course you had been waiting for *that* for a couple of hours; wondering when, where, and how it would come.

Bear in mind, though—if you have not bothered to think about it before—that my role was that of the pious, rational hero in a world of impious unreason. Three hundred years from now Santayana will speak of piety as "loyalty to the sources of one's being," and I would anticipate his insight for my own critique. The sources of my being were—we can list them—my father, and, through him, my reverence for the state of Denmark—we can call it England now: and at a deeper level still there was the warm feeling for decorum itself, especially for that version of it which exhibits a loving relation between the thought, the word, and the deed. And reason itself; not the vicious *mere* reason, mere rationalism, which distresses my author just as it will distress the humanist Alexander

Pope in his *Dunciad;* but the act of the humane mind which realizes, as any sound Aristotelian, that it has the duty of controlling the will, the passions. So it was my motive in our play to restore the orders of piety and right reason to a world in which those glowing realities had been perverted. But since I had to be pious toward right reason—before anything else—I had to satisfy that reason that the Ghost was honest, that Claudius had indeed murdered my father.

You see, I was scrupulously pious, scrupulously reasonable: I could not emulate Claudius, or Laertes, or Pyrrhus himself, since it is part of the heartache that the race is to the swift, or the crude, or the impious. But my author had to bear in mind that *your* piety and *your* reason are less scrupulous than mine: you wanted me to catch the nearest way. The killing of Claudius would have gratified you: but, since that event had to be delayed, my author tricked you into acquiescence, kept you in the palm of his hand, by giving you several *minor* gratifications, each involving a local victory over our enemies. Since you could not have the major thrill of seeing me make a corpse of Claudius, he gave you the minor thrill of seeing me make a fool of Polonius: yes, and there were several other victories . . . when I fooled Rosencrantz and Guildenstern . . . when I tricked my mother into talking about "is" and "seems" . . . when I quibbled outrageously with Claudius . . . when I produced the Mousetrap so winningly . . . when I rubbed out the "vice of style" called Osric. And then of course there was my virtuoso piece, when I led Guildenstern such a merry dance with the recorders.

These incidents were gratifying to you in themselves; they prefigured the much richer gratification which-would come with the killing of Claudius; and they kept you moving along nicely in what Hopkins will call "sequences of feeling."

The greatest of these minor victories was the conversion of my mother in the Closet Scene: you responded warmly to my performance there without knowing the processes involved . . . since you are sound Aristotelians only by desire and intuition.

Gertrude played into my hands. You recall that I had just killed Polonius; and, turning aside from his corpse (as if passing from the role of Scourge to that of Minister), I confronted my mother:

> *Peace! sit you down*
> *And let me wring your heart; for so I shall*

> *If it be made of penetrable stuff;*
> *If damned custom have not braz'd it so*
> *That it is proof and bulwark against sense.*

Gertrude made a mistake in braving it out. Perhaps she relied too much on the traditional hierarchy of mother and son, recalling that Coriolanus was shattered by its disruption. Anyway, she rose to the challenge:

> *What have I done that thou dar'st wag thy tongue*
> *In noise so rude against me?*

And my answer came thundering out:

> *Such an act*
> *That blurs the grace and blush of modesty;*
> *Calls virtue hypocrite; takes off the rose*
> *From the fair forehead of an innocent love,*
> *And sets a blister there ...*

You caught the tone, remember? It was my author's version of the "high" style, which Aristotle and Cicero have prescribed for *moving* an audience. I was trying to appeal to those emotions which would colour my mother's judgement and prompt her to a corresponding course of action. Aristotle discusses it in terms of pathos. He also outlines, under the heading of logos, an appeal to the audience's reason. So I appealed to Gertrude's reason to see, to acknowledge, the difference between my father and Claudius; my father, a man endorsed by the gods; Claudius, a mildew'd ear blasting his wholesome brother. And showing her the two pictures, I argued very severely indeed, appealing to intellectualist values which have always been dear to my author; values involving right reason and will, the judgement and the blood, and the relations between the several levels of existence, vegetative, animal, human, and so on. You probably understood the words, even the technical terms like "sense" and "motion"; but it would have been enough even if you had understood only the fury in the words, and not the words.

Gertrude understood both the fury and the words, and she begged me,

> *O Hamlet, speak no more!*
> *Thou turns't mine eyes into my very soul,*
> *And there I see such black and grained spots*
> *As will not leave their tinct.*

But I had my own idea of justice; so I twisted the knife, translating her "black and grained spots" into *animal* terms, the more to nail down her fall from the *human* level of existence:

> *Nay, but to live*
> *In the rank sweat of an enseamed bed,*
> *Stew'd in corruption, honeying and making love*
> *Over the nasty sty!*

My father's ghost entered; but Gertrude, since she could not see it, denied that it was there; protesting like any positivist. She thought me mad!—so I had to prove my reason—all over again—by appealing to hers (persuasion by Logos). You recall I challenged her term "ecstasy":

> *Ecstasy?*
> *My pulse as yours doth temperately keep time*
> *And makes as healthful music. It is not madness*
> *That I have utt'red . . .*
> *. . . Mother, for love of grace,*
> *Lay not that flattering unction to your soul,*
> *That not your trespass but my madness speaks.*
> *It will but skin and film the ulcerous place,*
> *Whiles rank corruption, mining all within,*
> *Infects unseen. Confess yourself to heaven;*
> *Repent what's past; avoid what is to come;*
> *And do not spread the compost on the weeds*
> *To make them ranker.*

I was facing two ways at that point. I was reminding you, my Elizabethan audience, of one of my deepest preoccupations in Claudius's Denmark, the unreliability of appearance as image of reality, the unreliability of what "seems": and the most pointed version I could recite was one which recalled to you the wonderful traditional metaphor of the "body politic." So I linked together all sorts of things: disease in our state, a grim hint about civil war, the overthrow of reason by sexual passion, the splitting apart of thought, word, and deed. I was telling *you* these things, not just my mother; since my author is not above giving timely warnings when an opportunity arises.

You probably felt that my tone at that point was harsh; and you began to resent the "holier than thou" ingredient in my attitude, especially in the last few imperatives, where it rather got out of hand. But I saw your frowns, and in unbending a little to Gertrude apologized a little to you. Not too much, of course; because after all I *was* holier than thou: my role was the sort of thing you are meant to live up to. If you chose to identify yourselves with me, you were indulging your vanity. There is no point now in mincing words. But I needed you on my side then, so I ingratiated myself with you—and with Gertrude—by exhibiting magnanimity, generosity, and so on. Aristotle was again my mentor, recommending persuasion (this time, by Ethos). So I asked Gertrude—and you—to forgive me this my virtue: I kept repeating the gentle, magical phrase "Good night": I said I must be cruel, only to be kind. Best of all I insinuated the assumption that Gertrude—and you—were now firmly on my side.

So I triumphed. Not only with Gertrude, but with you. Gertrude's conversion was complete: so was your fulfilment, at least for the time being. I had rescued my mother from the disease of Claudius; just as Antony cured the Roman mob after their infection by Brutus.

My task in the later scenes was easier. Claudius could have none of your sympathy after he had arranged to have me murdered in England. The rabble fastened on Laertes as King, but my author condemned both: anyway it was a flagrant breach of custom and antiquity. Your part, then, was to rise above such pettiness, and to sneer at Laertes in your own turn when he raved:

> *To hell, allegiance! vows, to the blackest devil!*
> *Conscience and grace, to the profoundest pit!*
> *I dare damnation. To this point I stand,*
> *That both the worlds I give to negligence,*
> *Let come what comes; only I'll be revenged*
> *Most thoroughly for my father.*

Rubbish! Was this the kind of vengeance you would have had me perform on Claudius? Nor indeed was there much courage in it, since Laertes was very soon to anoint his sword with poison. (My author was counting on your sturdy notion of fair play.)

When I returned from England I ingratiated myself with you, obliquely, by reciting a humane version of mortality, by joking with the Gravedigger, by sneering with you at Osric, and even by losing my self-control when I saw that my fair Ophelia was dead. Aristotle himself would have condoned this. He would also have approved my new and deeply pious feeling for Providence. You recall I gave Horatio—and you—two mottos: "Let be"; and "The readiness is all." My associate Thomas Becket will offer a gloss on my words when he says, in Mr. Eliot's play,

> *Death will come only when I am worthy,*
> *And if I am worthy, there is no danger.*
> *I have therefore only to make perfect my will.*

Thomas will understand my piety, since he has his own: and perhaps his is even more secure than mine since it rewards him with a "tremor of bliss" which I did not feel. He will say, just before death, "All things proceed to a joyful consummation," thereby revealing that the Reality with which he identifies his will is clearer to him than mine to me. But we are both pious men: that is enough: let be.

I hope I pleased you in the last scene. My fencing match was a lively performance: I graciously forgave Laertes; and at last, but in my own good time, I killed Claudius. Some of the more squeamish among you were perturbed, as well as thrilled, when I forced the dying King to drink from the poisoned cup. It was a grim piece of work. And yet I prepared the way for it, by calling Claudius "thou incestuous, murd'rous, damned Dane," and by bitterly conceding to him and my mother, in death, the sexual union I would have denied them in life. There was a severe propriety, surely, in all this; some kind of poetic justice. I think you understood it (most of you) at the time, just as you understood my answer to Horatio when he wanted to be with me in death. "I am more an antique Roman than a Dane," he cried, capitalizing on our reverence for both antiquity and Rome; but I recalled him to an even higher law, that of humanity itself, which for us means order, degree, reputation, the health of the body politic, and several other glowing realities. "As th'art a man," I cried, "Give me the cup." I was never more pious than at that moment.

Horatio endorsed your response to my death by calling me a "noble heart," a "sweet prince." And Fortinbras completed your tribute when he said,

> *Let four captains*
> *Bear Hamlet like a soldier to the stage;*
> *For he was likely, had he been put on,*
> *To have prov'd most royally; and for his passage*
> *The soldiers' music and the rites of war*
> *Speak loudly for him . . .*

The statement is dry and somewhat formal; the decorous truth, and yet a truth which you yourselves might have recited more warmly. It is as if my author were leaving a gap to be filled by your feeling; and, filling it, you succumbed once more to his wit and witchcraft. Except that his, unlike Claudius's, was white magic.

Desdemona to Emilia

Othello asked, Emilia, that you should attend on me; but he did not foresee the extent of your service. He did not know that you would die for witnessing to my virtue; killed by your husband as I was killed by mine. Nor did he know that you would be my "reflector," directing your own pragmatic light on my perfection. I wonder do you yourself realize how liberally you served me and our play.

My author's problem was so to present me that my values would stand, palpable, in the centre of the play—proud, absolute, pure—making no protestations. Early on Iago said of me, "She must have change, she must," thus telling the audience that the essential "quality" of my perfection was its absolute unchangingness. My role was to represent the perfect, incredible marriage of *being* and *seeming:* I had very little to say, because my acts and my sufferance had absolute sanctions. Indeed, behind all the pathetic mutations of the play, behind Othello's sightless vision of what did not exist, I was to stand as the very proof that appearances can be reliable, that we may sometimes trust in what seems, that truth and constancy exist as well as the glowing idea of each. From the moment of my marriage I became the incredible emblem of that truth, that constancy: those ideas crystallized in me. I moved through the play, modestly, without rancour, a gentle reproach to everything partial, alloyed, relative: I was the concrete *thing,* enacting an absolute *idea,* of fidelity and privacy. I was a reproach to you too, of course; and that mattered.

Othello could not believe in an absolute, since the belief itself would have been an absolute faith. He could not believe in my absolute constancy, even though disbelief meant the sundering of his entire world. How easy it was, then, for Iago to capitalize on this failure, insinuating that what seems is inevitably a deceit: "She did deceive her father, marrying you," he warned Othello, "And when she seem'd to shake and fear your looks, / She loved them most" . . . "Why, go to then; / She that so young could give out such a seeming, / To seel her father's eyes up close as oak—." And so on; distorting the neutral state of *seeming,* identifying it with the falconer's cruel deceit: and even the sound of the words collaborated with his rhetoric.

Thus my role as the embodiment of an idea. But our audience could hardly be expected to understand it if Othello was unable to believe in it. My author left Othello to his own pathetic devices, but he had to be gentle with his audience. So he arranged that you, wife to Iago and therefore to some extent involved in his world, would bridge the gap: he arranged that you would mediate between me and our audience, representing a way of life nearer their own, perhaps identical with their own, asking the crude, muscular questions.

You recall our conversation in the third scene of Act IV: it was hardly a conversation at all, you did most of the talking, but while you talked about yourself you were in fact defining *me.* We spoke about constancy, and wives, and husbands, and the selling price of virtue. And I recalled the death of my mother's maid Barbara and the song she sang about the willow. So Barbara's death scene aroused in the audience appropriate feelings for mine—which would come in its own good time—and it also enlarged the scope of my constancy, giving it the grandeur of a deathbed profession. So when I asked (thinking of men abusing their suffering wives), "Wouldst thou do such a deed for all the world?"—I was able to support the question with a lifetime's perfection: I was able to make it ring out—suggestively, with grandeur and mystery, and entirely without arrogance. You answered, in your own voice and perhaps in that of the audience, "The world is a huge thing: 'tis a great price / For a small vice."

It was not my place to lecture you or to pour scorn on a set of relative values, especially as I had to monopolize the ardour of an audience nearer to those values than to mine. So I merely repeated my vow, gently: "Beshrew me, if I would do such a wrong / For the whole world." And then you rounded on husbands, in language that anybody could understand:

> *Let husbands know*
> *Their wives have sense like them: they see and smell*
> *And have their palates both for sweet and sour,*
> *As husbands have. What is it that they do*
> *When they change us for others? Is it sport?*
> *I think it is: and doth affection breed it?*
> *I think it doth: is 't frailty that thus errs?*
> *It is so too: and have not we affections,*
> *Desires for sport, and frailty, as men have?*
> *Then let them use us well: else let them know,*
> *The ills we do, their ills instruct us so.*

A plain, ungarnished tale: no one could mistake your drift. And yet it had very little to do directly with my situation, or with yours, since neither Othello nor Iago had been unfaithful. All that my author wanted was that you would bridge the gap between my grand absolutes and the easier attitudes of the audience. He realized that it is very difficult to understand an absolute, and therefore difficult to have it throb with felt life: an absolute is too far away from the audience, too far out there in a stark world whose grandeur one can merely take on trust. So it did not matter what you said, so long as your saying it helped to bridge that gap, helped to render my perfection less abstract, less marmoreal. It was not necessary that you should cut me down, sneer at my perfection, or degrade it; but that you should draw that perfection into a context warm with human motive, alive, throbbing. Lacking that involvement, my perfection would have been gratuitous, cold, almost without a source in human feeling at all; just as, three centuries hence, André Gide will puzzle his readers by exhibiting men dealing out evil for its own pure, absolute sake; gratuitously.

Henry James will understand this necessity of bridging gaps that are too vast. In *The Wings of the Dove*, Milly Theale will move through the story with a superb allegiance to absolute values: she will be hurt, as I was hurt, and as I forgave, so she. And just as I have had you, Emilia, to define my values by enacting their rejection, so Milly Theale will have the relativist Kate Croy to render her beauty warm and glowing by involving it in a human situation. And just as Milly spreads her wings over Merton Densher, changing him utterly, so I will persist as an *eikon,* an exemplary instance, of constancy. But my constancy would have been merely a cold idea without your rough-and-ready presence. You, Emilia, were the means of opening to the audience the closed, absolute world of my perfection: and bear in mind how severe an absolute constancy is. My role, strictly speaking, had little to do with love or passion in themselves, but only as vehicles for an absolute that could persist even without them: and there is something forbidding about such an absolute, so austere, so stark in its perfection.

My author placed a great burden on you, and yet he did not depend on you entirely: there was always my death scene, which he could exploit so as to modulate my absolute into something vibrant. Having presented me as an exemplary instance of constancy, and an adept of sufferance, he devoted the last act to my participation in the most intimate human gesture. That is why the deathbed scene was almost Wagnerian in its passionate humanity; but it could take that tone only because I had already registered my claim to a more austere role. I could now afford this sweet modulation. So I asked you to lay my wedding sheets on my bed: later I said,

> *If I do die before thee, prithee, shroud me*
> *In one of those same sheets.*

When Othello came into my bedchamber he spoke of my blood and my skin, thereby endorsing the Wagnerian tone:

> *Yet I'll not shed her blood,*
> *Nor scar that whiter skin of hers than snow*
> *And smooth as monumental alabaster.*

He spoke of plucking my rose, and (kissing me) was almost persuaded to break the sword of seeming justice. In turn I quibbled about dying and deathbeds, as if in response to his lovemaking. Indeed my death scene was so warmly human now that Othello could without endangering its resonance say, "Cold, cold, my girl! / Even like thy chastity." And when he stabbed himself he fell on my body, saying

> *I kiss'd thee ere I kill'd thee: no way but this,*
> *Killing myself, to die upon a kiss.*

Thus our bodily union, resumed at last with ritual fervour: too late for either of us, and yet not too late to endorse our whole lives or to acknowledge my constancy.

So Othello at last acknowledged by a symbolic gesture what you had already protested on my behalf; and it was fitting that you, a relativist in these matters, should rise to proclaim my absolute guiltlessness, carrying the audience with you. Hence the splendour of your own death, reflecting the splendour of mine. You asked,

> *What did thy song bode, lady?*
> *Hark, canst thou hear me? I will play the swan,*
> *And die in music.*

Then you sang "Willow, willow, willow," just as I had done, just as Barbara had done. And, dying, you bore witness once again:

> *Moor, she was chaste; she loved thee, cruel Moor;*
> *So come my soul to bliss, as I speak true;*
> *So speaking as I think, I die, I die.*

Was there not here a yielding up of the relative values which you had sustained so lithely throughout the play? So speaking as I think: it doesn't sound much, and yet it came from one who had said,

> *Why, the wrong is but a wrong i' the world; and having*
> *the world for your labour, 'tis a wrong in your own*
> *world, and you might quickly make it right.*

Anyway, you were already my adjunct, before you died; bearing witness to the reality of truth as I to that of constancy. The justice of it pleases.

You see now that your role was like Barbara's. I invited the dead Barbara into our play so that the audience, feeling how closely my tragedy resembled hers, would give me the warmth of their sympathy. I wanted to take unto myself the audience's feeling for injured innocence — not just mine, but Barbara's, and that of millions of wronged women. And when I was dead you took Barbara's place, existing not for your own sake now but for mine; demanding that the audience pity me, weep for me, acknowledge my absolute merit.

My own death was the culmination of my role as sufferer. Othello suffered also, in the second phase of his "tragic rhythm," but that phase was the substance of my entire being. Mine was the third of those "offices" which Cicero assigned to the orator, to *move* an audience, to register the highest claim on their feelings; this, rather than to teach, or to delight. Hence, no matter how urbanely I spoke, I lived and died in the appropriate "grand" style. In that sense my role, unlike Othello's, was lyric: when I had arrived at my profound state of sufferance, that arrival was definitive, it *defined* the essential nature of my role. Thereafter I could only transcend this role by dying. And at that stage the "sequence of feeling" involving me and my sufferance was complete: formal perfection was achieved. Again the justice of it pleases.

From *Studies*, Winter 1958.

SHAKESPEARE IN THE SONNETS

There are at least four ways of reading the sonnets.

One: they are formal exercises. The sonnet is a poem of fourteen lines, available in three main rhyming orders, a lyrical form found by various poets to be suitable for the expression of such sentiments as love, desire, resentment, and so forth. A few poets, notably Sidney, Spenser, and Shakespeare, did more elaborate things with the form by stringing a number of sonnets into a sequence. Petrarch was the great precursor in the genre, and Ovid the supreme provider of themes and motifs. Question: what is Shakespeare doing in the sonnets? Answer: he is writing sonnets, working out the possibilities of the form, a procedure as deliberate and as inventive as Bach's in the *Goldberg Variations*. He is not unlocking his heart or confessing his follies.

Northrop Frye reads the sonnets in this way. In *Fables of Identity* (1963) he says that "about all that one can get out of the sonnets, considered as transcripts of experience, is the reflection that pederastic infatuations with beautiful and stupid boys are probably very bad for practicing dramatists." If the sonnets tell a story, it is as abstract as stories about Narcissus, Eros, Pygmalion, and Priapus.

Stephen Booth takes much the same line in his *Shakespeare's Sonnets*

(1977). "William Shakespeare was almost certainly homosexual, bisexual, or heterosexual: the sonnets provide no evidence on the matter." To assume that the poems "reflect particulars of Shakespeare's sex life is to be as unreasonable as Hamlet would be if he assumed that the first player was a chum of Hecuba's." The dark lady, like the male friend, "may be a literary creation." As for the rival poet, Shakespeare may not have had any particular poet in mind.

John Crowe Ransom doesn't even advert to such matters. His essay in *The World's Body* is concerned with Shakespeare's habits of style, and especially of diction where description and analogy are in question. Who is speaking to whom about what is not a question to be raised.

Two: they are a bundle of poems in an order which may or may not be authorial, to be read without assuming for them a particular context, real or imagined. The poems are therefore available for any purpose; they can be taken as texts for a theory of poetry, for instance, as in Murray Krieger's *A Window to Criticism* (1964), or for a thesis about poetic subjectivity, as in Joel Fineman's *Shakespeare's Perjured Eye.*

Three: they are poems more or less in a telling sequence, related in a rather distant sense to a lovers' triangle or quartet which may well be imaginary. In "A Poetics for Infatuation"—his contribution to Edward Hubler's *The Sense of Shakespeare's Sonnets* (1952)—R. P. Blackmur took such a situation uninsistently for granted, didn't trouble himself about its real or imaginary status, and assumed that the main emotions were infatuation and jealousy. But he also thought that Shakespeare in several of the poems was addressing himself in one or another of his multiple selves, that the rival poet need not have existed "save as an aid to Shakespeare's poetics," and that Shakespeare may have moved "among the coils and recoils of the various selves that thrive and batten upon the psyche" in order to declare "his uncommitted anonymity."

John Berryman, too, in "Shakespeare at Thirty"—it is reprinted in *The Freedom of the Poet* (1976)—maintained that "the sonnets do not tell a story, still less do they follow a fashion, though a habit of sonnet writing will produce occasional exercises; they reflect interests, pieces of living, two passions."

Four: they are poems in which Shakespeare transcribed his own experience. In some interpretations, the experience is that of a lowly actor-poet and his aristocratic patron, complicated by the poet's involvement with a married woman: Shakespeare, the Earl of Southampton, and Emilia Lenier, according to A. L. Rowse's *Shakespeare's Sonnets: The Problems*

Solved (1973). Or the experience is entirely sexual, as in Joseph Pequigney's *Such Is My Love.*

Professor Pequigney believes that Shakespeare wrote 154 sonnets, put them in a certain order, and arranged to have Thorpe publish them in that order in the Quarto of 1609. The poems tell a story of homoerotic passion, complicated and indeed disgraced by heterosexual lust; the story is rough, and roughly as follows. Sonnets 1–19: a poet, fascinated with a beautiful young man whose initials are W.H., urges him to marry and have children. Then he falls in love with W.H., and offers him poetic rather than sexual or procreative immortality. Sonnets 20–99: the poet and W.H. have an affair which goes through the standard phases of bliss, dependence, doubt, resentment, jealousy, and recrimination. W.H. is unfaithful to the poet, perhaps with a rival poet and/or with other men and perhaps a woman. The poet has his own lapses—two, to be precise. He confesses and begs his lover's forgiveness. Sonnets 100–126: the end of the affair. Sonnets 127–154: the poet has lustful dealings with a dark lady, who may already have been involved with W.H. The lady is married, promiscuous, and besides, the poet is not in love with her: he mostly feels self-disgust, bitterness, and occasional flares of desire. The affair, any psychoanalyst would say, won't last much longer.

Up to this point, Pequigney's interpretation isn't especially novel: the association of Shakespeare and homosexuality has a long history. Pequigney scorns the attempt to regard the relation between the poet and W.H. as exemplifying "Renaissance friendship." The "I" of the poems is bisexual, but his fundamental sexual category is homoerotic; his heterosexual activities are merely degenerate outbreaks. Who the "I" is, Pequigney is indeed ready to say. For a while, he refers to him as "the poet," often as "the persona," then as "Shakespeare's persona," but on page 118 he names him as Shakespeare: "Shakespeare (and I will now shift to using the proper name for the textual 'I') is not at all concerned with a poetic triumph; he is vying only for the prize of the fair friend." But I note, with dismay, that on page 136 Pequigney says that in Sonnets 109–112 "Shakespeare depicts himself (or the persona, if one prefers) as a committer of recent infidelities." The infidelities don't bother me; but why has Pequigney allowed me a preference he has already set aside? If one prefers "the persona," the whole case falls: then it becomes entirely permissible to think that stoutly heterosexual W. Shakespeare imagined the whole thing.

Pequigney doesn't think it was all in Shakespeare's head. He offers many "reasons to suppose that Shakespeare sonnetized his own amorous experiences." But on the same page 220 he lets the argument wobble:

> If the Sonnets create the dual impression of a rich flow of spontane-
> ous feeling and thought and of imaginative design, the effect may
> well derive from Shakespeare's rendering of his own life-experiences
> under the shaping power of art. His artistic shaping power need not
> distort or obscure the contours of the experiential love and lust that
> might lie behind the work.

I know not "might" and "may well." On page 97 Pequigney says:

> It is not improbable, though, that the remarkable pre-Freudian
> insights into the dynamics of homoerotic love derive from self-
> awareness, elicited by the amorous relationships reported. A good case
> can be made for the rendering of autobiographical experience in the
> Sonnets, but it would here be digressive, and so I defer it till later.

But later doesn't make the case, or make the implied one better. It isn't convincing to say that Shakespeare's sense of the dynamics of homoerotic love was so extraordinarily acute that he must have been gay—especially as the emotions attendant upon homoerotic love don't seem to differ much from the ones I'm more familiar with. The plays show that Shakespeare could imagine nearly anything, so why not the dynamics of homoerotic love? Besides, it isn't hard evidence to say that what the sonnets show of jealousy coincides with what Freud said of it in various essays, even though Pequigney makes much of Freud and describes his own reading of the sonnets as psychoanalytical.

Pequigney is a spirited writer, and he drives a severe bargain: he insists on reading the sonnets as truth-telling autobiography. Every poem is drawn into the record. Differences of tone aren't allowed to count. Sonnet 62—"Sin of self-love possesseth all mine eye"—seems to me an elaborate metaphysical conceit of rather slight voltage, but Pequigney won't let me get away with that: "In Sonnet 62 the persona, though old, borrows narcissistically and with a sense of guilt the physical qualities of the fair youth." Well, yes, if you insist: but why insist that all the poems are on the same level of intensity?

The main consequence of Pequigney's interpretation is that the experience of the sonnets is deemed to be entirely private, personal, and sexual. There is to be no recognition of a public world, nor of the four participants as having any life but their sexual one. No talk of patrons and money. The beautiful young man is not an aristocrat, so he is not in a position to do the poet any favours, except sexual ones.

The book is a formidable essay in debunking. Instead of enhancing the situation by calling it Renaissance friendship and giving a glowing account of that sentiment, Pequigney rejects this high-minded interpretation, translates the words into their most available physical sense—hence his constant reliance upon Eric Partridge's *Shakespeare's Bawdy* (1969) and E. A. M. Coleman's *The Dramatic Use of Bawdy in Shakespeare* (1974)—and then says, in effect, that the sexual story is just as uplifting as any told by Douglas Bush or A. L. Rowse.

Sometimes the case is persuasive. Sonnet 4, for instance, could be read in a lordly way as having to do with patronage and generosity—or even with the young man's niggardliness in keeping himself to himself. "The bounteous largess given thee to give" could cover much of this. The poem could even be read as saying, For God's sake don't be such a narcissist! But Pequigney takes it as saying: "You should really marry and have children: masturbation is no good." The bounty is semen. Stephen Booth glanced at that interpretation, but merely to list it as possible. Pequigney insists on it; and certainly the sonnet's references to "spend / Upon thyself" ... "why dost thou abuse ..." and "having traffic with thyself alone" are hard to keep high-minded. On the other hand, I can't be persuaded that Sonnet 33's reference to the basest clouds riding "with ugly rack on his celestial face" is about fellatio.

There is no clear way to settle this. Empson remarks, in *Some Versions of Pastoral*, that Swift's case, especially in *A Tale of a Tub*, was fearful because he couldn't get out of his mind the thought that everything spiritual has a gross and revolting parody, very similar to it, and having the same name. If you wanted to defend the established church against the reformers' inner light, you had to lay out all the terrible possibilities, high-minded and obscene, and work hard distinguishing between them:

> Mixed with his statement, part of what he satirised by pretending (too convincingly) to believe, the source of his horror, was "everything spiritual is really material; Hobbes and the scientists have proved this; all religion is really a perversion of sexuality."

Worse: "the language plays into his hands here, because the spiritual words are all derived from physical metaphors; as he saw again and again how to do this the pleasure of ingenuity must have become a shock to faith." Even someone as high-minded as Emerson saw this, but he didn't force it to Swiftian vertigo.

"Spirit" was one of Swift's dreadful words, impossible to keep pure from wind, farting, and drink. It was also one of Shakespeare's, as in Sonnet 56's lines ". . . and do not kill / The spirit of love with a perpetual dullness." Pequigney has a long paragraph in which he plays elaborately fair with the interpretation, but in the end takes the spirit of love as semen:

> The "spirit" of "love" may be taken to allude to its "soul" or "spiritual element," to feelings toward the other such as tenderness and wonder, for these inform eros and also depend on it, since they will not, it is feared, survive the permanent subsiding of desire. However, "spirit" again can = "semen," along with the closely allied physiological "spirit generative" that the word also conveys, and it may possibly = "the male member." Annotated thus, "the spirit of love" would have reference not to affectionate sentiments but to sexual sensations, and it would be deadened when no phallic reactions arose as a result of gazing on the beloved.

Pequigney's style, you see, is rather courtly: there is some discrepancy of tone between the debunking project and the air of patient explication which enforces it. Sometimes, too, he makes the heaviest weather establishing interpretations already fairly current; his dealings with a hard line in Sonnet 51, "Shall neigh no dull flesh in his fiery race," amount to his agreeing with George Steevens's reading, available since 1780.

Not that I can fault the project. But I think it has two difficulties. The first is that Pequigney takes the sonnets as annotations on Shakespeare's life, speculative chapters of a biography otherwise unwritten. He doesn't take them as poems in any other respect: they are documents in evidence for a case being made. The second is that the scope of the sonnets has to be kept narrow, for the sake of the story they are supposed to tell. There is no room for anything but sex, and the few emotions that issue from it.

I should try to show this by comparing two accounts of a sonnet. "They that have pow'r to hurt, and will do none" (94) is the subject of a chapter in Empson, and of a fairly long commentary in Pequigney. Here is the poem:

> *They that have pow'r to hurt, and will do none,*
> *That do not do the thing they most do show,*
> *Who moving others are themselves as stone,*
> *Unmoved, cold, and to temptation slow—*
> *They rightly do inherit heaven's graces,*
> *And husband nature's riches from expense;*
> *They are the lords and owners of their faces,*
> *Others but stewards of their excellence.*
> *The summer's flow'r is to the summer sweet,*
> *Though to itself it only live and die;*
> *But if that flow'r with base infection meet,*
> *The basest weed outbraves his dignity.*
> > *For sweetest things turn sourest by their deeds;*
> > *Lilies that fester smell far worse than weeds.*

Empson thinks the poem is talking about many sorts of people—stealers of hearts as well as of public power—and feeling many things about them. He assumes, too, that one of the important aspects of Shakespeare's sonnets is that they enabled or incited him to invent feelings which he developed later in the plays, as he developed in Prince Henry, Troilus, and Angelo several feelings about the attraction of coldness which occupied him in Sonnet 94. More specifically, Empson takes the sonnet as involving an Elizabethan feeling about the Machiavellian, "the wicked plotter who is exciting and civilised and in some way right about life." The feelings whirling about this figure are complicated: the speaker is recommending some degree of hypocrisy, and is aghast to find himself doing so. There is also an implication that whatever W.H. does is likely to be lovely because he is lovely. And so on. "The root of the ambivalence, I think, is that W.H. is loved as an arriviste, for an impudent worldliness that Shakespeare finds shocking and delightful." The flower is difficult, because the reasons why W.H. treated the poet badly "are the same as the reasons why he was fascinating, which gives its immediate point to the profound ambivalence about the selfishness of the flower." In the same way, Prince Henry's soliloquy promising to ditch Falstaff "demands from us just the sonnets' mood of bitter complaisance; the young man must still be praised and loved, however he betrays his intimates, because we see him all shining with the virtues of success." Empson doesn't mention it, but a lot of this feeling gets into *This Side of Paradise, The Great Gatsby,* and *The Last Tycoon*. Warren Beatty capitalized upon it in *Shampoo*. Empson doesn't mention that the speaker is giving W.H. the opposite advice to the one he gave him in the first sonnets: give up the single life, get married, have a child. Here he is saying: keep away from every entanglement, because they are all base and putrid in the end.

But Empson's reading of the poem opens it to a wide range of application: W.H. is a type, not a born aristocrat but a social climber, beautiful and elegant of course and therefore to be loved and protected from cads and from the worst parts of his own disposition. He shares much with Bassanio, and is encouraged to go the way of Prince Henry and Angelo.

Pequigney reads the poem more narrowly: it is not a sermon addressed to W.H., but W.H. is expected to overhear it and take it to heart. The sermon is about sexual fidelity, and the speaker is worldly enough to think most people faithless. If you have power, especially sexual power, choose not to use it: let others be attracted to you, but keep your distance from them. That way, you "husband nature's riches from expense." Pequigney interprets nature's riches as physical perfections, especially the treasure of one's semen, to be husbanded, not squandered in orgasms. Such husbandry means self-possession, appropriate to "the lords and owners of their faces" rather than to the mere stewards of their—the lords'—excellence. Pequigney doesn't make as much as Empson does of the summer's flower: presumably its being sweet to the summer means that one's instincts are in the right relation to their situation—integral, authentic, unvulgar, making whatever flourish its beauty entails but never making a show of itself. The lines

> *But if that flow'r with base infection meet,*
> *The basest weed outbraves his dignity*

are botched in *Such Is My Love*, "basest" being printed as "bravest." Pequigney interprets base infection as having "a suggestion here of vene- real infection." Empson was puzzled by "meet," but it would fit Pequigney's interpretation quite well in its suggestion of the casual sexual encounter:

> *For sweetest things turn sourest by their deeds;*
> *Lilies that fester smell far worse than weeds.*

Of these, Pequigney says:

> The "sweetest things" that "turn sourest by their deeds" can hardly
> be flowers, which admit of "sweet" and "sour" but not of "deeds."
> The verse is laden with sexual innuendo. Since "sweet" can =
> "sensually delectable," "deeds" can = "coital" and probably other
> "sexual acts," and "things" can = "genital organs," the things that do
> the deeds would seem to be rather phallic than floral.

The *OED* defines "fester" as "to putrefy, rot; to become pestiferous or
loathsome by corruption." It seems a violent word for a flower which in
Sonnet 12 was allowed to go quietly "past prime." I know that rotted
lilies have a peculiarly bad smell, but Pequigney could have made a bigger
claim for it as it carries further the infection of line 11.

Finally, I'm surprised that neither Empson nor Pequigney makes
anything of the third line. Aristotle, in Book 8, Chapter 6 and thereafter,
of the *Physics,* describes the first principle as the Unmoved Mover. In the
Christian tradition it became the divine attribute. God is omnipotent,
even if he doesn't choose to use his power on any occasion that seems to
call for it. Christ in the desert was "as stone / Unmoved, cold, and to
temptation slow"—cold when faced with a tempting Satan, not cold by
divine nature. So the beautiful young man, divine in his secular way,
should hold himself aloof from his inferiors. What the poem seems to be
saying is that the kind of equilibrium that comes easily to a god is hard
for humans to maintain, subject to decay and to sundry waywardnesses as
they are. It is easy for a god to combine incongruous powers, but men can
only do it as a tour de force. That being so, we do most good not, as
Empson says, by fulfilling our natures but by knowing our most complete identity—as the summer flower does—and by living up to it.

In the end I think those readers who will be fully convinced by
Pequigney's book must start out reading it already half convinced. A
disposition to start with an open mind is fine, but I doubt if such purity
of heart is possible. I start with a prejudice against the argument that a
work of literature transcribes an experience already in place. It seems to

me that much of what appears on the page was discovered in the process of writing, come upon as a linguistic opportunity not to be passed up. I feel this prejudice especially about the sonnets, which are extraordinarily tricky. I don't see how any experience could correspond to those words, or be thought to coincide with their virtuosity. A reader who begins the book already half convinced that the sonnets are autobiographical will find his sense of them confirmed and sharpened at every turn. Some of Pequigney's detailed readings seem to me to plod: too long, they don't assume a lively reader or a darting mind. But the full effect upon a congenially disposed reader is bound to be decisive.

Joel Fineman isn't much interested in this question: he has an elaborate argument, but it has nothing to do with autobiography. Just to get the matter out of his way, he remarks in a footnote that many details in the poems suggest "at least some dimension of private, personal reference," but that nevertheless very little autobiography can be derived from them. He accepts the 1609 order of the sonnets as authoritative "even if it is not authorial." The love quartet is agreed, too, "because it has already been accepted by literary tradition." But the story is "the projection of Shakespearean material imagination."

That last rather odd phrase points the reader toward Fineman's subject. The sonnets were written at a time when "the orthodox tradition of epideictic poetry" was exhausted. Shakespeare could not continue writing the poetry of praise. Instead, he established an ironic relation to it by resorting to the mock encomium: the poetry of praise became the poetry of the paradox of praise.

What Shakespeare wrote, therefore, belongs not to the history of his feelings and passions—or if to that, only by the way—but to the history of poetry and, more particularly, to the definition of "a new first-person poetic posture." The difference between the sonnets to W.H. and those to the dark lady is a mutation in ontology and expression. The sonnets to W.H. are predicated upon an ideal presence, "a poetics centered on the visionary fullness of subject and object." The fact that such presence, such fullness is no longer possible to Shakespeare is acknowledged, even in the sonnets to the young man, but the poet's sense of belatedness is not overwhelming. The sonnets to the dark lady, on the other hand, show how the tired tradition of epideixis may be revived, given a new because different life, "when it turns into a poetics centered instead on the resonant hollowness of a fractured verbal self."

The relation between feeling and form, according to this argument, is not that feeling searches for its proper form, but that a given form requires for its development a corresponding set of feelings. Epideixis is the governing cause of an increasingly subjective poetics rather than a consequence of it or an instrument for its expression. Fineman doesn't say anything about the choice of epideixis in preference to any other available style. It is there, like the sonata. But there is a vocation of form—to use Focillon's phrase—corresponding to a vocation of substance; so it could be argued that Shakespeare's taking up the poetry of praise wasn't an arbitrary choice but, however circuitously, an opportunistic one. A traditionalist would say that he "knew" he could express his feelings by moving between a moribund form and a knowingly belated semblance of it. Of course any consideration of form can be deflected in this way.

For the purposes of Fineman's argument—which owes something to Derrida and to Girard—it is necessary to start with a poetry of praise; to posit an original presence featuring a visionary subject fully present to his object, to himself, and "to all the speech he speaks." The enabling analogies are visual and visionary, their motto a line from Sonnet 23—"To hear with eyes belongs to love's fine wit." The language of such presence is "the iconic, autological discourse of visionary speech" in which words are the very things of which they speak. This is a discourse of presentation, not of representation, and it culminates in the presexual world of Shakespearean comedy.

The sonnets to W.H. intermittently, and those to the dark lady continuously, "give the lie" to this original true sight: they are the ruins of that firstness. They "merely represent the things of which they are the sign," and for that reason they are bound to seem a semiotic lie. They are a discourse not of the eye but of the tongue, "fallen words that have lost their visionary truth." Because as speech they forswear vision, "these words are what Shakespeare calls 'forsworn.'" They point, therefore, to the structures of character in the tragedies.

Fineman describes the relation between the sonnets to W.H. and those to the dark lady as "structural pathos."

Language re-presents what vision presents, and yet this repetition produces something different from that which it repeats, for the truth of language is that, compared to vision, it is false.

Language "lies" against sight. In the sonnets, "linguistic difference predicates sexual difference."

> Thus the young man is "fair," "kind," and "true" (105) and the sonnets addressed to the young man regularly invoke visual imagery of identificatory likeness when they characterize their poet's desire for the young man. In paradoxical contrast, the lady, as she is given to us, is foul because both fair and foul, unkind because both kind and unkind, false because both true and false.

The young man sonnets feature likeness, "specular homogeneity," homosexual truth, Platonic desire. The dark lady sonnets feature difference, the semiotic lie, linguistic heterogeneity, lust as the corresponding passion, and "an outspoken poetics of erotic desire" which Shakespeare, according to Fineman's insistence, "invents." Indeed, Shakespeare in the sonnets invents a poetics of subjectivity which ended with Freud.

> The Shakespearean subject is *the* subject of our literature, the privileged and singular form of literary subjectivity since the Renaissance. And this in turn will suggest why it is that Shakespeare's canon has historically been institutionalized by and within a larger literary canon for which subjectivity, as authorial presence, novelistic characterology, introspective interiority, has always seemed—or at least has always seemed since Shakespeare—a significant literary feature.

"A significant literary feature"; is that all? I thought Fineman's claim was going to be far larger than that, and that I would either have to see his bet or throw in my cards. If the bet is as it appears, quite small, I can stay in the game. I don't see, and Fineman hasn't shown me, how the story of the Fall, Shakespeare's "poetic subjectivity" in the sonnets, differs from, say, Wyatt's in "They Flee from Me That Sometime Did Me Seek," or many earlier poems.

In fact, Fineman's interest in the sonnets is—as it is entitled to be—opportunistic. He is eloquent and vivid in describing the paradox of the fortunate fall from sameness into difference, from vision into representation and reference. The fact that he finds the fall in the sonnets, their "characterology" neatly diverging from the young man to the dark lady, is a felicity, but he is chiefly interested in the mythic event itself, and would be equally committed to it if it were to be discovered elsewhere.

Allen Tate came upon it not only in Shakespeare but in Emily Dickinson, both of whom had the immense advantage of writing at a time when a coherent body of sentiment had broken down but was still sufficiently there to be invoked. So long as it lasted, it "dramatized the human soul" and provided terms in which the drama could be understood. In Shakespeare, it was what Tate calls "medievalism"; in Dickinson it was New England puritan theocracy. The names hardly matter. What matters is that such a situation makes it possible for a poet to invoke the body of sentiment for all it continues to be worth, if only as the ruins of its first form. Emerson says in "Self-Reliance" that "in every work of genius we recognize our own rejected thoughts; they come back to us with a certain alienated majesty." He could have said the same of the rejected thoughts of an age, a genre, a style, and found alienated majesty even in the late irony with which a Shakespeare or a Dickinson resorts to the ruins. I mention this comparison to account for my feeling that the interest of Fineman's argument is largely intrinsic. The story he tells is gorgeous because it testifies to the possibilities which live in the ruins of what people have discarded.

It follows that, given such an interest, Fineman's reading of the 154 sonnets can't be microscopic. He is a splendid reader, but his close work is rare: he has other obligations to observe, in literary history and the definition of subjectivity. But I should say something of his dealings with Sonnet 138, because they are typical if more detailed than usual.

> When my love swears that she is made of truth,
> I do believe her though I know she lies,
> That she might think me some untutored youth,
> Unlearnèd in the world's false subtleties.
> Thus vainly thinking that she thinks me young,
> Although she knows my days are past the best,
> Simply I credit her false-speaking tongue:
> On both sides thus is simple truth suppressed.
> But wherefore says she not she is unjust?
> And wherefore say not I that I am old?
> O love's best habit is in seeming trust,
> And age in love loves not to have years told.
>> Therefore I lie with her, and she with me,
>> And in our faults by lies we flattered be.

The poem brings together two archetypes—the aged lover with his young mistress, and the Cretan liar who says that all Cretans are liars. It is a matter of choice whether a reader brings the poem closer to what he conceives the situation of the sonnets as a whole to entail. I suppose a rudimentary sense of the poem would construe it along these lines. When my love swears that she is faithful to me, I delude myself into believing her. I do this, hoping that she will take my naïveté as an attractive sign of a young man's spirit, and treat me as a woman of the world treats such a lover. So I vainly persuade myself that to her I seem young—although she must know that I am old. I pretend to believe her, though I know what she says is false. In this way each of us is lying to the other. Why don't we both tell the truth? Oh, it's best, on the whole, to keep up the appearances of trusting each other. As for me, I certainly don't want to have my age spelled out. So I make love with her as if I believed her faithful, and she with me as if she thought me young. We deceive each other equally: a vice in each of us gratifies the other.

Fineman emphasizes that 138 uses the same kind of rhetorical and syntactic doublings that we find in the young man sonnets, but uses them "to support and to confirm the poem's explicit theme rather than, as in the young man sonnets, to undermine it."

> Thus the hard rhyme of "truth" and "youth" is explicated rather than ironically duplicated by the homophonic innuendo of "lies" and "subtleties." The enjambed assonance of "old" and "O" is the instantiation rather than the belying of an authentic sigh. The questioning iterations of "But wherefore says she not she is unjust? / And wherefore say not I that I am old?" are answered rather than problematized by the emphatic, "plain-style" "therefore" of the couplet.

Every detail, according to Fineman, ratifies the falsehoods the poem speaks about. The theme of the poem is comic and sophistic, but the poem itself "seems to mean precisely what it says."

But Fineman also assimilates the poem to his thesis:

> By the conventions of the sonneteering mode, the dark lady is as much the poet's Muse as she is his love, and so the old lover who admits he feigns his youth is equally the voice of an old poetics that "knows my days are past the best." In both cases, as poet and as lover,

the speaker of the poem will purchase the revival of desire with the outspoken travesty of praise, his perjured admiration presented as the literal embodiment of his lust.

It doesn't seem plausible. If we are to apply the poem to literary history, the speaker seems to me to be an old war-horse, a John Wayne type in his last movies—call him Language if you like—showing that while he's not as young as he was, he can still turn a trick or two and keep things going by being wiser than his younger self. He is not purchasing the revival of desire, but settling for what he can get. It is a relief to him to have someone—the disinterested reader—whom he doesn't have to deceive and who knows how hard it is even to pretend to believe or credit anything.

Review of *Such Is My Love: A Study of Shakespeare's Sonnets,* by Joseph Pequigney, and *Shakespeare's Perjured Eye: The Invention of Poetic Subjectivity in the Sonnets,* by Joel Fineman. From *Raritan,* Summer 1986.

THE VALUES OF *MOLL FLANDERS*

In the first scene of *The Life and Strange Surprising Adventures of Robinson Crusoe* a wilful Robinson Kreutznaer is about to commit his first verifiable sin; he rejects his father's middle-class code by running off to sea. The ancient Kreutznaer speaks for Defoe in praising "the middle station of life," or "what might be called the upper station of low life"; this is "the best state in the world," free at once from the hardships of "the mechanic part of mankind" and the tempting pride of "the upper part of mankind." Those in the middle station are ideally placed to receive the most reliable virtues and satisfactions, "temperance, moderation, quietness, health, society, all agreeable diversions, and all desirable pleasures." They glide through life with the blessings of God and Nature. The virtues which fall upon them are, in modern terms, the bourgeois attainments, and these are the only qualities which Defoe admired. He was not Scott Fitzgerald, he had no eyes for the beauty and "style" of wealth; he thought luxury an excellent thing for trade and therefore a politic necessity, but for its devotees a dangerous aspiration. He found in the mechanic part of mankind neither virtue nor happiness; his charity moved reluctantly toward the poor. The middle-class virtues accounted for the finest achievements of modern England in trade, in social organization, in behaviour, even in language.

Specifically, the finest type of Englishman was the middle-class trader. In the *Review* (January 3, 1706) Defoe declared: "If we Respect Trade, as it is understood by Merchandizing; it is certainly the most Noble, most Instructive, and Improving of any way of Life."[1] The "true-bred Merchant" held a glowing place in English society. "Trade is the Animal Spirit to this great Body, which having passed thro' many Decoctions, is at last arriv'd to a Moral Capacity of enlivening the whole Frame."[2] In trade the prudential virtues were of the greatest importance; there might be other virtues, but their existence was chimerical unless verified in the processes of trade.

Defoe would claim for this morality not only the support of common sense but the assent of Nature. "Nothing obeys the Course of Nature more exactly than Trade, Causes and Consequences follow as directly as Day and Night."[3] And, commingling Nature and God, Defoe asserts: "Generally speaking, all the Innumerables of Trade, come under these two Heads, Natural Produce, and Manufacture. The different Climates and Soil in the World have, by the Wisdom and Direction of Nature Natureing, which I call GOD, produc'd such."[4] Several years later in the *Review* Defoe sings a hymn to "the Harmony of the Creation, and the Beauty and Concern of Providence, in preparing the World for Trade."[5]

Defoe was well aware of the local implications of this view of life and he was prepared to face them. If religion and trade could proceed happily together, like Plato's horses, well and good; but if a dispute arose, religion must yield, we are a trading nation, we must be loyal to our calling. This is the rhetoric of *Mercator* and the *Review*. In *The Complete English Tradesman* he acknowledged that "Custom, indeed, has driven us beyond the limits of our morals in many things, which trade makes necessary . . ." and he glanced at the circumstance in which "if our yea must be yea, and our nay, nay, why then it is impossible for tradesmen to be Christians": but this was a dark patch of existence which he did not choose to enter; it could be relegated to a future in which he would think about it if he had nothing more pressing to think about at the time. Meanwhile, there were certain issues which impinged upon the life of trade and therefore could not be postponed. Luxury and Vice, for instance. Defoe agreed that luxurious living was wrong, but on the other hand it was the very life of trade.

How then can the Gentlemen of the Pulp't find in their hearts to Preach against Riot and Luxury, against the Pride and Vanity of the Age, against Drunkenness and Excesses in a trading Nation, whose Commerce being lately removed from the essential necessaries of Life depends now upon the Vice and Luxurious way of Living taken up by the People, and which it is plain, whenever they leave off, we shall be beggared and undone?[6]

Trade was also *Realpolitik*. In April 1711, Defoe made one of the most thoroughgoing statements of his view of life:

> 'Tis our Trade in many circumstances makes the war necessary, and that Necessity only makes it Just: What matter'd it to us, who possess'd Spain, if the Vent of our Manufactures, on which the Employment and Bread of our Poor depends, did not make it absolutely necessary to keep it out of the hands of France?[7]

Trade was "one of the great businesses of life." It must be pursued "with a full attention of the mind, and full attendance of the person; nothing but what are to be called the necessary duties of life are to intervene; and even those are to be limited so as not to be prejudicial to business."[8] It is apparent that Defoe considered trade the most important activity in life: but trade was a method, not an ethic; hence its appropriate idiom was that of ways and means, efficiency, anticipation, acumen; its terms were not ethical or moral, they were strategic. Defoe does not hesitate to show that a trader's success often demands certain qualities of character which are morally valuable, but if immoral qualities are necessary for trading success, he eases himself out of the dilemma by pointing to the inviolacy of trade; God does not require extreme sacrifices.

Up to a point, Defoe's ethic of trade was acknowledged by many Puritans. It was commonly felt that trading success was a sign of God's approval; "one could make profits for the glory of God," as a modern critic observes.[9] If your trading ventures turned out well, you had God's approval or, in Crusoe's case, his forgiveness for earlier sins. In the first years of the eighteenth century God was clearly on the side of the middle-class trader. Industry was a splendid thing; the sin of sloth was punished by trading loss. The "proof" of Roxana's sins was that "the blast of Heaven" was directed against her comfortable circumstances; ". . . and

I was brought so low again that my repentance seemed to be only the consequence of my misery, as my misery was of my crime." Defoe assented to Christian ethics only to the extent that it proved amenable to the analogies of trade. This brought him much further along the commercialistic line than, say, Richard Baxter, a more "representative" Puritan. Baxter's view of these matters is quite consistent. Although Solomon said, "Labour not to be rich," Baxter argued that "it is no sin, but a duty, to labour not only for labour sake, formally resting in the act done, but for that honest increase and provision, which is the end of our labour; And therefore to choose a gainful calling rather than another, that we may be able to do good, and relieve the poor."[10] But he warned against "a secret hypocritical hope of reconciling the World to Heaven, so as to make you a felicity of both; and dreaming of a 'compounded portion or of serving God and Mammon.' "[11] If Mammon conflicted with God, Mammon had to yield, restraining itself; on this there could be no compromise. Baxter spoke an ethical language and was pleased to find that in many respects it was also the language of profit and trade. Defoe spoke a commercial language and was not prepared to change it when the problem of ethical translation became acute.

Robinson Crusoe, for instance, is entirely devoted to the analogies of trade. Religion is a transaction; God is an excellent trading connection. When Crusoe comes upon barley growing and thinks it a gracious miracle, a blessing from God, he has the appropriate feelings of wonder and gratitude; but when he finds the source in the "bag of chicken's meat" which he brought from the wreck, he erases the entry from God's account and registers "no sale." This is the basis upon which he conducts all his personal relationships. When he takes Xury and the Moor to sea and throws the Moor overboard, he muses: "I could have been content to have taken this Moor with me and have drowned the boy, but there was no venturing to trust." When the boy proves himself loyal, Crusoe sells him to the Portuguese captain. In the encounter with the cannibals Crusoe rationalizes the situation in favour of taking no action; the "barbarous customs" become intolerable only when the victims are European and Christian.

The conditions of Crusoe's life on the island afford him plenty of opportunity for meditation; especially when he is ill, his thoughts range in a far wider circle than, say, those of Moll Flanders. True, he will try tobacco steeped in rum before resorting to prayer and the Holy Bible, but in comparison with Moll he is almost a philosopher. The significant aspect of his thought, however, is that it is conducted entirely through the analogies of trade. He interprets "Call on me in the day of trouble" as a promissory note: God's Covenant is literally understood as a commercial bargain. The "rhythm" of Crusoe's feelings is conveyed in a typical paragraph.

> It was now calm, and I had a great mind to venture out in my boat to this wreck, not doubting but I might find something on board that might be useful to me; but that did not altogether press me so much as the possibility that there might be yet some living creature on board, whose life I might not only save, but might, by saving that life, comfort my own to the last degree; and this thought clung so to my heart that I could not be quiet, night or day, but I must venture out in my boat on board this wreck; and committing the rest to God's providence, I thought the impression was so strong upon my mind that it could not be resisted, that it must come from some invisible direction, and that I should be wanting to myself if I did not go.

By the time we reach this paragraph we have already registered Crusoe's moral obtuseness. His idiom is morally null; so much so that his seeming concern for the lives of other people is an amazing novelty: but we have hardly taken the point of this concern before we have to delete it, when the next clause dissolves it in the idiom of utility and selfishness. This is the familiar Crusoeland, a dead-level plain of transactions in which God is invited to participate on the strict understanding that he will abide by the primacy of commerce. This is a capitalistic idiom: "that I should be wanting to myself" has nothing to do with subtleties of moral feeling; it expresses the fear that one might let himself down, missing something that might be to his advantage.

It may be argued that we are meant to take this ironically; as if Defoe were nudging us and pointing conspiratorially in Crusoe's direction. But this is incredible. Precisely the same moral obtuseness is disclosed in Defoe's own journalism, where there is no question of irony. One passage will stand for many: in the *Review* (May 22, 1712) Defoe is discussing the treatment of slaves:

> He that keeps them in Subjection, whips, and corrects them in order to make them grind and labour, does Right, for out of their Labour

he gains his Wealth: But he that in his Passion and Cruelty, maims, lames, and kills them, is a Fool, for they are his Estate, his Stock, his Wealth, and his Prosperity.[12]

It is typical of Defoe to use a term like "Right" without the slightest feeling that moral connotations hover about its edges. It is simply a term of strategy, opposed not to Wrong but to the "foolishness" ascribed to the imprudent master. Indeed, far from exerting a critical irony in *Crusoe,* Defoe's attitudes are strictly continuous with Crusoe's; there is no irony at all.

Similarly in *Roxana:* the heroine occasionally indulges herself in genteel pangs of conscience, "dark reflections which came involuntarily in and thrust in sighs into the middle of all my songs," but we cannot take this darkness seriously; it is shadowboxing with the Self. Again the sensibility disclosed is obtuse; the heroine who speaks of the catastrophe of marrying a fool gives as her husband's culminating defect that he was a bad businessman. The moral sensibility displayed in Roxana's ruminations is precisely the same as that illustrated by her putting Amy to bed with her own lover. In *The Life of Colonel Jack* the hero displays more humanity than his associate Will, and he restores to the old woman the money he stole from her—this scene points toward sentimental comedy, teetering on the brink of tears—but Jack makes up in smugness for what he lacks in cruelty. The "just reflections" which in the pages of his story he declares "the utmost felicity of human life" are focussed upon his own gratifications; his association with Job learning to abhor himself in dust and ashes is a predictable last-page gesture. When he gives the Spaniard's wife a gift, he fixes his eye—like all of Defoe's heroes—upon its cash value. The Spaniard, he says, "was extremely pleased with the nicety I used, and I saw him present it to her accordingly, and could see, at the opening of it, that she was extremely pleased with the present itself, as indeed might very well be; for in that country it was worth a very considerable sum of money." On the next page Jack bows toward God and Nature. As for Defoe's Cavalier, the nearest he comes to an act or an attitude of moral reference is to recognize "fatality of circumstances in this unhappy war."

Moll Flanders, born a waif, aspires to the condition of a gentlewoman. This design is the source of the book's unity; without it, we should have merely a picaresque anthology. A miscellany of husbands, children, thefts, and crises traces the course of Moll's aspiration; this is the scale of their importance. The aspiration itself is personal, isolated, and omnivorous.

For Moll, at the beginning, a gentlewoman was merely a person who worked for herself and got enough to avoid going to service. But after living for a year with the local Mayoress, Moll acquired a new idea; being a gentlewoman now meant living "great and high." In later years she would modify her demands under great stress, but the condition of a gentlewoman was at all times to be identified with happiness.[13] "She has a lady's hand, I assure you," says the Mayoress, unaware that this ambiguous synecdoche will account for most of Moll's distresses. The "form" of Moll's life will be social rather than moral or ethical; ethical considerations will arise from time to time, considerations of a vaguely defined "Nature," but the form and pressure of her life will be social. Moll demands that she be allowed to "raise herself" out of her waif condition; the necessary means will be other people, acumen, good looks, and money. The social end requires a miscellany of social means. That is why Moll recurs constantly to her isolation—a condition not, as in *Crusoe,* the occasion of splendidly Puritanical self-reliance, the frontier spirit, but the cause of exposure, friendlessness, fear, "want of friends and want of bread." Isolated, Moll is imprisoned in the circle of her own condition, a social castaway.

Money, or at least the appearance of money, and thence a "good" marriage: this is Moll's original plan. One of her first lessons is that "money only made a woman agreeable"; a whore must be "handsome, well shaped, have a good mien and a graceful behaviour," but for a wife "the money was the thing." Money, marriage, and virtue were therefore linked in a chain of analogies: "money's virtue, gold is fate." A good marriage was the female equivalent of a successful business transaction; it required the same "virtues," acumen, persistence, foresight, patience. It was "a subtle game"; it might even require a woman to "change her station" and "make a new appearance in some other place," but these exigencies, however regrettable, were in the normal course of competitive trade. In one of her happiest meditations Moll thinks of the "wild company" in which she had played a social part:

The case was altered with me; I had money in my pocket, and had nothing to say to them. I had been tricked once by that cheat called love, but the game was over; I was resolved now to be married or nothing, and to be well married or not at all.

Being well married was simply the condition of a gentlewoman:

> I was not averse to a tradesman; but then I would have a tradesman, forsooth, that was something of a gentleman too; that when my husband had a mind to carry me to the court, or to the play, he might become a sword, and look as like a gentleman as another man; and not like one that had the mark of his apron-strings upon his coat, or the mark of his hat upon his periwig; that should look as if he was set on his sword, when his sword was put on to him, and that carried his trade in his countenance.

This may seem disloyal to Defoe's ideal, the middle-class trader; but proof of middle-class commercial success was precisely the ability to "invade" upper-class circles now and again, secure in money and free from the dangerous exorbitance of the great. When Moll's draper husband carries her on a lordly trip to Oxford and plays the grandee, this is meant to be impressive in its way, and Moll concedes that he "carries it off," but it is absurd because he can't afford the £93—Moll's money—squandered in twelve pretentious days. If he could have afforded it, it would have been a stylish performance, the free manipulation of the best of all worlds. Far from abandoning a middle-class role, he would have given a proper display of middle-class prowess.

We have seen that Defoe's vision of life was a network of analogies drawn from the priority of middle-class trade. This meant that certain qualities and feelings had to be sacrificed to the main commercial chance. These were profitless luxuries. In the same way Moll has to set aside many feelings and attitudes which she cannot afford. Conscience, for example; in the disposal of her tenth child Moll expresses her scruples at surprising length and makes a temporary contribution of £5 a year to secure that the child will not be abandoned, but these stirrings of conscience are rare. In her strategic liaisons she is not at all troubled by her conscience, "for I was a stranger to those things," and even when one of her husbands turns out to be her brother, she is distressed only because "the action had something in it shocking to nature." The formula which covers all these occasions is Necessity; "necessity, which pressed me to a settlement suitable to my condition, was my authority for it." Necessity, poverty, and the Devil were interchangeable terms.

Another sacrifice was Feeling. Beyond noting that one lover was agreeable and another lovely, Moll lives a life crowded with event and absolutely bare of feeling. The normal pattern of her marriages is that she enters into them with all the energy of successful strategy and willing "Nature"; difficulties arise, the marriage lapses, and she assesses her gains and losses before setting out for a new scene. The "value" is money. There is one partial exception to this rule; Moll expresses much more affection for Jemmy than for any of her earlier or later protectors. But this does not prevent her from concealing her true name or from maintaining a quiet correspondence with "my friend at the bank," a more durable lover who would one day prove useful. In her later years Moll is entirely closed against feeling: when her thieving accomplice is arrested, Moll is terrified lest he should be able to direct the law toward her:

> This filled me with horrible apprehensions. I had no resource, no friend, no confidant but my old governess, and I knew no remedy but to put my life into her hands; and so I did, for I let her know where to send to me, and had several letters from her while I stayed here. Some of them almost scared me out of my wits; but at last she sent me the joyful news that he was hanged, which was the best news to me that I had heard a great while.

This is much more characteristic of Moll than her local eruptions of conscience. Indeed, her entire emotional life—to the extent that she reveals it—is compounded of fear, self-preservation, and the occasional gratifications of success. In Moll, and in Defoe himself, life is a matter first of survival and thereafter of competition: there is no recognition of any "promises of life" beyond the next meal or the next marriage. The relation of the soul to God is null: the relation of person to person is jungle war. Defoe does not push his vision of life to the extremes of putrefaction and deformity certified by Swift; his images merely declare that life is a narrow and grim affair in which evil means loss and good means gain and there is nothing more to it. There is no point in praising the accuracy, the "realism," of Defoe's style unless we remark that these are, in Defoe's eyes, equivalent to good bookkeeping and important for that sole reason. And if trading practices had required a more "fluid" or a more Latinical kind of bookkeeping, we may be quite sure that Defoe's fictional style would have reflected this need. In the same way Defoe's famous verve and gusto are qualities of successful trading in the first instance and literary qualities thereafter; there is no difference, in Defoe's case, between the man who suffered and the writer who created.

Moll Flanders is a fascinating book. It could have been extremely dull, one liaison after another, each indistinguishable, one theft, then another, and so on. It is commonly argued that the pleasures of the book arise from Defoe's realism, the lists, the details, and the character of Moll. But—to take the last point first—Moll cannot be said to have a character at all, if we mean a figure with a rich interior life, full of individuality. In her we are given little more than a set of predictable responses, each enclosed within a remarkably narrow circumference. Within this circumference Moll is given a recognizable "voice"—

> But all this was nothing; I found no encouraging prospect. I waited; I lived regularly, and with as much frugality as became my circumstances; but nothing offered, nothing presented and the main stock wasted apace.

—this is her tone, her idiom, her rhythm; the syntax registers the gap between the reasonable expectations based on good management practice and the null returns—a bad investment of "virtue" for which no one could be blamed. This is a distinct voice. But we do not find in Moll the total individuality, the rich moral contingency, which we think of as "character" in fiction: it is not a serious injustice to place Moll in the category of rogue heroines and leave her there. The book could not be sustained by Moll's character. Or even by the justly praised realism: the shopping lists have the kind of interest we find in old photographs, but this is a small part of the art of fiction.

And yet the book stands; in spite of Defoe's awkwardness, his carelessness, the book is engrossing. I think the reason is that it is utterly faithful to its own terms. This is what we mean when we speak of an author inventing an entirely individual world, a world which bears his sole patent; when we speak of the "world" of William Faulkner, for instance, and mean that the region is moral rather than topographical. The coherence of a fictional world is fascinating in itself; this is the fascination of *Moll Flanders* and of *As I Lay Dying;* each book declares its own identity, its loyalty to its own terms. A novel which is utterly faithful to its own terms can hardly fail in the first requisite of fiction, to be—it is James's word—*interesting.* In discussing the quality of the novel, of course, the quality of the terms themselves must be strictly considered, and the human image which they declare.

We need a text. Here is one of the most important passages in *Moll Flanders:*

> This was evidently my case, for I was now a loose, unguided creature, and had no help, no assistance, no guide for my conduct; I knew what I aimed at, and what I wanted, but knew nothing how to pursue the end by direct means. I wanted to be placed in a settled state of living, and had I happened to meet with a sober, good husband, I should have been as true a wife to him as virtue itself could have formed. If I had been otherwise, the vice came in always at the door of necessity, not at the door of inclination; and I understood too well, by the want of it, what the value of a settled life was, to do anything to forfeit the felicity of it; nay, I should have made the better wife for all the difficulties I had passed through, by a great deal; nor did I in any of the times that I had been a wife give my husbands the least uneasiness on account of my behaviour.

This speech it utterly loyal to its own terms. It is the idiom of Toleration.[14] Even when it uses terms like "true," "virtue," and "vice" it neutralizes their ethical implications and assimilates them to a purely social image, that of the solid comfort of the good trader. "Loose," for instance, has nothing to do with sexual behaviour; it simply means "unsettled," blown about in the social storm, lacking the security of an equable society. The demands which the speaker makes upon life are few and, in her eyes, modest: she proposes only a social end and assumes that the relation between means and end is direct, even if it is now frustrated. Life is painful, but not complex; this is not the "world" of Dostoevski. Vice is Necessity, a matter of entrances and departures enforced by grim circumstances. Virtue is "a settled state of life," a resting place, a haven to which one comes all the more willingly for the difficulties one has passed through. Problems which in another vision of life would be ethically complex are here simplified by assimilation to the idiom of physical space and movement, comings and goings, transits between condition A and condition B. Ethics does not survive the journey. Clearly, what this prose "is" and what Moll is "saying" are identical; the language verifies the "settled state of living" for which Moll strives. This is what I mean by the coherence of the book, its remarkable loyalty to its own basic terms, its "values." This is the chief difference between Defoe's style and that of a writer like Deloney, the best of Defoe's bourgeois precursors. Deloney did not commit himself to any terms, even those of middle-class morality; his view of life was insecure, his bourgeois allegiance was not sufficiently strong to give him a style or to protect him from the prevailing winds emanating from Italy, the Court, and the Universities. Hence the fluid nature of his fiction—its mixture of interludes, verses, and fractured plots; hence also his lurching into wildly different styles. Deloney was quite capable of writing simple, vigorous sentences. He was also capable of "realism." But he was not capable of developing a simple, vigorous style flexible enough to serve a reasonable variety of occasions. We have seen Defoe achieving a "voice" for Moll Flanders; there is nothing comparable in Deloney, nothing of such identity and coherence. His use of euphuistic dialogue is a case in point. When Jack of Newbury "raises himself" by marrying his widow employer, the preliminary wooing is conducted with simple speech on the woman's part and euphuistic speech on his; this registers the widow's social condescension and Jack's sense of inferiority.15 This is an acceptable convention. But euphuistic speech is called upon to serve many other occasions, where there is no question of inferiority or patronage. In one of the interludes in the same novel a young and wealthy Italian merchant courts Gillian, the wife of a poor weaver. The woman rejects his advances, he departs, and she has second thoughts:

When he was gone, the woman began to call her wits together, and to consider of her poor estate, and withal the better to note the comeliness of her person, and the sweet favour of her face: which when she had well thought upon, she began to harbour new thoughts, and to entertain contrary affections, saying, "Shall I content myself to be wrapped in sheep's russet that may swim in silks, and sit all day carding for a groat, that can have crowns at my command? No," quoth she, "I will no more bear so base a mind, but take Fortune's favours while they are to be had. The sweet rose doth flourish but one month, nor women's beauties but in young years: as the winter's frost consumes the summer flowers, so doth old age banish pleasant delight. O glorious gold," quoth she, "how sweet is thy smell! how pleasing is thy sight! Thou subduest princes, and overthrowest kingdoms, then how should a silly woman withstand thy strength?" Thus she rested meditating on preferment, minding to hazard her honesty to maintain herself in bravery; even as occupiers corrupt their consciences to gather riches.[16]

Gillian will retreat before it is too late, and she will confess her theoretical sins to her husband in even more strikingly euphuistic terms. In both speeches the euphuism has nothing to do with social considerations; nor is it a tip from the author to watch out for Gillian's absurdity. Deloney's modern editor has shown quite clearly that it is a sign to the reader to take Gillian's moral struggle seriously.[17] But it obviously cannot work for all these occasions. The "eloquence" in Deloney's fiction is autonomous, a manipulation of available styles rather than style itself, and the manipulation normally has no particular relation to the characters to whom the words are attributed. This is the frustration of reading Deloney; just at the point at which you think he is now at last going to turn his materials into coherent fiction, he dissipates the entire work in verbiage and pedantry. It is apparent that the novel as a literary form could not develop beyond the stage of picaresque anecdote until it committed itself to the invention of a single, unified world. This is precisely Defoe's contribution to English fiction; in *Moll Flanders* and *Robinson Crusoe* he committed all the energies of the case to the disclosure of fictional "worlds," each book a world constructed according to its own terms. "Eloquence" yielded to coherence; with some loss and—on the whole—a great gain.

The terms of this coherence can be given very briefly. First, the rhetoric of the Plain Style as the equivalent of Plain Dealing: "I am a plain dealer, and will die so," Defoe affirmed in the *Review*. Second, a commitment to what he called "the naked prospect of fact." Third, a commitment to the present tense. (*Moll Flanders* is a novel entirely without memory, without perspective, without tradition. For Moll there is only the present fearful moment forcing itself toward a future in which she may—*must*—become a gentlewoman.) Finally, the analogies of capitalistic trade provide the sole "form" of human action. These terms are enough to make of *Moll Flanders* a remarkably unified world; this is the excitement of the book, and its significance in literary history.

But the terms themselves are fearfully narrow. It is difficult to generalize about an art as various as fiction, beyond saying that the great novelist places his rendered actualities—of behaviour and relation—in a perspective of human possibility. If he renders his people and denies them at least the vision of possibility, in memory, hope, or illusion, he distorts the evidence or is blind to it. This is not a question of providing happy beginnings, middles, or endings. We do not ask that Moll Flanders marry Simon Eyre and wind up as Lady Mayoress of London. What Defoe says about life, in *Moll Flanders,* is true, so far as it goes, but the book is based upon a set of terms which ignores two-thirds of human existence; these terms cancel all aspects of human consciousness to which the analogies of trade are irrelevant. The terms assume that whatever cannot be measured does not exist. As a result, the book cannot even conceive of human action as genial, charitable, or selfless; hence it cannot survive comparison with a novel like *Portrait of a Lady* in which the enabling vision of life is wide, generous, answerable to human possibility.

NOTES

1. *Defoe's Review,* introduction by A. W. Secord, Facsimile Text Society (New York: Columbia University Press, 1938), III, 5.
2. *Ibid.,* V, 459.
3. *Ibid.,* II, 26. Cf. "Giving Alms No Charity": "Trade, like all Nature, most obsequiously obeys the great law of cause and consequence."
4. *Ibid.,* III, 5.
5. *Ibid.,* IX, 109.
6. *Ibid.,* IX, 82.
7. *Ibid.,* VIII, 25.
8. *The Complete English Tradesman,* p. 550.
9. Cf. Kenneth Burke, *Attitudes Towards History* (rev. ed.; Los Altos: Hermes Publications, 1959), p. 137.
10. *A Christian Directory: or, A Summ of Practical Theologie and Cases of Conscience* (London, 1673), Book IV, pp. 146–47.
11. *Ibid.,* III, 631. Cf. also R. H. Tawney, *Religion and the Rise of Capitalism* (London: Murray, 1944 reprint); Roland N. Stromberg, *Religious Liberalism in Eighteenth-Century England* (London: Oxford University Press, 1954); and Christopher Hill, *The Century of Revolution,* 1603–1714 (Edinburgh: Nelson, 1961).
12. *Review,* VIII, 730.
13. Writing of the England of about 1739—when Montesquieu visited the country—Tocqueville observes, "England was the only country in which the system of caste had been not changed but effectively destroyed. The noble and the middle classes in England followed together the same courses

of business, entered the same professions, and, what is much more significant, intermarried. The daughter of the greatest noble in England could already marry without a 'new' man.... For several centuries past the word 'gentleman' has entirely changed its meaning in England, and the word 'roturier' no longer exists.... In each century it ('gentleman') is applied to men placed ever a little lower in the social scale." *L'Ancien Régime*, trans. M. W. Patterson (Oxford: Blackwell, 1952), pp. 89–90.

14. Howard Mumford Jones has noted, in "American Prose Style 1700–1770," "an interesting correlation of two facts: the appeal for the avoidance of controversy or (viewed from its positive side) for toleration: and the appeal for a simple, lucid, and direct prose style." *Huntington Library Bulletin,* No. VI (1934), p. 134.

15. I owe this point to Merrit E. Lawlis. Cf. his *Apology for the Middle Class: The Dramatic Novels of Thomas Deloney* (Bloomington: Indiana University Press, 1960).

16. Merrit E. Lawlis (ed.), *The Novels of Thomas Deloney* (Bloomington: Indiana University Press, 1961), pp. 63–64.

17. Cf. *Apology for the Middle Class,* p. 102.

From *The Sewanee Review,* Vol. LXXI (1963).

Swift and the Association
of Ideas

Nor in the stagnant bay of Marsh's library where you read the fading prophecies of Joachim Abbas. For whom? The hundred-headed rabble of the cathedral close. A hater of his kind ran from them to the wood of madness, his mane foaming in the moon, his eyeballs stars. Houyhnhnm, horse-nostrilled. (James Joyce, *Ulysses*)

But now I would battle in the interests of orthodoxy, even of the commonplace; and yet could find nothing better to say than: "It is not necessary to judge every one by the law, for we have also Christ's commandment of love."

He turned and said, looking at me with shining eyes: "Jonathan Swift made a soul for the gentlemen of this city by hating his neighbour as himself." (W. B. Yeats: "The Tables of the Law")

In March 1934 F. R. Leavis published "The Irony of Swift," the essay which, more than any other, has persuaded readers that Swift's mind is characterized by a peculiarly intense animus not accounted for by its objects. It is widely agreed that there is a quality of exorbitance in Swift's work, a force which issues, as if unprovoked, from the mind itself.

It is my impression that only one of Leavis's arguments has failed to gain much credence. The comparison of Swift and Blake, to Blake's advantage in point of intelligence, has not been taken up as a matter that can be profitably discussed. But the main burden of the essay, that the general effect of Swift's irony is a sense of extraordinary energy turned upon negation, has been received as the crucial issue to be argued, though not indeed as the last word upon it. In my experience students fasten with evident satisfaction upon the sentence in which Leavis says that we have in Swift's writings "probably the most remarkable expression of negative feelings and attitudes that literature can offer—the spectacle of creative powers (the paradoxical description seems right) exhibited consistently in negation and rejection."[1]

The sentence is more regularly quoted than analyzed: in particular, what remains unexamined is Leavis's distinction between positive and negative sentiments, a distinction he seems to regard as self-evident. But it is clear that an ideological imperative is at work. The distinction, we might say, thrives in the vicinity of satire but not of irony. It is one of the marks of irony that it makes the reader doubt that the situation in hand can be adequately judged by appeal to a distinction between negative and positive impulses. Indeed, one's satisfaction in such discriminations and lucidities is what irony was devised to undermine.

To be fair to Leavis, he tells us precisely what he has in mind in making the distinction: it is by comparison with Gibbon and the fifteenth chapter of *The Decline and Fall of the Roman Empire* that he feels justified in saying that Swift's irony is negative. "The decorously insistent pattern of Gibbonian prose," he says, "insinuates a solidarity with the reader (the implied solidarity in Swift is itself ironical—a means to betrayal), establishes an understanding and habituates to certain assumptions." It is also understood that the positive standards which Gibbon calls upon "represent something impressively realized in eighteenth-century civilization." Gibbon, that is to say, invokes certain positive continuities of attitude and conviction which he is deemed to share with his readers and with the culture they together constitute. "Gibbon's irony, then, habituates and reassures, ministering to a kind of judicial certitude or complacency. Swift's is essentially a matter of surprise and negation: its function is to defeat habit, to intimidate and to demoralize" (p. 75).

Leavis's terms of reference are strange. In another context it would be taken as a mark of a writer's moral incapacity if the tendency of his work were to habituate and reassure, or to minister to the reader's complacency. It would also be a sign of an artist's creative power if his work were directed to defeat habit or at least to make it doubt itself. Leavis's account of Donne's poems, in *Revaluation,* acts upon that assumption. But in writing of Swift his moral sense is perturbed to find evidence (in the writing, line by line) of intensities not already sanctioned by the society Swift addresses. Egotism to the degree of insanity is the only explanation he offers.

I can put the matter briefly by referring to a distinction which Wayne Booth makes in *The Rhetoric of Irony* between stable and unstable irony. Stable irony is such that a competent reader who deals with an ironic text by making certain well-understood moves of interpretation finds himself on steady hermeneutic ground. Unstable irony is such that the reader, whatever moves he makes, finds himself in a hermeneutic void: there is no secure place. In Leavis's account Gibbon's irony is valid because stable, Swift's is unstable and therefore vicious.

I propose to look at the passage upon which Leavis's diagnosis mainly relies, the section of the "Digression on Madness," in *A Tale of a Tub,* about the state of being a fool among knaves. Leavis's analysis offers to show that Swift's reader is being lulled into the security of thinking that the object of attack is "curiosity" (a pretentious or vain insistence upon prying beneath the surface of things) and that the positive values being called upon are those of a contented residence among the "common forms" and external appearances:

Yesterday I ordered the Carcass of a *Beau* to be stript in my Presence; when we were all amazed to find so many unsuspected Faults under one Suit of Cloaths: Then I laid open his *Brain,* his *Heart,* and his *Spleen;* But, I plainly perceived at every Operation, that the farther we proceeded, we found the Defects encrease upon us in Number and Bulk: from all which, I justly formed this Conclusion to my self; That whatever Philosopher or Projector can find out an Art to sodder and patch up the Flaws and Imperfections of Nature, will deserve much better of Mankind, and teach us a more useful Science, than that so much in present Esteem, of widening and exposing them (like him who held *Anatomy* to be the ultimate End of *Physick*). And he, whose Fortunes and Dispositions have placed him in a convenient Station to enjoy the Fruits of this noble Art; He that can with *Epicurus* content his Ideas with the *Films* and *Images* that fly off upon his Senses from the *Superficies* of Things; Such a Man truly wise, creams off Nature, leaving the Sower and the Dregs, for Philosophy and Reason to lap up.[2]

The reader's assumption that the object of attack is curiosity, Leavis says, "has become habit, and has been so nourished that few readers note anything equivocal to trouble them in that last sentence: the concrete force of 'cream off,' 'sour,' 'dregs,' and 'lap up' seems unmistakably to identify Swift with an intense animus against 'philosophy and reason' (understood implicitly to stand for 'curiosity' the anatomist)" (p. 83).

In fact there is nothing equivocal in Swift's sentence. The motif of the outside and the inside, with which the passage began, has implied that the inside is best taken for granted. If we don't trouble it, it won't trouble us. The metaphor is certainly dismissive, because it says that there is much in life we should throw away so as to retain the better part. It is true, as Leavis says, that the reader's place is with Swift; but only an extraordinarily sacramental sense of life would find itself affronted by the recognition that some things in life are waste matter. "The trap," Leavis says, "is sprung in the last sentence of the paragraph": "This is the sublime and refined Point of Felicity, called, *the Possession of being well deceived;* The Serene Peaceful State of being a Fool among Knaves." "What is left?" Leavis exclaims. The positives disappear. Swift "never found anything better to contend for than a skin, a surface, an outward show" (p. 84).

I think we can agree that when Swift begins a sentence with the words "sublime" and "refined" an ironical tone is intended. Whether the irony is stable or unstable, or whether that distinction is going to suffice or not, is to be decided. The sentence is ironical. But it might still be possible to read it as saying that if it comes to a choice between being a fool or a knave, an honest man will choose to be a fool, and will then make the best of his situation: the best being in all probability more than it is worth. Dustin H. Griffin has pointed out that Swift borrowed the famous phrase from Rochester: "Artemisia to Chloe" has "the perfect joy of being well deceived."[3] It is not necessary to quarrel about the degree to which Rochester's manner infects Swift's: the high-pitched pleasure which Rochester expresses when libertinage and cuckoldry are invoked is not one of Swift's notes. Cuckoldry provides the general context in which fools are distinguished from knaves, but Swift is not infatuated with the theme. He is more interested in taking command of a space of sentiment by enforcing the terms upon which the discourse may be allowed to proceed. It is regularly a mark of his irony that it insists upon a desperate choice between two values or two predicaments, as if the situation admitted of no other and no more. We are allowed to choose only between those claimants: if we want to invoke a third value, or a different set of alternatives, we put ourselves out of the discourse.

In the present case there would appear to be two possibilities. One is that the choice is no choice, since the conditions of fool and knave are equally repugnant to an honest reader. In *The Structure of Complex Words* (London, 1951) William Empson maintains that Swift's sentence is the earliest use of a distinctively modern feeling. "The modern use of fool I think gets its power from a suggestion of nausea, which is a new stock reaction to the presence of a lunatic (not even an eighteenth century reaction)." Empson thought it likely that Swift for personal reasons felt "all our present-day revulsion from lunacy" (p. 110). Leavis's interpretation is much the same as Empson's, though he is far more outraged by the evidence than Empson is.

Empson adverts to the second possibility when he quotes a passage from Enid Welsford's *The Fool: His Social and Literary History* (London, 1935), where she says that "the first thing to be remembered is that the words 'fool' and 'knave' were constantly coupled together, but not always in quite the same way; for sometimes they were treated as synonyms, sometimes emphasis was laid on the distinction between them." She has been discussing Sebastian Brant's *Narrenschiff* and Barclay's loose English version of it: "To religious moralists such as Brant and Barclay, a knave was simply a fool regarded 'sub specie aeternitatis,' for he was neglecting his true, ultimate self-interest, and what could be more ridiculous than that? In view of Hell and Heaven, the worldly man is penny wise and pound foolish" (p. 237). Presumably if you took an earthy view of these alternatives you would hold them apart by saying that at least the knave lives up to his dramatic possibilities while the fool misses them. Welsford's discussion makes it clear that if you think of fool and knave as different you can see them as (to use Empson's phrase) covering the whole field between them; even if in practice you let one of them be the first of two stout contenders. Knave here, as Empson remarks, is the biblical fool who says in his heart "There is no God." If you think of them as the same you still have to decide whether to express their common character in genial or sinister terms.

Erasmus took the genial way. In the *Encomium Moriae* Stultitia gives a lively account of herself, and shows that you can live a decent life under her auspices. Ultimately what Erasmus is defending is the Christ-like way of being a little child. In the long run being one of Christ's fools will prove to have been the right way, and even in the meantime there are pleasures to be found. Sophisticates only seem to have a good time, and besides, their end is nigh.

It seems to be widely assumed that Swift's meaning cannot have coincided with Erasmus's, or drawn upon a similar set of feelings. Empson thought the Erasmian sentiments no longer available, probably because Freud has told us that children are not as innocent as they look. The argument is a poor one, if only because Christianity is still alive and it could not exist without the Christ-like sentiment and the paradoxes of the Sermon on the Mount. Erasmus's Stultitia is ingenious in showing how much of the best in life is compatible with being, in her special sense, a fool; she allows us to feel, too, how much of the worst in life goes with the unspecial sense of fool. Erasmus's contribution to the conceit is his smiling amusement at those worldlings who are dismayed by the evidence.

There is no reason why Erasmus and Swift must be regarded as living in different worlds. Leavis despised Swift's religious position, thought it mere show, and I agree that an age which was willing to settle for Occasional Conformity was well on the way towards letting politics take the place of religion. After the Restoration it was widely felt that the only security against another civil war was to have a consensus broad and strong enough to sink theological differences or evade them. The true-born Englishman was a safer bet than an enthusiast, an apostle, or a fanatic. Peace on earth and goodwill to men should begin with peace between Englishmen.

There is no reason why Swift could not have settled for the amenities that the philosophers available to him offered. An artist could sidestep the issues, just as Bolingbroke did. In *Praisers of Folly* (London, 1964) Walter Kaiser says of the passage about fools and knaves that Swift "would without hesitation strike through the mask of deception" (p. 75). The striking phrase comes from *Moby-Dick,* and it seems incongruous. Why should we think that Swift must have forced every issue of theology and philosophy further than David Hume did? Hume accepted that knowledge depends upon "those impressions, which arise from the senses," and that "their ultimate cause is, in my opinion, perfectly inexplicable by human reason, and 'twill always be impossible to decide with certainty, whether they arise immediately from the object, or are produc'd by the creative power of the mind, or are deriv'd from the author of our being." If so, Hume advises, "where Reason is lively, and mixes itself with some propensity, it ought to be assented to."[4] Nothing in the *Treatise* encourages anyone to strike through the mask.

What Swift seems to be saying in the contested sentence is that if we force the issue we are all necessarily deceived by appearances, so it is a question of behaving ourselves decently or not. A fool is indeed thoroughly deceived, if the strictest epistemological criteria are insisted on, but he will be justified in the end, and in the meantime he should live accordingly. A cuckold is unfortunate, but he has the second chance of acting decently despite his predicament. A knave will never be justified. The irony is that this advice, too, is arrived at only upon otherwise bewildered reflection: it is not given by nature.

Leavis assumes, and I have left the assumption unquestioned, that the one who is saying these things in the "Digression on Madness" is Jonathan Swift. He does not advert to any of the questions raised by reference to implied authors or personae. I have long believed that most of the difficulties of the *Tale* arise from the fact that some of the sentiments it puts on show are silly, vain, pretentious, or (as we might say) modernist; but many of them are not, and the difference is rarely signalled. Many years ago I speculated on the possibility that Swift was capitalizing upon the discrepancy between words issuing from a particular speaker and words issuing anonymously and as if spontaneously from a printing press. If you wanted stability you could find it in the notion of personal identity and a conversible style audible in its vicinity. It must have seemed a bizarre thing to be able to set words loose from the voice of a speaker responsible for them and instead to let a printing press deliver them with unquestioning impartiality. In *The Counterfeiters* Hugh Kenner considers the consequences, for eighteenth-century literature, of a language which theory has separated from its speakers. It does not seem implausible to me that a writer might choose to effect such a separation, in a wickedly intermittent and unsignalled way, as in digressions where an impression of unmoored and arbitrary authority could be enforced, to the dismay of his readers.

I can think of two theoretical vocabularies which would give this argument some credence. One is Derrida's distinction (he made it in his lecture "Structure, Sign, and Play in the Discourse of the Human Sciences") between two kinds of interpretation:

> There are two interpretations of interpretation, of structure, of sign, of freeplay. The one seeks to decipher, dreams of deciphering, a truth or an origin which is free from freeplay and from the order of the sign, and lives like an exile the necessity of interpretation. The other, which is no longer turned toward the origin, affirms freeplay and tries to pass beyond man and humanism, the name man being the name of that being who, throughout the history of metaphysics or of ontotheology . . . has dreamed of full presence, the reassuring foundation, the origin and the end of the game.[5]

Now suppose a book were to be written in which the narrative parts, allegorical indeed, were stable, coherent, and turned towards a meaning in the history of Christian sects since the Reformation; and in which the digressions practised what we may now call Derridean play in a void between persons and things, between voices and the mechanisms of a printing press. I can imagine such a book, and that it might coincide with *A Tale of a Tub*.

The second vocabulary might be deduced from Leavis's essay, but he does not make the deduction. He remarks that in Swift's irony "we more often, probably, feel the effect of the words as an intensity in the castigator than as an effect upon a victim: the dissociation of animus from the usual signs defines for our contemplation a peculiarly intense contempt or disgust" (pp. 76–77). This is true, but it is not clear why Leavis thinks it scandalous. His view seems to depend upon an abstract notion of equipoise, a balance supposedly fair between a mind's attention and the object under attack. But unless we are to ban every prejudice, or the pretence of prejudice, from the domain of irony, we must put up with the discrepancy. Henry James said, in an early letter to Thomas Sergeant Perry, that a prejudice is "a judgement formed on a subject upon data furnished, not by the subject itself, but by the mind which regards it."[6] It would be idle to plead that a writer, more especially an ironist, should not resort to such a discrepancy.

A few pages later in the essay Leavis says that "the only thing in the nature of a positive" that most readers of Swift will find convincingly present "is self-assertion—superbia" (p. 80). But Leavis does not pursue the matter beyond a point which I suppose he took as sufficiently conclusive. His clear implication is that Swift's form of irony is corrupt because of the self-assertion that animates it: it is damaging because it testifies to nothing beyond the energy it develops. No value or conviction at large in the world is invoked. Various attempts have been made to refute Leavis's argument by finding in Swift's work values which might count as positives: usually they amount to the commonplaces of an unexactingly defined Christianity. But there is at least one theory of irony according to which irony cannot be other than a produced *superbia*. It may appear that Kierkegaard's theory does not recognize unstable irony, because he says that in irony "the phenomenon is not the essence but the opposite of the essence": the word is not the meaning, but the opposite of the meaning. That would bear upon stable irony, since a reader would soon learn to construe a meaning by taking it as its opposite. But Kierkegaard goes on to allow for unstable irony (he does not call it that) by saying that in irony "the subject is negatively free": if what I say is neither my meaning nor the opposite of my meaning "then I am free both in relation to others and in relation to myself."[7] This marks the exclusiveness of irony, since even if it is understood at last it is not directly or immediately understood. The delay between the utterance and its being understood corresponds to a certain subjective freedom. The ironist, since he does not coincide with his meaning, has within his power the possibility of a beginning which is not "generated from previous conditions." The ironist masters every moment by travelling incognito. The purpose of irony is to enable the ironist to feel free to move in any direction he chooses: he is not intimidated by any object in view.

The sign of that freedom is superior detachment not from this or that but from the whole actuality of his time and situation. Irony therefore "has an apriority in itself, and it is not by successively destroying one segment of actuality after another that it arrives at its total view, but by virtue of this that it destroys in the particular." It is not this or that phenomenon but the totality of existence "which it considers *sub specie ironiae*" (p. 271).

What follows from this is Kierkegaard's distinction between satire, comedy, and irony. Satire proposes to destroy the phenomena it hates. Comedy (and I think Kierkegaard means, shall we say, Shakespearean rather than Jonsonian comedy) hopes to reconcile the conflicting forces. But irony "reinforces vanity in its vanity and renders madness madder"

(p. 274). It is as if the ironist required an object as universal as the "being-for-itself of subjectivity" which is Kierkegaard's characterization of irony: required it, so that his superiority to it may be correspondingly complete. If the vain phenomenon is merely local it must be enormously enlarged to make it appear to be worth the ironist's attention. But Kierkegaard emphasizes that for the ironist the object never acquires any reality, either in its own corrupt right or in its malign transformation. The ironist enforces his freedom by talking every object out of its reality: the object merely provides yet another occasion on which he may detach himself from a situation too specious to engage his interest. Finally Kierkegaard says that irony is healthy "insofar as it rescues the soul from the snares of relativity." But it is a sickness "insofar as it is unable to tolerate the absolute except in the form of nothingness" (p. 275).

It is true that Kierkegaard's idea of irony is derived from the example of Socrates, and that Socratic poise is the last quality one would associate with Swift. But Swift's irony answers to Kierkegaard's description in several respects. The animus to which Leavis refers is indeed the sign of Swift's appalling insistence on being free and superior to the whole world his mind encounters. If there is sickness, it is there, in his Kierkegaardian inability to tolerate the absolute except in the form of nothingness. But this allows us to say that Swift protected himself against a doomed absolutism by resorting, day by day, to the common forms of an undemanding Protestantism and a conventional epistemology. I do not suppose that he resorted to these with conviction, or that they are adequate as values in their own right and to be contended for. His relation to the commonplaces of religion and philosophy was, I would assume, chiefly strategic: better those (or at least safer) than news from nowhere or from the abyss. I am not bound to claim that his recourse to these commonplaces gave him, moment by moment, the stability he wanted.

The point can be made by comparing Swift and Locke on a subject of concern to both of them, the force of Enthusiasm in religion. Locke deals with it mainly in Book IV, Chapter 19, of the *Essay Concerning Human Understanding,* and Swift in *A Tale of a Tub* and *The Mechanical Operation of the Spirit.* There is good reason to think that each of them regarded Enthusiasm as vanity of a peculiarly vulgar and disgusting kind, and dangerous, too. Locke's way of dealing with it was to adjudicate between Reason, Revelation, and Enthusiasm. Reason is natural revelation, the means by which God discloses to men such truth as comes within the reach of their natural faculties. Revelation is natural reason enlarged by direct communications from God: it is the work of reason to determine that these communications indeed come from God. So it is necessary to maintain one's reasoning capacity even in the presence of such deliveries. As for Enthusiasm:

> This I take to be properly Enthusiasm, which though founded neither on Reason, nor Divine Revelation, but arising from the Conceits of a warmed or over-weening Brain, works yet, where it once gets footing, more powerfully on the Perswasions and Actions of Man, than either of those two, or both together: Men being most forwardly obedient to the impulses they receive from themselves; And the whole Man is sure to act more vigorously, where the whole Man is carried by a natural Motion. For strong conceit like a new Principle carries all easily with it, when got above common Sense, and freed from all restraint of Reason, and check of Reflection, it is heightened into a Divine Authority, in concurrence with our own Temper and Inclination.[8]

The notion of Enthusiasm as a noxious vapour rising from the conceit of a warmed or overweening brain and taking possession of the whole man as if it were a revelation from God is common to Locke and Swift. But Locke's account of it is subdued to the decorum of exposition and discrimination. If Enthusiasm is vanity, he must take it seriously as a motive for action. Swift is not obliged to take it seriously or to rebuke it; he plays fast and loose with it so that his imagination may take supreme freedom to itself:

> Upon these, and the like Reasons, certain Objectors pretend to put it beyond all Doubt, that there must be a sort of preternatural *Spirit,* possessing the Heads of the Modern Saints; And some will have it to be the *Heat* of Zeal, working upon the *Dregs* of Ignorance, as other *Spirits* are produced from *Lees,* by the Force of Fire. Some again think, that when our earthly Tabernacles are disordered and desolate, shaken and out of Repair; the *Spirit* delights to dwell within them, as Houses are said to be haunted, when they are forsaken and gone to Decay.[9]

"Our earthly Tabernacles" is blasphemous to a Christian who believes that by the Incarnation the human body was indeed accorded spiritual privilege. It is the force of Swift's rhetoric to reduce the body to its decrepit form, and tabernacles to houses, so that he can effect a corresponding reduction of spirits to ghosts. As haunters of houses they are bugbears, sustained only by superstition. In *Some Versions of Pastoral* (London, 1962) Empson raised the possibility that Swift's ironies released in him a force of doubt of which he may have been unconscious: as if to say, "could it be the case, truly, as etymology suggests, that everything spiritual is merely a sublimation of something physical or mechanical?" "What Swift was trying to say is a minor matter; he was rightly accused of blasphemy for what he said; his own strength made his instrument too strong for him" (p. 62). The value of that remark is that it testifies to the impression we often have of Swift: that his style ran away with him. If he divined a verbal possibility it became at once a necessity; he could not set it aside out of consideration for propriety or justice. He said more than he intended, and in some sense had to believe (and often to fear) what he had said. The words compelled the dismay they preceded.

I am suggesting that Swift indeed resorted to the common forms of attitude and belief, but as a matter of strategy rather than of conviction. His aim coincided with his greatest need, to hold himself free. The ideas he negotiated were commonplaces, and his sense of them was mostly opportunistic, but there were a few ideas which troubled him and could not easily be disposed of within common forms. One of these, I think, provided some of the impulse towards *Gulliver's Travels*.

Let us assume that Swift's irony is well enough indicated by Kierkegaard's assertion that the ironist, since he does not coincide with his meaning, has the power of beginning again at any moment, independently of previous conditions. Now suppose a helpful colleague (it might be Gay, hardly Pope) were to argue that the sentiment of being free from previous conditions is a delusion, since those conditions have already secreted themselves in Swift's mind as its contents. If that were the case, one's mind would be not an independent power but a bundle of images, the result of chance and circumstance. What then would the sentiment of freedom amount to? Suppose further that Swift already feared that the argument might be true, since it was in keeping with the reductive bias of his mind, the grim pleasure he knew he took in saying that high A was nothing but low B. Then he might express his fears, and do something to control them, by projecting a man of whom these dreadful things could truly be said.

Swift sends Lemuel Gulliver voyaging into several remote regions, and gives him a meagre supply of capacities: some competence in medicine, navigation, mathematics, and a smattering of several languages including Italian, Portuguese, and Dutch. As for a mind, Gulliver has a simple frame of reference, modest expectations, the disposition of a practical man. But these capacities are as much as most Englishmen of his day could claim. Gulliver may or may not be as God made him, but he is definitely as England made him. If there is an English stereotype in education, politics, and morality it is inscribed on him, and is evident in a temper that recognizes limits and regards as vanity most of the interests which occupy more experimental or more pretentious people. To put the matter briefly: Gulliver has been brainwashed to become what he is. England has indeed made him. It follows that he stations himself in front of situations and reports them in penurious prose. The first irony of the book is the fact that a mind programmed to observe nothing more than ordinary events is forced to bring its rudimentary considerations to bear upon situations inordinate and bizarre. Trained to report certain limited categories of experience, Gulliver's mind has never been prepared to deal with monsters. Johnson's remark that when once you have thought of big men and little men it is very easy to do all the rest is not quite apt: the real problem is to attract into the orbit of big men and little men a mind capable of surviving experience without understanding it.

In the first three voyages the comedy is fairly simple; it is the comedy of disproportion which arises from the difference between ends and means, essence and existence. In the fourth, Gulliver sees the Yahoos and thinks them hideous brutes. After a while he comes to think himself much akin to them except that he wears clothes: he hates Yahoos because they force him to see himself in a monstrous form. The Houyhnhnms regard him as a Yahoo, though remarkably teachable for such a brute. However, they show him that in many untrivial aspects he is more wretchedly endowed than the Yahoos.

Gulliver does not defend himself in these comparisons; gradually he finds them convincing. It is true, for instance, that a being whose eyes are placed directly in front, one on each side of his nose, cannot look on either side without turning his head, a disability from which the Yahoo is free. Gulliver is compelled to admit that such comparisons are valid. A mind already brainwashed by the England that made him is ready to be brainwashed again by his new masters, the Houyhnhnms. Appropriately, the first sign of this readiness is that Gulliver comes to regard the English language as barbarous by comparison with that of the Houyhnhnms. Before he has spent a year in their country he has contracted, he says, "such a Love and Veneration for the Inhabitants, that I entered on a firm Resolution never to return to human kind, but to pass the rest of my Life among these admirable *Houyhnhnms* in the Contemplation and Practice of every Virtue; where I could have no Example or Incitement to Vice" (*Works,* XI [revised 1959], 258). After a while he comes to think it wonderful that these horses should condescend to distinguish him from the rest of his species, meaning the Yahoos, and he cannot bear the reflection of his body in a lake: he begins to imitate the trotting of the horses, and to speak with a whinnying voice. When he is forced to leave the country of the Houyhnhnms he prostrates himself to kiss his master's hoof, and thinks it sublime that his master does him the honour of raising the hoof to his mouth. When it looks as if he will be rescued by a passing ship he sails off in another direction, choosing rather to live with barbarians than with European Yahoos. Taken up by the Portuguese Captain and brought to Lisbon he can walk the streets only if his nose is "well stopped with Rue, or sometimes with Tobacco" (p. 288). Restored to his home he is embraced by his wife, "at which," he reports, "having not been used to the Touch of that odious Animal for so many Years, I fell in a Swoon for almost an Hour" (p. 289). His favourite company is that of two horses and their groom, "for I feel my Spirits revived by the Smell he contracts in the Stable" (p. 290). Gradually the effect wears off: the next phase of brainwashing begins. At the end Gulliver is becoming an Englishman again, though he will remain for a long time incensed by the vanity and pride of his countrymen.

The *OED* defines brainwashing as "the systematic and often forcible elimination from a person's mind of all established ideas, especially political ideas, so that another set may take their place." The first recorded use of the word is in 1950, a phase of the "Cold War" which we associate with the trial of Cardinal Stepinac and the publication of novels of brainwashing such as *The Manchurian Candidate.* The dictionary also says that brainwashing is "a kind of coercive conversion practised by certain totalitarian states on political dissidents." Many of us recall television pictures of brainwashed victims confessing their guilt, praising their captors, and denouncing their native country. But the degree of coercion required in each case depends upon the degree of resistance offered by the victim. Gulliver's resistance is slight: nothing is more revealing than his susceptibility to new images. He does not need to be forced. *Gulliver's Travels* is only superficially about big men and little men: it is really about entrapment, and how the mind escapes from one prison only to enter another.

There is a passage in Abram Tertz's *A Voice from the Chorus* in which the Russian writer, imprisoned in Lefortovo in 1966, recalls the books he read as a child, including *Gulliver's Travels.* Tertz makes the point that Gulliver is well fitted to represent mankind in general precisely because he has no personality, he has no permanent characteristics, and everything depends upon the circumstances in which he is placed. "He is short or tall, clean or unclean only by comparison; he is a man by comparison and a non-man by comparison; he is a giant among Lilliputians, a Lilliputian among giants, an animal among the Houyhnhnms, a horse among men."[10]

According to Tertz, Swift is saying that man is a fiction, a sham. But there is another way of phrasing the conclusion. Man is a function of his environment, trapped in whatever structure holds him. His only escape is into another structure, where the brainwashing begins again, but this time according to a different set of ideas and principles, equally arbitrary. The only alternative to this progress from one prison to the next is that of the Struldbruggs, those people in Luggnagg who are immortal in the horrifying sense that they get older but cannot die.

The word "brainwashing" is modern, but the history of rhetoric shows that its techniques have been understood and practised for centuries. The main technique is repetition (Iago's "Put money in thy purse") because it gradually makes its victim feel that the entire space of reality is occupied and possessed by the repeated injunction. No other experience is felt to count. Brainwashing, in any terminology, is the overt form of violence which changes the composition of the mind and leaves the body in every visible respect virtually intact. If we think of the process as categorical (a susceptibility of the mind which only good luck keeps in a tolerable form) rather than deliberately enforced, we do not call it brainwashing; we call it the association of ideas.

The chapter "Of the Association of Ideas," which Locke added in 1700 for the fourth edition of the *Essay Concerning Human Understanding,* was an inevitable consequence of his rejection of innate ideas in favour of a theory of experience largely based upon Boyle's corpuscular physics and Newton's optics. But Locke was much disturbed by the tendency of certain ideas to run together for no good reason:

> Some of our Ideas have a natural Correspondence and Connexion one with another: It is the Office and Excellency of our Reason to trace these, and hold them together in that Union and Correspondence which is founded in their peculiar Beings. Besides this there is another Connexion of Ideas wholly owing to Chance or Custom; Ideas that in themselves are not at all of kin, come to be so united in some Mens Minds, that 'tis very hard to separate them, they always keep in company, and the one no sooner at any time comes into the Understanding but its Associate appears with it; and if they are more than two which are thus united, the whole gang always inseparable shew themselves together (p. 395).

Locke thought the association of ideas a real phenomenon, and a dreadful one, a form of madness, because it prevented the mind from reasoning. The reference to "gang" makes his dismay clear. He held the association of ideas responsible for virtually all the mischief and folly in the world, including sectarian violence. In the *Essay* he urged parents and teachers to try to prevent such associations from forming in their children, so that a clear space might be available to the mind for dealing with impressions according to rational proeesses.

But the association of ideas remained a problem. If you argue, as Hartley does in his *Observations on Man* (1749), that knowledge is the result of repeated juxtapositions of corpuscular vibrations, you expose the possibility that these could be enforced. In the *Inquiry Concerning Human Understanding* (1748) Hume gives a copious account of the principles upon which ideas rush into association. There are three, he says: resemblance, contiguity in time or place, and cause or effect. He thought we could not survive without the association of ideas, because it prompts us to believe, and to act upon our beliefs. But the association of ideas makes nonsense of the axiom that man is a reasoning animal. What we regard as knowledge is entirely irrational, because there is no good reason to link the impressions which habit and custom insist on linking. In the chapter "Of the Reason of Animals" in the *Inquiry* Hume reduces the supposed difference between animals and men by arguing that animals, like men, learn by experience; that men and animals believe and act upon the deliveries of custom rather than upon ratiocination; that some parts of knowledge, in animals as in men, are derived "from the original hand of nature" (we call them "instincts"); and finally:

> The experimental reasoning itself, which we possess in common with beasts, and on which the whole conduct of life depends, is nothing but a species of instinct or mechanical power that acts in us unknown to ourselves, and in its chief operations is not directed by any such relations or comparison of ideas as are the proper objects of our intellectual faculties.[11]

It was for this reason that in the 1748 edition of the *Philosophical Essays* Hume sketched a non-Aristotelian theory of epic poetry, history, and tragedy, predicated upon the affections and the association of ideas rather than upon an Aristotelian theory of *mimesis*. He was afraid that the claims of cognitive independence, vested in the mimetic act, were specious.

Hume does not consider the possibility that one of the principles of the association of ideas (that is, contiguity) might be ordained (or, as we say, programmed) rather than circumstantial. The figure of metonymy could be enforced by repeated insistence upon it. Worry on this score has become explicit from time to time. In the *Enquiry Concerning Political Justice* Godwin considered it a scandal that every idea, however complex, offers itself to the mind under the conception of unity. The blending of many impressions into one perception was, he conceded, a law of nature, but the mind's prejudice in favour of unity made thinking virtually impossible. Standard education, which he thought had a deplorably vested interest in maintaining unity, was, as we would now say, a form of brainwashing.

The only way of eluding the dismal implications of the association of ideas (or, more accurately, the association of images) is by showing that cognition is indeed an independent power, however frustrated it may be by unconscious gangs of images. In 1805 the notion of the association of ideas was still so rife that Hazlitt had to attack Hartley's version of it directly in the hope of claiming autonomy for mind, imagination, and volition. In the *Essay on the Principles of Human Action* he insisted that volition could not be explained "from mere association."[12] All would be well if associations of ideas could be attributed not to chance or custom but to the first gestures of cognition. C. S. Peirce tried to remove the irrational harm from these associations by arguing, in "Some Consequences of Four Incapacities" (1868), that what is called "the association of ideas" is in reality an association of judgements amounting to inference:

> The association of ideas is said to proceed according to three principles—those of resemblance, of contiguity, and of causality. But it would be equally true to say that signs denote what they do on the three principles of resemblance, contiguity, and causality. There can be no question that anything is a sign of whatever is associated with it by resemblance, by contiguity, or by causality: nor can there be any doubt that any sign recalls the thing signified. So, then, the association of ideas consists in this, that a judgement occasions another judgement, of which it is the sign. Now this is nothing less nor more than inference.[13]

This ingenious attempt to turn a psychological embarrassment into an entirely respectable form of judgement to be understood by a theory of semiotics did not end the matter. Yeats worried about what he called "a new naturalism that leaves man helpless before the contents of his own mind," and he thought of Pound's *Cantos* and Joyce's *Anna Livia Plurabelle* as "works of an heroic sincerity, the man, his active faculties in suspense, one finger beating time to a bell sounding and echoing in the depths of his own mind" (*Essays and Introductions* [London, 1961], p. 405). Remy de Gourmont thought that all associations of ideas must be exploded, else the ostensibly rational faculty could not proceed: his essay on the dissociation of ideas was a programme of demolition. If the mind is not a capacity in some sense independent of its contents, the next questions arise: how did its contents come to be those and not other, and who put them there?

It is not necessary to maintain that Swift was a behaviourist, but only that he feared that something like behaviourism might be true, or at least more probable than the axiom that there is an inviolable human essence and that it consists of the distinctive power of reasoning. I accept, as most readers do, R. S. Crane's account of the rhetorical and ironic structure of Book IV of *Gulliver's Travels,* that it exhibits a simple reversal of the conventional distinction, common to textbooks of logic from Porphyry to Burgersdicius, between man as the reasoning animal and the horse as the whinnying animal.[14] But Crane does not quite say (it is perhaps implicit in his demonstration) that what Swift is mocking is essentialism as such. If you turn Porphyry's tree upside down you still get an essentialism, though a humiliating one. But Swift goes further, as if to say "and in any case if you take your essentialism seriously, and preen yourself upon your typology as the reasonable animal, I'll show you what your vanity entails." It is hard to say how seriously Swift took the distinction, which he conveyed in a letter to Pope and Bolingbroke, between man as reasoning animal and man as merely an animal capable of reasoning.[15] He seems to have felt that the author of the *Essay on Man* was not taking him seriously enough, and that the production of a wide-ranging thought might make him pay attention. Bolingbroke told him that the distinction would not stand scrutiny, and I suppose it does not, but Swift was serious in rejecting essentialist notions. He was not much interested in philosophy, but I think he felt that essentialist definitions, and especially the enhancing ones, did a lot of damage and made people vainer than they would otherwise be. My reading of Swift suggests that he was irritated by high-minded essentialist claims for man and his cognitive powers, but that he was dismayed, too, by the readiest alternative notion, that the mind is merely the sum of its arbitrary and haphazard contents. *Gulliver's Travels* mocks the euphemistic typology (as in the *Essay on Man*) which elides the differences between one man and another by providing a category, Man as such, in which they are transcended. His serious thinking is far closer to Locke's remark, in the *Essay,* that while "the difference is exceeding great between some Men, and some Animals," if we "compare the Understanding and Abilities of some Men, and some Brutes, we shall find so little difference, that 'twill be hard to say, that that of the Man is either clearer or larger" (p. 666). The descents, and the ascents, in the scale of being are very gradual. Rochester seems to have felt much the same: the famous line in the "Epilogue" of the "Satyre against Mankind" ("Man differs more from man, than man from beast") seems to say that the moral difference between the best people and the worst is greater than that between the best people and the general run of animals.

But a lot depends upon the particular animal you have in view. If you merely want to make a thundering attack on man you do not need to specify the animal you prefer: I'd be a dog, a monkey, or a bear, Rochester says in the "Satyre," or indeed anything rather than that vain animal,

man, who is so proud of being rational. Nearly any animal would do, if
you wanted to attack man's self-conceit. But if you wanted to make a
more pointed case the particular animal might make a difference. Empson
argues, in *The Structure of Complex Words,* that in the seventeenth and
eighteenth centuries it was common to feel that animals "blow the gaff"
on human nature, and the thought is either dreadful or not, depending
on the animal. He thinks that it was tolerable if you had dogs in mind,
rather than monkeys, even though it was agreed that among the lower
animals the elephant, the ape, the dog, and the horse are intelligent in that
descending order. In any case it was sound strategy to think of yourself as
the most triumphant of the animals rather than as the most fallen angel. If
you thought of the dog you could start building yourself into a man, and
not hate yourself: "The important point about the noble animal is that he
is a deeply reassuring object to contemplate. The fact that he can be
patronized as no more than fundamental makes you think better of the
race of man" (p. 170).

Empson makes the point that Swift refused this genial sentiment:
"The fact that monkeys were so like men was 'sadly humbling' to Boswell;
Monboddo only dared to say what many had suspected, and Johnson
agreed he was not a fool. Swift might fall back on the Houyhnhnm in
accepting this about the Yahoo, but that was a refusal of humanity; the
only real animal to use was the dog" (p. 170).

But Swift could not have used the dog, man's faithful friend, without making Book IV a cosy fireside thing. He had to pick an animal
sure to keep his distance even in a domestic setting. It was an advantage
that in Greek mythology and in Plato's *Republic* horses were given wings
splendid enough to make them fly as poetic inspiration or as the noble
soul. It has always been possible to say, as D. H. Lawrence did in many
poems, that virtually any organism (bird, beast, or flower) is more
completely itself than man is. The most recent version of this is Stanley
Cavell's assertion that what is splendid in the horse is his willingness to
be known:

> The horse, as it stands, is a rebuke to our unreadiness to be understood,
> our will to remain obscure. And the more beautiful the horse's
> stance, the more painful the rebuke. Theirs is our best picture of a
> readiness to understand. Our stand, our stance, is of denial. We feel
> our refusals are unrevealed because we keep, we think, our fences

invisible. But the horse takes cognizance of them, who does not care about invisibility.[16]

Gulliver's Travels does not require us to think that horses are finer than we are—or than some of us are. The Houyhnhnms do not, in fact, exhibit ideal powers of reasoning: if they did they would distinguish at once and without fuss between their leader's hospitality to Gulliver and Gulliver's relation to the other Yahoos. It is enough for the irony of the book that the Houyhnhnms are more intelligent than Englishmen who quarrel about matters entirely indifferent and run wild into factions and sects. There is no need to drive the matter to superlatives; comparatives are enough. Reason has a better chance, a clearer run, among the Houyhnhnms because it meets fewer obstacles: they are more content than we are, because they propose to themselves fewer wants. But they, like Gulliver, are what they are not by some essentialist or categorical imperative but as a consequence of the experiences which have made them.

I do not claim that this was Swift's settled position: clearly, it could be tipped in either of the available directions. He was far more determined to hold himself free and to convince himself that he, at least, had escaped the humiliation of the association of ideas. The practice of irony was his way of retaining that consolation, despite every consideration that told against it.

NOTES

1. *The Common Pursuit* (London, 1952), pp. 73–88.
2. Quotation is from *The Prose Writings of Jonathan Swift*, ed. Herbert Davis and others, 16 vols. (Oxford, 1939–74), I, 109–10.
3. *Satires against Man: The Poems of Rochester* (Berkeley and Los Angeles, 1973), p. 280.
4. *A Treatise of Human Nature*, ed. T. H. Green and T. H. Grose (London, 1886; reprinted Aalen, 1964, in two volumes), I, 385.
5. *Writing and Difference*, trans. Alan Bass (Chicago, 1978), pp. 278–79.
6. Henry James, *Letters*, I, 1843–1875, ed. Leon Edel (London, 1974), p. 45 (Letter of November 1, 1863).
7. *The Concept of Irony*, trans. Lee M. Capel (Bloomington, Ind., 1968), pp. 264–65.
8. *An Essay Concerning Human Understanding*, ed. Peter H. Nidditch (Oxford, 1975), p. 699.
9. *A Discourse Concerning the Mechanical Operation of the Spirit*, *Works*, I, 185–86.
10. Trans. Kyril Fitzlyon and Max Hayward (London, 1976), p. 21.
11. Ed. Charles W. Hendel (Indianapolis, 1955), p. 116.

12. *Works of William Hazlitt,* ed. P. P. Howe, 21 vols. (London, 1930–34), I, 73.
13. Charles S. Peirce, *Selected Writings,* ed. Philip P. Wiener (New York, 1958), p. 67.
14. *The Idea of the Humanities,* 2 vols. (Chicago and London, 1967), II, 261–82.
15. *The Correspondence of Jonathan Swift,* ed. Harold Williams, 5 vols. (Oxford, 1963–65), III, 121 (Letter of December 14, 1725).
16. Letter to Vicki Hearne, quoted in Vicki Hearne, "Tracking Dogs, Sensitive Horses, and the Traces of Speech," *Raritan,* V, No. 4 (Spring 1986), 1–35 (p. 34).

From *The Yearbook of English Studies,* Vol. XVIII (1988).

TRISTRAM SHANDY

In Volume IX, Chapter 4, of *Tristram Shandy* Toby and Trim arrive within twenty paces of Mrs. Wadman's door. If plot means anything, the attack should now begin. Military preparations have been ample. But Toby hesitates. Perhaps the Widow will take it amiss. Trim encourages him. The Widow will take it, he says, "just as the *Jew's* widow at *Lisbon* took it of my brother *Tom*" (p. 603). As soon as Tom is mentioned, however indecorously, his tragic fate is recalled, Trim cannot leave the case. If Tom had not married the Jew's widow, he would not have been dragged off to the Inquisition. " 'Tis a cursed place," Trim says: "when once a poor creature is in, he is in, an' please your honour, for ever." So the Corporal moralizes the occasion. Nothing can be so sad as confinement for life, nothing so sweet as liberty. Toby agrees. Then Trim, rising to the new note, begins a sentence: "Whilst a man is free," he says; but he ends the sentence with a flourish of his stick (p. 604). The flourish is not described; but by the magical resources of the printing press it is represented in a fine gesture, a brave flourish of print halfway down the page. We are reminded of Locke's chapter "Of the Imperfection of Words" in the *Essay,* where he suggests that "words standing for things which are known and distinguished by their outward shapes should be expressed by little draughts and prints made of them." Sterne's bold flourish of print stands for Trim's feeling, his impression, his idea, far more accurately than mere words. Of course it is possible to describe the joy of freedom, using nothing but words. Sterne makes a fair shot at this mark in the *Sentimental Journey,* a set piece in the chapter "The Passport: The Hotel at Paris." " 'Tis thou, thrice sweet and gracious goddess," he says, "whom all in public or in private worship, whose taste is grateful, and ever will be so, till NATURE herself shall change" (p. 199). These words are useful enough if freedom is to be invoked; or even for the more delicate purpose of indicating Yorick's general sense of freedom. But they are imperfect, in Locke's sense. We are led to think that they do not fully render the idea, the impression in Yorick's mind; or they render it as a general sentiment, a commonplace of feeling. The requirement in this respect is severe. The sign on the page should mark the feeling with preternatural intimacy. The ideal sign is the painting of Socrates, already praised in *Tristram Shandy.* Raphael's painting is so faithful to its occasion that, when you see it, you know precisely what Socrates was saying at that moment. The words are embodied in the gesture. Given the gesture, we require no remarkable imagination to set out the Socratic argument, as indeed Sterne sets it out in Volume IV, Chapter 7. The sinuous line on the page in Volume IX mimes the movement of Trim's stick, which in turn mimes the movement of his feeling. Sterne is not describing freedom; he is giving the exact figure in which Trim's sense of freedom is enacted.

I have gone into this episode in some detail because it is an exemplary moment in *Tristram Shandy.* Ostensibly, the topic is freedom, but what the words serve is Trim's feeling. Freedom provides the raw material, subject to the qualification that many other abstractions would have answered as well. If we refer to Trim's sense of freedom, we write "sense" in italics, "freedom" in roman. The sense is the thing. The proof is that nothing in this episode tells us anything about freedom, if we separate the common ideal from Trim's particular possession of it. But everything, including the printing press, conspires to reveal Trim in this gesture. The direction of our interest is from object to subject, from form to feeling. We are not allowed to rest until that sequence is fulfilled.

It is usual to say that this is according to Locke. Sterne has said it already. The *Essay,* he says, "is a history-book, Sir . . . of what passes in a man's own mind" (II, 2, p. 85). We postpone consideration of the silent question, whether any other history matters. It is according to Locke that

we remark the propriety of Trim's flourish. We suppose that many ideas
or impressions of freedom came into the sensorium of an old soldier, a
corporal. We know that his powers of reflection are consistent with his
vocation. So it is proper that the scale of those reflections is represented in
a splendid gesture. Nothing less would be enough. If the gesture has more
of Trim than of freedom in it, that too is proper, and some philosophers
argue that it is inevitable. In the second Book of the *Essay* Locke says that
the first source of our mental life is our senses, which "conversant about
particular sensible objects, do convey into the mind several distinct
perceptions of things, according to those various ways wherein those
objects do affect them." And then, "the other fountain from which
experience furnisheth the understanding with ideas is, — the perception of
the operations of our own mind within us, as it is employed about the
ideas it has got." But Locke does not say how much of our mental life is
sensation and how much reflection. There are men in whom the proportion
of reflection to sensation is inordinate; inordinately small or inordinately
large. In fiction, Walter Shandy is one of these; his sensory experience is
limited, but his reflective activities are comically exorbitant. We may say
of Toby's sensory experience that it is enough to fill a book of adventure,
and would require a larger book if his reflections upon that experience
were not so sparing. Sterne says that "REASON is, half of it, SENSE," but
he disturbs the symmetry at once by saying that "the measure of heaven
itself is but the measure of our present appetites and concoctions" (VII, 13,
p. 494). This is the idiom of sense, in Sterne's representation here the
better half. But if we define reflection in generous terms, we find the
rhetoric of the book proposing that what enters our minds by sense is
casual; we are really defined by our reflection, it is our very own. The
philosophic bearing is idealist. In the first volume of *The Philosophy of
Symbolic Forms,* Cassirer says that "the spirit is purely passive in relation
to its simple impressions, and need merely receive them in the form given
from outside, but when it comes to combining these simple ideas, it
represents its own nature far more than that of the objects outside it."
It follows, then, that language "is not so much a reflection of material
reality, as a reflection of mental operations." This is congenial to the
language spoken at Shandy Hall, which is not entirely according to
Locke. In Shandy Hall words are more intimately related to their speaker
than to the official objects of their reference. Material reality is the spur to
mental operations, but the reflective effect is greater than its cause. Trim

may talk of freedom, but the words are primarily interested in revealing Trim. In Volume III, Chapter 9, Dr. Slop looks at his obstetrical bag, and then he has a modest thought. "But here, you must distinguish," we are told; "the thought floated only in Dr. *Slop's* mind, without sail or ballast to it, as a simple proposition; millions of which, as your worship knows, are every day swimming quietly in the middle of the thin juice of a man's understanding, without being carried backwards or forwards, till some little gusts of passion or interest drive them to one side" (p. 167). The justification of passion, as of interest, is the part it plays in the mechanical operation of the spirit; it is a form of energy, propelling a man's reflection, so that he may the better reveal himself. Words declare their speaker, in the first instance, and their ostensible object only insofar as that is compatible with their first inclination.

It is tempting to say, for the moment, that what enters a man's mind through his senses is of no account in its nature and quality; it is essential that it come, since otherwise the reflective faculty is idle, but its character is perhaps indifferent. Sensations are needed as material, but we are defined by the nature of our reflection, which includes association, combination, relation, not to speak yet of Walter Shandy's hypotheses. No event, no sensation is sufficiently powerful in its own right to impose itself upon man's reflective capacity. The character of the sensation is one thing, the nature of its reception another. This is one of the sources of comedy. Some of Sterne's richest effects come from this disparity. An event may appear to be irrefutable in its character, and perhaps we cannot think of receiving it on any terms other than its own, but we are deceived. In Volume V, Chapter 2, of *Tristram Shandy* the news of Bobby's death is brought to his father, to Toby, Trim, and the rest. Walter is at that moment riding his hobbyhorse somewhere between Calais and Lyons; his reflection takes the form of an elaborate speech, the soothing commonplaces of oratory on the slight differences between good and evil. Trim makes a speech from a different tradition of rhetoric, richer in gesture and therefore more successfully pathetic. To Susannah, the death means mourning clothes, and her reflection is a mental tour of the wardrobe. To the scullion, Bobby's death is a striking reminder that she herself is alive. Trim ends his speech, and as talk of one death leads to talk of another, he gives the full history, the life and death of the Lieutenant. One impression incriminates another; thus life is lived. We live by passing time which, as Samuel Beckett says, would have passed anyway. The mind lives by instantaneous translation of its experience into esoteric and mutually incompatible languages.

The point to emphasize is that every object of experience is translated into the diverse terms of its perceiving subject; of the object itself, independent of the perceiving consciousness, nothing remains, except an ambiguous report. When Sterne calls *Tristram Shandy* "this rhapsodical work," he means that the governing terminology is the idiom of subject and process. The novelist is the contriver of process. In March 1762, Sterne wrote to Garrick: "I cannot write—I do a thousand things which cut no figure, *but in the doing*" (*Letters,* p. 157). It is almost a motto for the entire work, where everything is known in the doing, not in the thing seen as done. Considering the relation between subject and object, we acknowledge that there are, indeed, objects; we read of noses, knots, whiskers, deaths, clocks, fortifications, and widows. We take these things at Sterne's word. But they are entertained rather than acknowledged: a novelist in this tradition of fiction condescends to his ostensible materials, they are his minions. They are received and allowed on the understanding that, after that service, they will make no other demand. The objects are treated as happenings; they have everything except rights. Like the Siege of Namur and the Treaty of Utrecht, they are so colored by subjectivity that their objective status cannot hope to be recovered. We say of this, somewhat rudely, that the objects are invited only to be insulted, thrown aside when the spirit has done with them. But in this tradition of literature and philosophy the spirit has always denied the seeming solidity of objects, their claim to remain impervious. Sterne is as extreme in this inclination as Borges in our own time, who likes nothing better than to be seen using the language of impervious objects, subject to the consideration that the impervious quality is merely ostensible. In Sterne's comedy things are dissolved, then made into hobbyhorses; concepts in Walter Shandy, battles in Toby. The book itself is Sterne's hobbyhorse, as he acknowledged in a letter of 1760. Writers have always known that to use language in one way is to celebrate, as the greatest thing, a world outside the book; to use it in another way is to dissolve the world for the book's sake. In the age of print it became still easier to give the book this degree of precedence, as in *Tristram Shandy,* where the development of characters is far less compelling than the progression of chapters. Time may have more subtle divisions, but the divisions that count are the end of one chapter and the beginning of the next. A dangling participle may keep the whole world dangling.

The first law of subjectivity is that we move from one moment to another by responding to the chances of association. Words jump from one hobbyhorse to another. Any sentence with the word "siege" in it sets Toby translating it into his own terms. Trim can recite the Fifth Commandment, if he is allowed to start at the First. Walter Shandy's recourse to speculation and hypothesis is like a nervous tic, reducing all associations to one, the association of the mind with itself. Walter's mind is reflexive in the sense that it defines itself in one gesture, it reduces everything to itself. Tristram says at one point in Volume II: "It is the nature of an hypothesis . . . that it assimilates every thing to itself as proper nourishment; and, from the first moment of your begetting it, it generally grows the stronger by every thing you see, hear, read, or understand. This is of great use" (p. 151). It is of great use because it saves energy; so long as the mind is moving in that way, it is not tempted from the track of its business. So Walter is right, meaning logical, when he asks, "What is the character of a family to an hypothesis?" "Nay," he goes on, "what is the life of a family?"—a question as interesting as it is unanswerable (p. 69). Tristram called this rhetoric the *Argumentum ad Verecundiam, ex Absurdo, ex Fortiori* (p. 71).

We think of this as a hobbyhorse, but it would be enough to call it a habit. Samuel Beckett says in his essay on Proust that habit is "the generic term for the countless treaties concluded between the countless subjects that constitute the individual and their countless correlative objects." "If habit is a second nature, Proust says, it keeps us in ignorance of our first." Habit, then, is a generic term, an abstraction. Locke says in Book II, Chapter 11, of his *Essay* that in abstraction "ideas taken from particular beings become general representatives of all of the same kind." Habit saves us the labour of dealing with every impression as if it were new. Our second nature saves us the labour of living by our first. It is assumed, of course, that there is a difference between the two. If there is no difference, the single nature is a comic humour. The first thing we feel about a comic humour is the logical nature of his activities; there are no contradictions. Sterne's art delights in the possession of comic humours. We come round to Walter Shandy, logician of hypotheses.

Walter is entirely logical, for instance, in calling upon language to aid him in the manufacture of hypotheses. The auxiliary verbs which he praises in Volume V, Chapter 43, are self-engendering devices. "Now, by the right use and application of these," he says, "there is no one idea can enter [the] brain how barren soever, but a magazine of conceptions and conclusions may be drawn forth from it" (p. 406). He offers proof in the fruitful activity of white bears, incited by these verbs. Trim has never seen a white bear, but he can discourse upon them, because his inventive powers are sustained by corresponding powers in language itself. So language, whatever we hope to say of the relation between word and thing, is incorrigibly idealist and subjectivist, when invention is in question. There is the case of the Parisian barber in the *Sentimental Journey,* though this time Yorick is somewhat insular in his response to the French way of speaking. The Frenchman, praising his buckle, asserted that it would stand being immersed in the ocean. Yorick knows that an English barber would be content to say that the buckle would stand being immersed in a pail of water. He then argues in favor of his countryman that at least it would be possible to test the English assertion, but a Parisian, living in an inland city, would be hard pressed to find an ocean. Yorick's conclusion is that the grandeur of the French Sublime is magnificent, but "is *more* in the *word;* and *less* in the *thing"* (p. 159).

If the subjective law obtains, with the connivance of a subjective language, the necessity of plot is doubtful. "In *Freeze-land, Fog-land,* and some other lands I wot of" (p. 539) plot is considered essential in a novel, and cabbages are planted in straight lines and stoical distances, but in this climate of fantasy and perspiration, where every idea, sensible and insensible, gets vent, the case for adventure is weak. The place of real adventure is within the mind, where the strongest auxiliaries live.

It was usual to say, before we became accustomed to such things, that *Tristram Shandy* has no plot. But we are slow to make this a settled point of dispute. *Tristram Shandy* has enough plot, and enough adventure, to keep itself going, so long as the principle of its motion is maintained. Defoe's art would not survive upon that measure. The action of *Tristram Shandy* is to exhibit the comic freedom of the mind; the only requirement of plot is that it sustain that cause. A little plot goes a long way when it reaches a suitably inventive mind. Besides, a commitment to adventure would imply a certain independent power in the world at large, as if facts, things, and objects were indeed obdurate — an implication alien to Sterne, if it is severely enforced. But it is not severely enforced. Indeed, some of the most remarkable effects in *Tristram Shandy* are achieved by setting the ostensible mechanism of adventure against the irrefutable force of word or feeling. In Volume I, Chapter 22, Sterne gives a hint: "By this contrivance," he says, "the machinery of my work is of a species by itself; two contrary motions are introduced into it, and reconciled, which were thought to be at variance with each other. In a word, my work is digressive, and it is progressive too,——and at the same time" (p. 73). We say that the book is digressive in its first intention, and progressive in its second, but with an implication that both intentions are eventually fulfilled. The great advantage of a digressive manner is that any departures from it in the progressive way are likely to be momentous. In Volume V, Chapter 13, after Bobby's death, Walter Shandy makes a Socratic speech of desolation to Uncle Toby. Mrs. Shandy is outside the door, eavesdropping. At one point Mr. Shandy recites, " 'I have friends—— I have relations,——I have three desolate children,'——says *Socrates*": but Mrs. Shandy bursts in. "Then," she says, "you have one more, Mr. *Shandy*, than I know of." "By heaven! I have one less,——said my father, getting up and walking out of the room" (p. 370). Is not this one of those "familiar strokes and faint designations" (p. 73) which Sterne mentioned, far back in the book, designed to let the digression proceed while at the same time keeping the speaker's picture touched up, developed, modified? If it is, it is achieved not merely by having Mrs. Shandy interrupt her husband's rhetoric in the interests of truth, but by having Mr. Shandy break in upon rhetoric itself in the interests of a more poignant truth. The irony is that both are right.

In a later episode Mr. Shandy is wrong. At the end of Volume V, Chapter 32, Trim has been going through the Ten Commandments. Shandy is not impressed: "SCIENCES MAY BE LEARNED BY ROTE, BUT WISDOM NOT." He declares that Trim has not a single "determinate idea annexed to any one word he has repeated" (p. 393). The phrase "determinate idea" is the emendation which Locke inserted in the second, third, and fourth editions of the *Essay* instead of the "clear and distinct ideas" in the first edition. By determinate idea he means "some object in the mind, and consequently determined, i.e. such as it is there seen and perceived to be." "This, I think," Locke writes in the "Epistle to the Reader," "may fitly be called a determinate or determined idea, when such as it is at any time objectively in the mind and so determined there, it is annexed, and without variation determined, to a name or articulate sound, which is to be steadily the sign of that very same object of the mind, or determinate idea." Shandy is quizzing poor Trim as a strict son of Locke. Trim has

emitted the names or articulate sounds. Now he must declare the corresponding idea. What dost thou mean, Trim, by *"honouring thy father and
mother?"* It is a stern test, but Trim passes it triumphantly: "Allowing them,
an' please your honour, three halfpence a day out of my pay, when they
grew old." Words, forms, ideas, and charity are diversely great, but the
greatest of these is charity. Even Locke would yield at this point. The
relation between feeling and form is always indeterminate, but the moment
when the force of one clashes with the force of the other is peculiarly
moving. Interruption may come from either direction. A poem, it sometimes happens, seems unusually adequate to the feeling engaged; and when
we count the lines, lo, they come to fourteen and rhyme in ways proper to
the sonnet. Or a rhetorical structure seems wilfully determined to exclude
the world of telegrams and anger; and suddenly a telegram is delivered.

Sterne was peculiarly gifted in the apprehension of such moments,
especially of moments in which a rhetorical structure is suddenly waved
aside and we find ourselves, where we have an interest in being, on solid
earth, surrounded by people, places, and things. F. R. Leavis accused
Sterne of pretentious and nasty trifling, but I am not sure that the charge
will hold. I would maintain that a fine moral awareness is revealed when
the two worlds are allowed to collide. J. R. R. Tolkien distinguishes
between the Primary World, the given world in which we eat, sleep,
think, and work, and the Secondary World, different for each of us, the
world of art or of any structure which we delight to make. We do not live
in the secondary world; that world is fictive, the product of our need
and our imagination. It is possible to keep the primary world and the
secondary world apart, and there are strategic advantages in doing so, but
it is wonderful when, for a moment, the two worlds touch. This happens
when the primary world, perhaps in a "spot of time," seems wonderfully
responsive to man's need and therefore an enchanted place. Or in the
secondary world, when the fictive laws chime, for a moment, with the
daily laws of earth. In Volume VI, Chapter 34, of *Tristram Shandy* we are
told that when the Treaty of Utrecht was signed, Toby's fortifications
were left idle for several pacific months, except that occasionally he
would ride out to see that the Dunkirk machines were demolished,
"according to stipulation." Toby and Trim discuss the best way of effecting
the demolition, since that is in question. Toby offers an elaborate scenario,
ending with the whole harbour blown into the air. "And having done
that," he says, "we'll embark for *England*." "We are there, quoth the

corporal, recollecting himself." "Very true, said my uncle *Toby*—looking at the church" (p. 465). This may be a trifle, but the art is not trifling; nor is its feeling. There is no attempt, on Sterne's part, to shame one world in the sight of the other. What is remarkable is the flow of feeling between the two worlds, the subjective world of hobbyhorses and auxiliary verbs, and the historical world in which wars are fought, treaties are signed, and an English queen is shy with her allies.

Of course it is not necessary to maintain that in *Tristram Shandy* a just regard is continuously held for the rival claims of subject and object. The dominant procedure is subjectivist. But often, when we least expect it, the objective world, the primary world, is suddenly acknowledged, and the effect is momentous. For Sterne's comic purpose it is enough to allow that objects are not given to consciousness, as Cassirer says, "in a rigid, finished state," but that "the relation of representation to object presupposes an independent, spontaneous act of consciousness." Sterne finds the act of consciousness fascinating and, in many of its transactions, wonderfully comic. He does not quarrel with realists or empiricists, but he finds it comic to proceed upon a different assumption. If we think him "modern" in a sense in which Pope, Swift, and Johnson are not, the reason is that his axioms are psychological rather than moral. He is modern in the assumption that the important events take place within the individual sensibility. Pope, Swift, and Johnson assume that the important events take place in the public world, the given world of time and place.

Subject to these qualifications, we ascribe to Sterne a position in the first instance subjective and idealist. But he is a peaceful man by nature, and a comedian by vocation; in both characters hospitable to rival claims. Ascribing to him a double acknowledgement, we look for a suitably peaceful terminology. There is a strange letter, dated November 15, 1767, in which Sterne writes of the *Sentimental Journey,* "which shall make you cry as much as ever it made me laugh—or I'll give up the Business of sentimental writing—& write to the Body" (*Letters,* p. 401). It is an odd phrase. Sterne's idea of sentimental writing is explained in a letter of November 12: writing is sentimental when it runs most "upon those gentler passions and affections" which teach us to love the world and our fellow creatures. But what is writing to the body? Pornography, perhaps. But then it also means, presumably, *Tristram Shandy,* where the language of wit is certified by the sprightliness of the body. The soul may be a Christian, but the body is a pagan; a dualistic fact crucial to comedy.

True, *Tristram Shandy* also invokes the heart. In Volume IV, Chapter 26, Yorick has some thoughts on preaching; he favours the direct approach, despises ostentation. "For my own part," he says, "I had rather direct five words point blank to the heart" (p. 317). Sterne endorses this preference when he compares Walter Shandy's rhetoric unfavourably with Trim's, though to modern taste Trim's performance is scarcely more winning than Walter's. Trim is supposed to go "strait forwards as nature could lead him, to the heart" (p. 359), but Nature's rhetoric is pretentious on this occasion. Presumably the heart is the force in domestic things which, in sublime things, is called genius—an original gift, like instinct in animals. There is a passage in Garat's *Mémoires historiques sur la vie de M. Suard* (Paris, 1820, II, 148–49) which reports Sterne on this matter. Suard asked him to describe the natural and the acquired characteristics of genius. Sterne's answer is couched in subjective terms. He speaks of "le principe sacré qui forme l'âme, cette flamme immortelle qui nourrit la vie et la dévore, qui exalte et varie subitement toutes les sensations, et qu'on appelle *imagination, sensibilité,* suivant qu'elle représente sous les pinceaux d'un écrivain ou des tableaux ou des passions." The idealist tradition urges that the constitutive factor is the imagination, the power within. It follows that the idealist develops an elaborate idiom, different names for this inner power in its several manifestations. Cassirer has pointed out that in the seventeenth and eighteenth centuries this tradition was focussed in a single centre. "Both in thought and language," he says, "the new motion of a spiritual life far surpassing mere empirical-psychological reflection was epitomized in the concept of genius." The classic text is Diderot's *Lettre sur les sourds et muets,* where the concept of genius is "the point of ideal unity," as Cassirer calls it, towards which the spirit strives; in that centre, all dichotomies of subject and object are resolved. The aim of such thought is to transform "the passive world of mere *impressions,* in which the spirit seems at first imprisoned, into a world that is pure *expression* of human spirit." Poetry has always aspired to this transformation, as if it resented the evidence of an impervious world. This desire is found even in more empirical traditions. Bacon's famous account of poesy in the *De Augmentis* reflects this inspiration: "Whence," he says, "it may be fairly thought to partake somewhat of a divine nature; because it raises the mind and carries it aloft, accommodating the shows of things to the desires of the mind, not (like reason and history) buckling and bowing down the mind to the nature of things." There is no desire of the mind more fundamental than that of transforming the world, making the impressions which we receive from Nature appear as expressions of our own spirit. In descriptions of sensibility, the transforming power is often called the heart.

In Sterne, the first result of this idiom is that Nature becomes amenable to the inclinations of the mind. In Volume IV, Chapter 17, Tristram throws his wig in the air. Exasperated, he is then relieved. "Nor," he says, "do I think any thing else in *Nature,* would have given such immediate ease: She, dear Goddess, by an instantaneous impulse, in all *provoking cases,* determines us to a sally of this or that member — or else she thrusts us into this or that place, or posture of body, we know not why" (p. 293). The impulse is right, because Nature endorses the heart. The corresponding metaphors are familial and maternal. The *Sentimental Journey* itself, as Sterne says in one of the Versailles chapters, is "a quiet journey of the heart in pursuit of NATURE, and those affections which rise out of her, which make us love each other — and the world, better than we do" (p. 219). So the subjective terms begin to accrue: heart, genius, sensibility, affection, and (in a necessarily limited sense) Nature.

But the crucial word is Feeling. If the world is to be transformed, impressions appearing as expressions; if Locke's resistant world is to become the more susceptible world of Shaftesbury, Hume, and Diderot; feeling is the essential force. Feeling is the heart in motion, process personified; life itself, when life is understood in moving terms. "So much of motion, is so much of life, and so much of joy," Tristram says in Volume VII, Chapter 13, p. 493, surrounding life with two of the most powerful subjective terms. First among Sterne's values is the endless mobility of feeling, a delight in the self-creative plenitude of feeling. If the grace of mobility looks very like the dance of whim, Sterne is willing to bear that imputation, since whim, too, is subjective. Mobility of feeling is his way of circumventing the otherwise static relation between the mind and its materials. This is why Locke's account of the mind is not, to Sterne, enough. In Locke's world the relation between the mind and its materials is static because there is no allowance for the dynamic terminology of action. Impressions come unbidden to the sensorium, and there they are formed into arrangements or relationships governed by reflection, association, abstraction, or chance. But these transactions do not permit anything more dynamic than arithmetical progression; one thing, then another, then another. If Sterne is a transitional figure, the reason is that

he is moving toward a terminology of feeling, so that the mind's imprisonment in Locke's world, once recognized, may be broken. Feeling does in
one way what genius or imagination do in their own ways; it transcends
the limitations of historical experience, creating far other worlds and
other seas of feeling. If life is determined by chance impressions, in the
first instance, this restriction may be conceived as a kind of inner Fate, but
the human spirit may still elude that determinism by its own resources.
Sartre has said that the final aim of art is to reclaim the world by revealing
it as it is, but as if it had its source in human liberty. In Sterne, the only
liberty he takes is the liberty of endless feeling. The aim is to confound
the historical determinism of experience by engaging the multiplicity of
one's own powers. This makes a virtue of necessity; in this tradition a
necessity transformed by feeling becomes the virtue of freedom. In his
sermon on time and chance Sterne again makes a virtue of necessity by
representing the offerings of chance as hidden decisions of a providential
God. Those things "which to us seem merely *casual*" are "to him, certain
and determined" (*Works,* V, p. 133). So God, too, is subject, Nature is
subject, man is subject; and feeling is the proof.

The result is that many things are justified in this tradition which, in
a rival tradition, are suspect. Passion is justified because as a vital force it
operates within. After the "Maria" chapters of the *Sentimental Journey,*
Sterne has a famous apostrophe to sensibility.

> Dear sensibility! source inexhausted of all that's precious in our joys,
> or costly in our sorrows! thou chainest thy martyr down upon his
> bed of straw — and 'tis thou who lifts him up to HEAVEN — eternal
> fountain of our feelings! — 'tis here I trace thee, — and this is thy
> divinity which stirs within me —— not, that in some sad and
> sickening moments, *"my soul shrinks back upon herself, and startles at
> destruction"* — mere pomp of words! — but that I feel some generous
> joys and generous cares beyond myself — all comes from thee, great
> — great SENSORIUM of the world! which vibrates, if a hair of our
> heads but fall upon the ground, in the remotest desert of thy creation
> [pp. 277–78].

The idiom of subjectivity could hardly be more extreme. The difference
between joys and cares is not important; the crucial point is the continuity
of feeling, whatever the feeling is. If life is identified with feeling, the

place of action in other traditions is taken by the flow of feeling in this one. We admit this when we say that the *Sentimental Journey* is a book of impressions rather than a travel book. We make the point more accurately if we say that it is a book of expressions. What it expresses is the world as feeling.

We approve of this tradition, or we disapprove. Generally, the English moralists have found Sterne in some measure offensive; he is either trivial or subversive. Certainly, he is alien to the English spirit, if that spirit is embodied in a literature which is largely social, political, and historical. We may assume that this is what Johnson meant when he told Boswell, "Nothing odd will do long. *Tristram Shandy* did not last." The English moral tradition does not approve of works which seem, even at a glance, odd. Coleridge's attack upon the cult of sensibility is only a more elaborate version of this distaste. Sensibility, "a constitutional quickness of sympathy with pain and pleasure," is based upon certain "parts and fragments of our nature" rather than upon the whole. It is therefore false. "All the evil achieved by Hobbes and the whole school of materialists will appear inconsiderable," Coleridge writes in *Aids to Reflection,* "if it be compared with the mischief effected and occasioned by the sentimental philosophy of Sterne, and his numerous imitators." "The vilest appetites," he continues, "and the most remorseless inconstancy towards their objects, acquired the titles of the *heart, the irresistible feelings, the too tender sensibility:* and if the frosts of prudence, the icy chains of human law thawed and vanished at the genial warmth of human nature, who could help it? It was an amiable weakness!" Virginia Woolf thought Sterne wonderful, except that he kept the joke of *Tristram Shandy* running too long. The *Sentimental Journey* was somewhat soft: Sterne was too much concerned with "our good opinion of his heart." "The mood," she maintains, "is subdued to one that is too uniformly kind, tender and compassionate to be quite natural." Perhaps it would be more accurate to say that in the *Sentimental Journey* Sterne is too readily delighted with a subjective idiom and its mobility. It is common to argue that the book is ironic, but the argument is weak. If we find the book soft, we must put up with it in that character and reflect that softness is inevitable in a work dedicated to the values of sensibility.

But perhaps the tradition is not, after all, as vulnerable as this account suggests. I have already proposed that Sterne's world need not be regarded as subjectively closed. But another defence is possible: that subjectivity is one of the perennial demands of the mind. I note that

Susanne Langer in her recent book, *Mind,* proposes to treat the entire psychological field, "including human conception, responsible action, rationality, knowledge," as "a vast and branching development of feeling." True, she speaks of feeling, not of sensibility, but the difference is hard to establish. One idiom shades into the other. The argument is that the organism, "*in toto* and in every one of its parts, has to 'keep going' "; and in the subjective or idealist tradition it goes by feeling. So we should not underestimate the natural potentialities of a subjective idiom. The Man of Feeling is too often regarded as a mere historical phenomenon, a moment in the history of literature and psychology. In fact, he is perennial; irrefutable because always possible. He is always possible because he represents certain desires of the mind upon which the mind insists. The Man of Feeling is perennial because of the continuity of his sensations and the self-delighting power of his reflections. His only limitation is that he can never know whether feeling is enough, or whether its sole merit is that it keeps the organism employed. Psychological answers tend to be tautological. The Man of Feeling can never know when his feeling is adequate, because he cannot know what an adequate feeling would be: adequate to what? There are no criteria in feeling; there is only the satisfaction of its presence, or the despair of its end.

We are moving toward comedy, in the modern manner exemplified by Joyce and Beckett. Sterne employs the images of fact, time, and place; and he acknowledges them to the extent of that employment. He often uses them as a relief from the importunities of his feeling; as the most resolute idealist is pleased to be refuted, perhaps, by a Johnsonian stone. To Sterne, things are real, and their reality is comic: there is no contradiction. The relation between the mind and the things outside the mind is a relation of need and relief, a comic need, and a comic relief. Beckett says in the essay on Proust that "exemption from intrinsic flux in a given object does not change the fact that it is the correlative of a subject that does not enjoy such immunity." By heart and sensibility Sterne makes up for the frustrations of the flux, bridging the gap between subject and object by subjective energy, by the continuity of feeling. If feeling is continuous, the fluidity of subject does not matter. Sterne defeats frustration by taking it as it comes, making virtues of necessities. If you say with Beckett that the observer infects the observed with his own mobility, you may say it ruefully or you may say it as a comic gesture. *Tristram Shandy* and the *Sentimental Journey* make the same assumptions about human nature, the mind, the body, the sensorium; but the tone of one differs from the tone of the other. Suppose a man were to write a novel treating every characteristic mode of the mind as an amiable and necessary foible; might it not turn out like *Tristram Shandy,* given Sterne's genius? And suppose he were to write another book to suggest that all men share in the possession of amiable foibles and could not live without them; might it not turn out like *A Sentimental Journey,* given the same genius? Kenneth Burke has remarked that "the progress of humane enlightenment can go no further than in picturing people not as *vicious,* but as *mistaken."* "When you add," he continues, "that people are *necessarily* mistaken, that *all* people are exposed to situations in which they must act as fools, that *every* insight contains its own special kind of blindness, you complete the comic circle, returning again to the lesson of humility that underlies great tragedy."

We speak of Sterne as our contemporary, but the word is ambiguous. We say that Sterne is modern and that Swift, Pope, and Johnson are not. Boswell recalls an occasion on which Johnson teased his friend "the lively Miss Monckton." The lady had insisted that some of Sterne's writings were very pathetic. Johnson denied it. "I am sure," Miss Monckton maintained, "they have affected *me."* "Why," said Johnson, smiling and rolling himself about, "that is because, dearest, you're a dunce." Johnson is not denying that some readers find Sterne's writings affecting. Still, he insists that by common or public standards Sterne's writings fail. They fail, we may assume, because in their oddity they devote themselves to the exception rather than to the rule. Johnson represents that general sense of life in which reality is deemed to be tangible, verifiable, and public. He knows that there are obstacles to this view, but he refuses to give them more allowance than is appropriate to local difficulties. Sterne is fascinated by the obstacles, he prefers them to the truth they impede. As a comedian he loves to rebuke the axioms of common sense. We think of this as a modern stance, critical, comic, and subversive. But we should not push the difference too far. There is no reason to speak of Sterne as if he were Kafka, Musil, or Beckett. He is a man of his time, though he complicates our sense of that time. Indeed, it may be maintained that the differences between Sterne and Johnson allow for a body of feeling, since that is the crucial term, common to both. There is no reason to think that Sterne merely denied, or that Johnson merely asserted; their differences are not incorrigible. Sterne's comic intransigence is not, after all, prohibitive.

He does not undermine the common assumptions of his age, though it is the nature of his comedy to ensure that those assumptions are not too glibly held. Perhaps what is exemplary in Sterne is the urbane tone which suffuses his intransigence, as if in that urbanity the acerbities of true and false, subject and object, might still be appeased.

From Arthur H. Cash and John M. Stedmond (eds.), *The Winged Skull: Papers from the Laurence Sterne Bicentenary Conference at the University of York* (Kent, O.: Kent State University Press, 1971).

A VIEW OF *MANSFIELD PARK*

Henry James spoke of Jane Austen's "light felicity," thereby patronizing a novelist whom he was happy to admire provided he was not required to take her too seriously. "Light felicity" is a term of praise, in its way, but it does not accord with the image of Jane Austen which modern readers recognize and sponsor. "Everybody's dear Jane,"² like James's mistress of felicity, has been replaced by the astringent figure outlined in D. W. Harding's famous essay "Regulated Hatred." Professor Harding's Jane Austen is a systematic ironist, writing of a society which she accepts, but only subject to the critical rigour for which she makes, in her fiction, an assured place. She votes for the society when it is a question of voting, but meanwhile she insinuates general and specific critiques, brisk summaries of disenchantment; many of these hover on the edge of subversion. This view of Jane Austen is agreeable largely, I think, because it exemplifies a position in society which many of us would wish to hold. We want to participate in a social order while purifying it, privately, by mental reservations; and we want to feel that this way of life is intelligent, humane, and artistic, that it has a certain finesse, a meticulous propriety of conscience. Jane Austen discloses this happiness.

But, not, I think, invariably. The modern image of Jane Austen corresponds accurately enough to the narrative voice of *Emma,* for instance, where the formative vision of life is systematically ironic; but these are not the terms in which we would speak of *Mansfield Park.* In *Mansfield Park* the irony is local, a sharpening of the instrument now and again, rather than a constant imperative.

There is, for example, the announcement of Mr. Norris's death:

> The first event of any importance in the family was the death of Mr. Norris, which happened when Fanny was about fifteen, and necessarily introduced alterations and novelties. Mrs. Norris, on quitting the parsonage, removed first to the park, and afterwards to a small house of Sir Thomas's in the village, and consoled herself for the loss of her husband by considering that she could do very well without him, and for her reduction of income by the evident necessity of stricter economy. (ch. 3)

The critical voice is sharper here than generally in *Mansfield Park,* but even here we are invited to attend not to the voice itself but to the narrated facts, the events, almost as if they had not yet become verbal. We can readily believe that Jane Austen disliked such people as Mrs. Norris, and we are meant to register the parody of feeling in the widow's consolation, but the narrative voice is as "neutral" as it can well be: it is content with an enabling role, it does not declare itself as the object of primary interest. The relation between Mrs. Norris's husband and the reduction of her income is a rhyme of syntax, indisputably verbal; but as soon as we have taken the weight of the juxtaposition, we are free to let the words go. This is to say that the words do not insist upon themselves beyond the moment at which the delivery of the "facts" is made. But listen to the announcement of Mrs. Churchill's death in *Emma:*

> It was felt as such things must be felt. Every body had a degree of gravity and sorrow; tenderness towards the departed, solicitude for the surviving friends; and, in a reasonable time, curiosity to know where she would be buried. Goldsmith tells us that when lovely woman stoops to folly, she has nothing to do but to die; and when she stoops to be disagreeable it is equally to be recommended as a clearer of ill-fame. Mrs. Churchill, after being disliked at least twenty-

five years, was now spoken of with compassionate allowances. In one point she was fully justified. She had never admitted before to be seriously ill. The event acquitted her of all the fancifulness, and all the selfishness of imaginary complaints. (ch. 45)

This is Professor Harding's mistress of regulated hatred. We are still in clichés of feeling; the mechanical slide from tenderness to curiosity, the automatic compassion, the provisional obscurity of gravity and sorrow. Indeed the ironies, word by word, are dazzling; we read this prose as we read the verse of the *Dunciad*. Clearly a much larger proportion of the effect depends upon the narrative voice in this case than in the paragraph from *Mansfield Park;* the ironist is listening to the sounds and relishing their brilliance. In the passage from *Mansfield Park* the dominant assumption is that the meaning, the human "point," lies in the facts themselves, apart from any incidental force attributable to the voice of the narrator. But in the passage from *Emma* the locus of significance and value is far less in the "facts" and far more in the voice of a narrator deemed to be superior to any facts. The voice is nearly everything; the facts, the events, are merely the occasion of its performance. It is like opera in a foreign language when the singing is magnificent.

We are already exaggerating. But a modest distinction is valid: the witty and superior voice of Jane Austen is the commanding presence of *Emma, Pride and Prejudice,* and *Sanditon;* but in *Sense and Sensibility, Northanger Abbey, Persuasion,* and *Mansfield Park* there is far less irony, far less "voice," the meaning is entrusted to facts which largely speak for themselves. Jane Austen, indeed, wrote two quite distinct kinds of fiction. *Mansfield Park* is not an unsuccessful attempt to repeat the success of *Pride and Prejudice;* it is a different kind of novel and, in that kind, a masterpiece. The reader is free to prefer *Emma* or *Pride and Prejudice* but the preference counts for little until *Mansfield Park* is acknowledged as a major work in a different genre.

A common view of *Mansfield Park* is vigorously given in Marvin Mudrick's *Irony as Defense and Discovery.* The novel is the triumph of mere gentility. Fanny Price is a dull prig. Mary Crawford is so charming and vital that she threatens to overthrow the novel and compels Jane Austen to betray her in the end. "In *Mansfield Park,*" Professor Mudrick says, "the most notable omission is irony." I should deflect the blow a little by saying that it is not an omission; if *Pride and Prejudice* strives towards the condition of French classical comedy, *Mansfield Park* is cousin to the Morality plays.

Jane Austen knew that *Pride and Prejudice* was a masterpiece and something of a *tour de force*, but I think she felt that it was slightly operatic in its brilliance. In the famous letter to Cassandra (February 4, 1813), she says: "The work is rather too light, and bright, and sparkling: it wants shade, it wants to be stretched out here and there with a long chapter of sense, if it could be had; if not, of solemn specious nonsense, about something unconnected with the story; an essay on writing, a critique on Walter Scott, or the history of Buonaparté, or anything that would form a contrast, and bring the reader with increased delight to the playfulness and epigrammatism of the general style."[1] I think she felt something factitious in *Pride and Prejudice,* as if it were too dazzling to be true; and she was beginning to think a good deal about the nature of truth. In *Mansfield Park* she would propose a sterner discrimination, even at the risk of being, as she said, "not half so entertaining."[2] In *Pride and Prejudice* life allowed the novelist to declare the marvellous union of Wit and Wisdom, but this was one liberty in a thousand restrictions. The more general rule of life is that Wit and Wisdom are cut adrift and often in that severance Wit becomes corrupt and Wisdom a little dull; and if it must be a choice, then one must choose Wisdom, because (as Jane Austen wrote to Fanny Knight in November 1814) "Wisdom is better than Wit, and in the long run will certainly have the laugh on her side."[3] This is more English than French; like Cowper's indigenous morality in "Tirocinium" when he refers to "wit's eccentric range." *Mansfield Park* is written in the same idiom; it is concerned with Wisdom, with Truth, with the moral sense and the possibility of improving it or corrupting it.

We know what Jane Austen means by Wisdom; at least when she sets it off against Wit. We know that by "Truth" she means, in human relationships, a direct correlation of speech and action. In the great argument between Emma and Mr. Knightley (ch. 18) about Frank Churchill's behaviour, Emma speaks for charm and wit, but Knightley will listen only to duty and truth. Several chapters later Emma adopts his idiom. Speaking to Mrs. Weston of Frank Churchill's secret engagement, Emma says: "Impropriety! Oh!—Mrs. Weston—it is too calm a censure. Much, much beyond impropriety!—It has sunk him, I cannot say how much it has sunk him in my opinion. So unlike what a man should be!—None of that upright integrity, that strict adherence to truth and principle, that disdain of trick and littleness, which a man should display in every transaction of his life" (ch. 46). Each of Jane Austen's novels has at least one major occasion on which the demands of Truth are flouted: Frank Churchill's secret engagement to Jane Fairfax; in *Sense and Sensibility,* the secret trip of Marianne and Willoughby to Allenham (ch. 13), which mimes a marital relation to which they have no claim; in *Pride and Prejudice,* Lydia's elopement with Wickham; in *Persuasion,* the bland secrecies of Mrs. Clay; in *Lady Susan,* the sexual strategies from beginning to end; in *Northanger Abbey,* Isabella Thorpe's duplicity with Frederick Tilney; and in *Mansfield Park,* the chain of deceit which leads to Henry Crawford's elopement with Mrs. Rushworth and Julia's with John Yates. But *Mansfield Park* moves the issue into the centre of the novel; nothing less than Truth is at stake in the crucial chapters which deal with the amateur theatricals.

We first hear of the playacting in ch. 13. The notion is opposed by Edmund and, with natural silence, by Fanny. But the stronger party consists of John Yates, Tom Bertram, Maria, Julia, the Crawfords, Mrs. Norris, and the indolent Lady Bertram. Edmund's argument is that "in a *general* light, private theatricals are open to some objections," but "as *we* are circumstanced," they would be "most injudicious." They would show a certain lack of feeling for an absent father: Sir Thomas would not wish his daughters to act plays; the business would be particularly imprudent now that Maria is engaged to Mr. Rushworth. Besides, the play itself, *Lovers' Vows,* is objectionable in detail. Edmund is rather vague in specifying the scandalous implications, and Fanny, of course, is silent, but as the arrangements proceed the issues become clear enough, although they are never debated. Private theatricals were a frequent amusement in the Austen home; acceptable enough, indeed, so long as their innocence was guaranteed by the privacy of the family. But privacy was always vulnerable. In 1787, for instance, Eliza de Feuillide, wife of a French aristocrat, arrived at Steventon. Soon she was taking part in the family theatricals. Some years later, when her husband was executed in Paris, she turned her thoughts again towards the Austen family; towards Henry, in particular, whom she married in 1797. Jane Austen's feeling on this occasion may have made its way into *Mansfield Park,* though there is no evidence of direct transcription. In any event, innocence did not hold when, as in *Mansfield Park,* the players included people who were likely to become emotionally involved with one another. Mary Crawford will not marry the infatuated Edmund because she despises penniless clergymen, but she is ready to make love to him, vicariously, by miming the part of Amelia in *Lovers' Vows*. Julia wants to play the part of Agatha, the lover of the Baron, played by John Yates—with whom she eventually elopes, in the "fact" of the fiction. Edmund refuses to join, but when there is talk of inviting Charles Maddox to take his place, he objects that this will put an end to "all the privacy and propriety"—his phrase—and to prevent this he agrees to play. But now he himself, within the play, is what he longs to become, "outside," Mary's successful lover. Perhaps Fanny was justified in thinking of her hero's "unsteadiness." Maria, engaged to Rushworth, is in love with Henry Crawford: the rehearsals enable her to avoid Rushworth and to spend a lot of time with Henry. The implications are clear, the playacting is corrupt. If the great question in Jane Austen's fictive world is the relation between human feeling and the social forms in which it is certified or distorted, then the theatricals at Mansfield Park are corrupt because they obscure the forms and evade the ethical sanctions which the forms sustain. Above all, the theatricals are an offence against Truth. That is why Fanny will always associate Henry Crawford's behaviour during the rehearsals with his deceitful stratagems at Sotherton.

We are dealing with a stern ethic. Indeed, *Mansfield Park* seems to associate itself with those letters in which Jane Austen expressed an increasing respect for the seriousness of the Evangelicals. She had started off by simply not liking these people, and even in her later years she would remain cool to the idiom of Regeneration and Conversion, but there is a revealing letter in which she says, "I am by no means convinced that we ought not all to be Evangelicals, and am at least persuaded that they who are so from Reason and Feeling must be happiest and safest."[4] This is close to the spirit of *Mansfield Park,* a novel which dramatizes many of the leading moral issues from Shaftesbury to Adam Smith, Cowper, and Johnson. *Mansfield Park* is Jane Austen's most committed novel: the free play of irony is only one of its resources, and not the greatest. When the novelist said that her subject in *Mansfield Park* would be "ordination," she was concerned to focus upon the bristling relation between truth, the moral sense, and the integrity of the self.

There are two great commitments in *Mansfield Park:* Edmund's choice of the priesthood, and Fanny's love for Edmund.

Of the first: Halévy's *History of England in the Nineteenth Century* gives many reasons for the low status of ministers in the Church; enough to show that Mary Crawford's contempt for the clergy was a common and sustainable view, however corrupt. But it was, indeed, corrupt. In *Sense and Sensibility* Edward Ferrars mentions (ch. 19) that he wished to become a minister, but that this profession "was not smart enough for my family." And his brother Robert laughs "most immoderately" (ch. 47) at the vision of Edward "reading prayers in a white surplice, and publishing the banns of marriage between John Smith and Mary Brown." We are to understand that when Edmund Bertram insists upon becoming a clergyman and taking up all the duties of rural ministry including that of residence, there can be no deeper commitment. William James, speaking of the consciousness of self, mentions the common situation in which we are compelled to choose, to stand by one of our empirical selves and relinquish the others. Edmund Bertram is in love with the fascinating Mary Crawford, and to be her husband is one of the "selves" he most strongly wishes to achieve, but he stands by the greatest of these, his role as minister, and he eventually relinquishes the role which impedes this self. One of James's sentences happens to give the situation precisely: "the seeker of his truest, strongest, deepest self must review the list (of selves) carefully, and pick out the one on which to stake his salvation."[5] For similar reasons, Fanny commits herself to Edmund, once for all, despite the persuasions of Sir Thomas, Henry Crawford, Mary Crawford, and Edmund himself. Bishop Butler argues in his *Analogy* that personal identity is established by the similarity, on different occasions, of one's consciousness: through a multitude of whirling circumstances Fanny Price is conscious of loving Edmund, and this consciousness is inescapable. In *Persuasion* Anne Elliot's love for Captain Wentworth is of a similar order; and in *Sense and Sensibility*, Elinor's commitment to Edward. This is what Jane Austen means by "Truth" in personal relations.

The two great temptations which lie across the path of truth in Jane Austen's fiction are "charm" and selfishness.[6]

It is possible, of course, for charm to be good, as it is in the miracle of Elizabeth Bennet. But Jane Austen often felt, and particularly after *Pride and Prejudice*, that the dangerous people were those whose charm was at once irrefutable and corrupt. She would always relish charm, even in a Henry Crawford; there is a letter of March 1814, in which she refers to her brother: "Henry is going on with 'Mansfield Park.' He admires H. Crawford: I mean properly, as a clever, pleasant man."[7] What she means is that we cannot ignore or despise the cleverness or the pleasantness of such a man. These virtues render his corruption the more lamentable, the more insidious. She would never have approved Lord Chesterfield's advice to his son, but she knew the force of charm, she relished it, and— I feel sure—feared it. Clearly she was afraid of charming, worthless, clever men like Willoughby, Wickham, Crawford, and Frank Churchill. She knew that charm in such men is notoriously beguiling; even Elizabeth was greatly taken by Wickham's charm in chs. 16 and 17 of *Pride and Prejudice,* and poor Edmund in *Mansfield Park* is so bewitched by Mary Crawford's charm that he forgets the civilities due to Fanny, especially at Sotherton. This is one of the great successes in *Mansfield Park,* Mary Crawford's charm; we are constantly aware of it, partly under its spell, even though the text is strewn with hints of its corruption. She openly criticizes her uncle (ch. 6), comes very close to an obscene pun (ch. 6), boasts of knowing only admirals (ch. 6), sneers at prayer (ch. 9), despises the clergy (ch. 9), takes London as her moral standard (ch. 9), makes unforgivable remarks about Maria's impending marriage (ch. 11), is quite insensitive to natural beauty (ch. 22), and changes her mind about Edmund when it seems likely that Tom will die and Edmund will inherit his father's wealth. Perhaps the earliest and strongest hint of Mary's character is in ch. 6, at Mansfield, when she demands a cart to bring her harp from Northampton and cannot understand the conditions of rural life which make this demand particularly unwelcome at harvesttime. But the charm persists and cannot be neutralized until at last it reveals its corruption to Edmund; when Mary speaks of the adultery of her brother and Mrs. Rushworth as mere folly: "She saw it only as folly, and that folly stamped only by exposure" (ch. 48).

The second temptation in the path of truth is selfishness. Jane Austen was not a pupil of Mandeville or Hobbes but she was sufficiently wry to acknowledge that selfishness, whatever the cause, is a common effect in human action. But if truth means commitment—so her argument would run—the movement of feeling cannot be self-engrossed, it must go out in full acknowledgement of other people. There are many versions of selfishness in Jane Austen's fiction, some deadlier than others; in *Sanditon,* Sir Edward Denham's plan to seduce Clara Brereton; Lady Susan's entire life; William Elliot's advances to Anne, in *Persuasion* (ch. 20); in *Sense and Sensibility* (ch. 27), Marianne's rudeness to Mrs. Jennings; Mr. Bennet's systematic contempt, in *Pride and Prejudice;* Emma's snobbery. These are not morally identical. But they are all, in their differing degrees, reprehensible. In Jane Austen's fiction the rule is that extreme cases of selfishness must be punished, and the milder versions—since most of us exhibit them—must be neutralized and if possible transformed into love and wisdom. The greatest example of this conversion of force into style is Emma: her rudeness to Miss Bates, her repudiation of Robert Martin, her patronage of Harriet Smith; these must be neutralized, Emma must be brought to the point of saying, as she does towards the end of the book, "It would be a great pleasure to know Robert Martin." At this point force becomes style, which is energy without aggression. All the analogies now flow together to enrich the marriage of Emma and Knightley—the "sweet" English landscape (ch. 42), Hartfield and Highbury rather than London, an ethic of principle and truth. But where selfishness has been extreme, there is no forgiveness. In *Sense and Sensibility* Lucy Steele is repudiated, by Jane Austen if not by Edward Ferrars. The same punishment is dealt to Isabella Thorpe in *Northanger Abbey*. In *Mansfield Park* the most extreme act of selfishness is Henry Crawford's decision to make Fanny fall in love with him. This is the culmination of a chain of selfish acts on his part, beginning with his remark at Sotherton (ch. 9), "I do not like to see Miss Bertram so near the altar." Thereafter he flirts with the engaged Maria, behaves like a boor towards Rushworth, and plays with the feelings of Maria and Julia. When he decides to make Fanny fall in love, it is to amuse himself "on the days that I do not hunt" (ch. 24), and even when he is really in love with her, he continues to think of his emotion as a favour (ch. 30) and to exhibit what Fanny, despite her gratitude on other grounds, calls "a want of delicacy and regard for others" (ch. 20). This being so, even in his finer moments he cannot speak the language of true grace. When Fanny is visited by her brother William and her happiness is clear to everyone, Henry Crawford is greatly taken by the picture:

It was a picture which Henry Crawford had moral taste enough to value. Fanny's attractions increased—increased two-fold—for the sensibility which beautified her complexion and illumined her countenance, was an attraction in itself. He was no longer in doubt of the capabilities of her heart. She had feeling, genuine feeling. It would be something to be loved by such a girl, to excite the first ardours of her young, unsophisticated mind! She interested him

more than he had foreseen. A fortnight was not enough. His stay
became indefinite.   (ch. 24)

There is a characteristic deterioration of feeling here. The first notes are
of eighteenth-century weight and civility. They are Jane Austen's terms,
and she is prepared to lend them to Crawford to the extent that he merits
them; terms like "moral taste," "insensibility," "the capabilities of the
heart," and "feeling." This is one of the tests which Jane Austen imposes
upon her characters; some will speak this language gracefully, and these
are her saints. But Henry Crawford handles the words awkwardly and
soon slips into the easier idiom of conquest and triumph. It would be
"something" to be loved by such a girl, he muses, but the "something"
has nothing to do with the higher "value" sponsored by his moral taste; it
is a public prize, the success of strategy. The "interest" of the occasion is
in direct proportion to the pride of victory. It is the kind of interest
which Mary Crawford offers Fanny in the possession of Henry, several
chapters later. When Fanny refers to the gallantries in which Henry has
indulged himself, Mary points to "the glory of fixing one who has been
shot at by so many; of having it in one's power to pay off the debts of
one's sex!" "Oh, I am sure it is not in woman's nature to refuse such a
triumph" (ch. 34). Henry shares this language of prizes, triumphs, debts,
and—the word is now defined—"interest": like his sister, he is a capitalist
of the sensibility. He may read Shakespeare well, and this is in his favour,
but he has said so much in the language of fashion and power that he
cannot bring himself to learn the idiom of truth and love. He speaks it as
a foreign language, too recently acquired. At the end of the book he is
still the same. When he meets Maria Rushworth and is received "with a
coldness which ought to have been repulsive," he becomes again a man of
mere power, winning, and winning nothing. Jane Austen's last word is a
blank cheque. We may fairly consider, she says, "a man of sense like Henry
Crawford, to be providing for himself no small portion of vexation and
regret—vexation that must rise sometimes to self reproach and regret to
wretchedness—in having so requited hospitality, so injured family peace,
so forfeited his best, most estimable and endeared acquaintance, and so
lost the woman whom he had rationally, as well as passionately loved"
(ch. 48). In *The Beast in the Jungle* Henry James takes up where this
sentence leaves off: John Marcher realizes, too late, when May Bartram is

dead, that he has "lived" in "the chill of his egotism and the light of her use." Fanny Price is preserved by Edmund, by Jane Austen, and by a chosen "self" which demands nothing but its own small space. Henry Crawford is preserved, to the extent that he is preserved, merely by not being deemed worthy to suffer in John Marcher's way.

Clearly there is a problem. Jane Austen cannot allow her world to be divided between charming scoundrels and dull saints. She must discriminate between the charm of Wickham and the vivacity of Darcy, between the force of Frank Churchill and the style of Knightley. She must set up a rivalry of spirit between Mary Crawford and Fanny Price, letting Fanny lose the battles and win the war. The central question is the moral sense. What is it, and what is its function?

Jane Austen's treatment of this matter corresponds very closely to the position of "orthodox" English moralists in the eighteenth century. She assumes the operation of a moral sense, an "inner sense," a power deemed to be innate in every person, as Shaftesbury said, "a first principle in our constitution and make."[8] Hutcheson argued that the moral sense is universal and uniform because there are "some actions or affections which obtain the approbation of any spectator or observer, and others (which) move his dislike and condemnation." Furthermore (and this bears directly upon *Mansfield Park*), it is assumed that while the moral sense may be, as Burnet says, "improveable into more distinct knowledge,"[9] it may also be depraved, notably by "Custom, Habits, false opinions, Company,"[10] as Hutcheson says, or—in Shaftesbury's account—"from the force of custom and education in opposition to Nature"[11] or through "licentiousness of practice."[12] In Adam Smith's *Theory of Moral Sentiments* the idea of sympathy plays a much larger part than in the writings of moralists like Burnet, Shaftesbury, Butler, and Hutcheson, but it is all the more revealing that he speaks in similar terms "of the influence of Custom and Fashion upon Moral Sentiments." The following paragraph from *Theory* might almost have been written to prepare us for the Crawfords of *Mansfield Park*:

Those who have been educated in what is really good company, not in what is commonly called such, who have been accustomed to see nothing in the persons whom they esteemed and lived with, but justice, modesty, humanity, and good order; are more shocked with whatever seems to be inconsistent with the rules which those virtues prescribe. Those, on the contrary, who have had the misfortune to be brought up amidst violence, licentiousness, falsehood, and injustice, lose, though not all sense of the impropriety of such conduct, yet all sense of its dreadful enormity, or of the vengeance and punishment due to it. They have been familiarized with it from their infancy, custom has rendered it habitual to them, and they are very apt to regard it as, what is called, the way of the world.[13]

Hence, in *Mansfield Park,* the importance of education, one of the leading themes of the novel.

Mansfield Park begins with arrangements by which Fanny Price is brought to Mansfield as Sir Thomas's ward, and it ends with similar arrangements in favour of Susan, Fanny's agreeable sister. The main difference is that Susan arrives under better auspices; Sir Thomas, who has been primarily interested in preserving the social differences between Fanny and his daughters, is now concerned only with the proper education of character, with what Jane Austen calls "the sterling good of principle and temper" (ch. 48). The sins of Julia and Maria have been prefigured, from the beginning of the novel, by instances of their defective education. "To the education of her daughters," we are told, "Lady Bertram paid not the smallest attention" (ch. 2). As for Sir Thomas, he had handed over his daughters' education to Mrs. Norris. As a result, "it is not very wonderful that with all their promising talents and early information, they should be entirely deficient in the less common acquirements of self-knowledge, generosity, and humility. In everything but disposition, they were admirably taught" (ch. 2). Julia's education was entirely superficial: Jane Austen speaks of "the want of that higher species of self-command, that just consideration of others, that knowledge of her own heart, that principle of right which had not formed any essential part of her education" (ch. 9). Maria's education was even worse, giving her nothing but "self-consequence" (ch. 48). Indeed, towards the end of the novel, when Sir Thomas's eyes have been opened, we are told that "the anguish arising from the conviction of his own errors in the education of his daughters, was never to be entirely done away." At this point, thinking of "the most direful mistake in his plan of education," Sir Thomas has a meditative passage which begins with an extreme speculation and goes on to translate the tropes of eighteenth-century moral philosophy into his own experience:

Something must have been wanting *within,* or time would have worn away much of its ill effect. He feared that principle, active principle, had been wanting, that they had never been properly taught to govern their inclinations and tempers, by that sense of duty which can alone suffice. They had been instructed theoretically in their religion, but never required to bring it into daily practice. To be distinguished for elegance and accomplishments—the authorised object of their youth—could have had no useful influence that way, no moral effect on the mind. He had meant them to be good, but his cares had been directed to the understanding and manners, not the disposition; and of the necessity of self-denial and humility, he feared they had never heard from any lips that could profit them.   (ch. 48)

These sentences are in the idiom of English educational and moral theory from Burnet to Adam Smith. In considering the possibility that his daughters' moral sense may have been "wanting" from the beginning, Sir Thomas questions the fundamental optimistic assumption of moral theory. This is the degree of his horror, beyond the issue of defective education.[14] Edmund's horror arises from the same fear in regard to Mary Crawford: when he has finally broken with her, he decides that "hers are not faults of temper . . . hers are faults of principle, Fanny, of blunted delicacy and a corrupted vitiated mind" (ch. 47). Before this, he has assumed that Mary's faults are the result of bad education. In the middle of the novel, when he has been distressed by her contempt for the clergy, he still considers her "disposition" faultless but that she has been educated in corruption by her aunt and uncle. Even at the end, when he blames the world for Mary's defects, he says to Fanny, "This is what the world does. For where, Fanny, shall we find a woman whom nature had so richly endowed?—Spoilt, spoilt!" (ch. 47). The same explanation is offered to account for Henry Crawford; his education at the hands of a corrupt uncle. Finally, Fanny's love for Edmund is closely related to his share in her education: she thinks of him as having "directed her thoughts and fixed her principles." As early as ch. 2, when Fanny has just arrived at Mansfield Park, Edmund becomes her guide and counsellor:

Miss Lee taught her French, and heard her read the daily portion of History; but he recommended the books which charmed her leisure hours, he encouraged her taste, and corrected her judgement . . .

This sounds formidably explicit, but we should not take these sentences as mere moral ballast for a smoothly running novel. The question of education figures in the book because Jane Austen is tracing the hazards of the moral sense when confronted by widely varying experiences. Education is an inextricable part of the story because it is "added" to the moral sense: the addition bears immediately upon the nature of the chosen self and its probable fate in the world at large. It is at least as important as marriage. Jane Austen's account of this issue in *Mansfield Park* is remarkably deft; some of her most delicate moral perceptions ring the changes upon the theme and reverberate through the novel. I shall mention one or two.

When the play is first proposed, Edmund laughs it aside. Julia rebukes him, "Now, Edmund, do not be disagreeable . . . Nobody loves a play better than you do, or can have gone much farther to see one." And Edmund answers: "True, to see real acting, good hardened real acting; but I would hardly walk from this room to the next to look at the raw efforts of those who have not been bred to the trade, — a set of gentlemen and ladies, who have all the disadvantages of education and decorum to struggle through" (ch. 13). The irony is Jane Austen's, not Edmund's; Edmund, after all, is only asking that these people assent to what they are; his tone is like Sir Henry Harcourt-Reilly's in *The Cocktail Party*. "You must accept your limitations." This prepares us to find the playacting gauche and the participants silly, but the result goes far beyond this; the emotions released by the playacting are corrupt, and the source of this corruption is the failure of education to engender a proper truth, a genuine decorum.

Education in *Mansfield Park* is such a crucial issue that we may expect to find it featured in practically all the situations involving change and progress. Two people, Fanny and Edmund, have chosen the ground of their characters; the others veer according to whim, pride, or greed. This is the structural figure of the novel. Jane Austen is concerned with ethical changes, so she presents several instances of changes which are casual or wild. Many of these belong to the same "family" as the word "education" itself. The most incisive example of this linkage is the topic of "improvements." Clearly there are many possibilities in juxtaposing one kind of "improvement" against another: think of a passage like this from Humphrey Repton's *Fragments on the Theory and Practice of Landscape Gardening* (1816):

> In a House entirely new, Character is at the option of the Artistic Proprietor; it may be Gothic or Grecian, whichever best accords with the face of the country; but where a great part of the original structure is to remain, the additions should doubtless partake of the existing character.[15]

The terms of landscape gardening are drawn from an aesthetic-moral world, implying that one's house and gardens have a "character" corresponding to one's own, the character of one's moral choice. One cannot speak of "improving" one's estate without implicating the analogy of moral education, an improvement of a much more fundamental kind. In English literature we find this implication in Jonson's "To Penshurst," in Marvell, Goldsmith, Wordsworth, Ruskin: it is active in *Howards End* and in Charles Tomlinson's *A Peopled Landscape,* to take examples at random. "Improvement" is one of the crucial terms in those late-seventeenth- and early-eighteenth-century English moralists whom we have invoked, especially in optimists like Burnet and Shaftesbury. Locke's *Treatise on Education* is an important text in a sterner tradition, and naturally he will not use the term with such weight. But if, like Burnet, you posit a moral sense, "a principle of distinguishing one thing from another in moral cases, without ratiocination," and if you admit that the moral sense in children is at first weak and obscure, then you must allow that it may be developed into full vision, as Burnet says, "according to the Improvement that is made of it."[16] Blake had this term in mind when, in *The Marriage of Heaven and Hell,* he derided the optimistic and prudential ethic which it implies: "Improvement makes strait roads; but the crooked roads without Improvement are roads of Genius." Jane Austen's code is more orthodox, old-fashioned. Like most people in 1813, she did not subscribe to the view that the tigers of wrath are wiser than the horses of instruction. Some of the most incisive local ironies in *Mansfield Park* arise from the concern of several characters with improvements of a superficial kind, at a time when there is room for considerable improvement in their principles and actions. This applies to the great chapters devoted to the improvements at Sotherton Court.

We first hear of these in ch. 6. Rushworth has been visiting a friend who has recently had his grounds laid out by an improver. Rushworth "was returned with his head full of the subject, and very eager to be improving his own place in the same way." Maria advises him to hire Mr.

Repton. Babbling on, Rushworth toys with the notion of cutting down some of the old trees at Sotherton, and Fanny, remembering Cowper's lament in *The Task,* pities their fate. The talk of improvements continues: Edmund, Fanny, Mary, Julia, Mrs. Grant, even Henry Crawford are drawn in. When Julia asks Henry whether he is fond of improving an estate, Henry, speaking of his own, answers:

> Excessively, but what with the natural advantages of the ground, which pointed out even to a very young eye what little remained to be done, and my own consequent resolutions, I had not been of age three months before Everingham was all that it is now.   (ch. 6)

Julia's reply shows again how easily this idiom slips into the language of moral action. "Those who see quickly," she says, "will resolve quickly and act quickly." At this point Henry's assistance is sought on Rushworth's behalf: the upshot is that the entire party will make a trip to Sotherton to enable Henry to see what improvements are desirable. Edmund "heard it all and said nothing." On the trip the deceptions begin. Julia and the engaged Maria conduct a silent battle over the possession of Henry Crawford. At Sotherton, when they are shown the chapel, and Rushworth's mother says:

> It is a handsome chapel, and was formerly in constant use both morning and evening. Prayers were always read in it by the domestic chaplain, within the memory of many. But the late Mr. Rushworth left it off.   (ch. 9)

Mary Crawford says to Edmund, with a smile, "Every generation has its improvements." Walking through the wilderness, Mary challenges Edmund on his decision to become a clergyman. Henry Crawford and Maria Bertram connive in getting rid of Rushworth, to whom Maria is engaged: the ambiguities of improvement allow Henry to make an elaborate pretence of caring for Maria. When she asks him what he thinks now of Sotherton, he says, "I find it better, grander, more complete in its style, though that style may not be the best":

> "And to tell you the truth," speaking rather lower, "I do not think that *I* shall ever see Sotherton again with so much pleasure as I do now. Another summer will hardly improve it to me."

After a moment's embarrassment the lady replied, "You are too much a man of the world not to see with the eyes of the world. If other people think Sotherton improved, I have no doubt that you will."

Henry answers:

"I am afraid I am not quite so much the man of the world as might be good for me in some points. My feelings are not quite so evanescent, nor my memory of the past under such easy domination as one finds to be the case with men of the world."   (ch. 10)

Henry and Maria are walking through Sotherton, discussing the improvements, but between the lines of the conversation they are indulging themselves in illicit emotions which will lead to adultery by way of the theatricals at Mansfield Park. This scene at Sotherton is one of the finest achievements of Jane Austen's art. It is like the second act of *The Three Sisters,* where the idiom of moral choice seeps through the surface of social convention. Indeed, if we respond to this in Chekhov it is not because we have been schooled in these epiphanies by Shakespeare and Strindberg but because we recognize them in the ostensibly casual progression of the novel; especially in Jane Austen and Henry James.

My argument is that we must receive *Mansfield Park* in the ethical idiom in which it is cast. Macaulay would have us approach it by way of *Evelina, Cecilia,* and *Camilla,* with a glance ahead at *The Absentee.*[17] This is sound advice, but there is a lot to be said for approaching *Mansfield Park, Sense and Sensibility, Northanger Abbey,* and *Persuasion* by way of the eighteenth-century English moralists. These are the sources of the great abstractions which Jane Austen places across the paths of her characters, pointing to centuries of judicious experience held in poise. If we look ahead we see on one side the continuity of the English novel and, on another, *Culture and Anarchy* and *The Education of Henry Adams.* Indeed, when Arnold in *On Translating Homer* rebukes Chapman and remarks that the characteristic virtue of English thought is force and its characteristic defect the want of lucidity, he makes the same point which Jane Austen dramatizes in *Mansfield Park.* The moral history of English force is written on her two inches of ivory. As for Henry Adams, the conversion of force into style was his great chimerical hope, a style of expressive equilibrium without naïveté or arrogance; a style like that of St. Thomas's Gothic where the equilibrium "is visibly delicate beyond the line of safety; danger lurks in every stone"—as Adams said on the last page of *Mont Saint-Michel and Chartres.*

But in the meantime we have to put these matters back into *Mansfield Park,* to see how they are made to function not as inert blocks of morality but as values in a magnetic field of personal relationships. We need a scene which is all composition, if not composure, where the clash of values is all the more dramatic because of the formality, the minuet of the occasion which reveals them, and the noise of arms is audible only to some of the participants, and to the reader. One of the most revealing occasions is in ch. 23, the card playing at the Grants'. Two games are in progress: Whist, a sober square game played by Sir Thomas, Mrs. Norris, Dr. and Mrs. Grant; and at the round table there is Speculation, played by Lady Bertram, Mary Crawford, Fanny, Henry Crawford, Edmund, and William, Fanny's brother. William is an innocent player, with the resilient concentration which reminds us that outside the Parsonage and beyond the Park there is a world in which midshipmen hope for promotion. Lady Bertram is in the group to remind us that the Schoolmen describe the condition of vegetative being as having the powers of local motion and growth but nothing else. She is marvellously uncomprehending and silent, one kind of silence setting off the other kind, Fanny's, making Fanny's appear all sensibility, which it nearly is. The game is Speculation, which is based on two principles, the first, the purchase of an unknown card on the calculation of its probable value when known, the second, the purchase of a known card on the chance of no better appearing in the course of the game, some cards in the pack not being dealt. So already we have something to conjure with in the idiom of valuation, price, and competitive risk. This, in an almost Dutch interior.[18]

The games begin. At Speculation, Henry Crawford is in command, guiding Lady Bertram and Fanny, directing their play as well as his own. Like all card games, this one has an air of engrossment which can be used to parody genuine care or to cast a delicately respectful glance in its direction; it brings several people together to testify to the observances of their society. An artist can use the observances to show how different these people are, the limits of their community. Henry Crawford talks of Thornton Lacey, which is to be Edmund's residence when he is ordained. It must be greatly improved, or so Henry insists; the house must be turned to front the east instead of the north, there must be a new garden, and so forth. This is a splendidly brash performance, in the course of which Henry throws out a few remarks which we can pick up as we please. He says, for instance, "I never do wrong without gaining by it," and again that he never inquires about anything, he always tells people. But Edmund has his own resilience, and tells Henry that in the matter of improving Thornton Lacey he has in mind something far more modest; he will make the house comfortable and give it "the air of a gentleman's residence"; that will be enough. All this time Mary Crawford has been listening while playing her cards, and suddenly she disposes of William Price by taking his knave at an exorbitant rate, exclaiming, "There, I will stake my last like a woman of spirit. No cold prudence for me. I am not born to sit still and do nothing. If I lose the game, it shall not be from not striving for it." There is more, but this is enough for the moment.

The "plot" of the scene is designed to set off Edmund's values against those of Henry and Mary Crawford; and indeed a few moments later Mrs. Norris will speak of the Rushworths in almost the same terms as those of the Crawfords, and the Crawfords will find it hard to recover from that infection. Later on, we will have to discriminate between Henry and Mary, giving Henry at least the merit of having been in love—to the limit of his character, and the most we can allow to Mary, apart from charm, is that she has a certain right to feel that Edmund has wounded her. Henry's speeches at the card game are practically insolent, and it says a lot for Edmund's civility that he puts up with them; but Mary supplies a vigorous theory to endorse Henry's practice. She will stake her last like a woman of spirit. No cold prudence for her. Jane Austen knew as well as anyone how compelling this idiom is, how attractive and strong. Mary Crawford is a formidable person because she is the only one in the book who could use this heroic language without absurdity. At a later stage we reflect that she urges this spectacular way of life on others while fixing her own eyes on the main chance. If I lose the game, she declares, it shall not be from not striving for it. Yes, but Jane Austen's next sentence is: "The game was hers, and only did not pay her for what she had given to secure it." If this were our motto for the entire novel, we should add a gloss to the effect that heroic gestures are fine in playing cards, but in life they invariably take the form of trading on other people, and—Jane Austen would say—in these transactions the price is never right.

In the same scene there is more talk of improvements, and the conversation roams a little. In his sturdy way Sir Thomas supplies the answer to the moral questions we have been considering, questions about the priority of action, the sitting still and doing nothing, the staking all like a woman of spirit. What Thornton Lacey amounts to, in Mary Crawford's eyes, is a desire "to shut out the church, sink the clergyman, and see only the respectable, elegant, modernized, and occasional residence of a man of independent fortune." But Sir Thomas, now that his Whist is finished, joins the group at the round table and speaks of Thornton Lacey in quite different terms, offering a theory to support Edmund's quiet practice. "He knows," Sir Thomas says, "that human nature needs more lessons than a weekly sermon can convey, and that if he does not live among his parishioners and prove himself by constant attention their well-wisher and friend, he does very little either for their good or his own." This is unanswerable. Life may be in some respects a game of cards, but some of the cards—as in Speculation—are not dealt, and there are certain respects in which the metaphor is simply an impertinence. When Sir Thomas speaks of a man's duty to his parishioners, the card game comes to an end. *Homo ludens* is only part of the truth.

What stays in the mind from this scene is a wonderfully perceptive art in which the movements of a social occasion provide, for some of the participants, all the meaning there is; and, for others, sufficient form to contain the visible feeling but not the turbulence. The two card tables, the Parsonage, the rules of the game, the encounters; on these the waves of individual feeling break, declaring themselves, then falling back. This is the art of the thing. But it would be fruitless to effect a neat separation between this art and the morality which gives the composition its gravity and composure.

NOTES

1. Jane Austen, *Letters,* ed. R. W. Chapman (2nd ed.; London: Oxford University Press, 1952), pp. 299 ff.
2. *Ibid.,* p. 317.
3. *Ibid.,* p. 409.
4. *Ibid.*
5. William James, *The Principles of Psychology* (London: Macmillan, 1907), I, 310.
6. Cf. Erich Fromm, "Selfishness and Self-Love," *Psychiatry* (1939), II, 507–23.
7. *Letters,* p. 375.

8. Anthony Ashley Cooper, Earl of Shaftesbury, *Characteristics of Men, Manners, Opinions, Times* (London, 1727), II, 44.

9. Thomas Burnet, *Third Remarks upon an Essay Concerning Human Knowledge* (London, 1699), p. 8. Quoted in Ernest Tuveson, "The Origins of the 'Moral Sense,'" *Huntington Library Quarterly* (1948), XI, 241–59.

10. Francis Hutcheson, *An Essay on the Nature and Conduct of the Passions and Affections, with Illustrations on the Moral Sense* (London, 1727), p. xi.

11. *Characteristics*, II, 45.

12. *Ibid.*, II, 46.

13. Adam Smith, *Essays Philosophical and Literary*, Part V, ch. 2.

14. In *Billy Budd*, Melville, to whom speculation on these matters is a natural activity, elucidates Claggart in somewhat similar terms: "Now something such was Claggart, in whom was the mania of an evil nature, not engendered by vicious training or corrupting books or licentious living, but born with him and innate, in short, 'a depravity according to nature'" (ch. 10).

15. Quoted in R. W. Chapman's edition of *Mansfield Park* (London: Oxford University Press, 1953 reprint), p. 351.

16. *Third Remarks*, p. 8.

17. Macaulay, *Works* (London: Longmans, Green, 1907), IV, 70.

18. For other implications in this scene, see P. R. Lynch, "Speculation at Mansfield Park," *Notes and Queries*, New Series, XIV, No. 1 (January 1967), 21–22.

From B. C. Southam (ed.), *Critical Essays on Jane Austen* (London: Routledge and Kegan Paul, 1968).

SHELLEY'S WAY

This is a fine book, but I wish William Keach had supplied a more explicit context for it. Apart from saying that Shelley's language hasn't been adequately described, he relies on the reader to know how the critical debate stands. He assumes too much, so I'll mention some of the matters he takes for granted.

The case against Shelley has been stated so insistently by modern critics that you would imagine they had invented it. But Arnold, Eliot, Leavis, and other opponents have merely refined what Hazlitt said in 1821 and Mary Shelley said, among more laudatory things, in 1824. The gist of it is that Shelley's sense of reality is immature. "His bending, flexible form," as Hazlitt put it, "appears to take no strong hold of things, does not grapple with the world about him, but slides from it like a river." Shelley's style—Hazlitt still—"is to poetry what astrology is to natural science—a passionate dream, a straining after impossibilities, a record of fond conjectures, a confused embodying of vague abstractions." Mary Shelley's note on the poems of 1822, like her note on "The Witch of Atlas," observed that Shelley couldn't "bend his mind away from the broodings and wanderings of thought, divested from human interest, which he best loved."

The sustained academic defence of Shelley began with two books by Carl Grabo, *A Newton among Poets* (1930) and *The Magic Plant* (1936): fighting books, but no match for Leavis's dismissive account of Shelley in *Revaluation* (1936). Herbert Read, G. Wilson Knight, Frederick Pottle, and many other defenders argued that Shelley's poetry is sustained by the coherence of its imagery, and that the work as a whole shows an extremely intelligent mind fully in touch with the philosophy and science available to him. More recently, scholars have made much of his relations to Locke and Hume rather than to Plato.

The most formidable defence of Shelley is Harold Bloom's *Shelley's Mythmaking* (1959). Bloom dealt with the case by shifting its ground. We are to read Shelley as "an agnostic mythmaker": "from his concrete I–Thou relationships, the poet can dare to make his own abstractions, rather than adhere to formulated myth, traditionally developed from such meetings." Bloom's authority was Martin Buber's distinction, in *I and Thou*, between the two primary words, *I–Thou* and *I–It:*

> When *Thou* is spoken, the speaker has no thing for his object. For where there is a thing there is another thing. Every *It* is bounded by others; *It* exists only through being bounded by others. But when *Thou* is spoken, there is no thing. *Thou* has no bounds.

Bloom translated the distinction into his own terms: Experience and Relation. The act of I–It can only annotate a fallen world of experience. I–Thou projects a new relation. Shelley's poems don't willingly allude to an experience with the aim of recalling it or sharing it with the reader. They don't even imagine a new experience on the analogy of an earlier one possessed and remembered: if they do, they report a vision lost. Time is not for Shelley the mercy of eternity but an affront to the endlessness of desire. His poems propose relations by virtue of the mind's typical capacity to project new instances of itself: as the fruit, in "The Witch of Atlas," turns the light and dew

> *by inward power*
> *To its own substance.*

What such poetry presents is the force of desire rather than any images it would be adequate to cull from experience. Bloom says: "The image Shelley seeks is one which can embody the confrontation of life by life, the living which is a meeting of Thous, relationship as dialogue, in which experience and its necessary objects disappear." So it's beside the point to say, with Donald Davie in *Purity of Diction in English Verse,* that in "The Sensitive Plant" and "The Witch of Atlas" Shelley "takes a common object such as a rose or a boat, and the more he describes it, the less we remember what it is." Or to refer, with Leavis, to Shelley's "weak grasp upon the actual." There is no merit in urging Shelley to buck up and look hard at a rose or a boat. The disability of any image, settled upon as an act of I–Thou, is that it loses its ideal character at once and becomes an *It.* As Bloom says, "the rational event quickly runs its course; the image cannot hold the Thou." Besides, "the deep truth is imageless." Poetry is lost in the poem, as Shelley concedes in *The Defence of Poetry.*

There is also a moral question. An image is bound to be a nuisance, if the "Thou" Shelley wants to invoke is nothing less than Life itself. Bloom makes an enormous concession to his opponents when he says that "Shelley far too often forgets that you confront an ultimate Thou only through a particular thou." The question of Shelley's sense of a particular thou would be returned to the critical agenda, and could only be answered, as Leavis insisted, by a critical analysis of language in each poem. The unmediated vision that Shelley seeks is impossible, as he often bitterly admitted, and the pursuit of it raises a question of vanity. It is a moral consideration that I–Thou must not be allowed to lapse into the Narcissism of I–I. Yeats thought that Shelley kept his poetry intact by differentiating his symbols, so that the tower and the cave in "Laon and Cythna" suggest "a contrast between the mind looking outward upon men and things and the mind looking inward upon itself." But Yeats is not an impeccable witness, he had his own problems with caves and towers, and looked to Shelley for endorsement.

This is a point of crisis in Shelley's poetry. In his essay "On Life" he rejects "the shocking absurdities of the popular philosophy of mind and matter," and he adopts, as Keach and other scholars have noted, "the intellectual philosophy" most clearly given in Sir William Drummond's *Academical Questions.* Keach quotes the passage in which Shelley's position, at least for the moment, is clear: "Nothing exists but as it is perceived. The difference is merely nominal between those two classes of thought which are vulgarly distinguished by the names of ideas and of external objects." That the thoughts which are called real or external objects differ "but in regularity of recurrence" from hallucinations and dreams was a position Yeats, too, accepted in his Shelleyan moods. In the *Defence* Shelley seems to think the classes differ only as "vitally metaphorical" words gradually become dead metaphors. Another version of the predicament is Hume's in the *Treatise of Human Nature,* that since we can never conceive anything but perceptions, we must make every thing resemble them.

Shelley accepted the condition, and not as a predicament. In the *Defence* he insists that "poetry defeats the curse which binds us to be subjected to the accident of surrounding impressions." The only disability is that idealism must fail in the end: the world refuses to be transformed. In "Julian and Maddalo" Shelley deals with his misgiving by giving it a separate hearing. Keach aptly refers to "Julian's belief in the power of mind to dissolve and transform all impediments to ideal self-realisation, and Maddalo's dark pessimism about the soul's blindness and limitation." What Leavis and Davie resent is that most of Shelley's poems—except for "Letter to Maria Gisborne" and "Peter Bell the Third," which might have been written by a good Augustan—were written by Julian rather than by Maddalo. Such readers have always wanted "heard melodies" to sound for "those unheard," and they deride as spiritual vanity any apparently direct raid upon the Absolute. They are epitomists, and have common sense and much of the character of language on their side.

But there are other readers who are not even convinced that the asserted relation between heard melodies and the words in which they are to be apprehended is at all secure. For such readers, what Bloom calls Shelley's "search for a Thou which would not become an It" should not be derided by the assumption that the proper words for every Thou are already sensibly in place. Keach's book, as I read it, intervenes at this point. But it is a reply to Empson rather than to Leavis or Davie. In *Seven Types of Ambiguity* Empson remarks that Shelley "seldom perceived profitable relations between two things, he was too helplessly excited by one thing at a time, and that one thing was often a mere notion not conceived in action or in an environment." Empson's positivism doesn't allow any room for doubting what a thing is, or what differentiates one such thing from another, or how a notion fails to be a thing, or how an action and an environment acquire the stable forms he gives them. The ambiguity he has in view "occurs when the author is discovering his idea in the act of writing, or not holding it all in his mind at once, so that, for instance, there is a simile which applies to nothing exactly, but lies half-way between two things when the author is moving from one to the other." One might, he says, "regard as an extreme case of the transitional simile that 'self-inwoven' simile employed by Shelley, when not being able to think of a comparison fast enough he compares the thing to a vaguer or more abstract notion of itself, or points out that it is its own nature, or that it sustains itself by supporting itself." Empson didn't think much of Shelley's procedure, but he conceded that "even with so limited an instrument as the short-circuited comparison, he could do great things," and silently gave an example from "The Triumph of Life":

> And others mournfully within the gloom
> Of their own shadow walked, and called it death.

It is Keach's aim to show the great things Shelley could do with self-inwoven figures, and their source in his general theory and practice of language.

The book begins with a study of *The Defence of Poetry,* emphasizing the mixture of buoyancy and scepticism in Shelley's sense of language. Sometimes Shelley regarded words as the mere phonetic shadows of thought; sometimes, like Asia in *Prometheus Unbound,* he believed that Prometheus "gave man speech, and speech created thought." Shelley's idealism asserted the constitutive power of language; his scepticism noted not only the habit by which a Thou congeals into an It but the fact that the triumphs of poetry are but partial and fleeting. This mixture of idealism and scepticism in Shelley has made him a hero to adepts of Deconstruction. In *Deconstruction and Criticism* (1979) J. Hillis Miller associated Shelley in this character with "the co-presence in any text in Western literature, inextricably intertwined, as host and parasite, of some version of logocentric metaphysics and its subversive counterpart," and quoted the passage in "The Triumph of Life" about the bubble of the phenomenal and historical world:

> Figures ever new
> Rise on the bubble, paint them as you may;
> We have but thrown, as those before us threw,
> Our shadows on it as it passed away.

Keach emphasizes that only in an ideally transformed world could language have constitutive or Orphic power; in the world as he found it, Shelley knew, with Bacon, that words, "as a Tartar's bow, do shoot back upon the understanding of the wisest, and mightily entangle and pervert our judgment." He learned his style more from that despair than from the hope it affronted.

Keach's main interest is in those images which, as Shelley noted in the Preface to *Prometheus Unbound,* "have been drawn from the operations of the human mind, or from those external actions by which they are expressed." Defining reflexive images as those "in which an object or action is compared, implicitly or explicitly, to an aspect of itself, or is said to act upon or under the conditions of an aspect of itself," Keach remarks that such images "call unusual attention to the act of mind they presuppose in the writer and provoke in the reader, an act of mind in which something is perceived as both one thing and more than one thing; as both itself and something other than itself." I'd prefer to say that a thing is seen, by a reflexive act of mind, not as a unitary object but as a tissue of aspects, none of them in principle privileged. But in any case Keach's account of reflexive imagery in "Alastor," "The Triumph of Life," and *Prometheus Unbound* is fine criticism. Perhaps he could have made even more of "Alastor," and of the passage in the Preface to it where Shelley says of his hero:

So long as it is possible for his desires to point towards objects thus infinite and unmeasured, he is joyous, and tranquil, and self-possessed. But the period arrives when these objects cease to suffice. His mind is at length suddenly awakened and thirsts for intercourse with an intelligence similar to itself. He images to himself the Being whom he loves.

Much of Shelley's poetry asks to be construed as searching among objects and situations for an intelligence similar to his own. If one is found, it is invoked only or chiefly in that capacity: its being otherwise a rose or a boat isn't allowed to matter much. When nothing answerable is found, a virtual object is posited, as Shelley projected Intellectual Beauty and hymned it. The act needn't be self-indulgent or tautological, because the imagination can choose to project difficult rather than easy forms of itself—as G. Wilson Knight says in *The Starlit Dome* that in "The Witch of Atlas" we watch Shelley's myth-making faculty at work, "that queer business of using one's imaginative experience to create something surprising to oneself." Self-objectification "may prove uncanny and revelatory": not necessarily cannily obscurantist.

When such critics as Leavis, Empson, and Davie find Shelley's poetry scandalous or vain, it is usually because—in Davie's version—"the sensuousness is of his peculiar sort which makes the familiar remote." But Shelley's only interest in an object is to involve it in further relations to his imagination: in that ghostly setting, its familiarity constitutes a menace. So he compares the physical to the spiritual, or in any event to some quality less accessible than its familiarity. In "Stanzas Written in Dejection, Near Naples" he writes:

> *I see the waves upon the shore,*
> *Like light dissolved in star-showers, thrown:*

and the removing simile doesn't intend making the waves more fully known but giving them a further imaginative relation to the speaker. More than most poets, Shelley knew that it is possible to propose relations which have, as Wordsworth said in the "Essay upon Epitaphs," "another and a finer connection than that of contrast"; or even that of plausible similarity. Keach says of the lines from "Stanzas Written in Dejection" that they "offer the synaesthetic image of light dissolved in water, but also of light dissolved into a shower of light, as in a shower of meteors . . . the effect is of a transient, momentary display of light on the verge of extinction . . . The image of 'light dissolved in star-showers' grows out of the opening impression of the sun shining brilliantly in 'The purple noon's transparent might,' and yet spins away from that impression as it anticipates the speaker's desire to 'weep away the life of care.'" But the image also depends upon our being willing to read "see" as "imagine," a concession we readily make since we've already made it for

> *I see the Deep's untrampled floor*
> *With green and purple seaweeds strown.*

In any positivist sense Shelley can't see the floor, but we know he can imagine it. So the question to ask about the light dissolved in star-showers is not, in what respect is it like the waves on the shore? but rather:

can I imagine myself "seeing" the waves, as Shelley does, in that relation?

It follows that Shelley's common style is a kind of euphemism, since the direction is always from the physical object or manifestation to some spiritual aspect in which the intelligence seeks intimations of itself. The apparent stability of the object is what the intelligence least wants to recognize. Indeed, "the volatility of perception and intuition," as Keach refers to it, is at once the sign of its value and the mark of its mortality. The image always takes a route of evanescence. No wonder Shelley is especially tender toward a sentiment which, as Arthur Symons wrote of a dance, "lasts only long enough to have been there." An idealizing stance has every virtue except that of persisting. Thinking is swift, indeed the type and paradigm of speed, in Shelley's poetry—as Keach observes—but the fate of thinking is that it makes its image disappear.

Sometimes the force of Shelley's images is in what they leave behind them, the afterimages to which the reader's sense aspires. As in the description of the contents of the bower in "The Witch of Atlas":

> Carved lamps and chalices, and vials which shone
> In their own golden beams—each like a flower,
> Out of whose depth a firefly shakes his light
> Under a cypress in a starless night.

He emphasizes, not the stability of the lamps, chalices, and vials, but the dream-transience they share with flowers, fireflies, and light. Their impression of stability merely provokes Shelley to spiritualize them, giving them a character closer to that of perception.

"The mind's evanescent access to power or beauty" is Keach's theme in the later chapters, which concentrate on images of physical transformation: freezing, melting, dissolving, evaporation, condensation. It is a fairly standard theme now, but he develops it well. I thought at one moment he would compare Shelley with Rilke in this respect, on the authority of the *Duino Elegies* and Rilke's letter of November 13, 1925, to his translator Witold von Hulewicz. The whole letter is a post-Shelleyan defence of poetry, though I am persuaded by Paul de Man's *Allegories of Reading* that there is a deconstructive motive in Rilke, too.

The only point I would think of adding to Keach's description is that the crisis for Shelley's style always comes when desire has to be embodied. Bloom has remarked that Shelley's poems "generally begin in relationship, are defeated, and end as artifice." The reality which concerns Shelley can be divined only while it remains unspecified. Any attempt to embody desire, as in an allegorical object, is doomed: the object can't be better than a paltry substitute for the desire it is supposed to appease. That is why Shelley's favourite image, as Yeats was I think the first to note, is the elusive Morning Star, which lends itself to desire in general rather than to any particular form of it. It also explains why the Hermaphrodite, in "The Witch of Atlas," is merely, as Bloom says, a robot, an object for the Witch to experience. The Hermaphrodite has incited the kind of argument which used to be provoked by Swift's Houyhnhnms as type of perfection, but the Houyhnhnms are better suited to Swift's purpose because their perfection is mainly negative: it is what life would be like if it were to be rid of the passions which afflict and yet, we know, sustain us. The Hermaphrodite is a thing entirely alien to pathos, an artifice of eternity. Shelley's style can resort only to such a thing, if to any device of an embodying intention. It is satisfactory only in process and transformation, like desire itself dying at last of its own too much.

Keach's book arises, in a general sense, from the recuperation of Romantic poetry which has been proceeding, mainly against Eliot's authority, for the past fifty years. More specifically, it takes part in the current assumption that the image of Shelley as beautiful ineffectual angel is specious, a libel upon the poet who is such a force in the poetries of Browning, Tennyson, Swinburne, Yeats, Hardy, Frost, and Stevens. The image of Shelley as angel, by the way, is Arnold's, but André Maurois's version of it—"Shelley angelic, too angelic"—in his *Ariel* (1923) sent it aloft again and has done much to keep it there. Many readers have derived from it their definitive image not only of Shelley but of the life of a poet: this, or something like it, is how a poet should live and die. *Ariel* was the first Penguin ever published: on July 30, 1935, in a batch of ten, price 6d. To celebrate the 50th anniversary, Penguin Books are issuing it again, with the first dust jacket. I have always assumed that the first line of Stevens's "The Planet on the Table"—"Ariel was glad he had written his poems"—came more directly from Maurois's book than from *The Tempest* or the name of Shelley's boat.

There is no merit in claiming that Shelley is a poet for all seasons. There are moods in which it is repellent that he thought the Poet too good for this world. But there are other moods in which his ambition seems wonderfully noble. I think of Valéry, who said that "the self flees all created things: indeed, one might apply the word 'universe' to that in which the self refuses to recognize itself." No English poet speaks more eloquently than Shelley to that sentiment.

Review of *Shelley's Style,* by William Keach (London: Methuen, 1985), and *Ariel: A Shelley Romance,* by André Maurois and Ella D'Arcy (London: Penguin, 1985). From *The London Review of Books,* Vol. 7, No. 16 (1985).

EMILY BRONTE: ON THE LATITUDE OF INTERPRETATION

uthering Heights is my example, but there must be a certain delay in reaching it. I assume that in any work of fiction a double pressure may be felt: on the one hand, a certain force exerted by the genre, the particular type or category of fiction which the individual work acknowledges and perhaps qualifies; on the other, the force exerted by the configuration of the writer's entire *oeuvre*, liaisons of image, grammar, syntax, diction, rhythm. It is a maxim of modern criticism that in reading a work of fiction the reader must begin by establishing the genre; otherwise he is bound to run off the rails. We are largely indebted to Northrop Frye for this maxim. But I shall argue that the establishment of genre, in any given instance, is a more difficult matter than we have allowed and that the decision, once made, may lead us too far. I sometimes wish that we might be permitted to postpone the decision until the end, so that we might be free to make our own mistakes; that wish is perverse, but it arises from the feeling that the ascription of genre, if made too soon and too blithely, prevents us from seeing the words on the page. We easily see the words when they embody our genre, less easily when they qualify it or threaten to refute it. I propose to leave this problem until later. As for the configuration, the grand pattern of choices and affiliations to be discerned in the writer's entire work, the loyalties of a lifetime, perhaps, it is my understanding that these choices are establishing themselves as one work follows another and that in an author's works still unwritten the choices are waiting to be disclosed, as if written in invisible ink. Each new work, to stay with the fancy, brings some of the invisible marks to the surface. So I would look at Emily Brontë's work as a whole, a network of relationships, and then settle upon her fiction.

I

Her poems were first published in *Poems by Currer, Ellis, and Acton Bell* (1846). When the second edition of *Wuthering Heights* was issued in 1850, in a volume which also contained *Agnes Grey* and a selection of poems by Emily and Anne, Charlotte Brontë added a biographical notice of the two sisters. Of Emily's poems she wrote:

> One day, in the autumn of 1845, I accidentally lighted on a MS. volume of verse in my sister Emily's handwriting. Of course, I was not surprised, knowing that she could and did write verse: I looked it over, and something more than surprise seized me,—a deep conviction that these were not common effusions, nor at all like the poetry women generally write. I thought them condensed and terse, vigorous and genuine. To my ear, they had also a peculiar music—wild, melancholy, and elevating.

Some of the poems were written as early as 1834, when Emily Brontë was sixteen. Between that date and 1846, she wrote about two hundred poems, most of them short pieces, and some fragments. In February 1844 she transcribed a selection of verses into two notebooks: one contained thirty-one poems, autobiographical lyrics; the other, forty-four poems from the Gondal saga, a childhood legend propounded by Emily and Anne. Charlotte speaks of one volume, but the first printed poems come variously from both sources, the personal poems as well as the Gondal pieces; no distinction is announced. This has caused some confusion. The reader who comes upon "The Night Is Darkening Round Me" in, say, W. H. Auden's anthology *Nineteenth Century Minor Poets* is likely to assume that it is a personal lyric, unless he happens to know that it is a dramatic lyric spoken by the guilty Augusta in the Gondal saga. The paralysis of will which is represented in the poem is Augusta's, not Emily Brontë's. Again, "Heavy Hangs the Raindrop" does not express the relation between Emily Brontë and Nature; it marks a moment in the relation between the imprisoned Arthur of Exina and the little fair-haired girl who loves him.

In fact, most of Emily Brontë's poems, including several of her most celebrated pieces, are Gondal poems.[1] We are to think of a mythical island in the North Pacific, divided into several hostile kingdoms. Julius Brenzaida, Prince of Angora in Northern Gondal, is loved by Rosina, Princess of Alcona in the south. He conquers the kingdom of Almedore and sacks the city of Zalona. Then he secretly marries Geraldine Sidonia, daughter of a conquered family. Soon, however, he leaves her, possibly to return to Rosina. Geraldine has a child, Augusta Geraldine Almeda, and she decides to bring the infant to Julius. But on the voyage the ship is wrecked, and Geraldine is drowned. The child is saved and brought to Julius, who arranges to have her reared in the mountains of Angora. Julius then marries Rosina. A child is born to them, a beautiful boy. Julius captures the city of Tyndarum. Shortly after, he betrays Gerald of Exina, and casts him into prison along with Gerald's son Arthur. But a rebellion is raised against Julius, and he is murdered. (Rosina mourns him in the famous threnody "Cold in the Earth, and the Deep Snow piled above Thee.")

The personal poems issue directly from Emily Brontë's experience; many of them testify to her isolation, her sense of decay and mutability, the melancholy to which Charlotte referred, Emily's "dark world," her dreams, visions, fancies, Branwell's tragedy. A few poems are direct invocations of her muse, sometimes called Imagination as opposed to "stern Reason," the admonishing voice of daylight and law. These are moorland poems, in the sense that they praise the visionary power by which the bleakness of the moors is transformed and enriched. "My sister Emily loved the moors," Charlotte wrote; yet, as Charlotte remarked in the introduction to *Wuthering Heights,* the moors do not provide the desired beauty from their own resources; rather, they provoke it in the perceiver, compelling the visionary power to invent it. "If she demand beauty to inspire her," Charlotte wrote, "she must bring it inborn; these moors are too stern to yield any product so delicate." That product must come from within. "The eye of the gazer," Charlotte said, "must *itself* brim with a 'purple light,' intense enough to perpetuate the brief flower-flush of August on the heather, or the rare sunset-smile of June; out of his heart must well the freshness, that in latter spring and early summer brightens the bracken, nurtures the moss, and cherishes the starry flowers that spangle for a few weeks the pasture of the moor-sheep." Finally, "unless that light and freshness are innate and self-sustained, the drear prospect of a Yorkshire moor will be found as barren of poetic as of agricultural interest." But to Emily Brontë's imagination, absence and bareness were just as provocative as presence. Her characteristic powers were innate and self-sustained; they did not delight in a given plenitude, if the gift seemed independent of her imagination.

We distinguish between these autobiographical poems and the Gondal poems, but we should not push them too far apart. Beneath the overt difference, there is continuity. Demonstrably, and in more than the obvious sense, every poem issues from a single imagination, bearing Emily Brontë's signature. Moving from *Wuthering Heights* to the Gondal saga and then to the autobiographical poems, we mark the obvious differences of genre, but we are also aware of a landscape of feeling shared by all these works. The landscape is given in certain pervasive images, recurring figures, patterns, rhythms. Some of these are so distinctive that they assert themselves. When Emily Dickinson read Emily Brontë's poems, she found one stanza lodging in her mind; it struck her as somehow definitive, and she quoted it in several letters:

> *Though Earth and Man were gone*
> *And Suns and Universes ceased to be*
> *And thou wert left alone,*
> *Every existence would exist in thee—*   (p. 243)

The first line should read "Though Earth and Moon were gone"; but it hardly matters. What matters is a certain gesture. Emily Dickinson recognized it as Emily Brontë's particular sign, ostensibly a syntax of excess, of hyperbole, but in the declared case not excess at all, since the feeling lives up to the declaration. It is a characteristic cadence, especially in the verve with which All is identified with One. The cadence is memorable in the poems, and it is one of the definitive tropes of *Wuthering Heights,* as in Chapter IX, where Catherine says of Heathcliff: "If all else perished, and *he* remained, *I* should still continue to be; and if all else remained, and he were annihilated, the universe would turn to a mighty stranger: I should not seem a part of it." It is typical of Emily Brontë's imagination that it runs to the extreme case, or to the extreme form of a common case, and that it is impatient with mediate things, relative or provisional moods. It is also typical of her imagination to define character by its extremity, and to make extremes meet. So Augusta, the fatal heroine of the Gondal saga, is a trial account of Cathy in *Wuthering Heights;* when we add Julius to that account, we see that Heathcliff is already in a measure defined. Emily Brontë did not possess, in any Shakespearean sense, a dramatic imagination. Her characters, in the novel as in the poems, are functions or projections, if not of herself, then of certain forces which belong to her as intimately as her desires. These forces are few, but each is definitive. Each is absolute. The novel and the poems are continuous in this respect, that they release these forces, at whatever cost to other forces which are ignored. Emily Brontë's limit is the outer limit of those forces which she releases, separately or in powerful conjunction. Her fictive world is not, indeed, complete. It is not, in the common sense, rich, diverse, plenary. Rather, it compels by the power of its limitation. Many images of life are absent, but we are forced to feel that they are absent because they have been rejected as irrelevant. Whatever beauty she needs, she invents, but her necessities are not of that order. Her deepest need is to make a clear space for her imagination; what she demands of space is that, for her sake, it be empty.

Indeed, her imagination is so exclusive that it discloses itself in a certain pattern, a plot. The plot is a fiction; it is not to be found in any single poem or in the novel, but in the configuration of her whole work. It suggests itself as an abstract or virtual fiction, compounded of a few typical figures and motifs. It is often said of Shakespeare's plays that they constitute a single work, a single poem. The remark is not fanciful. Emily Brontë's entire work constitutes a single poem, a single fiction. Its plot runs somewhat as follows. The story begins in childhood; the young spirit is in harmony with nature, delighting in "the splashing of the surge, / The changing heaven, the breezy weather." "Laughing mirth's most joyous swell" is delightful for the same reason, the swell, the great sense of life as motion and action. Spirit conceives itself as action, and recognizes action in every natural appearance. Indeed, life itself is unified by this terminology, so that no gap is disclosed between consciousness and experience. But in the next period a change occurs. Natural events are felt to have changed their character. The terminology of action persists, but its characters and signs are altered. Breezes become storms, malignant because independent; change becomes decay. The splashing of the surge now denotes the violence and hostility of nature; there is no kinship:

> O cold, cold is my heart!
> It will not, cannot rise;
> It feels no sympathy
> With those refulgent skies. (p. 108)

Everything is felt as external. Sometimes this feeling is embodied in imagery of imprisonment, severance, and burial. The spirit feels itself defeated by a "tyrant spell." "I hear my dungeon bars recoil." The hidden God has turned tyrant. In other moods, the feeling comes as a sense of guilt, either a categorical feeling of guilt as innate and original, or else guilt arising from a specific sin, perhaps a sinful passion. Both feelings now merge in an archetypal figure, to be discussed later in the present essay, the child lost in a forest. The child is lost, abandoned, either because of a malicious God or because of an original sin. In the next period there is a corresponding desire for rest, release, silence, calm. The terminology of action is given up altogether, since it has proved itself fallacious. The pervasive images in this new period are quietist:

> How still, how happy! Those are words
> That once would scarce agree together; (p. 96)

But now they agree together. In this condition the ideal imagery features the loss of definition and character; states once welcomed as separate and therefore rich are now dissolved. Sometimes the old images of rigour, ice, and snow are melted; there is consolation in nullity, when all things are returned to an original, undifferentiated source. The earth itself is tolerable when bare and silent, but the only joy is in absence. Finally, there is a movement of feeling beyond earth and time; the things of earth and time are transcended, or retained only as shadows of themselves. The relative appearances offered to the senses are translated into their absolute equivalents, so that the appearances themselves may be discarded:

> But first a hush of peace, a soundless calm descends;
> The struggle of distress and fierce impatience ends;
> Mute music soothes my breast—unuttered harmony
> That I could never dream till earth was lost to me.
> Then dawns the Invisible, the Unseen its truth reveals;
> My outward sense is gone, my inward essence feels—   (p. 239)

Death is the only good thing, after all; the spirit frees itself from the heard melodies of time, since the divine malice resides in melody itself. "O for the time when I shall sleep / Without identity." The motto for this period is given in one of the poems: "I'm happiest when most away" (p. 63). In another, the spirit speaks of the terror felt when, after such happiness, the senses reassert themselves:

> Oh, dreadful is the check—intense the agony
> When the ear begins to hear and the eye begins to see;
> When the pulse begins to throb, the brain to think again,
> The soul to feel the flesh and the flesh to feel the chain!
>
> Yet I would lose no sting, would wish no torture less;
> The more that anguish racks the earlier it will bless;
> And robed in fires of Hell, or bright with heavenly shine,
> If it but herald Death, the vision is divine.   (p. 239)

The vision is divine; specifically, these transcendental desires are addressed toward an angelic figure, variously called messenger, idol, "visitant of air," or "Strange Power." Sometimes the power is invoked as God, sometimes it is identified with the creative power of the imagination. Under any name, its place is "the steadfast, changeless shore," otherwise "Eternity" or "Immortality." One poem begins with "Death" and ends with "Eternity" (pp. 224–25), a characteristic sequence, but Eternity here has nothing to do with the Christian hope of resurrection. The tone is different. The dominant feeling is deemed to be fulfilled in rest, calm, obliteration, as in those Renaissance manuals of iconography in which Night is featured as a woman with black wings, "in one, a sleeping white child to signify Sleep, in the other a black one that seems asleep, and signifies Death."[2]

The only validity I would ascribe to this plot or *figura* is that of forming a qualitative context for the fiction and poems of Emily Brontë. It does not determine the particular plots, the stories. Perhaps its main use is to suggest the grand rhythm of her work as a whole, within which we hear the more specific rhythms of the individual poems and the novel. But the matter may be brought further. The grand rhythm, as I have described it, is one of the marks of an imagination intensely subjective. Indeed, Emily Brontë's imagination is remarkably true to the Romantic archetype that Georges Poulet describes in *Les Métamorphoses du cercle:*

> Peut-être ne pourrait-on mieux définir, sinon le romantisme, au moins l'un des côtés les plus importants de celui-ci, qu'en disant qu'il est une prise de conscience du caractère fondamentalement subjectif de l'esprit. Le romantique est un être qui se découvre centre. Peu importe que le monde des objets soit hors de portée, il sait qu'au fond de lui-même il y a quelque chose d'inassimilable à un objet, et qui est le moi-sujet, la partie de son moi la plus authentique, ou celle qu'il reconnaît le plus volontiers pour sienne. Privé de la périphérie, le romantique va longuement se familiariser avec le moi, avec le centre.[3]

One way of describing the *figura* in Emily Brontë's work is to say that it marks the gradual discovery, on her part, that the periphery was lost, the world of objects a deceit. In her "first" moments she was herself part of the sustaining periphery; progressively, as the world of objects lost its consoling force, she discovered that her own imagination must occupy the creative centre of whatever circle might be drawn. The result is that her characteristic poems do not explore the objective world; they do not even define or test a sense of the world as already formed. These poems act on the assumption that the world of objects is, indeed, given, but given as foreign and indifferent. To know the world in greater depth or in richer detail would not alter that new sense of its character; it would merely confirm it. Emily Brontë has already passed sentence upon the world. In "The Night Wind" and "Shall earth no more inspire thee?" the genius of Earth woos her, persuading her to return to his favor and protection. But the spirit answers that the music of Earth has no power over her; her feelings run in another course. Emily Brontë writes, in fact, as if a knowledge of the world were not in question; before speech begins, that knowledge is present. She writes as if, on that theme, there is nothing further to be said. A knowledge of the world is already her possession, and therefore her fate. What each poem proposes, therefore, is not so much to confirm her sense of the world but rather to define the self in which that sense has been formed. Inevitably, her sense of the world comes to seem crucial because it is her nature, not because it bears upon such an object. Emily Brontë's romanticism is indeed her subjectivity, her sense of herself as centre.

The more this sense was developed, the more inward it appeared. The inward essence is increasingly distinguished from the outward sense; the distinction is, in several poems, between God and man. Whether the ostensible object of invocation is the imagination, fancy, or the angelic messenger, it is in fact a function of Emily Brontë's nature. Finally, the imagination must identify itself with God, if the logic of the imagery is to prevail. The distinction between God and man may persist as an interim rhetoric, but it cannot remain when the one centre becomes All. At that moment the only relevant circle is the new circle formed by the centre which expands itself, occupying ground laid waste for that purpose. The centre begins to expand when "the world without" is sharply and critically distinguished from "the world within." In "To Imagination" the creative power within is invoked to "call a lovelier life from death, / And whisper with a voice divine / Of real worlds as bright as thine" (p. 206). The principle is Coleridgean—the imagination as the secular version of the divine power, the infinite I AM. In "No Coward Soul Is Mine" Emily Brontë writes:

> *O God within my breast,*
> *Almighty ever-present Deity*
> *Life, that in me has rest*
> *As I Undying Life, have power in thee.*   (p. 243)

The theology itself is circular, as it must be when the only vivid terms move about an ever-expanding centre. In another poem to Imagination, Emily Brontë writes:

> *And am I wrong to worship where*
> *Faith cannot doubt nor Hope despair*
> *Since my own soul can grant my prayer?*   (p. 209)

It could hardly be a more explicit assertion. In this idiom poetry and religion become one, faith and aesthetics become one. A new world arises when the old world, discredited, is transcended. The old world was based upon the primacy of object; the new world is based upon the primacy of subject.

This goes some distance to explain why Emily Brontë's efforts to establish a liaison between herself and the objective world were few, and those few perfunctory. This child, lost in a forest, repudiates the forest; a certain subjective hauteur is operative. Hélène Tuzet has discussed this motif in *Le Cosmos et l'imagination:*

> Un enfant perdu dans la forêt: ce thème qui a souvent, parfois merveilleusement, inspiré la fantaisie romantique est peut-être la meilleure image de l'homme dans le cosmos, tel que le voit cette même fantaisie. Le plaisir que goûte le Romantique à s'insérer dans l'Univers n'est plus celui de se sentir à sa place, mais bien de se sentir égaré. Il y a une volupté à ne *pas* embrasser l'ensemble, à ne pas comprendre, à s'avouer dépassé, débordé, à fermer des yeux éblouis ou épouvantés, à s'abandonner aux Puissances paternelles et terribles.[4]

But this pleasure, this vertigo, as Hélène Tuzet describes it, is available only when the child-spirit feels that it may invent a new world, emanating from the self as centre. The child does not then negotiate with the forest, since to deal with the world in those terms is to be compromised. The answer to loss is wilful disengagement:

> *Fall, leaves, fall; die, flowers, away;*
> *Lengthen night and shorten day;*
> *Every leaf speaks bliss to me*
> *Fluttering from the autumn tree.*
> *I shall smile when wreaths of snow*
> *Blossom where the rose should grow;*
> *I shall sing when night's decay*
> *Ushers in a drearier day.* (p. 82)

The ultimate ideal is to answer one rejection by another, the spirit transmuting everything into itself:

When I am not and none beside —
Nor earth nor sea nor cloudless sky —
But only spirit wandering wide
Through infinite immensity.

(p. 63)

When we speak of the expansion of the centre to fill the entire circle, we posit a continuous act of will. Nothing less will answer. If the objective world is maintained by God or by some other force, the subjective world is maintained only by the subject — the imagination, endlessly creative, sustained by that form of itself which is called the will. It is a commonplace that *Wuthering Heights* is a fiction remarkable for its representation of life in terms of will; indeed, the novel owes little to any other manifestation of human life. We make the point when we say, and it is again a commonplace, that Heathcliff and Cathy are more readily understandable as forms of energy than as characters, absolute because self-sustaining. Their identity, upon which Cathy insists, is the centre, the vortex, from which the relevant forms of energy issue. It is in this sense that passion in *Wuthering Heights* is given as a natural force, natural and therefore immune to the moral considerations of men and women in the historical world. Heathcliff is a purer form of energy than Cathy, a point made in the novel by the multiplicity of considerations which are deemed irrelevant to him. Indeed, what gives the book its uncanny power is the verve with which so much of human life is set aside as irrelevant. Here again the continuity between Emily Brontë's imagination and Heathcliff as one of its characteristic projections is clear. Both are defined by the nature of their wills; in both, sublimity is egotistical.

There is a famous passage in Hazlitt's lecture on Shakespeare and Milton, one of the *Lectures on the English Poets,* in which Hazlitt speaks of the "generic quality" of Shakespeare's mind, "its power of communication with all other minds — so that it contained a universe of thought and feeling within itself, and had no one peculiar bias, or exclusive excellence more than another." He goes on: "He was the least of an egotist that it was possible to be. He was nothing in himself; but he was all that others were, or that they could become." Keats extended Hazlitt's description of the Shakespearean imagination, distinguishing it from the Wordsworthian or egotistical sublime. "When I am in a room with People," he wrote to Richard Woodhouse on October 27, 1818, "if I ever am free from speculating on creations of my own brain, then not myself goes home to myself:

but the identity of every one in the room begins to press upon me [so] that I am in a very little time annihilated." It is the special mark of Emily Brontë's imagination that it resists annihilation by maintaining itself at the centre of its circle. So her Gondal poems are not, or not entirely, dramatic monologues: they are in another sense soliloquies, diverse only in their settings. What is different, in each case, is the circumstance. The difference does not require a variation in the demonstrated character of the world, only in the feeling of the perceiver. To Emily Brontë, even in the Gondal poems, soliloquy is a mode of introspection; the circumstance provides the occasion, but it does not offer itself as the object of consciousness. If we distinguish between the Gondal poems and the personal poems, the distinction should admit the consideration that, at a certain level of description, the local differences tend to disappear. It is not necessary to force the argument. Hazlitt rebuked certain contemporary poets for trying to "reduce poetry to a mere effusion of natural sensibility," surrounding the meanest objects "with the morbid feelings and devouring egotism of the writers' own minds." In Emily Brontë's imagination there is, indeed, a trace of the morbid, but she does not parade her sensibility: she is concerned with sensibility only as a form of the will. She takes no pride in the expression of will; the will is supreme because innate and categorical.

Her imagination, that is to say, does not allow the identity of an object to assert itself in her presence. The ideal moment, for that imagination, is when the plenary objects of the world are either hidden or transcended. Emily Brontë is a lunar poet, if we distinguish between poets lunar and solar. The solar poet delights in the manifold richness of objects. The lunar poet waits until night, when objects lose their force, the earth withdraws, and the imagination proceeds to fill the empty space between itself and the stars. The muse invoked in "The Prisoner" is akin to Emily Brontë's muse in the poem "Stars":

> *O Stars and Dreams and Gentle Night;*
> *O Night and Stars return!*
> *And hide me from the hostile light*
> *That does not warm, but burn—*
>
> *That drains the blood of suffering men;*
> *Drinks tears, instead of dew:*

Let me sleep through his blinding reign,
And only wake with you![5]
(pp. 226–27)

But my account is too general if it does not specify the choice poems and observe them. Henry James complained, in "The Lesson of Balzac," that the romantic tradition associated with the Brontës had virtually prevented any critical attention to their works. The image of "their dreary, their tragic history, their loneliness and poverty of life" stood as a force "independent of any one of their applied faculties." That image, he maintained, had supplanted the works themselves, had offered itself more insistently than *Jane Eyre* or *Wuthering Heights,* so that the question of the Brontës "has scarce indeed been accepted as belonging to literature at all." Literature, he argued, is "an objective, a projected result; it is life that is the unconscious, the agitated, the struggling, floundering cause." The case is somewhat different now, but there is always, and preeminently in the consideration of Emily Brontë, a disposition to allow the causes to speak for the results. Indeed, the best claim I can reasonably make for the paradigm, the *figura* as I have called it, in Emily Brontë's poems is that it mediates between cause and result, between the original agitation and the resultant forms. The paradigm is not merely agitation; but it is not yet form. It is a mediating fiction, no more. Its chief merit may be that it recalls the agitation and foresees its probable forms.

A reasonable showing among the two hundred poems would include these, listed in no particular order but with an implication of weight and representative merit: "Sacred watcher, wave thy bells"; "Fall, leaves, fall"; "A little while, a little while"; "How still, how happy"; "The night is darkening round me"; "If grief for grief can touch thee"; " 'Tis Moonlight"; "Aye, there it is"; "In Summer's Mellow Midnight"; "I See Around Me Tombstones Grey"; "The Day Is Done"; "How Clear She Shines"; "Well Hast Thou Spoken"; "The Linnet in the Rocky Dells"; "When Weary with the Long Day's Care"; "O Thy Bright Eyes"; "Enough of Thought, Philosopher"; "Cold in the Earth"; "Death, That Struck When I Was Most Confiding"; "Heavy Hangs the Raindrop"; "How Beautiful the Earth Is Still"; "Often Rebuked"; "In the Dungeon Crypts"; "Silent Is the House"; "No Coward Soul." One of these will help to show some of Emily Brontë's "applied faculties":

Aye, there it is! It wakes to-night
Sweet thoughts that will not die
And feeling's fires flash all as bright
As in the years gone by!

And I can tell by thine altered cheek
And by thy kindled gaze
And by the word thou scarce dost speak,
How wildly fancy plays.

Yes, I could swear that glorious wind
Has swept the world aside,
Has dashed its memory from thy mind
Like foam-bells from the tide—

And thou art now a spirit pouring
Thy presence into all—
The essence of the Tempest's roaring
And of the Tempest's fall—

A universal influence
From Thine own influence free—
A principle of life, intense,
Lost to mortality.

Thus truly when that breast is cold
Thy prisoned soul shall rise,
The dungeon mingle with the mould—
The captive with the skies.   (p. 165)

The motif is characteristically Romantic. The wind is invoked as the
natural force of action, the Aeolian lyre, the "correspondent breeze," life
itself as motion and spirit. Spirit is universal, wind is the form it takes, and
the form of the poem is the process by which, from first word to last,
every objective image is transformed into spirit. This interchange of state
is the motive of the poem. The wind, waking sweet thoughts and feelings
in the recipient, begins the process of changing him into its own terms.
The first signs of change are the "altered cheek," the "kindled gaze," of

the second stanza. In the second stage of transformation the terms of earth and time are dissolved, "the world" and its memory. The change is complete when the recipient is entirely spirit. At that stage wind and recipient are one, alike in function and power: "And thou art now a spirit pouring / Thy presence into all"; like the original wind itself. Appropriately, existence is purified to essence, while essence retains, like the wind, its proper terminology of action; "The essence of the Tempest's roaring / And of the Tempest's fall." In the next stanza the terms are moral rather than philosophical. Just as the recipient's existence was purified, transformed into its proper essence, so now his finite "influence" is transformed into that "universal influence" which is spirit in its moral idiom. "From Thine own influence free"; free, as prefiguring the freedom from mortality invoked in the next lines. "A principle of life, intense"; intense, since principles and absolutes do not obliterate the manifestations they transform, in this case manifestations of force and power. The last stanza is a vision of the future, the transformation complete, soul released to the skies. This is more than freedom, commonly understood, since it enforces the victory of a subjective terminology over every alien power.

The poem is, then, a ritual, designed to break the chains of time, place, and body. Most of the work, so far as the language goes, is done by the verbs; assertively in the third stanza, where the "glorious wind / Has swept the world aside, / Has dashed its memory from thy mind." "Glorious" is not a mere tag, given that the wind's achievement is martial and heroic. In fact all the verbs are verbs of transformation, changing every state into its spiritual equivalent: wakes, flash, plays, swept aside, dashed, rise, mingle. The verbs testify to a formative principle of change and are themselves, preeminently, the vehicles of that change. The nouns are, for the most part, the great subjective terms—feeling, fancy, memory, mind, spirit, presence, influence, soul, principle, essence—with their descriptive cousins—fire, wind, cheek, gaze, breast, thought. The adjectives are those of human and natural relations, with a supporting air of extremity and change: sweet, bright, wild, kindled, glorious, intense. But in saying that the main work is done by the verbs we should also remark that the essential movement of feeling is a stanzaic movement, where each stanza is a lyric moment, sustained and effected by the action of the verbs, for the most part, up to that point. Within each stanza there is little change; rather, a change is registered, defined in the stanza. The plot of the poem, if the term is permissible, is a sequence of lyric moments, each stanza marking a certain stage in the large cadence of feeling. The process is subjective, but only because the relevant transformation is personal, an act of will. Nature does not, in this case, enforce itself: it is invoked in that character. The movement of feeling arises from within the soul of the speaker; the transformation is effected by calling upon a natural force already hospitable to such changes. This explains the typical grammar of the poem. Emily Brontë begins with the indicative, "Aye, there it is"; simple because true. But gradually she uses indicatives as if they were imperatives: or rather, a poet with less confidence in the transforming power of will and the subjective idiom generally would be obliged to use imperatives where Emily Brontë uses indicatives. "And thou art now a spirit" means "Be thou now a spirit," but it is unnecessary to change to the imperative mood, since the indicative already has the air of an assumption. "Already with thee!" is Keats's equivalent in the "Ode to a Nightingale." The point is that Emily Brontë's poem is doing the traditional work of metaphor, but in slow motion, and by degrees. The process of metaphor is the process of transformation, metamorphosis. Metaphor acts suddenly, in a flash; the poem achieves a metaphorical object, but slowly, earning the right to do so as it moves along, stanza by stanza.

But a critical difficulty persists. I have reached the stage of describing Emily Brontë's poems as soliloquies; but if they are soliloquies, they cannot be dramatic lyrics, Gondal monologues. So, according to the logic, the Gondal saga is irrelevant, at best a romantic smoke screen. I hope to show that the contradiction is more apparent than real, but it must be faced, perhaps along the following lines.

It is clear that Emily Brontë's imagination found in Gondal sustenance not available in the daily life of Haworth. Gondal was an invented kingdom, neither England in general nor Haworth in particular; that it was the joint invention of Emily and Anne increased its distinction, giving the invention a note of conspiracy. It made, for the two sisters, a "world elsewhere": that world is the source of the "peculiar music" which Charlotte heard in Emily's poems. Gondal was a fiction, not necessarily better than historical fact in every respect but certainly better in respect of freedom. To Emily it offered a world in which she could play roles far more diverse than those available to her at Haworth. The roles she chose to play are now male, now female, now adult, now child: but, more important, the roles are played in an aboriginal world. We are to think of Gondal as a place not yet marked out by conventions, laws, morals, society. These forces have not yet arrived: to Emily Brontë, so much the better. The only laws are those of passion and will: punishment is primitive, but natural. Gondal is anthropological, Haworth is historical. Like *Wuthering Heights,* it proposes a mode of life which exists, powerful and intransient, beneath the accretions of manners, morals, and society. That Emily Brontë's imagination needed such a world can hardly be disputed.

But the creation of Gondal did not really extend her imagination: it fulfilled the needs of that imagination without changing its nature or composition. Emily Brontë could not suppress herself in favour of her invented characters: could not, or would not. The characters, once invented, are allowed to move and live in Gondal, but they are still extreme functions of Emily Brontë's own personality. She does not release them: she endows them not with free will, but with her own will in diverse forms. When they speak, therefore, what we hear is a kind of ventriloquism. There is no precise term for this, as far as I know. "Dramatic monologue" will not do, because this proposes a strict separation of speaker and poet. "Soliloquy" will not do, because this implies a speaker communing with her own feelings. The term we need is somewhere between these two phrases; but where, precisely, and what word?

Perhaps we can approach it by noting a certain sequence. We call that imagination "Shakespearean" which delights in registering modes of feeling not its own. We may call another kind of imagination "Yeatsian" if it has a particular flair for registering modes of feeling related to its own by contrast and opposition: we have in mind, for this description, Yeats's account of the imagination as operating in terms of mask, role-playing, anti-self, and so forth. *A Vision* and "Ego Dominus Tuus" are the theoretical occasions. There is also, for a third stage, the imagination which we may call "Proustian," thinking of a remark by Roland Barthes in *Le Degré zéro de l'Écriture* that "a character of Proust materializes into the opacity of a particular language, and it is really at this level that his whole historical situation . . . is integrated and ordered." Finally, there is an imagination which we call "Eliotic," which delights in secreting "characters" from materials entirely verbal, the characters therefore being merely virtual or ostensible. Thus Hugh Kenner has observed in *The Invisible Poet* that "J. Alfred Prufrock is a name plus a Voice: he isn't a 'character' cut out of the rest of the universe and equipped with a history and a little necessary context, like the speaker of a Browning monologue." So there are several identifiable positions between the two extremes, soliloquy and drama; more, indeed, than the standard critical terminologies encourage us to recognize. Josiah Royce has shown in his *Lectures on Modern Idealism* that it was characteristic of nineteenth-century idealists to develop by way of dialectics, truth being a process, the grappling of opposites. Arnold spoke, in his Preface to the 1853 edition of his *Poems,* of "the dialogue of the mind with itself" as constituting the modern element in literature. But Emily Brontë does not commit herself to these procedures. The relation between her and, say, Augusta in the Gondal poems is not Shakespearean; Emily is not willing to suppress herself for Augusta's sake. Augusta is established only in the sense that Emily's subjective imagination secretes her: her fictive existence is not independent; it depends upon Emily's will and is, indeed, an extreme manifestation of that will. In the Gondal poems generally Emily Brontë's will sets an outer limit beyond which her imagination, in the creation of characters, may not go. In detail, the same limit is marked by the opacity of the language; the comparison with Proust may be retained but need not be forced. In *Wuthering Heights* the minor characters are equably released from the control of her will; with Joseph, Zillah, Lockwood, and Mrs. Dean, Emily Brontë's will takes a holiday, they present no danger to her imaginative world. But upon the central characters she exerts a particularly imperious claim, requiring them to contain themselves within her circle. She cannot release them.

II

It is natural to think of *Wuthering Heights* in an essay on the latitude of interpretation. The history of its reception is a record of extraordinary divergence. Every reader agrees that it is a masterpiece, but agreement ceases at that point. F. R. Leavis stated a position in one sentence of *The Great Tradition* (1948): "I have said nothing about *Wuthering Heights* because that astonishing work seems to me a kind of sport." He did not go further, there was no necessity. His case was that "the great tradition of the English novel" is represented by Jane Austen, George Eliot, Henry James, Conrad, and D. H. Lawrence. In that company, it seemed clear, Emily Brontë could figure only as a freak of nature, a maverick genius. To Leavis, the central tradition of English fiction is empirical, "realistic," temporal, historical; it is concerned with the relations between men and women in a palpable society. Its first cousin is politics; its natural form is the novel. In such a tradition, *Wuthering Heights* is bound to appear a wild thing, an aberration of genius, an astonishing work, indeed, but marginal, "a sport." In the *Anatomy of Criticism* (1957), however, Northrop Frye proposed a method of reading fiction in which we would attend to a far wider range of genres than "the Novel," the first advantage being that works of maverick genius would be recovered and retained within their proper genre. He proposed, in short, several great traditions rather than one. He mentioned, for instance, that *Wuthering Heights* is in the tradition of the romance rather than the tradition of the novel: it is related to the tale, the ballad, rather than to realistic narrative:

> The romancer does not attempt to create "real people" so much as stylized figures which expand into psychological archetypes. It is in the romance that we find Jung's libido, anima, and shadow reflected in the hero, heroine, and villain respectively. That is why the romance so often radiates a glow of subjective intensity that the novel lacks, and why a suggestion of allegory is constantly creeping in around its fringes.

Frye has not written of *Wuthering Heights* in detail, but he has implied a reading of the book which is, I think, clear enough. Indeed, some of the detail is available in Lord David Cecil's *Early Victorian Novelists* (1934), where *Wuthering Heights* is interpreted as a metaphysical fiction, a drama of warring principles, light and dark, rather than, in the empirical sense, a novel. The merit of this reading is that it attends to certain major elements in the book; its defect is that, in its haste to underline these elements, it ignores other elements, such as the hard, concrete detail. Lord David is concerned with principle at some cost to particle. If we read the book as a romance, or as a metaphysical drama, we find many chapters answering to those assumptions, but we are likely to miss the indissoluble detail, the impression of a dynamic life proceeding in place and time, the apple-picking, the harvest, Linton's crocuses, Mrs. Dean sweeping the hearth, the sound of Gimmerton's chapel bells, the ousels. Briefly, we miss Gimmerton in our urge to recognize the metaphysics. So it is not enough, and it may be seriously misleading, to decide that *Wuthering Heights* is a romance.

Other readers have run to the other extreme. In his *Introduction to the English Novel* (1951) Arnold Kettle interprets *Wuthering Heights* as, in effect, a realistic novel, its theme the nature and quality of life in early nineteenth-century England. Heathcliff is born in the slums of Liverpool, and his subsequent life is to be understood in terms of the class struggle, the Industrial Revolution, the later history of capitalism in England. What is Gothic for one reader is historical for another. But the result is that Kettle makes *Wuthering Heights* sound like *Dombey and Son,* and this cannot be right. Recently, Q. D. Leavis has made another effort along similar lines, as if she were determined to bring *Wuthering Heights* within the terms of her husband's "great tradition." She reads the book as a "realistic novel"; its conventions are historical, social, political, personal. In *Lectures in America* (1969) she interprets the book as if it were really a novel called *Thrushcross Grange,* toning down the metaphysical element, treating much of Heathcliff's story as intractable material left over from an earlier version or as part of an inadequately assimilated Gothic tradition. She refuses to allow the characters a metaphysical dimension; she insists upon motive, cause and specific effect, continuity between personal and social considerations. So she counts it a flaw in the book that we are not shown due cause in the relationship between Catherine and Heathcliff: "A real flaw however is wholly inadequate illustration of the shared life and interests of himself and Catherine that makes it plausible that on his return she should be so absorbed in conversing with him as to cut out immediately and altogether her young husband." The relation between Catherine and Heathcliff is treated as "not love but a need of some fundamental kind that is quite separate from her normal love for Edgar Linton, a love which leads to a happily consummated marriage and the expectation of providing an heir."

I do not wish to abuse Mrs. Leavis's interpretation; it is formidable and, in many details, unerring. But it requires us to play down several parts of the book and to write other parts in italics. Heathcliff and Catherine are scaled down to make room for Mrs. Dean, Joseph, and the younger Cathy. Everything which tells against this reading is relegated as primitive or residual. The Gondal element in Emily Brontë is set aside entirely. I should argue, therefore, that Mrs. Leavis's interpretation is inadequate because it does not allow all the evidence to be heard, it resorts to suppression, it alters the book to accommodate the critic.

I would maintain, however, that it is proper to begin with the recognition of *Wuthering Heights* as a novel, even if we find it necessary to admit other elements which are uncomfortable in that description. If we take the book, in the first instance, as a novel, we acknowledge the fact that it is firmly grounded in a particular society, the Yorkshire moors, at a particular time, the years from 1757 to 1803. C. P. Sanger has demonstrated in detail the care Emily Brontë took to anchor the book in place and time.[6] We are made to feel that between Wuthering Heights and Thrushcross Grange there is solid land, a distance of four English miles, and it is only a short way to Gimmerton, and beyond Gimmerton there are other villages and towns. In this land people live and die, farm their acres, furnish their homes, hire lawyers to make wills, act as magistrates, walk to Pennistone Crags, and scandalize the neighbors. Six men carried Heathcliff's coffin; we know nothing more of them, but we are not allowed to forget that, behind the violent events at Wuthering Heights and Thrushcross Grange, there are ordinary people going about their business. It is the novel's business, too. Manners, morals, families, relations, houses, property: these are the novel's traditional instruments. In *Wuthering Heights* much of this concern reaches us through Mrs. Dean. It has often been maintained that she is an unreliable guide; if she is, it follows, according to the argument, that Emily Brontë means us to think of the domestic moralities as inadequate, irrelevant, beside the point. At least one reader has thought of Mrs. Dean as the villain of the whole piece. But this is perverse. Mrs. Leavis has no such doubts: "Nelly Dean is most carefully, consistently and convincingly created for us as the normal woman, whose truly feminine nature satisfies itself in nurturing all the children in the book in turn." This is reasonable. Mrs. Dean is not the omniscient narrator, the detached observer; she has her likes and dislikes, in the quarrel between Earnshaws and Lintons she is a Linton, she has been cruel to the child Heathcliff. But she is undoubtedly a reliable witness: we know her faults only because she confesses them. Finally, there is no reason to think that Emily Brontë wants us to hold aloof from Isabella's testimony, in Chapter XIII, when she says, "How did you contrive to preserve the common sympathies of human nature when you resided here?"—meaning Wuthering Heights. It seems clear that Mrs. Dean maintains the common sympathies; this is her chief function in the narrative. While others aspire to the metaphysics, she consults the physics, she is the spirit of the English novel.

But Emily Brontë does not confine her imagination to these matters. Living at Haworth, she invented Gondal by an act of will, insisting upon this wild place free from clergy and morality. Correspondingly, there are forces in the novel which strain to be released from empirical allegiance. In terms of genre, *Wuthering Heights* is mixed: novel and romance. The novel strains toward the romance, to transcend its own nature. Mrs. Leavis thinks it a flaw that the relationship between Catherine and Heathcliff is not substantiated, we ought to have been shown their "shared life and interests." But this misses the point; the cause is not a question of shared life and interests but of merged natures, merged identities. Heathcliff's character is irrelevant to Catherine; she knows his cruelty, but it is irrelevant. She identifies herself with his nature as with a reality far more profound. The identification is so complete that it determines her life even when she perceives every vice in his character. She warns Isabella against him, in Chapter X, but the vices disclosed make no difference to herself; to him she responds in terms which have nothing to do with character, personality, vice or virtue. "Your bliss lies in inflicting misery," Catherine tells Heathcliff in Chapter XII: true or false, the charge is irrelevant, since it can only be relevant to morality, and morality is irrelevant. To respond to this part of the book it is necessary to acknowledge modes of being which act at a level beneath the patterns of ethics and morality: of the identification of Catherine and Heathcliff it is necessary to say that the gap separating it from considerations of morality and society is absolute. We begin to recognize this gap when, using the word "nature," we sense possibilities in its presence so primitive, so much a matter of instinct and consanguinity, that they render moral considerations irrelevant. Catherine and Heathcliff are not united by love, or even by passion; they are united by nature, and nature is unanswerable.

It may be argued that this is not made clear in the book. The requirements of morality are prescribed by Mrs. Dean and other characters: they are continuous with our awakened sense of an ordered life in society. But where are we shown the laws of primitive Nature as a separate category, an imperative absolute in its independence? I would answer: we are shown one absolute condition by analogy with another, the absolute separation of soul and body. In Chapter XII Catherine cries to Edgar, "What you touch at present you may have; but my soul will be on that hilltop before you lay hands on me again." Thereafter, body is associated with the palpable life, morality, custom, marriage, the values of Thrushcross

Grange; soul is the essential spirit, the identifying power, the purest form of will. To Catherine and Heathcliff, soul is absolute; and absolutely separate from the mere body. In the great Chapter XV, when Heathcliff is wilful and intractable, Catherine says to Nelly, "Well, never mind. That is not *my* Heathcliff. I shall love mine yet, and take him with me; he's in my soul." Immediately after, she speaks of "this shattered prison," meaning first her body and thereafter the entire finite condition, which she yearns to leave. Throughout these chapters, the body is associated with the things of time, the daily proprieties, moral considerations. Mrs. Dean comments at one point in Chapter XV:

> Well might Catherine deem that heaven would be a land of exile to her, unless with her mortal body she cast away her moral character also.

The witness speaks more wisely than she knows, for Catherine's moral character is, indeed, like her body—dispensable, ultimately a superficial part of her being. Heathcliff speaks the same language. In the same chapter, a few hours before Catherine's death, he cries to her,

> Do I want to live? What kind of living will it be when you—O God! would *you* like to live with your soul in the grave?

In the next chapter:

> Be with me always—take any form—drive me mad—only *do* not leave me in this abyss, where I cannot find you! O God! it is unutterable! I *cannot* live without my life! I *cannot* live without my soul!

And, near the end of the book, when yearning for death, Heathcliff says to Mrs. Dean:

> I'm too happy; and yet I'm not happy enough. My soul's bliss kills my body, but does not satisfy itself.

I take this to mean that the soul, separated from the body, cannot be at rest until the dying animal is consumed; then, all is soul. What separates Catherine and Heathcliff from the other characters in the book is not fully explained as a more violent passion than any other; rather, they are leagued against all the other characters by living in terms of nature, identity, consanguinity. No public law can endorse these terms, because they are clearly destructive of any code or pattern of society which may be conceived; the aura of incest which surrounds their relationship is a mark of this destructive power. Society cannot bear such a relationship; so it must live in the cellar, until it transcends society in death.

To support this reading, I would point out that it is consistent with the notion of a mixed genre, the novel under stress of romance. It is also consistent with the paradigm which I have already described in relation to Emily Brontë's work as a whole. The first chapters of the book, after Heathcliff's arrival, describe the childhood of Catherine and Heathcliff, together, roaming the moors. In Chapter VII they are separated, Cathy staying for five weeks at Thrushcross Grange, a breach recalled and transfigured in dream in Chapter XII when Catherine says to Mrs. Dean:

> But, supposing at twelve years old I had been wrenched from the Heights, and every early association, and my all in all, as Heathcliff was at that time, and been converted at a stroke into Mrs. Linton, the lady of Thrushcross Grange, and the wife of a stranger, an exile and outcast thenceforth from what had been my world—you may fancy a glimpse of the abyss where I grovelled!

Thereafter, Catherine's feeling strains beyond the finite world. Mrs. Dean reports of her in Chapter XV:

> The flash of her eyes had been succeeded by a dreamy and melancholy softness; they no longer gave the impression of looking at the objects around her; they appeared always to gaze beyond, and far beyond—you would have said out of this world.

Later in the same chapter Catherine says to Mrs. Dean:

> I'm tired of being enclosed here. I'm wearying to escape into that glorious world, and to be always there—not seeing it dimly through tears, and yearning for it through the walls of an aching heart, but really with it and in it.

That glorious world is beyond time, beyond morality: "outward sense" is gone, "inward essence" revealed, matter transcended in spirit. Finally it is death itself. Catherine and Heathcliff meet in death, souls united. Death becomes that "existence of yours beyond you" to which Catherine referred in Chapter IX. When Heathcliff dies, Mrs. Dean tries to close his eyes, "to extinguish, if possible, that frightful, life-like gaze of exultation before any one else beheld it." This death is a *Liebestod,* sexual union transfigured, the soul's inward gaze seeing nothing but itself and its shared identity.

Catherine and Heathcliff are allowed to persevere in their natures; they are not forced to conform to the worldly proprieties of Thrushcross Grange. Conformity is reserved for the next generation. But this is too blunt as an account of the later chapters of the book. The juxtaposition of Wuthering Heights and Thrushcross Grange is inescapable, but it is not simple. The values of the Grange are social, political, personal, compatible with the emerging England, the cities, railways, the lapse of the old agricultural verities. Wuthering Heights is, in this relation, primitive, aboriginal, bohemian; it rejects any pattern of action and relationships already prescribed. Finally, Emily Brontë accepts the dominance of Thrushcross Grange, since the new England requires that victory, but she accepts it with notable reluctance. Wuthering Heights has been presented as, in many respects, a monstrous place, but its violence is the mark of its own spirit, and Emily Brontë is slow to deny it. The entire book may be read as Emily Brontë's progress toward Thrushcross Grange, but only if the reading acknowledges the inordinate force of attraction, for her, in the Heights. We mark this allegiance when we associate the Heights with childhood, the Grange with adult compulsions. The Heights is also the place of soul, the Grange of body. Imagination, the will, the animal life, folk wisdom, lore, superstition, ghosts: these are at home in the Heights. The Grange houses reason, formality, thinner blood. Much of this opposition is directed upon the question of education. Heathcliff is not a reader, Edgar is despised for his bookishness; but, at the end, the new generation resolves its quarrel in a shared book. I take this to mean that you must learn to read if you want to marry and live in the Grange. The young Cathy teaches Hareton to read, and thus redeems him. Emily Brontë endorses the change, but again with some reluctance, as if the Gutenberg civilization, inevitably successful, meant the death of other values dear to her. The end of the book is an image of concord, but we are meant to register the loss, too. This is implicit in the composition of the book. The fiction is Emily Brontë's composition, her assertion, and in a sense her act of defiance—set against the demonstrable success of fact, time, history, and the public world. At the end, Catherine and Hareton are to marry and, on New Year's Day, to move to the Grange. As for Wuthering Heights, another writer would have burnt it to the ground, but Emily Brontë retains it, in a measure. Joseph will take care of the house, meaning the living rooms, "and perhaps a lad to keep him company." As Mrs. Dean says, "they will live in the kitchen, and the rest will be shut up." The tone of this passage makes it clear that much of Emily Brontë's imagination remains at Wuthering Heights, not as a ghost to haunt it, but as a mind to respect it. It has been argued that we are not to choose between the two houses, but rather to hold them together in the mind. At the end, we choose, as Emily Brontë chose, as Cathy and Hareton chose; but we make the choice with reluctance and with a sense of the values which are inevitably lost. Wuthering Heights is not merely the terrible place of Lockwood's visits, not merely the result of rough manners, bad education, a gnarled landscape. Its chief characteristic is that it exists in its own right, by a natural law formulated, as it were, centuries before the laws of man and society. To that extent, it is closer than Thrushcross Grange to those motives and imperatives which, helplessly, we call Nature. That is its strength. We should not feel embarrassed by the violence of the first part of the book; it is neither melodramatic nor spurious. The energy dramatized there has nothing to sustain it but itself: hence its association with the elements, especially with wind, water, and fire, and with animals, dogs, snow. It is linked also to the landscape, the firs permanently slanted by the wind. "My love for Heathcliff," Catherine says, "resembles the eternal rocks beneath—a source of little visible delight, but necessary." The sentence provides a motto for the entire book, the acknowledgement of quality and character followed by appeal to an older law: necessity.

The sole guardian of this law is Emily Brontë's imagination. At the end, it assents to fact, time, history, an emerging pattern of life for which it is not responsible. At the beginning, it asserted itself by inventing a fiction consistent with its nature; readers who find most of Emily Brontë in the first part of the book are right. The first part is an act of assertion, a declaration of Romantic rights, embodied in fiction as such; the second part begins a long process of accommodation which is fulfilled in Thrushcross Grange. But at that point, history has been compelled to recognize the forces it has to control. In the last paragraph of the book Lockwood, a chastened witness, stands in the churchyard looking at the three graves:

> I sought, and soon discovered, the three head-stones on the slope next the moor: the middle one grey, and half buried in heath: Edgar Linton's only harmonised by the turf and moss creeping up its foot: Heathcliff's still bare.
>
> I lingered round them, under that benign sky; watched the moths fluttering among the heath and harebells, listened to the soft wind breathing through the grass, and wondered how any one could ever imagine unquiet slumbers for the sleepers in that quiet earth.

This is meant to lay the ghosts, letting the dead bury their dead. But it is not meant to be any more conclusive than that: the previous paragraph has referred to "coming autumn storms," as if to warn the reader that the soft wind is temporal and provisional. The purpose of these last sentences is to restore the reader, like Catherine and Hareton, to historical time, in a condition apparently conscientious. One of the purposes of fiction is to tell fact it lies. Another, hardly to be distinguished from the first, is to rebuke the arrogance with which fact wields its power.

NOTES

1. The contexts of the poems are clarified in *Emily Jane Brontë: Gondal Poems,* ed. Helen Brown and Joan Mott (Oxford: Basil Blackwell for the Shakespeare Press, 1938); *The Complete Poems of Emily Jane Brontë,* ed. C. W. Hatfield (New York: Columbia University Press, 1941); and *The Complete Poems of Emily Brontë,* ed. Philip Henderson (London: The Folio Society, 1951). The poems quoted in the present essay are taken from the Hatfield edition, and the numbers in parentheses after each quotation are page references to that text. The Gondal saga is reconstructed in Laura L. Hinkley, *The Brontës: Charlotte and Emily* (London: Hammond, 1947), pp. 273–82, from which the present synopsis is taken. Fannie E. Ratchford argues in her *Gondal's Queen* (Austin, Texas: University of Texas Press, 1955) that all of Emily Brontë's verse "falls within the Gondal context."
2. Jean Seznec, *The Survival of the Pagan Gods,* trans. Barbara F. Sessions (New York: Pantheon Books, 1953), p. 291.
3. "Perhaps there could be no better definition, if not of Romanticism, at least of one of its most important aspects, than to say that it is a taking possession by consciousness of the basically subjective character of the mind. The Romantic is one who discovers himself to be a centre. It does not matter

very much that the world of objects may be out of reach; the Romantic knows that deep within himself there is something which cannot be assimilated to an object. That is the subjective and most authentic part of the self, the part which he most willingly recognizes as his own. Deprived of the periphery, the Romantic will gradually familiarize himself with the self, the centre." Translated by the author from Georges Poulet, *Les Métamorphoses du cercle* (Paris: Librairie Plon, 1961), p. 136.

4. "A child lost in the forest: this motif which has often and sometimes wonderfully inspired the Romantic imagination is perhaps the best image of man in the cosmos, as this imagination sees him. The pleasure which the Romantic takes in inserting himself in the Universe is no longer that of feeling himself at home, but rather that of feeling himself displaced. There is a desire *not* to embrace the whole, not to understand, to acknowledge one's self superseded, overwhelmed, to close one's eyes, dazzled or dismayed, to yield one's self to the paternal and terrible Powers." Translated by the author from Hélène Tuzet, *Le Cosmos et l'Imagination* (Paris: Librairie José Corti, 1965), p. 121.

5. Fannie E. Ratchford (*Gondal's Queen*, p. 87) argues that this poem is to be read as part of the Gondal Saga, interpreting it as A.G.A.'s apostrophe to Julius. This seems to me a strained reading. It is probably better to take the poem as a personal lyric.

6. C. P. Sanger, *The Structure of Wuthering Heights* (London: Hogarth Press, 1926).

From Morton W. Bloomfield (ed.), *The Interpretation of Narrative: Theory and Practice* (Cambridge, Mass.: Harvard University Press, 1970).

THE ENGLISH DICKENS AND
DOMBEY AND SON

It is widely agreed that the account of Dickens which Edmund Wilson gave in *The Wound and the Bow* (1941) has had remarkable success with academic readers. It is hardly too much to say that we think of Dickens very largely in Wilson's terms. Santayana's Dickens in *Soliloquies in England* is an engaging figure, the novelist as man's best friend: we are to admire Dickens's "vast sympathetic participation in the daily life of mankind"; but it now seems a picture from a gone time. It would be foolish to disengage ourselves entirely from Santayana's Dickens or from Henry James's Dickens in the *Autobiography* ("the great actuality of the current imagination"), but these figures do not speak to us, it appears, with particular authority. *The Wound and the Bow* presents Dickens as a victim, a man of obsession, and for that very reason as a poet, an artist of modern fears and divisions. We are to think of his fiction in association with the novels of Dostoevski and Kafka. We do not hope to find him in our Christmas stocking; it is no longer common to speak of his novels in association with good cheer.

The first effect of this interpretation is that Dickens is no longer received in the first instance as a voluble presence, a large arrival (in James's phrase), an entertainer, or a comedian; he is of the modern dispensation now, a tragic hero. If this means that he is taken seriously as a major artist, companion of Shakespeare, George Eliot, James, Dostoevski, and Tolstoy, perhaps it makes a happy conclusion. But it is hard to avoid the impression that there is still something askew in our sense of Dickens's art. We seem to have run from one extreme position to another. If an instance is required, there is our failure with the comedy. We do not know what to make of it, now that we have moved the centre of our interest away from the famous comic scenes. We cannot relate the comedy, with any ease, to the main picture, we are almost in the miserable position of thinking the comedy an embarrassment. We have put aside Dickens's sentiment too; we share James's distaste for "the Little Nells, the Smikes, the Paul Dombeys." It is clear that we take Dickens not as we find him but as we improve him. To give ourselves more freedom, we detach him from the English tradition, forgetting that it was largely this tradition which made him what he became; we make him over now as a great European. I think we have gone too far. The similarities between Dickens and Kafka, for instance, are marginal, not central. For one thing Dickens is not a fabulist, he does not insist upon the claims of the imagination over and against every claim of fact or time, he is not intransigent. I would maintain that Dickens is great as Wordsworth is great, not as Kafka is great. In the relation between imagination and reality he does not think of imagination as the senior or the greater term.

Dombey and Son begins with father and infant son in the darkened room. The scene is composed around them, as if their force were already institutional and statutory. Mrs. Dombey's presence in the room is almost accidental; she is in a neglected corner of the picture. Florence is not in the picture at all. Dickens is relying upon the reader to receive these first pages with a sense of the perturbation in the given relationships. The image of this family is presented, set off against another image which is not yet given in fact: that of a properly operative family. The figure of the operative family is still merely virtual, indeed abstract; it is present merely by being denied in the particular case: that of the Dombeys. We hold the given picture poised against another which is not given. The first picture is actual: Dombey, the infant Paul, then the dying mother, and beyond these, Florence. The second image is not yet drawn; it is traditional and categorical, recalled now and present in our outraged sense of its absence. What is unnatural in the given case animates our sense of the natural in other cases; thus a writer knows what he does not need to put in: the other cases—they are there as shadows already. A few pages later Dickens defines the second image, making it actual in the Toodle family. The enforced relation between Dombey and the Toodles, a trading affair, is the first major juxtaposition in the novel; it makes public and overt what is given implicitly in the first picture, the scene in the darkened room.

Dombey is already linked with trade. "The earth was made for Dombey and Son to trade in, and the sun and moon were made to give them light" (p. 2).[1] Trade and money: Florence was "merely a piece of base coin that couldn't be invested—a bad Boy—nothing more" (p. 3). Dombey is "one of those close-shaved close-cut moneyed gentlemen who are glossy and crisp like new bank-notes" (p. 17). He teaches Paul that money "can do anything" (p. 92) or at least that "it could do all that could be done" (p. 93). The lesson is turned to account when Paul is put in the position of giving Walter Gay the money he "begs for" at Brighton. Trade, money, pride, power—in Dombey's world a man is defined by his possessions. If Dombey's wife should die, "he would find a something gone from among his plate and furniture, and other household possessions, which was well worth the having" (p. 5). He thinks Polly Toodle "a deserving object" (p. 16). "You know he has bought me," Edith Granger says to her mother later in the novel: "or that he will, to-morrow. He has considered of his bargain; he has shown it to his friend; he is even rather proud of it; he thinks that it will suit him, and may be had sufficiently cheap; and he will buy to-morrow" (pp. 393–94).

On a bleak autumnal day Dombey is "as hard and cold as the weather"; his house has "black, cold rooms" (p. 52). The Toodles, on the other hand, are a genuine family. Toodle is illiterate but sensitive, warm-hearted, and—above all—independent. When Miss Tox says that Polly in her mourning garb will be "so smart that your husband won't know you," Toodle answers briskly: "I should know her anyhows and anywheres" (p. 19). Dombey imposes upon Polly the name "Mrs. Richards" when he hires her milk to save the infant's life. If Toodle is a good man, Dickens says, Polly has a further merit: "She was a good plain sample of a nature that is ever, in the mass, better, truer, higher, nobler, quicker to feel, and much more constant to retain, all tenderness and pity, self-denial and devotion, than the nature of men" (p. 27). When she tells Florence a tale of death, the child speaks of "the cold ground," but Polly says, "No! The warm ground, where the ugly little seeds turn into beautiful flowers, and into grass, and corn, and I don't know what all besides" (p. 24). Polly knows by instinct and nature what Dombey learns only by a lifetime of error, defeat, and angelic ministry.

Dickens wants this first contrast between Dombey and the Toodles to reverberate throughout the domestic and the public worlds of the novel. The domestic contrast is the difference between two ways of life in terms of intimate relationships. The public equivalent is given as the first radical severance in the novel, the division of rich and poor. In Chapter 5 of *Hard Times* Stephen Blackpool speaks to Bounderby of the "black unpassable world betwixt yo," that is, between masters and men, the owners and the "hands." In Chapter 8 of *Bleak House* Esther Summerson and Ada Clare reflect upon the "iron barrier" which separates them from such people as the brickmaker whose house they enter. The subtitle of Disraeli's novel *Sybil* is *The Two Nations,* a striking phrase glossed in Book I, Chapter 5, when Stephen Gerard says that "there is no community in England; there is aggregation, but aggregation under circumstances which make it rather a dissociating than a uniting principle." "Two nations," he continues, "the rich and the poor; between whom there is no intercourse and no sympathy; who are as ignorant of each other's habits, thoughts, and feelings, as if they were dwellers in different zones, or inhabitants of different planets."

It may appear that in the first juxtaposition of Dombey and Toodle, Dickens is already taking sides, sponsoring the poor against the rich; but his attitude is not as simple as that account implies. Toodle is a good man, a worthy husband and parent, but he is clearly limited; he cannot be invoked to mark the range of human possibilities. His vitality is indisputable, his independence impressive, but there are crucial areas of human experience which he cannot think of encompassing. As for Dombey, hard and bleak as he is, he must not be destroyed; he is neither vicious nor deceitful. Indeed, he is a man of honor. Mention of Bounderby is enough to make the point that among Dickens's trading people there are moral distinctions to be drawn. Dombey is not Veneering. So it is not a case of Dickens as Robin Hood, robbing rich Dombey to pay poor Toodle. Dickens is not sentimental on this point, even though there are letters and speeches in which his vote for a "popular" England is clear. His account of Staggs's Gardens is the real evidence.

The Toodles live in the Gardens, and presumably they feel the traditional English loyalty toward one's own place. Their house is lively, vivid, full of children. Those who live in the Gardens think of the place as "a sacred grove not to be withered by railroads" (p. 64). We are not meant to smile too broadly at the ironic phrase; the Gardens are indeed a sacred grove to those who live there. Dickens registers this English sentiment and responds to its vitality, but he is convinced, nevertheless, that the human advantages of the new railway are worth their cost: "In short, the yet unfinished and unopened Railroad was in progress; and, from the very core of all this dire disorder, trailed smoothly away, upon its mighty course of civilisation and improvement" (p. 63). The tone in the last phrase is not ironic. Staggs's Gardens are destroyed, but the railway is a boon; the human cost is high but not, in the long term, exorbitant. I put the case too bluntly; Chapter 15 is entirely given to the development of the question. To put it more bluntly still, Dickens is letting the dead bury their dead. At one point he emits a preservationist's lament: "Oh woe the day when 'not a rood of English ground' — laid out in Staggs's Gardens — is secure!" (p. 219). But he continues:

> There was no such place as Staggs's Gardens. It had vanished from the earth. Where the old rotten summer-houses once had stood, palaces now reared their heads, and granite columns of gigantic girth opened a vista to the railway world beyond. The miserable waste ground, where the refuse-matter had been heaped of yore, was swallowed up and gone; and in its frowsy stead were tiers of warehouses, crammed with rich goods and costly merchandise.   (pp. 217–18)

Up to this point the sentiment could be interpreted, with some difficulty, as nostalgic on the whole, the narrator a Southern Agrarian, an English Fugitive. But the passage proceeds:

> The old by-streets now swarmed with passengers and vehicles of every kind: the new streets that had stopped disheartened in the mud and waggon-ruts, formed towns within themselves, originating wholesome comforts and conveniences belonging to themselves, and never tried nor thought of until they sprung into existence. Bridges that had led to nothing, led to villas, gardens, churches, healthy public walks.   (p. 218)

Dickens is coaxing his own feelings in the direction of that last sentence. He is persuading himself that all shall be well. Persuasion is necessary, since his devotion to the old England persists. The entire passage and the paragraphs which follow are designed to enable him to give the new railway his blessing. He speaks of the trains as containing "the secret knowledge of great powers yet unsuspected in them, and strong purposes not yet achieved" (p. 219). In one sentence, when he has now persuaded himself, he relates the new engines to the fundamental rhythm of human life: "To and from the heart of this great change, all day and night, throbbing currents rushed and returned incessantly like its life's blood" (p. 218). The railway is endorsed because it brings more life into play, it enriches the country by movement and action, it brings people together. Dickens is ready to conceive of the potentialities of social change in terms of the great perennial rhythms. He is not frightened of the new even when it appears, like the railway, in the form of power. The politics which sustains this sense of change is based upon the values of plenitude, variety; it is a popular Romanticism of bustle and hubbub. So it is not a case of an "organic society" destroyed by the Industrial Revolution, Chestertonian stagecoaches banished by steam engines: the circulation of life, effected by the railway, is as natural as the circulation of the blood. If we remark that Dombey and Jo Bagstock go to Leamington by train and that the railway is a congenial part of Dombey's world, we should also note that the railway has done the Toodles no harm; on the contrary, they enjoy a better life now that Toodle is an engine driver. The train destroys only those like Mr. Carker the Manager who are already damned.

The contrast between Dombey and the Toodles is sharp, then, but it is not blatant. Propaganda is not intended; Dickens's aim is to bring the two nations together at last. But the immediate obstacles must be acknowledged. Dombey and everything he represents must be seen as intractable, consumed with pride of station. In the encounters with Edith one form of pride meets another. Dombey's pride is categorical, Edith's is consistent with her sense of herself as fatally corrupted. Edith's pride is modern in the sense that it is self-aware, ironic; Dombey's is beyond self-criticism, coinciding too neatly with his character. But before these encounters Dombey is revealed in relation to his wife and children. The crucial passage comes in Chapter 3 after Mrs. Dombey's death. Dombey recalls the last scene, Florence and her mother clasped together:

Let him be absorbed as he would in the Son on whom he built such high hopes, he could not forget that closing scene. He could not forget that he had had no part in it. That, at the bottom of its clear depths of tenderness and truth, lay those two figures clasped in each other's arms, while he stood on the bank above them, looking down a mere spectator—not a sharer with them—quite shut out.   (p. 29)

The passage should be read with an earlier reference in mind—the last sentence of Chapter 1:

Thus, clinging fast to that slight spar within her arms, the mother drifted out upon the dark and unknown sea that rolls round all the world.   (p. 10)

Dombey is safe upon the bank, he runs no risk of drowning, but his safety is bought at the cost of always remaining on the surface of things. Here and throughout the main body of the novel he is held to the surface, cut off from the depths, the sources of life and feeling. Man of the City, he is alien to the Sea. What is appalling in him is the terrible penury of the symbolism by which he lives; he has so little in that way that he must hold to what he has with insistence of will. W. H. Auden has argued that most of the troubles of the world are caused by our "poverty of symbols"; we have to entrust our entire emotional lives to the few symbols we possess. The difference between Dombey and Florence is the difference between a wretchedly penurious symbolism and a symbolism at least adequately wide and deep—*adequately* meaning that Florence's symbols are enough to sustain the range and depth of her allegiance. Dombey has paid for what he has with what he is. Florence has committed herself to a life of feeling and to a correspondingly responsive symbolism. Note, for instance, of Dombey that Dickens never gives him a childhood, a father, a mother. Moving on a bleak surface, he is denied whatever makes for density of experience. He is thin and brittle. Florence and Paul, deprived in every domestic way, inhabit the depths. In Book 2, Chapter 7, of *Hard Times* Dickens says of James Harthouse and Louisa: "To be sure, the better and profounder part of her character was not within his scope of perception — for in natures, as in seas, depth answers unto depth." Dombey feels toward Florence, Dickens says,

an uneasiness of an extraordinary kind. He almost felt as if she
watched and distrusted him. As if she held the clue to something
secret in his breast, of the nature of which he was hardly informed
himself. As if she had an innate knowledge of one jarring and
discordant string within him, and her very breath could sound it.

(p. 29)

The knowledge is innate because it lives and moves far below the ostensible surface; when we think of Florence's patience and sensitivity, we
find her character in her symbols. Her kinship with Paul is a shared
symbolism, a secret lore.

Paul is constantly associated with depth, the sea, and death. Miss
Blimber reports that "he is singular (what is usually termed old-fashioned)
in his character and conduct" (p. 184) and Paul wonders what this "old
fashion" can be which others find in him. We have assumed, with Henry
James, that Paul is merely precocious and therefore obnoxious. But if we
repudiate Paul we separate ourselves from the fundamental symbolism of
the novel. The *OED* cites Miss Blimber's report for one meaning of "old-
fashioned," that is, "having the ways of a grown-up person; hence, precocious, intelligent, knowing." But in the novel it rather means having the
ways of a person born for death. Chapter 17 ends:

The golden ripple on the wall came back again, and nothing else
stirred in the room. The old, old fashion! The fashion that came in
with our first garments, and will last unchanged until our race has
run its course, and the wide firmament is rolled up like a scroll. The
old, old fashion—Death!

Oh thank God, all who see it, for that older fashion yet, of
Immortality! And look upon us, angels of young children, with
regards not quite estranged, when the swift river bears us to the
ocean! (p. 226)

If we choose to be embarrassed by this aspect of the novel, we must bear
the consequences. In fact Paul cannot be received on any terms but his
own. His life is a free-flowing current rushing to the sea. "Why, will it
never stop, Floy," he asks; "it is bearing me away, I think" (p. 222). He
sees a boat at sea and, in vision, his mother shining upon the water.

The symbolism is perennial. Emily Dickinson has a poem which begins: "My River runs to thee— / Blue Sea! Wilt welcome me?" (No. 162). Paul asks Florence: "The sea, Floy, what is it that it keeps on saying?" (p. 109). Florence does not gloss the waves; like old Glubb she probably "knows a great deal about it" (p. 152), but there are no translations for these sounds. Waves say whatever the listener is capable of hearing. Dr. Blimber hears them saying, "Gentlemen, we will now resume our studies"; to Mr. Toots they speak of a time when he was brighter; to Florence they recite Paul's story and finally the grand story of love, "eternal and illimitable, not bounded by the confines of this world, or by the end of time, but ranging still, beyond the sea, beyond the sky, to the invisible country far away!" (p. 811). To Paul the waves speak of death, "the old, old fashion," and then of immortality, but they also rehearse the movements of life, the succession of days and nights, the rhythm of the seasons, the mystery, the secret doctrine of things. His own feeling merges in the feeling of the sea. In "The Masthead" chapter of *Moby-Dick* Ishmael thinks of a young, absentminded Platonist manning the masthead, lulled "by the blending cadence of waves with thoughts" until, losing his identity, he "takes the mystic ocean at his feet for the visible image of that deep, blue, bottomless soul, pervading mankind and nature." Paul Dombey, a child Platonist, is old-fashioned in this sense too; the new fashion is temporal, empiricist, and wilful. So while Paul is associated with currents, rivers, seas, and death, his father is associated with surface and ice: "he might have been hung up for sale at a Russian fair as a specimen of a frozen gentleman" (p. 57). One glance from her father is enough to freeze Florence's tears (p. 30). When Captain Cuttle shakes Dombey's hand, "at this touch of warm feeling and cold iron, Mr. Dombey shivered all over" (p. 134).

Indeed the action of the book may be stated in these terms. The novel tells how Dombey's pride and his will are at last dissolved by the flow of Florence's feeling. At the end "the white-haired gentleman" playing with his two grandchildren loves to see them "free and stirring" (p. 878). More generally I would argue that this pattern of action is central in Dickens's fiction. His concern is to bring the two nations together by making them share certain perennial feelings and sentiments. Feeling could be shared, he believed, so fully that the sharing would dissolve the artificial barriers of class, money, and prejudice.[2] He was not alone in this conviction.

The fifth chapter of John Stuart Mill's *Autobiography* deals with a crisis in his "mental history." The crisis began in the autumn of 1826 when Mill felt that, as he wrote, "my love of mankind, and of excellence for its own sake, had worn itself out." This sense of attrition was related to his fear that "the habit of analysis has a tendency to wear away the feelings." The crisis, he says, left him in the condition which Coleridge describes in his "Dejection" ode. The first relief came when he was reading that passage in Marmontel's *Mémoires* where, after his father's death, the young boy assures his family that he will be everything to them, that he will "supply the place of all that they had lost." Mill's response to this passage was so strong that it released the flow of feeling which in the crisis had been frozen. From that time, he says, "I gave its proper place, among the prime necessities of human well-being, to the internal culture of the individual." He ceased "to attach almost exclusive importance to the ordering of outward circumstances, and the training of the human being for speculation and for action." The cultivation of the feelings became, he reports, "one of the cardinal points in my ethical and philosophical creed." Mill then goes on to say that his reading of Wordsworth's miscellaneous poems, in the two-volume edition of 1815, proved a crucial event in the development of his creed:

> What made Wordsworth's poems a medicine for my state of mind, was that they expressed, not mere outward beauty, but states of feeling, and of thought coloured by feeling, under the excitement of beauty. They seemed to be the very culture of the feelings, which I was in quest of. In them I seemed to draw from a source of inward joy, of sympathetic and imaginative pleasure, which could be shared in by all human beings; which had no connexion with struggle or imperfection, but would be made richer by every improvement in the physical or social condition of mankind.

It is a celebrated moment in the history of nineteenth-century sensibility. I place it now beside another occasion, hardly less celebrated and equally pertinent to the present consideration of Dickens. Wordsworth is writing in the preface to the second edition of *Lyrical Ballads:*

> If the labours of Men of science should ever create any material revolution, direct or indirect, in our condition, and in the impressions which we habitually receive, the Poet will sleep then no more

than at present; he will be ready to follow the steps of the Man of science, not only in those general indirect effects, but he will be at his side, carrying sensation into the midst of the objects of the science itself.

The two passages are congenial. Together they propose a function for poetry which is peculiarly relevant to the nature of nineteenth-century society. Mill and Wordsworth, starting from different positions, reach the same conclusion: that the principal function of literature in an apparently intractable age is the cultivation of the feelings. The pleasure of this cultivation, the "inward joy" available from that source, could be "shared in by all human beings." The artist's role in a new Age of Science rests upon this fact. I would maintain that this is essentially the role which Dickens proposes to himself, especially in his later novels. The more recalcitrant the conditions, the more urgent the medicine. Two nations, separated more rigidly than ever before, might still be brought together by sharing feelings common to all.

The continuity between *Lyrical Ballads* and Dickens's novels is based upon this conviction that the flow of feeling may still dissolve the frozen places of life. Feeling is a form of energy at once natural and occult; issuing from "the buried life," it transforms the daily rote of surface, like water in Auden's poem "In Praise of Limestone." Feeling, indeed, is a kind of religion, with one advantage in that comparison: that it is shared, in some measure, by everyone. There is never enough feeling to satisfy Dickens or to melt, with ease, a hard world; like Christianity, feeling often lies inert and terrified before its enemies. But it may be encouraged and provoked. Dickens and Wordsworth knew in their different ways and degrees that nineteenth-century society insists upon its industrial triumph and that it must be made to respect the old fashions, it must become sensitive to the human cost of its success; otherwise it would lose its soul. With whatever differences, Dickens and Wordsworth put their trust in feeling, as Henry Adams staked all, with less confidence, upon intelligence. Dickens and Wordsworth were luckier than Adams, because they had merely to provoke their society to increase and release and share the feelings it already had—free, unearned, and as yet unfulfilled. Adams had to demand that his society live by novelty, producing an active, governing intelligence where it had only promised to produce force and power. Dickens and Wordsworth asked society to remember its buried life and live for continuity and plenitude. Adams asked society to admit for its own salvation a force of sentiment which he called, in Chapter 25 of the *Education,* the Virgin. "Symbol or energy," he writes, "the Virgin had acted as the greatest force the Western world ever felt, and had drawn man's activities to herself more strongly than any other power, natural or supernatural, had ever done."

In such a program the first requirement was to curb the will. The will must be relaxed, assuaged. There is a relevant passage in Huysmans's *A Rebours* where Des Esseintes, at the Bodega, orders a glass of amontillado. A mental traveler, he has been thinking of London as represented in Dickens's novels, imagining various characters from *David Copperfield, Martin Chuzzlewit, Bleak House,* and *Little Dorrit.* But after living for a while in his London of the imagination, he looks at the glass of sherry, and he recalls Poe's story of the cask of amontillado. Dickens's novels now seem to him merely lenient and consoling by comparison with Poe's stories, abrasive and desperate. En route to Decadence, Des Esseintes abandons Dickens at this point, because Dickens proposes, at least as a final possibility, a continuous movement of feeling among his characters. The characters are isolated at the start because that is their hard condition, but some of them, at least, are reconciled at the end. Poe's characters are walled in dungeons, utterly dependent upon the violence of their wills; there is no question of mutual feeling or community. Des Esseintes, heading toward Baudelaire, Mallarmé, and Verlaine, finds Dickens first a consolation, then an amusement, but finally a scandal. To Dickens feeling can be questioned but cannot be doubted; its eloquence takes the form of action rather than knowledge, and like the sound of the waves it cannot be construed. Life is not naturally or necessarily, he asserts, a function of the predatory will. In Chapter 47 of *Dombey and Son* he writes:

> Not the less bright and blest would that day be for rousing some who never have looked out upon the world of human life around them, to a knowledge of their own relation to it, and for making them acquainted with a perversion of nature in their own contracted sympathies and estimates. (p. 648)

This is his characteristic note; the later novels strive to reach conclusions in which it is heard.

But the "true voice of feeling" must be defined by distinguishing it its false appearances. This is the purpose served by Mrs. Skewton in *Dombey and Son:* to represent in one character everything spurious which parades itself as "the language of the Heart." "I want Nature everywhere," she says (p. 289). "With all those yearnings, and gushings, and impulsive throbbings that we have implanted in our souls, and which are so very charming, why are we not more natural?" she asks Dombey, as if he knew or she cared (p. 293). Her praise of the past humiliates it; of Queen Bess she exclaims, "Dear creature! She was all Heart!" (p. 387). In *Little Dorrit* Mrs. Merdle is put to the same use, and Mr. Pecksniff in *Martin Chuzzlewit.* "I am very impressible myself, by nature," Mrs. Merdle says in Book I, Chapter 20, the great scene with the parrot. Dickens is anticipating criticism, making the obvious case first against himself. An exponent of true feeling must protect his truth by exposing falsity; otherwise his enemies are likely to undertake the task on their own terms. In Mrs. Skewton, Dickens takes the risk of showing his own values dangerously compromised, but temporarily and as a challenge, to deny his enemies the pleasure of casting the first stone. After Mrs. Skewton, no reader could accuse Dickens of being a slave to the language of delicacy. He is now free to represent the form of genuine feeling and its practical success in the world.

There is, as one example among many, Harriet Carker's success with Alice Brown. At the end, after years of bitterness, Alice is assuaged. In the last scene Harriet is associated with Christ as she reads to the dying Alice from the New Testament, "the blessed history, in which the blind lame palsied beggar, the criminal, the woman stained with shame, the shunned of all our dainty clay, has each a portion, that no human pride, indifference, or sophistry, through all the ages that this world shall last, can take away" (p. 826). There is also Florence's influence upon Edith, short of practical success. Chapter 30 describes again the nature of Edith's pride, and then asks: "Was this the woman whom Florence—an innocent girl, strong only in her earnestness and simple truth—could so impress and quell, that by her side she was another creature, with her tempest of passion hushed, and her very pride itself subdued?" (p. 423). In contrast, Dombey fails to "correct and reduce" Edith; she cannot be subdued by force of will (p. 646).

It is a common pattern in Dickens's novels, the simple, innocent girl who melts stern hearts; we cannot disown it. Florence's effect upon Edith is a minor version of the major success which she at last gains with Dombey. Constantly described as an angel, she becomes Dombey's Guardian Angel when she prevents him from killing himself. She melts his frozen heart. Taine says that Dombey becomes the best of fathers and spoils a fine novel, but this is unjust; Dombey cannot be separated from the angel who ministers to him or from the pattern of reconciliation which he embodies. It is hardly a question of character at all; it is the grand design of the book, already anticipated, in miniature, by several episodes before the end. The point to make is that Dickens is evoking certain sensations, associations, and states of feeling which move at a level far below the distinctions of society and class. The continuity of these feelings marks for him the essentially human element. Together in feeling, people may freely differ in opinion; it matters little. Everything beyond feeling is a later gloss upon the old text, the old fashion.

That Dickens was deeply disturbed by the venom of class and caste which embittered English society is clear in his later novels, especially in *Our Mutual Friend,* his most elaborate engagement with a question of class. But his rhetoric implies that England may still make a genuinely popular success of itself by retaining direct contact with its sources in feeling. Like Wordsworth's ballads, Dickens's novels hope to save the harsh world by stirring the fundamental rhythms of life; acting upon a realm of sentiment far below the divisions of telegrams and anger, Marshalsea Prisons, class, money, and Circumlocution Offices. Edmund Wilson has argued that in the later novels Dickens changes his political stance; the novelist now hopes that, as Wilson says, "the declassed representatives of the old professional upper classes may unite with the proletariat against the commercial middle class." But the essential movement of feeling on Dickens's part is beneath class altogether; he now wants to ground his appeal upon those sentiments and sensations which are common to all men regardless of class. The point about Dombey is that he takes so long to recognize his humanity. Like Wordsworth, Dickens asserts the essential basis of human life in terms of being and nature; in that context distinctions of class become secondary matters. Hopefully the two nations and all classes meet in the community of these feelings. In the last chapter of *Dombey and Son,* Dombey, old Sol, Captain Cuttle, and Toots join in drinking the last bottle of old Madeira, toasting Walter and Florence. In the City class distinctions persist, but in Sol's house the classes meet in goodwill. Classes persist, Dickens seems to say, but they do not matter, they do not touch the depths of humanity. He does not hope to rid England of class but to make the divisions of class as narrow as possible. People are not required to deny their "natural" class or to move above it, especially if the effort results, as it generally does, in the loss of natural feeling. Walter's role in *Dombey and Son* is important in this regard. "Awfully serene and still" (p. 508) now that his quality has been proved by experience, he is deputed to redeem the City, setting it moving again in a new spirit. Another firm of Dombey and Son is promised, rising "triumphant," but it will enjoy the triumph while retaining a sense of the human values within its care. Dickens is not offering an Arcadian pastoral, a return to cows instead of capital, bowers instead of dustheaps. He has no quarrel with railways or the City so long as they keep in mind the community they serve.

This marks the continuity between Dickens's novels, early and late, despite their obvious differences. The two Scrooges are not totally apart. The aim of Dickens's fiction applies to the entire body of his work: to bring people together by making them share those feelings which, except by denying their humanity, they cannot fail to possess. The same motive relates many things in the fiction: the good cheer represented in *Pickwick Papers* by the Christmas party at Manor Farm; Dickens's praise of wonder and fancy, banished by Gradgrind in Chapter 8 of *Hard Times;* the selfless vitality of Mr. Sleary's circus folk; the lenient image at the end of *Dombey and Son.* For the later novels one moment is especially significant. In *Our Mutual Friend* Eugene Wrayburn has married Lizzie Hexam; the marriage is scandalous to Society. The last chapter is called "The Voice of Society," the question being: who really speaks on such a matter with the voice of Society? The chapter recites several voices, each in a note of predictable hauteur. But Twemlow defends the marriage: "If this gentleman's feeling of gratitude, of respect, of admiration, and affection," he says, "induced him to marry this lady, . . . I think he is the greater gentleman for the action, and makes her the greater lady." "I beg to say," he continues, "that when I use the word gentleman, I use it in the sense in which the degree may be attained by any man." This moment is important in Dickens because it advances the concept of a gentleman as a moral term rather than a term of class. The morality can only be a matter of feeling. Toodle, for instance, is a gentleman by Twemlow's definition. So is Dombey, after Florence's ministry.

My account may suggest, however, that Dickens's design upon us is all too clear, too palpable, that his novels, if my view holds, strive to complete themselves as fables and parables. The question then arises: if so, what relation persists between the grand design and the novelist's sense of circumstance, his recognition of the unpredictable fact which threatens design and embarrasses parable? It has often been held that the books are full of irrelevant life, incidents which have nothing to explain their presence but the fact that Dickens's plenary imagination brought them forth. But the chief characteristic of the later novels is the remarkable balance which they maintain between these rival considerations. These novels are still rich in circumstance, but the circumstance always admits the pressure of a governing design. Admittedly if the design is meant to define the social function of feeling, it is capacious enough for almost any circumstance. But Dickens's artistic scruple is evident. Our impression persists that in these novels there is a splendid "wooing both ways" between incident and design. Incidents are rarely intimidated by the design; the relation is not harsh. On the contrary, incidents have an air of free development, short of total freedom.

To mention one example: Some readers have been scandalized by the fact that Florence continues to love her monstrous father. This can only be explained, they maintain, by the insistence of the fable. According to the Orphic design of the book, it is obviously necessary that Florence should love her father if she is to win him over at the end. Angels do not give up easily. Furthermore it may be urged that Florence loves her father, rigid and proud as he is, because it is natural for her to do so. In this she is indeed natural except that she is an extraordinary case of the natural. But in fact Florence's feeling is not so monolithic as those readers say. There are gradations. After Dombey strikes her, she continues to love him but not to expect anything from that love; it makes a difference. Even before that incident there are gradations, notably in a remarkable passage in Chapter 47 where Dickens describes how the picture of Dombey, to Florence's still loving eyes, has become abstract, receding from the present tense: "Florence loved him still, but, by degrees, had come to love him rather as some dear one who had been, or who might have been, than as the hard reality before her eyes" (p. 649). The paragraph which follows that sentence is one of the finest things in the book. Dickens's art, which has so often been supposed to deal in rough-and-ready effects, is here a matter of precise and delicate adjustment as Dombey's presence to Florence becomes dim and virtual. The adjustment is made by the grammatical forms which disengage the image of Dombey from the present tense until it recedes through the past to become, like the grammatical mood itself, subjunctive.

The point is that Dickens's sense of his large design is indeed imposing limits upon his freedom; his zest, his delight in gusto and proliferation, are curbed. But the restriction brings reward, for within these self-imposed limits he gains a new power of adjustment and nuance. As a novelist he assents to limitation; he does not chafe under restriction now. In *Little Dorrit,* for instance, the persuasions of design are strongly operative when the house falls upon Blandois, killing him; when Mrs. Clennam confesses her crime to Amy; when Amy marries Arthur. These events are rhetorically congenial, and the design requires them. But while a suggestion of parable hovers about Blandois's death, as about Carker's death in *Dombey and Son,* it does not inhibit Dickens's sense of circumstance too severely. One recalls the great moment when Mrs. Clennam says, "Flintwinch, it is closing in." Dickens is like a man who, believing in Destiny, chooses to call it Providence. The given world is still his oyster, but he lives in it now with a sense of providential will. He strives to accommodate himself to the will of Providence as to a structure of values independent of his consciousness. He assents to the structure because he has not made it; he has merely sensed its presence. Feeling is common to circumstance and to the grand design; palpable in the content of circumstance, it may be sensed in the design too. So Dickens reconciles man's individual feeling to a providential pattern in which the feeling suffers as little restriction as possible and gains in the end what it lacked of form and meaning. So too the narrator in *Dombey and Son* speaks as he does, not because he pretends to be God but because he assents to Providence and offers himself as its witness. Design or Form is the artistic correlative of Providence. Dickens trusts in the community of feeling because it is at once particular and general; there can be nothing more intimate than feeling and at the same time nothing more universal. The design is compounded of feeling; feeling aspires to the success of design. The art of Dickens's later novels is based upon his sense of the continuity of earth and sky, land and sea, fact and type. The "popular" nature of his art depends upon this sense.

If so much depends upon feeling, Florence's burden is enormous. She must feel nearly everything, and Dickens is bound to place her in a position to do so. She is present when her mother dies, when Paul dies, when her father comes home with a new wife, when contention arises between Dombey and Edith, when Walter comes back, when Dombey tries to kill himself, and so forth. She must feel everything whether she expresses what she feels or not. Like Fanny in *Mansfield Park,* she must contain within herself what other characters release in action and words. In the preface to *What Maisie Knew* James speaks of Maisie as "really keeping the torch of virtue alive in an air tending infinitely to smother it; really in short making confusion worse confounded by drawing some stray fragrance of an ideal across the scent of selfishness, by sowing on barren strands, through the mere fact of presence, the seed of the moral life." James's novel proves, if proof is demanded, what can be done by the mere fact of presence. In *Dombey and Son* Florence registers everything by holding it within herself. Nothing is ever lost or forgotten. Florence is given to us not as a remarkable "vessel of consciousness" but as someone who lives in the depths. She feels and fears and contains what Dombey merely confronts as obstacles on the surface.

In Chapter 35, for instance, Dombey and his wife have returned from their honeymoon. Edith has told Florence that she cannot teach her how to "become dearer to Papa." That night Florence dreams of Paul, her father, Walter, and Edith: "In every vision, Edith came and went, sometimes to her joy, sometimes to her sorrow, until they were alone on the brink of a dark grave, and Edith pointing down, she looked and saw— what!—another Edith lying at the bottom" (p. 508). Edith has admonished Florence "never seek to find in me what is not there," meaning presumably her better self, already corrupted and destroyed. Like Dombey in an earlier instance of the same figure, Edith is standing upon the brink looking at the self she has killed. The woman on the brink is the Edith who defeats Dombey by running off with Carker, whom she detests. The same figure is invoked on several occasions in the novel and especially when Edith sees in the depths of her hatred for Carker "the dark retaliation" she is about to practice upon Dombey. Florence feels this too and is confirmed in fear when she sees Carker coming from Edith's room.

It may be argued that poor Florence is simply incapable of sustaining these burdens. But we should not forget the narrator, who feels so strongly in her behalf that the effect is almost as if she were more than herself. The narrator goes before her, preparing her way, removing obstacles; what Florence feels is echoed and amplified in his feelings. He "sets the scene" for her. In Chapter 47, for instance, he arranges the action as a miniature drama in five acts, but he also introduces the play, prepares our minds to receive it. In the first paragraphs he comes before us as an orator, a preacher, but especially as an impresario. "Oh for a good spirit who would take the house-tops off, with a more potent and benignant hand than the lame demon in the tale,[3] and show a Christian people what dark shapes issue from amidst their homes, to swell the retinue of the Destroying Angel as he moves forth among them!" (p. 648). And lo the narrator proceeds to take the Dombey housetop off, revealing the dark shapes. And since the story has a moral, the impresario gives it at once: if Christians knew the truth, they would "then apply themselves, like creatures of one common origin, owing one duty to the Father of one family, and tending to one common end, to make the world a better place!" (p. 648). Now the housetop is lifted. Act 1: Edith and Florence. "Forgive me," Edith says, "for having ever darkened your dark home— I am a shadow on it, I know well—and let us never speak of this again" (p. 651). Act 2: at the dinner table, Dombey, Edith, Florence, and Carker. This act works up to a climax when Edith, throwing her jewels to the ground, leaves the room, but the climax is prefigured by the detail of the quarrel between Edith and Dombey. The quarrel is strong stuff, enlivened by the shift from direct speech to oblique speech when the participants address each other through the sinister agent, Carker; enlivened too by our sense of Florence's presence, silent and distraught, until Dombey orders her to leave the room. Act 3: Florence sees Carker on the staircase. Act 4: Florence, meeting Edith on the stairs, is "transfixed before the haggard face and staring eyes," as Edith shrieks, "Keep away! Let me go by!" (p. 662). Act 5: Edith has run off with Carker. Dombey strikes Florence, who rushes out of the house.

I have described this chapter as if it were a Victorian melodrama mainly to concede that the basis of Dickens's art is, as many readers have said, theatrical. Concession may go further. George Eliot complained that Dickens always stopped at the surface of things, never revealed the hidden self in his characters. Henry James agreed with her, compounding the charge by equating the hidden self with intelligence and intelligence with "nature." "Where in these pages," James asked in his review of *Our Mutual Friend,* "are the depositaries of that intelligence without which the movement of life would cease? Who represents nature?"[4] Now it is obvious that Dickens did not think of intelligence as having the place in life which James ascribed to it. He does not show his characters putting much trust in ratiocination. His art is most congenially employed when a character is revealed by action, gesture, idiosyncrasy. He seldom presents a character by showing him in relation to himself. His characters are not introspective by nature, though they may occasionally be forced to look within by circumstance. Normally a character in Dickens is disclosed in relation to other characters, or in relation to his setting, or in relation to certain figures and images which surround him. Normally too the characters depend for their lucidity upon the way in which the narrator presents them, the degree of light and shade which he allows them. They need not do everything for themselves. We are dealing, it is apparent, with a kind of fiction which delights in conditions and conventions; the impresario loves to be seen at work. Robert Garis has described this aspect of Dickens in *The Dickens Theatre.* The only point I would make is that Dickens's theatre, like most theatres, is animated by feeling rather than by intelligence. The most "intelligent" character in *Dombey and Son* is the narrator in the sense that he knows precisely what he is doing: deploying and controlling the figures, relationships, motifs. But Dickens does not believe that intelligence is the principle "without which the movement of life would cease." It would not cease, unless it were also deprived of feeling. In Chapter 47 none of the characters says anything remarkable; there is very little evidence of intelligence as the moving principle of life. Except for Florence these dark shapes are contorted in one degree or another; those are doomed who are congealed in their characters. But Florence escapes from the ruined house and "in the wildness of her sorrow" seeks old Sol's Midshipman, the only place which, she knows by instinct, will welcome her. So the principle of feeling is preserved—by Florence, Captain Cuttle, Mr. Toots, not least by Diogenes. All that Dickens asks of Florence is that in behalf of England she keep the lines of feeling open—silently, if silence is appropriate to her circumstance.

NOTES

1. Page references to *Dombey and Son* are to the New Oxford Illustrated Dickens ed. (London, 1950).

2. I use the word "feeling" in this essay to refer to "the primary feelings," in Alfred North Whitehead's phrase, except that I emphasize the sense in which the word is a verbal noun, a term of action, rather than a noun. In Part 3 of his *Process and Reality: An Essay in Cosmology* (Cambridge, 1929), Whitehead deals with the Theory of Prehensions, comprising the Theory of Feelings, the Primary Feelings, the Transmission of Feelings, Propositions

and Feelings, and the Higher Phases of Experience. "A feeling," he says, "is the appropriation of some elements in the universe to be components in the real internal constitution of its subject. The elements are the initial data; they are what the feeling feels. . . . The essential novelty of a feeling attaches to its subjective form. The initial data, and even the nexus which is the objective datum, may have served other feelings with other subjects. But the subjective form is the immediate novelty; it is how *that* subject is feeling that objective datum" (p. 327).

Whitehead then distinguishes "three primary types of feeling which enter into the formation of all the more complex feelings. . . . (i) that of simple physical feelings, (ii) that of conceptual feelings, and (iii) that of transmuted feelings." He continues: "In a simple physical feeling, the initial datum is a single actual entity; in a conceptual feeling, the objective datum is an eternal object; in a transmuted feeling, the objective datum is a nexus of actual entities. Simple physical feelings and transmuted feelings make up the class of physical feelings. In none of these feelings, taken in their original purity devoid of accretions from later integrations, does the subjective form involve consciousness. Although in a propositional feeling the subjective form may involve judgment, this element in the subjective form is not necessarily present" (p. 328).

To come to Dickens: the "primary feelings" are especially relevant to community and communication because, in Whitehead's terms, the "elements" are universal and universally available, and the process of appropriation is the same in kind for everyone, though different in degree. When people are divided by the machinery of society, the differences may be reduced by emphasizing the "natural" affinities between one man and another. Thus Dickens treats divisions as artificial, affinities as fundamental. In a full account of the matter it would be instructive to refer to two major works which throw strong if indirect light upon the politics of Dickens's fiction: Susanne K. Langer's *Mind: An Essay on Human Feeling* (Baltimore, 1967) and Otto Gierke's *Natural Law and the Theory of Society, 1500–1800* (Boston, 1957).

3. The lame demon is Asmodeus in Le Sage's *Le Diable Boiteux,* translated as *Asmodeus, or The Devil upon Two Sticks.* In Chapter 3 and thereafter Asmodeus, for Signor Leandro's edification and enlightenment, lifts the housetops and reveals the inhabitants, the springs of their actions, and their secret thoughts (I am indebted to Harry Stone for this ascription; see his *Charles Dickens' Uncollected Writings from "Household Words": 1850–1859,* 2 vols. [Bloomington, 1968], II, 488, n. 11).

4. *The Nation,* I (December 21, 1865), 787 (unsigned review).

From Ada Nisbet and Blake Nevius (eds.), *Dickens Centennial Essays* (Berkeley: University of California Press, 1971).

ARNOLD AS CRITIC

In 1970 Park Honan decided "to write a definitive biography—or as Painter said he attempted for Proust, a book close, full, and scholarly, accurate in every detail—for the Arnold specialist and general reader alike." I respect the ambition, though I wish it were not so boldly declared. It is not clear that the general reader has felt the need of such a thing. He may have been content with any of several books already available to him, books which have studied, in one spirit or another, the bearing of Arnold's private and public life upon his published work. Lionel Trilling's *Matthew Arnold* (1939) was "a biography of Arnold's mind," but it used the biographical materials open to Trilling at the time. A general reader would be hard to please if he could not find what he wanted in Trilling's book or in later books by E. K. Chambers (1947), Louis Bonnerot (1947), Douglas Bush (1971), and A. L. Rowse (1976).

But if we suppose that the general reader is indeed hard to please, and that he can be pleased only by being brought into contact with many more published and unpublished documents than were available to previous biographers, Professor Honan's address to such a person becomes reasonable and timely. A good deal of new material has come to hand in the past few years, mostly correspondence, diaries kept by the Arnolds and the Cloughs, letters from Thomas Arnold the Younger. There is also the material assembled in Miriam Allott's edition of Arnold's poems (1979) and in the eleven volumes of R. H. Super's edition of Arnold's prose (1960–77). So it is easy, after all, to justify a full-scale biography of Arnold. Professor Honan's book is not, in fact, as large as Painter's *Proust,* Ellmann's *Joyce,* or Edel's *James.* Large enough for any general reader I can imagine, it may not be large enough for all the needs a scholar will ask it to serve.

The broad outline of Arnold's life, except for one episode which Honan claims to elucidate, is already fairly well established. The young Arnold is seen mostly in relation to his father, Dr. Arnold of Rugby, and his equally vivid mother. But Honan has documented these relations far more fully than his predecessors: he has brought forward Arnold's mother, especially, and shown the quality of her presence and force. He has also given more detail on Arnold's schooling, his years at Oxford, and the verve with which he concealed his insecurity by playing the fop, the exquisite, the young man-about-town. Arnold's marriage to Frances Wightman is charmingly narrated, especially the months in which Frances's father forbade the girl to marry Arnold, and the man-about-town decided that it was time to be serious, get a respectable job, and give up playing the fool. But the most powerful chapter deals with the appalling trip Arnold and Frances made to the Grande Chartreuse at Isère in September 1851, three months after the wedding.

The value of these chapters consists mainly in the detail, the variety of reference and commentary. But the chapter in which Honan claims to have established something new concerns the "Marguerite" of Arnold's love poems. The standard account says that Marguerite was a French girl whom Arnold met at Thun in September 1848 and again in September 1849: little is known of her, apart from a few descriptive phrases in the poems and a couple of references in Arnold's letters to Clough which do not run to the extremity of supplying a name. Arnold told Clough that he planned to "linger one day at the Hotel Bellevue for the sake of the blue eyes of one of its inmates." Professor Honan argues that the blue eyes were Mary Claude's, and he thinks the identification "beyond any doubt." His main evidence is a letter from Arnold's brother Tom. On November 25, 1848, Mary Arnold wrote to Tom, who was then in New Zealand. Her letter has not survived, but Tom's letter of June 14, 1849, to his mother refers to Mary's and says that her "account of Matt's romantic passion for the Cruel Invisible, Mary Claude, amused me beyond every-thing." Mary Claude had already been in the Arnold-Clough set since 1845, when she met Anne Jemima Clough and became her best friend. Arnold had known her brother Louis for several years before 1847, when Mary became a familiar and frequent presence at Fox How. She was remarkably beautiful, pale, intense, an enthusiast, all for passion, espe-cially the passion of meditation. She is often mentioned in Anne Clough's diary and in letters between Hartley Coleridge and the Claude family.

Mary Claude is certainly a feasible candidate. There is no doubt that Arnold was for a time powerfully attracted to her. But there are difficul-ties in the identification. Mary did not, in fact, reach Thun in September 1848: her holiday was cut short. She may have made a date with Arnold to meet him in Thun, but she did not arrive. Nor was she there the fol-lowing September. I find it implausible that Arnold would have referred to her in such a coy phrase, in the letter to Clough, since she was already an intimate of the Clough family. If "Marguerite" were Mary Claude, I don't think Arnold would have written, even as late as 1887, his wife being still alive, an Introduction to Mary's *Twilight Thoughts* in the tone of these sentences:

> The breath of Westmoreland blows through [these stories]. They carry me back to the past days, when Westmoreland was the Westmoreland of Wordsworth and Hartley Coleridge . . . when the authoress of these stories moved in her youth and spirit and grace through that region, herself a vision worthy of it.

In 1969 Kenneth Allott reviewed the relation between Arnold and Mary Claude, on the basis of Tom Arnold's letter (which had been published in *New Zealand Letters of Thomas Arnold the Younger,* edited by James Bertram), Hartley Coleridge's letters, and the *Memoir of Anne Jemima Clough.* He concluded that Mary was "very unlike the French girl Marguerite with whom Arnold flirted at Thun in September 1848."

Park Honan has done well to bring Mary Claude so vigorously into the story of Arnold's life. I am not persuaded that she and "Marguerite" are one and the same pair of blue eyes. No matter. Mary is an important character in the play of feeling in Arnold's life in the few years before he met Frances Wightman. Biographies which don't mention her—A. L. Rowse's, for instance—are in that respect defective. She is especially important because she had some influence, difficult as it is to estimate, in turning Arnold towards Senancour, Richter, Chateaubriand, and Foscolo in his search for an aesthetic of inwardness, a life consecrated to the truth of feeling.

After Mary Claude, there are no surprises or proposals for surprise. The rest of Professor Honan's story is a more detailed version of the standard account. But it presents problems for the reader. It is my impression that he has composed his book mainly from an adversary relation to Trilling's, the only book to which he refers with asperity. "Trilling's factual errors," he says, "are less important than his remorseless politicizing of Arnold's thought, and his failure to see that Arnold came to Spinoza after very carefully reading Berkeley and Epictetus." I am not sure that the two parts of that sentence go well together, or that "remorseless" properly comes into the debate. It is true that Trilling, to a greater extent than Professor Honan, concentrates on the public issues, and keeps in mind the fact that a self is created and defined not in a vacuum but in a particular society and at a particular moment. Trilling gives more consideration to the Tractarians, the dispute between Dr. Arnold and Newman, Arnold's *England and the Italian Question,* and such matters. He gives six cogent pages to the dispute between Arnold and Bishop Colenso on the interpretation of the Pentateuch, an episode Honan disposes of in six lines. One of the great merits of Trilling's book is that it makes clear at every point why the proportions between one issue and the next are those and not other, so it enables the reader to follow the argument not passively but deliberately. It is much more difficult to maintain such an experience with Honan's study. The book is insufficiently lighted; or rather, all the lights are of the same wattage, so it is difficult to see where the emphasis is meant to fall or which of the many relations in the case are deemed uppermost. It would be inaccurate to describe the book as a psychological study, but Professor Honan, dealing with Arnold's feelings, allows the reader to think that the relation between inner and outer events or between self and world was, in Arnold's case, merely casual.

Two emphases are, however, clear enough, so clear that I wish they were more richly accompanied: Arnold as family man, and Arnold as a good European. Honan's account of Arnold's family life is splendid, full of significant detail and circumstance. Arnold was unostentatiously wonderful with his wife and children. The Arnolds had six children, three of whom they saw die; Basil in his second year, Thomas in his seventeenth, Trevenen in his nineteenth. Professor Honan's account of the Arnolds in those years of dyings and deaths is heartbreaking. His account of Arnold the European goes far beyond the common notion that Arnold beat the English bourgeoisie about the head with France and Germany. What Arnold said about provincialism is fully justified not only by its local force but by Honan's description of Arnold's diverse relations to his masters: an incomplete list includes Epictetus, Marcus Aurelius, Milton, Spinoza, Herder, Burke, Goethe, Wordsworth, Heine, Carlyle, Newman, Renan, and Sainte-Beuve. On these and other relations Honan is helpful, but there is often something missing, a final touch which would show precisely rather than vaguely what the particular relation amounted to. Let me give an example.

Like Trilling, Honan has much to say of Spinoza. Trilling emphasizes Spinoza's distinction between morality and speculative doctrine, a distinction as important to Arnold as to Coleridge. Morality is a product of the imagination, speculative doctrine is a product of the intellect. The distinction enabled Arnold to assert "the alliance between imagination and conduct" in *God and the Bible,* and to retain his hold upon intuition, faith, and the figurative character of language. Honan is more interested in the epistemological question: he maintains that Spinoza underwrites Arnold's philosophy of nature in his poems. "In our own time of advanced nuclear physics," he says, "Arnold's lyrics show a convincing respect for the complex independence of matter"; a judgement my ignorance of advanced nuclear physics does not permit me to question. But I can say with some confidence that the quotations from Arnold's poems which Honan offers in support of the judgement could more cogently be taken as ascribing purely human conditions and responses to the natural scene.

Honan's account of the relation between Arnold and Spinoza is in any case insufficiently pointed. Of the Spinoza who mattered to Arnold, there is a far more suggestive description in Kenneth Burke's *A Grammar of Motives* (1945), where the *Ethics* is read as "a noble philosophic accountancy whereby, through the cultivation of 'adequate ideas,' one could transform the passives (of human bondage) into the actives (of human freedom)." Arnold suppressed "Empedocles on Etna" because it failed to effect this transformation. The gesture by which passion is transformed into action or reinterpreted as action seems to me Arnold's most telling concern: how to construe suffering as an act of endurance, how to interpret necessity as freedom. The classic statement is in "Spinoza and the Bible," where Arnold says that "he who truly conceives the universal divine law conceives God's decrees adequately as eternal truths, and for him moral action has liberty and self-knowledge." The classic instance of such a transformation is Goethe in his relation to Spinoza, according to Arnold's version of it:

> Spinoza first impresses Goethe and any man like Goethe, and then he composes him; first he fills and satisfies his imagination by the width and grandeur of his view of nature, and then he fortifies and stills his mobile, straining, passionate, poetic temperament by the moral lesson he draws from his view of nature. And a moral lesson not of mere resigned acquiescence, not of melancholy quietism, but of joyful activity within the limits of man's true sphere.

The passage is clearly related to Arnold's search for the "joy whose grounds are true" in "Obermann Once More"; true as in true to life, true to nature, true to human feeling. In Arnold's definition of religion as morality touched by emotion, the first term points to constraint, law, or obligation, and the second lifts the phrase into freedom, as in the freedom of feeling and imagination.

The secular form of this freedom, so far as Arnold's social criticism represents it, is the willing accessibility of society to ideas. Professor Honan quotes Arnold so often on the power of ideas that he may consider a further explanation unnecessary; but I think he errs. It is not clear what Arnold meant by an idea. Did he mean an object of thought, or of imagination, or of perception, a notion, a concept, or what? In "Spinoza and the Bible" he distinguishes between a revelation received by the prophets through the imagination and anything that might be achieved as a mental process; a distinction used immediately to say that "only an idea can carry the sense of its own certainty along with it, not an imagination." In other places he uses the word in a more rudimentary sense. But if we take it that he means by an idea the form of certitude in which a particular mental process is completed, it is the secular version of a moral lesson. In *Culture and Anarchy, Friendship's Garland,* and *Essays in Criticism,* ideas are crucial because they are the only instruments of social redemption. A society in which ideas are not found alive and vivid is doomed.

If we retain the "philosophic accountancy" from Spinoza, we see that ideas, to Arnold, are the forms in which a society exercises its freedom, transforming human bondage into human liberty. More specifically: faced with the chaos of facts, modern man can deal with it or make his peace with it only by comprehending it, finding a principle of order and certitude in what is otherwise an appalling miscellany. We are delivered from chaos, as from anarchy, by comprehending its occult law: ideas are the vehicles of comprehension. "Deliverance" is Arnold's word in "On the Modern Element in Literature." The demand for deliverance arises, he says, "because the present age exhibits to the individual man who contemplates it the spectacle of a vast multitude of facts awaiting and inviting his comprehension." Deliverance begins "when our mind begins to enter into possession of the general ideas which are the law of this vast multitude of facts." And it is perfect "when we have acquired that harmonious acquiescence of mind which we feel in contemplating a grand spectacle that is intelligible to us."

Arnold's programme seems innocent, and perhaps noble. But it contains, I believe, an impurity of motive. In a benign light you could say that ideas are the certainties by which the chaos of facts is rendered intelligible. But in a sharper light you would say that Arnold wanted ideas to deliver him from the bewilderment and the insecurity of experience. He wanted not experience but release from it into a world characterized by the free play and currency of ideas. In Arnold himself the currency of ideas often takes the form of premature generalizations about France, Italy, Germany, Ireland, England, America, the three social classes, culture, democracy, and so forth.

The notion of ideas as a substitute for experience, or as an easier form of experience, explains, I believe, what Eliot had in view in a famous paragraph on Henry James. I cannot read the paragraph without thinking that he had in mind a contrast between James and Arnold:

James's critical genius comes out most tellingly in his mastery over, his baffling escape from, Ideas; a mastery and an escape which are perhaps the last test of a superior intelligence. He had a mind so fine that no idea could violate it. Englishmen, with their uncritical admiration (in the present age) for France, like to refer to France as the Home of Ideas ... England, on the other hand, if it is not the Home of Ideas, has at least become infested with them in about the space of time within which Australia has been overrun by rabbits. In

England ideas run wild and pasture on the emotions; instead of thinking with our feelings (a very different thing) we corrupt our feelings with ideas; we produce the political, the emotional idea, evading sensation and thought.

If we put beside this passage Henry Adams's remark in the *Education* that "the mind resorts to reason for want of training," we see that the question of ideas in Arnold is one with which a biographer who offers his work as definitive should have engaged.

Park Honan's claims for Arnold's poetry are notably high. *The Strayed Reveller*, he says, "seems a great thing—and a valuable rarity today—because for sheer lyrical beauty it is the best first collection of lyrics by an Englishman from Arnold's time to ours." That doesn't necessarily make it a great thing. Quoting the stanzas about Tiresias and the Centaurs, Honan remarks: "One may say that in our own century in English poetry only T. S. Eliot has equaled its intensity." "Empedocles on Etna" "is perhaps, as critics have said, the finest work of its length in Victorian literature." But Honan does not examine the poems, or look closely at their ways with language: he does not consider it a major disability, apparently, that they are so limited to one tone, that of "the sad probation," gloom, dismay, estrangement, "the burden of ourselves," and "immedicable pain"; that they are so demonstrably a function of low spirits. James's sense of them is better judged than Honan's. James says of the poetry:

> With its cultivated simplicity, its aversion to cheap ornament, its slight abuse of meagreness for distinction's sake, his verse has a kind of minor magic and always goes to the point—the particular ache, or regret, or conjecture, to which poetry is supposed to address itself.

Honan's reasons for praising Arnold's criticism are, as one would expect, more cogent. But he drives good reasons beyond the reach of debate. He enjoys, as everyone does, Arnold's vivacities of expression, enjoys them so much that he rarely pauses to consider whether they amount to an exorbitance. Arnold's rhetorical power, like F. R. Leavis's, was extraordinary. Like Leavis, too, he won many disputes not because he served the better cause but because he had more street knowledge than his opponent, and a determination to win at any price. I have never been persuaded by *On*

Translating Homer that Francis Newman's sense of Homer was inferior to Arnold's, but it hardly matters: what one recalls from the book is Arnold's swashbuckling prose, leaping about like Douglas Fairbanks.

Honan's comments on *On Translating Homer* are judicious: for once, he is not inclined to use superlatives. But a few pages later he says that Arnold's best essays "are emotionally as taut as scenes in Shakespeare; the emotive attitude to the idea, in Arnold, enriches the idea, so that we feel he is driving at the heart of human life." The tone of this avowal seems grandiose; something more discriminating is needed. The problem is that Professor Honan does not always ask himself the right questions, or allow other voices into his book to ask them. Eliot said of Arnold: "He had no real serenity, only an impeccable demeanour." Shouldn't a biographer consider whether this is true or not?

Honan's general sense of Arnold's critical achievement is appropriately vigorous. "An understanding of him," he says, "is really more useful to us than an understanding of any other Englishman of the last century." Not the only begetter of modern criticism, Arnold is the critic who, more than anyone else, shows what, in the way of energy and vigilance, a serious criticism entails. If we isolate a particular kind of criticism, we can easily find another critic who practises it more convincingly than Arnold does. Arnold's greatness consists in his making available, more completely than anyone else, the role of "the general critic," the man who directs the force of his intelligence upon the common life and its manifestations. The general critic thinks his own business hardly worth minding except so far as it coincides with everyone's business. If he is a literary critic, it is because the formal complexity of literature protects him from the naïveté of thinking that he has understood the common life when he has merely registered its most vociferous forms.

Arnold's achievement as a great general critic may be acknowledged, all due qualifications having been made, by assenting to the entirely proper claim he made in a famous passage in the first chapter of *Culture and Anarchy:*

> We have not won our political battles, we have not carried our main points, we have not stopped our adversaries' advance, we have not marched victoriously with the modern world; but we have told silently upon the mind of the country, we have prepared currents of

feeling which sap our adversaries' position when it seems gained, we have kept up our own communications with the future.

The style is deservedly high. It hardly matters that little of our thinking about literature and society is conducted, in fact, under the auspices of Arnold's reiterated phrases: sweetness and light; the study of perfection; Barbarians, Philistines, and Populace; Hellenism and Hebraism; the grand style; disinterestedness; the provincial spirit; to see the object as in itself it really is; poetry is at bottom a criticism of life. The phrases have not retained their power to compel. But Arnold is still compelling because of the force with which he kept up his communications with the future. It is chiefly because of Arnold that literary criticism has not become, to its impoverishment, entirely literary; that a general criticism is still practised by critics who nevertheless have a particular commitment to literature. I am thinking of such books as Leavis's *Education and the University,* Trilling's *The Liberal Imagination,* Kenneth Burke's *Attitudes Towards History,* and Nicola Chiaromonte's *The Worm of Consciousness.*

Review of *Matthew Arnold: A Life,* by Park Honan. From *The Times Literary Supplement,* August 28, 1981.

PATER'S RENAISSANCE

In 1965 René Wellek remarked that "today Pater is under a cloud; he is no longer widely read, and he is dismissed as an 'impressionistic' critic." The cloud has lifted. Most of Pater's books are still out of print, it is nearly impossible to find a set of the standard edition of his works, the Library Edition in ten volumes first issued in 1910; he is not yet widely read. But he is more vividly present today than at any time in the past fifty years.

Walter Horatio Pater (1839–94) was a Fellow of Brasenose College, Oxford, when he published his first book, *Studies in the History of the Renaissance* (1873). The book consisted of a Preface, a Conclusion, and eight chapters on Pico della Mirandola, Botticelli, Luca della Robbia, the poetry of Michelangelo, Leonardo da Vinci, Joachim du Bellay, Winckelmann, and two early French stories. Several chapters had already been published as essays. Part of the Conclusion had appeared as a review of William Morris's poetry, without stirring much interest. But when these disparate materials were brought together to make *Studies in the History of the Renaissance,* they caused a fuss.

Not the chapters, but mainly the Preface and the Conclusion, where Pater was understood as offering in high-minded sentences a blatant invitation to hedonism, if not to something unnamably worse. "Art for art's sake first of all," a phrase from Swinburne's *William Blake* (1868), was not scandalous in itself, but something in Pater's tone seemed to propose a particular temptation to the young men an Oxford bachelor don might be supposed to address. His style corresponded to an extremely pronounced self-consciousness, consistent with a man whose rooms at Brasenose had none of the usual Victorian clutter but, as a student remembered, "were panelled in a pale green tint, the floor was matted ... and a dwarf orange tree, with real oranges on it, adorned the table." Pater's book ended with these sentences:

> We have an interval, and then we cease to be. Some spend this interval in listlessness, some in high passions, the wisest in art and song. For our one chance is in expanding that interval, in getting as many pulsations as possible into the given time. High passions give one this quickened sense of life, ecstasy and sorrow of love, political or religious enthusiasm, or the "enthusiasm of humanity." Only be sure it is passion—that it does yield you this fruit of a quickened, multiplied consciousness. Of this wisdom, the poetic passion, the desire of beauty, the love of art for art's sake, has most; for art comes to you professing frankly to give nothing but the highest quality to your moments as they pass, and simply for those moments' sake.

The book was widely reviewed and, on the whole, much praised, though few understood that Pater's criticism aimed to reveal the continuity between a temperament and its manifestations; to go back from the manifestations, a painting, a sculpture, a phrase or two in poetry, to the temperament they at once reveal and conceal. Pater was interested in Botticelli, Michelangelo, and Leonardo as types or emblems of human feeling rather than as individuals. He was even more interested in the impingement of these types upon his own structure of feeling, in the quality of gesture and sentiment he associated with each or, to a high degree, projected upon each. Some reviewers felt that Pater had foisted his exquisite anxieties upon Renaissance artists who would not have recognized themselves in his account of them, but the book was acknowledged as formidable, perceptive, and handsomely written.

Within a few months readers who had forgotten the several chapters remembered the Conclusion. George Eliot thought the book "quite

poisonous in its false principles of criticism and false conceptions of life."
W. J. Courthope said that it was not criticism but "pure romance," not
fine but an exhibition of Pater's finery. The Bishop of Oxford quoted
part of the Conclusion in a sermon and warned undergraduates against
such scepticism. John Wordsworth, a colleague of Pater's at Brasenose, protested that the philosophy of the Conclusion was "an assertion that no fixed
principles either of religion or morality can be regarded as certain, that the
only thing worth living for is momentary enjoyment and that probably or
certainly the soul dissolves at death into elements that are destined never
to reunite." He called upon Pater to give up examining students in divinity.
W. H. Mallock in *The New Republic: or Culture, Faith, and Philosophy in
an English Country House* (1876) parodied Pater as Mr. Rose, who speaks
in an undertone and has only two topics, self-indulgence and art:

> I rather look upon life as a chamber, which we decorate as we would
> decorate the chamber of the woman or the youth that we love,
> tinting the walls of it with symphonies of subdued color. . . . We
> have learned the weariness of creeds; and know that for us the grave
> has no secrets.

It was clear in 1873 that Pater's *Renaissance* disavowed, in its elegant
fashion, such socially minded critics as Arnold and Ruskin. In many
important respects Pater was indebted to both men, but his advocacy of
"aesthetic criticism," and his cultivation of the values hovering about
such words as impression, sensation, beauty, pleasure, and consciousness
were incompatible with the social emphasis paramount, however differently worded, in his elders. It is now clearer than ever, from the evidence
gathered in Donald Hill's superlative edition of the 1893 text, that Pater's
affiliations are mainly with Hegel, Shelley, Gautier, Baudelaire, and
Swinburne. Many of his themes are common to Arnold, Ruskin, and
Newman, but his sense of them draws subversive force from sources
mainly German and French. Like Arnold, he thought English culture at
best incomplete, at worst crude, an uncomely choice among satisfactions.
But he went much further than Arnold in resorting to the more daringly
exotic thoughts and sensations he found in Greek, French, and German
sources. Arnold was restrained by what he construed as native good
sense. Pater, never insistently English, was stimulated by a whiff of

European corruption. It is the subversive Pater who appealed so strongly to Wilde, Yeats, Beardsley, Lionel Johnson, Arthur Symons, Dowson, and other writers of Yeats's "Tragic Generation."

The crucial term is consciousness. The desperate quality in the cult of consciousness in Pater and other late-nineteenth-century writers is explained not only by Romanticism and the attempt to hold some personal force secure from the aggression of science and technology but by the sense that freedom of action, in any public form, was illusory. The only remaining field of action was within the psyche; consciousness was its sign and mode. If you add, in Pater, an acute sense of mortality, of death as the mother of beauty, and of beauty as the fulfilment of desire, you have some indication of the desperateness with which consciousness is cultivated.

Pater was taken aback by the reception of his *Renaissance.* Accepting Emilia Pattison's criticism that the several chapters "are not history, nor are they even to be relied on for accurate statement," he changed the title, when the second edition was published in 1877, to *The Renaissance: Studies in Art and Poetry.* More important, he suppressed the offensive Conclusion lest "it might possibly mislead some of those young men into whose hands it might fall." He also toned down some phrases hostile to religious belief or too emphatic in their subjectivity. Pater's later writings were more prudent, but they did not recant or withdraw the hedonism he took greater care to define. In *Marius the Epicurean* (1885) he repeated the gist of the Conclusion to *The Renaissance,* mostly in the chapter called "New Cyrenaicism."

In any case, Pater was safer with *Marius,* a work of fiction, than with *The Renaissance,* which purported to deal with matters of fact and therefore revealed immediately Pater's own interventions. *Marius* is a novel of ideas, in the sense that it replaces fictional characters by ideas, and offers as events chiefly transitions from one sentiment to another.

Marius, like Pater, considers religion and philosophy as fine arts, and values the first for its ritual, the second for its charm. But his Cyrenaicism or Epicureanism is not a definitive creed but a moment of transition. The book tries to reconcile the apparent hedonism of *The Renaissance* with Christianity, "the old morality," by showing it as "an exaggeration of one special motive" in that morality. Marius's chief quality is the mobility of his feelings, as if perfection meant the capacity of frequent change. "Be perfect in regard to what is here and now" was suited to one moment, later becoming another for which the motto was "not pleasure, but fulness of life, and insight as conducting to that fulness." Perfection was Unity of Being, in Yeats's Paterian phrase for it, a state in which body is not bruised to pleasure soul. In an essay on D. G. Rossetti, published in 1883, Pater praised the poet for knowing "no region of spirit which shall not be sensuous also, or material."

By 1888, when the third edition of *The Renaissance* was published, Pater had decided that he had done enough to clarify what the Conclusion to the first edition meant, and to defend himself against misinterpretation. So he restored it, with minor changes, and it was accepted without much comment. In the same year he wrote an essay, "Style," invoking the criterion of truth along with that of beauty, and pointing to Flaubert for success in both. It is easy to say that he became prudent in later years and took precautions against offending anyone. He would claim that what he had always proposed was not pleasure but perfection, the highest possible organization of one's faculties; unity of feeling in the person and—though he had less to say of this—unity of culture in the society. Reviewing the second version of Wilde's *The Picture of Dorian Gray* in 1891, he distinguished Wilde's allegedly false Epicureanism from his own true Epicureanism, which "aims at a complete though harmonious development of man's entire organism." And he had the cheek to rebuke Wilde for ignoring the moral issue, although it was Pater who showed Wilde, in the first *Renaissance,* how it could be transcended or subsumed in an aesthetic state. The review scolds Wilde:

> To lose the moral sense therefore, for instance, the sense of sin and righteousness, as Mr. Wilde's heroes are bent on doing so speedily, as completely as they can, is to lose, or lower, organization, to become less complex, to pass from a higher to a lower degree of development.

Perfection as an available state of being is also invoked in Pater's last and finest book, *Plato and Platonism* (1893), especially in the chapter on the doctrine of number, where he insists that "the essence, the active principle of the Pythagorean doctrine, resides, not as with the ancient Eleatics, nor as with our modern selves too often, in the 'infinite,' those eternities, infinitudes, abysses, Carlyle invokes for us so often—in no cultus of the infinite, but in the finite."

Pater died in Oxford on July 28, 1894. Of his life, one might say, as he said of Leonardo's years at Florence, that his history is the history of his art, "he is lost in the bright cloud of it." He had lived mostly in his rooms at Brasenose. In 1869 he took a house in Bradmore Road, Oxford, and lived there with his sisters Hester and Clara. Vacations he spent mainly in France and Italy. In 1885 the Paters moved to a modest house in London, and he took up a mild social life. But in 1893 he went back to Oxford, as if to fulfil the logic of his life by dying there.

A few months after his death, Henry James said that Pater had had "the most exquisite literary fortune: to have taken it all out, wholly, exclusively, with the pen (the style, the genius) and absolutely not at all with the person." He is, James said, "the mask without the face, and there isn't in his total superficies a tiny point of vantage for the newspaper to flap his wings on." Perhaps not; and certainly not, by dramatic contrast with Ruskin, Wilde, Swinburne, and nearly everyone else. James thought of Pater as having one form of success, that of the artist in triumph, of whom we see only "the back he turns to us as he bends over his work." The phrase comes from James's preface to *The Tragic Muse* (1889), a novel about such artists, wonderfully lost in their work, though the particular example of Pater comes into it only when we bring it in.

After Pater's death, his styles and procedures, invited or not, went into the work of other writers; not only Yeats ("that extravagant style he had learnt from Pater") but Proust, Pound, Joyce's "epiphanies," Eliot, Forster, Stevens, and Virginia Woolf.[1] His books were regularly reprinted until about 1925, when the wind started turning against him. Eliot was influentially hostile, especially in the essay "Arnold and Pater" (1930), where he asserted that Pater had merely extended the secularizing damage Arnold had already done. Public taste, in any case, was moving away from Pater. In an England where, according to Auden, nobody was well, the illness seemed to call for social and political treatment, not for aesthetic refinement.

Why, then, has Pater emerged? Why for more than a few critics does he seem central rather than marginal to the definition of modernism, cousin to Mallarmé rather than to Arnold?

Some reasons are obvious. He is now seen as a crucial figure in the reconsideration of Romanticism which has been going on for the past ten or fifteen years; especially in its bearing upon the question of self and consciousness. But the question is obscure. Some critics have turned against the notion of consciousness because it seems to claim a high degree of spontaneity and originality: they want to see the Jamesian figure of the artist as hero eclipsed by the notion of the text—and not the personal and social experience with which the text is concerned—as the principal reality to be solicited. Pater gives them comfort in the Conclusion to *The Renaissance*:

> Analysis goes a step further still, and assures us that those impressions of the individual mind to which, for each one of us, experience dwindles down, are in perpetual flight; that each of them is limited by time, and that as time is infinitely divisible, each of them is infinitely divisible also; all that is actual in it being a single moment, gone while we try to apprehend it, of which it may ever be more truly said that it has ceased to be than that it is.

So the freedom of consciousness is even more desperate, because more spasmodic, than we have allowed. The notion of self as known only by the momentary appearances and disappearances of every evidence in its favour is congenial to some critics; though it is hard to square with the fact that Pater forces every object of attention into complicity with his highly distinctive style. Objects assume his mystery. What Byron said of Keats applies with better reason to Pater: "not indecent, but constantly soliciting his own ideas into a state." Yet it is Pater who speaks of "that strange, perpetual, weaving and unweaving of ourselves," a phrase dear to many critics who write of him.

Another reason for Pater's emergence is that his writing, blurring the supposed distinction between criticism and creation, encourages those critics (Geoffrey Hartman, Harold Bloom, Ihab Hassan, and others) who want to practise criticism as a fine art.

But the most telling reason is that Pater's understanding of language anticipated many of the axioms current again today. A passage from *The Renaissance* ascribes to language whatever impression of solidity is attached to objects: "of objects in the solidity with which language invests them." And there is a passage in *Plato and Platonism* which is virtually an anthology of currently received ideas:

> For in truth we come into the world, each one of us, "not in nakedness," but by the natural course of organic development clothed

far more completely than even Pythagoras supposed in a vesture of the past, nay, fatally shrouded, it might seem, in those laws or tricks of heredity which we mistake for our volitions; in the language which is more than one half of our thoughts; in the moral and mental habits, the customs, the literature, the very houses, which we did not make for ourselves; in the vesture of a past, which is (so science would assure us) not ours, but of the race, the species: that *Zeit-geist,* or abstract secular process, in which, as we could have had no direct consciousness of it, so we can pretend to no future personal interest.

Pater's dash from "clothes" to "vesture" to "shroud" should be questioned, but the passage is bound to please those critics who regard as delusion every claim to spontaneity or creativity.

Gerald Monsman is such a critic. Or rather, he has become one during the years in which he has written three books on Pater. His first, *Pater's Portraits* (1967), was concerned with a conflict in Pater's fiction between two principles: Dionysian and Apollonian, to use Nietzschean terms which Pater does not use. Monsman argues that he sought a dynamic relation between them rather than a war in which one of them would win. My own view is that what he sought was a term or a style capable of accommodating both. Monsman's second book, *Walter Pater* (1977), had a fairly innocent readership in view, and held to the immediate requirement of elucidation.

The new book has three tasks in hand. First: it seeks to show that Pater's entire work is disguised autobiography, the main disguise being the "imaginary portrait," part factual, part fictive. Second: it interprets Pater's works in psychoanalytical terms. Pater's father died when the boy was two and a half years old, his mother when he was four and a half. If you add to these misfortunes an elder brother, William, rival for his mother's affection, you have the makings of a story of guilt and expiation. Third: the book attempts to transpose the study of Pater's work into a discourse congenial to contemporary criticism.

Monsman's first book is still his most useful. It is far clearer than his second or third on Pater's desire to reconcile paganism and Christianity by providing a sentiment capable of holding them together or suffusing them with a glow of feeling in which their sharp edges are smoothed. Mostly, what emerges from the new book is a sense of some inner psychic drama working itself out in Pater's writings. I am not persuaded by Monsman's argument, mainly because it is heavily reductive.

That something odd is going on in Pater's work is clear enough, but I have never seen it explained. He often writes as if he had something at once to hide and to reveal, some crime or sin not quite committed, the guilt of which he needs to prolong by the expression of it. Eliot accused him of confusing life with art, but the charge may itself be confused, since art is part of life or a quality of life. Eliot was scandalized by anyone who practised life as a fine art or proposed to replace moral criteria by aesthetic criteria.

But it is hard to blame Pater for the "untidy lives" lived by Wilde, Dowson, Symons, and Johnson. They did not need his encouragement to see themselves as tragic heroes, fallen into dissipation and despair. It is not true that they practised what Pater preached. If they translated his style into a way of life, the translation was premature and inaccurate. Yeats, after all, was one of Pater's disciples, but he did not translate his style or his rhetoric directly into daily life.

Monsman's way of dealing with the issue is evasive. He wants to associate Pater's entire work with "those ultra-reflexive writers whose fictional worlds invariably lead back to the generative activity of art itself: Borges, Beckett, Robbe-Grillet, Leiris, Nabokov, Fowles, Barth, Barthelme, to name several." It is to name too many. If Pater is to be added to that list, we might as well forget him: no writer has come unscathed from such an association. It is far more to the point to see Pater where he mainly saw himself, in relation not only to Hegel, Goethe, Wordsworth, and Coleridge but to the wilder manifestations of Romanticism in its English, French, and German forms. The unity he sought was not available to him in any world his observation could confirm. His dream of a better world than the real one is what we mostly sense in his style, but it is still a problem and a worry what the constituents of that better world might be, and what would happen to our own constituents, were Pater's to prevail.

NOTE

1. Perry Meisel's *The Absent Father: Virginia Woolf and Walter Pater* (Yale, 1980) is an essay in the "anxiety of influence": it argues that Pater was Virginia Woolf's chief precursor, and that her work embodies her struggle to over-

come his authority. Meisel has convincingly established Pater's influence on Woolf, but I am not persuaded that it was, to the extent he maintains, a source of great creative anxiety.

Review of *The Renaissance: Studies in Art and Poetry* (*The 1893 Text*), by Walter Pater, edited by Donald L. Hill, and *Walter Pater's Art of Autobiography*, by Gerald Monsman. From *The New York Review of Books,* May 14, 1981.

HOPKINS

T his is not," Paddy Kitchen says, "an official or definitive biography of Gerard Manley Hopkins." It is a book for the general reader, an affectionate, spontaneous account of an extraordinary man. Hopkins is Ms. Kitchen's favourite poet, and the book is written in that spirit.

G.M.H. was born on July 28, 1844, to comfortably middle-class parents, professional people with a High Anglican tone. He went to a decent boarding school, did well, won a prize for poetry, and took the predictable road to Oxford, arriving in 1863. On October 21, 1866, he became a Roman Catholic. On May 11, 1868, he decided to become a Jesuit priest, and on the same day he burned his poems, as if to subdue one flame by another. For the next seven years he wrote no poems. On December 7, 1875, a ship, the *Deutschland,* was wrecked in the Thames, and five Franciscan nuns, exiled from Germany, were drowned. "I was affected by the account," Hopkins told his friend Canon Dixon, "and happening to say so to my Rector he said that he wished someone would write a poem on the subject." Hopkins set to work, and wrote "The Wreck of the Deutschland," the first of the major poems on which his reputation is based. He was ordained on September 23, 1877, and thereafter spent most of his time teaching. In 1884 he went to Dublin as professor of classics at University College. He died on June 8, 1889.

No collection of Hopkins's poems was published in his lifetime. A few early poems were published in anthologies, but nothing of any account appeared until 1916, when his friend Robert Bridges included some pages of Hopkins in an anthology, *The Spirit of Man*. In 1918 Bridges issued the first selection of Hopkins's poems in an edition of 750 copies, which took ten years to sell. Gradually, the poems began to attract the few readers who could cope with them. I. A. Richards wrote about them in *The Dial* in 1926. In December 1927 Yvor Winters read some of them to Hart Crane, who was astonished by their brilliance. Middleton Murry was an early reader. So was William Empson, guided to the poems by Richards.

In 1930 the second edition of the poems appeared, edited by Charles Williams, who added several poems to Bridges's selection. F. R. Leavis devoted a chapter to Hopkins in *New Bearings in English Poetry* (1932) and provided the context in which he is still discussed. In 1934 W. H. Auden referred to Hopkins as a major poet, a description which has remained, on the whole, intact. There have been a few dissenters. T. S. Eliot was never fully convinced of the scale of Hopkins's achievement. Winters gave up his first enthusiasm and wrote a detailed attack upon Hopkins's procedures. But his reputation is too strongly based to be undermined.

Still, Hopkins's presence in modern literature has odd features. His first readers (apart from the few friends, like Bridges, Dixon, and Coventry Patmore, who saw some poems in manuscript) read him alongside Yeats, Eliot, and Pound. If these poets seemed to constitute "Modernism" by their forms, structures, allusions, and themes, Hopkins's bizarre language put him in the same company. Readers of Leavis's *New Bearings* do not find it curious that chapters on Eliot and Pound should lead to a chapter on Hopkins, a poet who died while they were infants: he belongs to the New, just as they do. Even yet, it is hard to accept the idea that Hopkins is a Victorian and that his true fellowship is with Ruskin, Tennyson, Arnold, Newman, Meredith, Browning, Pater, and Swinburne. Or with Whitman, for reasons which Hopkins felt and acknowledged: "I always knew in my heart Walt Whitman's mind to be more like my own than any other man's living." Hopkins's modernity has been exaggerated because the common understanding of Victorian poetry has not made itself flexible enough to accommodate Whitman, Clough, Hopkins, or Emily Dickinson.

Much of the modern interpretation of Hopkins has concerned itself with the question of priest and poet: did his priesthood limit his experience, to the damage of the poems? It is hard to deal with this question crisply. Some poets, like Wallace Stevens, thrive on limitation, a little experience goes a long way with them, they could do nothing with freedom except lose themselves in it. Besides, experience is not circumstance but what we make of circumstance. If you read through Hopkins's poems and the five volumes of prose, you find it hard to believe that his sensibility was starved: even the chore of grading examination papers may not have been a dead loss.

True, he was often dispirited, he complained a lot and gave an impression of sickliness even when he was not sick, but he was also extraordinarily resilient, humorous, witty, and strong where it mattered. His letters to Bridges, Dixon, Patmore, Alexander Baillie, and other friends are wonderfully quirky, full of curious notions and hypotheses. None of these men understood him, Bridges least of all, but they provoked him to understand himself. In every way that counted he was remarkably self-possessed and on intimate terms with his genius. Like other people whose sensitivity is the kind we remark, he was naïve in his admiration of sturdy folk who live at ease with their bodies: soldiers and ploughmen, mostly. But the crucial thing is that, whatever happened to him, he made the most of it; starting with himself, his presence to himself in the world.

This sense of self was, if anything, dangerously sharp. Here are some notes he made for his retreat on August 20, 1880 (they are published in Christopher Devlin's edition of *The Sermons and Devotional Writings*):

When I consider my selfbeing, my consciousness and feeling of myself, that taste of myself, of *I* and *me* above and in all things, which is more distinctive than the taste of ale or alum, more distinctive than the smell of walnutleaf or camphor, and is incommunicable by any means to another man (as when I was a child I used to ask myself: What must it be to be someone else?) Nothing else in nature comes near this unspeakable stress of pitch, distinctiveness, and selving, this selfbeing of my own. Nothing explains it or resembles it, except so far as this, that other men to themselves have the same feeling. But this only multiplies the phenomena to be explained so far as the cases are like and do resemble. But to me there is no resemblance: searching nature I taste *self* but at one tankard, that of my own being.

If you feel yourself with such intensity, and if you become a priest, you need some principle by which the feeling is either curbed or transformed. Hopkins's early readers were on the lookout for evidence of tension between poet and priest. Empson in *Seven Types of Ambiguity* (1930) read Hopkins's "The Windhover" as a case of the seventh type, which occurs "when the two meanings of the word, the two values of the ambiguity, are the two opposite meanings defined by the context, so that the total effect is to show a fundamental division in the writer's mind." According to this reading, when Hopkins sees the bird he conceives it as the opposite of his own spiritual renunciation: he insists that renunciation is better than its opposite, but he can't really judge between them, and holds both with agony in his mind:

> *My heart in hiding*
> *Stirred for a bird—the achieve of, the mastery of the thing!*

The idea would be that in the poem Hopkins is trying to persuade himself that a life of devout renunciation is best, most beautiful, despite the opposite zest for mastery. The sestet of the sonnet—

> *Brute beauty and valour and act, oh, air, pride, plume, here*
> *Buckle! AND the fire that breaks from thee then, a billion*
> *Times told lovelier, more dangerous, O my chevalier!*

—would then be, in Empson's reading,

> a clear case of the Freudian use of opposites, where two things thought of as incompatible, but desired intensely by different systems of judgements, are spoken of simultaneously by words applying to both; both desires are thus given a transient and exhausting satisfaction, and the two systems of judgement are forced into open conflict before the reader.

A lot depends on the meaning and grammar of "Buckle," a famous point of dispute unlikely to be settled. I would think that the conflict might be resolved by coming to feel that renunciation, far from being abject, has the dangerous beauty and power ascribed to the bird. But a more fundamental recourse in Hopkins was to set up, in the poems as well as the priestly meditations, a continuous circuit of feeling, linking self, the world, and God. All the better if the circuit could be represented as speech, utterance, communication. Hopkins gave the principle of it in a note on August 7, 1882:

> God's utterance of himself in himself is God the Word, outside himself is this world. This world then is word, expression, news of God. Therefore its end, its purpose, its purport, its meaning, is God and its life or work to name and praise him.

The whispering which enables Hopkins to get from end to purpose to purport, and from word to expression to news, and from word to name to praise is the type of his poetry in general. If all goes well, a poet working in those terms could construe his entire experience in sounding terms, translating energy into communication. Kenneth Burke has pointed out that Hopkins as poet could devote himself to the world, filling his notebooks with minute observations of natural objects, because if he saw in them, or thought he saw in them, an essence derivable from God, "the more accurate his study in the empirical sense, the more devotional he could be in his conviction that these objects were signatures of the divine presence."

Hopkins could even devote himself to "that taste of myself," with impunity, since self could be regarded as a constituent of the circuit of devotion. When all goes well in praise and exaltation, the circuit holds; but when it breaks down, there is desolation. When this happens, it is like a believer's loss of faith, the self is alienated from itself because cut adrift from the circuit in which it has been transformed. Instead of the smell of walnutleaf or camphor, it becomes, in Hopkins's phrase, "Selfyeast of spirit a dull dough sours." Or it feels itself a eunuch:

> *birds build—but not I build; no, but strain,*
> *Time's eunuch, and not breed one work that wakes.*

The symptom of this state, in the poems, is fixation upon one word, battering it: in the last sonnets, the "terrible" sonnets, the words "patience," "comfortless," "tormented":

> *not live this tormented mind*
> *With this tormented mind tormenting yet.*

Lacking "the fine delight that fathers thought," Hopkins mostly lacked, in the last years, the metaphorical range of potency, productiveness, fatherhood. I recall Yeats's phrase, "honey of generation," to emphasize that the radical desire in Hopkins is generative, child-producing. Or work-producing, because in Hopkins you only need a flick of terminology to make one word become another; as self becomes soul in one context and imagination in another. Hopkins's need, as priest and poet, was to translate "different systems of judgments" into compatible terminologies.

This explains why Duns Scotus meant more than Aquinas to Hopkins. In the poem "Duns Scotus's Oxford" he writes:

> *Yet ah! this air I gather and I release*
> *He lived on; these weeds and waters, these walls are what*
> *He haunted who of all men most sways my spirits to peace.*

Hopkins valued Scotus for two main reasons. The first was that Scotus made a universal out of the recognition of particularity. Scotus's concept of "thisness," *haecceitas,* became even more engaging when expressed as Hopkins's "beholdness," *ecceitas.* He was touched by Scotus's account of intuition, *cognitio confusa,* the first act of knowledge; it was the secular version of faith. Later stages of knowledge could be pursued on the analogy of writing a poem, nudging one word into another, producing one's self under the guise of one's poem. Wasn't it Lionel Johnson who said that all God demands of us is attention? The English form of attention, from Scotus to Ruskin, encouraged Hopkins to do what he wanted to do in any case, look long and hard at objects. What you look hard at seems to look hard at you, Hopkins rightly noted, and the experience seemed to verify the zeal for communications. Scotus encouraged Hopkins to believe that in the act of attention, eye, mind, and soul were equally and spiritually engaged, it was a form of prayer.

The second reason for Scotus's presence to Hopkins was his voluntarism, he was one of the few philosophers in Christendom to speak for the Will in its relation to Knowledge. Hannah Arendt has represented his work in this way in the second volume of *The Life of the Mind.* She also points to Scotus's emphasis upon contingency, quoting his remark that "those who deny that some being is contingent should be exposed to torment until they concede that it is possible for them not to be tormented." In Hopkins, the relation between will and knowledge is extremely complex: to know something was not to be lucidly detached from it or superior to it but to be provoked by its contingency into experiencing a mutual "stress of selving." Here is a case in point, the first lines of "Spelt from Sibyl's Leaves," in which evening is represented as moving to become night:

> *Earnest, earthless, equal, attuneable, vaulty, voluminous, . . .*
> *stupendous*
> *Evening strains to be time's vast, womb-of-all, home-of-all, hearse-of-all night.*

To most eyes, the movement of evening into night is calm, so gradual that you hardly notice that night is upon you. To Hopkins, evening strains because everything strains, feels the stress of its selving, wills itself to become its ultimate possibility. Hopkins coined the words "inscape" and "instress" partly to justify his way of seeing things: he explains the words differently in different contexts, but I take inscape to be the individual quality of form or shape in an object, and instress the recognition of energy in the object. To inscape something is to register it as form, to instress it is to feel it as energy or force. In "The Wreck of the Deutschland" Hopkins writes of Christ:

> *Since, tho' he is under the world's splendour and wonder,*
> *His mystery must be instressed, stressed.*

The theme of Hopkins as poet and priest figures largely and justly in Paddy Kitchen's book. She is apparently not a religious believer, but she doesn't repeat the old assertion, common in the first generation of Hopkins's Cambridge critics, that his becoming a priest killed him as a poet. If he hadn't joined the Jesuit Order he would have written more poems, but not necessarily better poems. Empson says in *Milton's God* that the basic complaint of Hopkins's last sonnets is "that the severe Jesuit training doesn't seem to have made him any better." But if Hopkins had claimed that he felt improved by the regimen, it would have shown that he wasn't. The point of the training is not to make you feel better but to turn your will towards God. It's not like jogging.

Another theme which Ms. Kitchen touches with due delicacy is Hopkins's sexuality, for which the evidence is slight and hard to assess. I gather that some unpublished manuscripts at Campion Hall, Oxford, point in a homosexual direction, but no one has suggested that they go beyond desire and latency. The question has been raised before now. In April 1934, Auden, reviewing E. E. Phare's *Gerard Manley Hopkins* for *The Criterion,* said that reading Hopkins's poem "The Bugler's First Communion" "suggests a conflict in Hopkins between homosexual feelings and a moral sense of guilt," and he speculated that the poem fails "because the guilt is unacknowledged." Another poem, "On the Portrait of Two Beautiful People," is deemed to succeed because, Auden says, the guilt "is transformed into the unspecified moral danger which Hopkins fears for the subjects of the poem."

Ms. Kitchen hasn't added much to our knowledge here, but she has provided a very interesting account of Hopkins's friendship with Digby Dolben, a distant cousin of Bridges's whom Hopkins met in Oxford, and she agrees with Humphry House that the poem "The Beginning of the End" makes better sense in relation to Dolben than to some unknown woman, the object of a brief obsession on Hopkins's part. Dolben was drowned at the age of nineteen: a dreamy, charming youth, poetic and devout, he seems to have fascinated Hopkins for a time, though it is impossible to measure the fascination. Of Hopkins's sexuality, Ms. Kitchen says that "since he was to become a celibate, and since his life as an undergraduate was apparently very chaste, it may fairly be claimed that his sexual orientation was never conclusively evolved." It's a modest claim, but the question is difficult. Hopkins was highly susceptible to beauty in any form, and he convinced himself that God was just as truly present in beauty as in truth, so it was not too difficult to be fascinated by a handsome youth and call the state of feeling by a spiritual name.

The last theme I want to mention is hardly touched at all in Paddy Kitchen's biography: Hopkins's language. Her book does not run to literary criticism, but the question of language has implications for a biographer. There is clearly a relation between Hopkins's language and the "stress of pitch, distinctiveness, and selving" which preoccupied him in the examination of conscience and soul. But, to be specific, I think there is also a relation between Hopkins's conversion to Catholicism and his determination to become a particular kind of poet. Isn't it curious that his special way of being English was to go back beyond the Reformation for his thought, and back beyond the Norman Conquest for his language?

Austin Warren emphasized, in his *Rage for Order,* Hopkins's preference for the Anglo-Saxon element rather than the Latin and Romance elements in English. In 1873 Hopkins took notes from G. P. Marsh's *Lectures on the English Language* (1859), which advocates the recovery of forgotten native words. Victorian philology includes a fairly strong opposition to the Latin factor in English. Warren mentions E. A. Freeman, F. J. Furnivall, R. C. Trench, and the poet William Barnes, who urged writers to replace Latin words by compound synonyms from Anglo-Saxon. On November 26, 1882, Hopkins referred to Barnes's *An Outline of English Speech-Craft* in a letter to Bridges:

> It makes one weep to think what English might have been; for in spite of all that Shakespeare and Milton have done with the compound I cannot doubt that no beauty in a language can make up for want of purity. In fact I am learning Anglosaxon and it is a vastly superior thing to what we have now. But the madness of an almost unknown man trying to do what the three estates of the realm together could never accomplish! He calls degrees of comparison pitches of suchness: we *ought* to call them so, but alas!

Hopkins's earliest notebooks are full of etymologies, dialect words, lost sounds. Until he died he kept up correspondence with Baillie and others on linguistic problems. He pestered W. W. Skeat until Skeat told him his life wasn't long enough to answer such questions. The basic question was English: how to keep up the language, restore its lost values, restore its Anglo-Saxon power. Critics have emphasized Hopkins's praise of Dryden for maintaining "the naked thew and sinew of the language," but they have not gone far enough to consider a kind of poetry which deliberately turns degrees of comparison into pitches of suchness. Such words as sake, pied, dapple, fell, and wuthering gave Hopkins an alternative language which, in some poems, amounted to an adversary language, an escape from the standard feelings enclosed in Standard English. So whenever he felt the need to "call off thoughts awhile elsewhere," he had a language in which it might be done:

Soul, self; come, poor Jackself, I do advise
You, jaded, let be; call off thoughts while
Elsewhere; leave comfort rootroom; let joy size
At God knows when to God knows what; whose smile
's not wrung, see you; unforeseen times rather—as skies
Betweenpie mountains—lights a lovely mile.

The English language that Hopkins needed had to be a sinewy vernacular, gathering up its history with particular care for experiences otherwise lost; having root room instead of mere space; stirring forgotten meaning in the verb "to size"; and allowing a poet to use "betweenpie" as a verb. Bright sky seen between two mountains makes each dappled or pied; another sign of God's grandeur.

Review of *Gerard Manley Hopkins: A Biography*, by Paddy Kitchen. From *The New York Review of Books*, September 27, 1979.

OSCAR WILDE

Oscar Wilde was born at 21 Westland Row, Dublin (not the best address), on October 16, 1854. He died in the Hôtel d'Alsace, Paris, on November 30, 1900. The novelist George Moore said of him: "I do not think anybody would have troubled about him if the Marquess of Queensberry had not written him a postcard." A harsh judgement, but not absurd: if Wilde had not, on March 1, 1895, sought and obtained a warrant for Queensberry's arrest, there would have been no trials, no imprisonment, no *Ballad of Reading Gaol,* no disgrace. Our interest in his life would have coincided, as it now does not, with an interest in his plays. He would belong to the history of the English theatre, but he would not be a continuing issue, involving morals, homosexuality, law, Victorian society. We would comfortably compare him with Shaw, distinguish his comedies from those of Congreve, and enjoy the plays as they come. We would certainly not say of him, as Richard Ellmann does in his biography, that "Wilde is one of us."

A word about the postcard. It is generally agreed that Wilde, who married Constance Lloyd on May 29, 1884, remained heterosexual until he felt it necessary, sometime in 1886, upon discovering that the syphilis he had contracted from a prostitute at Oxford was not entirely cured, to discontinue having intercourse with his wife. In the same year he met Robert Ross, who seduced him into homosexuality. Wilde, as Ellmann remarks, "was not attracted to anal coition, so Ross presumably introduced him to the oral and intercrural intercourse he practiced later." In June 1891 (though a date a few months earlier had been suggested), Wilde met Lord Alfred Douglas, one of the Marquess of Queensberry's sons, and fell in love with him.

Mutual fidelity was neither expected nor required; each of the lovers was promiscuous. But the relation persisted, in England and on vacations in Italy and Algeria. The Marquess demanded that his son bring the scandal to an end. Alfred refused. On February 28, 1895, one of the porters at the Albemarle Club in London handed Wilde a postcard that the Marquess had left for him ten days before. The message, hard to decipher, reads: "To Oscar Wilde posing Somdomite [*sic*]." The culmination of several blows from Queensberry, the postcard seemed to Wilde the ultimate provocation. "I don't see anything now but a criminal prosecution," he wrote to Ross a few hours after he had received it. On March 1 he obtained a warrant for Queensberry's arrest on a charge of criminal libel.

The case came to trial on April 3, and two days later Queensberry was acquitted. But the evidence produced at the trial was so damaging to Wilde—it described him soliciting more than twelve boys, of whom ten were named, to commit sodomy—that he had to be arrested and charged under Section XI of the Criminal Law Amendment Act, 1885: "Any male person who, in public or private, commits, or is a party to the commission of, or procures or attempts to procure the commission by any male person of, any act of gross indecency with another male person, shall be guilty of misdemeanor, and being convicted thereof, shall be liable, at the discretion of the court, to be imprisoned for any term not exceeding two years with or without hard labor." On May 1 the jury disagreed and a new trial was ordered: it couldn't have been avoided, since the names of several men in high place, including Lord Rosebery, had been mentioned in evidence. If Solicitor General Lockwood had dropped the case, he would have been accused of a cover-up. The new trial began on May 20; five days later Wilde was found guilty and sentenced to two years' hard labor. He served his full term. Released on May 19, 1897, he went immediately to France, then to Italy, Sicily, Switzerland, and back to Paris, resuming the homosexual life that had sent him to jail.

Wilde was much concerned with biographical commentary. Reviewing Joseph Knight's biography of Dante Gabriel Rossetti in 1887, he said: "We sincerely hope that there will soon be an end to all biographies of this kind. They rob life of much of its dignity and its wonder, add to death itself a new terror, and make one wish that all art were anonymous." In "The Critic as Artist" he wrote: "Every great man nowadays has his disciples, and it is always Judas who writes the biography." Alfred Douglas was Wilde's Judas, publishing lies until death stopped him. And another of Wilde's associates, Robert Sherard, demonstrated in several books that he did not understand anything, least of all his friend Wilde. But there have been decent biographies: by Hesketh Pearson in 1946, a better one by H. Montgomery Hyde in 1976.

Now Wilde has found in Richard Ellmann a most affectionate disciple. The new biography is the work of many years. Ellmann interrupted his research from time to time to publish other books, but this biography was his main commitment since 1959, when he published his life of Joyce. There are signs of constraint in the new book. Ellmann told me several years ago that the biography of Wilde would be a much longer book than that of Joyce; in the event it is about 200 pages shorter. I assume that when Ellmann became ill (he died last year of Lou Gehrig's disease), he knew that he would have to finish the work even at the cost of leaving a few issues unresolved.

If Ellmann had lived, I think he would have expounded and justified his sense of Wilde, offering more evidence in its favor. He regarded Wilde as a good man, warmhearted, generous, the best of company, as I am sure he was. On more doubtful ground, however, he exonerates Wilde from the charge of corrupting the boys he paid for sex: "They were already prostitutes." Wilde "got to know the boys as individuals, treated them handsomely, allowed them to refuse his attentions without becoming rancorous, and did not corrupt them." It's a poor argument. Wilde took part in the corruption, and maintained it.

I should say that Ellmann's biography is written, as one would expect, with consummate elegance and grace. It is fluent, often witty, always urbane. Most of the episodes are narrated so compellingly that the question of dissenting from Ellmann's sense of them hardly arises. But I think that his recourse to standard notions about Victorian society is often facile. He believes that Wilde was brought down by the hypocrisy of Victorian law and government. The second trial, he writes, was "a farce." "The society whose hypocrisies he had anatomized now turned against him: Victorianism was ready to pounce." The book ends with a ringing assertion: "Now, beyond the reach of scandal, his best writings validated by time, he comes before us still, a towering figure, laughing and weeping, with parables and paradoxes, so generous, so amusing, and so right."

The last word, "right," has a footnote sending the reader to *Other Inquisitions,* where Borges, more judicious than Ellmann on this theme, refers to "the provable and elementary fact that Wilde is almost always right." *The Soul of Man Under Socialism,* according to Borges, "is not only eloquent; it is just." The miscellaneous notes that Wilde lavished on the *Pall Mall Gazette* and the *Speaker* "are filled with perspicuous observations that exceed the optimum possibilities of Leslie Stephen or [George] Saintsbury." These claims are valid. But Ellmann goes beyond Borges: in his version, Wilde was *always* right, and the people who brought him down were monstrous hypocrites, true epitomes of the society they maintained.

The trouble is that such an argument can be sustained only by a more fundamental one: that an artist should never be subject to the law or charged with a crime. (Besides, the argument runs, if every man who engaged in homosexual practices were to be thrown into jail, Victorian clubs and drawing rooms would have been emptied.) But Ellmann ignores the fact that Wilde brought the law upon himself. The police took no interest in his private life until irrefutable evidence came to light in the case that Wilde brought against Queensberry. The truth is that Wilde did an incredibly stupid thing; he should have ignored Queensberry's postcard and every other such missive. There is no evidence that Victorian institutions of power had their evil eye on him.

Ellmann concedes that Wilde was imprudent, but he exculpates him otherwise at every turn. Exemplifying what Lionel Trilling once referred to as "the modern tendency to locate evil in social systems rather than in persons," Ellmann glosses over the fact that Wilde lied both in and out of court. He lied to the lawyer he employed to defend him. On November 8, 1893, he wrote to Lord Alfred's mother urging her to send her son to Lord Cromer in Cairo for five or six months, for the good of his health. It is now clear that the scheme was a stratagem that Oscar and Alfred concocted together to remove Alfred, at his mother's expense, from the scene of an imminent scandal. It involved a schoolboy named Philip Danney, who went from Ross's bed to Douglas's and extended his trip to

Wilde's, before returning to London to sleep with a woman at Douglas's expense. The boy's father got wind of these activities and wanted to prosecute every offender, but he was dissuaded by his lawyer: "They will doubtless get two years, but your son will get six months." Wilde's name was kept out of it, but Douglas had to be spirited out of the country. Egypt was a haven just far enough away. All this is clear, thanks to Ellmann's own research; the scandal is one of several new items in his book. But he doesn't remark how shoddily Wilde emerges from it.

The new materials in Ellmann's book are not immediately obvious, but they are worth a search. There is amassed detail about Queensberry, including a new letter that shows him in one of his coarsest moments. Montgomery Hyde's explanation of Queensberry's vendetta against Wilde—that his eldest son, Drumlanrig, killed himself to avoid the disclosure of his involvement in a homosexual tangle with his master, Lord Rosebery—is accepted and developed in Ellmann's book. Queensberry was determined that, having lost one son to homosexuality, he wouldn't lose another one in the same cause: the interpretation seems plausible, especially when we reflect that Queensberry was rich enough to survive any indignity and demented enough to risk it.

Ellmann treats the trials themselves pretty briefly; they have already been fully described in several books by Hyde. But Wilde's unfortunate wife, Constance, is more persuasively described by Ellmann than by any of his predecessors. She turns out to have been a woman of notable courage and spirit, indeed of magnanimity. When Wilde's mother died in 1896, Constance set out from Bordighera to bring the sad news to Wilde in prison, and to comfort him in his distress. The meeting between Constance and Oscar is one of the most touching episodes in the entire story. It may be true, as Ellmann thinks, that Constance had fallen in love, in the summer of 1894, with Arthur Humphreys, the manager of Hatchard's bookstore; if the affair was brief, one hopes that it was also gratifying.

There are still a few gaps in the biography. How did the notorious "Hyacinthus" letter from Wilde to Lord Alfred ("I know Hyacinthus, whom Apollo loves so madly, was you in Greek days") get into Queensberry's hands? The relation between Wilde and W. E. Henley, culminating in Henley's attack on The Ballad of Reading Gaol in 1898, needs more elaborate study than Ellmann gives it; it touches upon political and imperial motives not otherwise clear. Henley was an ardent imperialist, and he convinced himself that Wilde and his decadent friends were a threat to the empire. One of his most famous poems begins:

> What have I done for you,
> England, my England?
> What is there I would not do,
> England, my own?

No wonder that he loathed Aestheticism, and took pride in publishing, as editor of *The Scots Observer* in 1890, Charles Whibley's attack on *The Picture of Dorian Gray*. Wilde, in turn, had a low opinion of Henley as a writer ("his prose is jerky, spasmodic, and he is incapable of the beautiful architecture of a long sentence"), but the relation between them is more interestingly complex than I have made it seem; they rose to moments of affection and admiration in the intervals of conflict.

Then there is the question of the cause of Wilde's death. Ellmann says:

> His ear developed an abscess: he had otitis media. This the doctor now diagnosed, according to Turner, as a "tertiary symptom" of syphilis. It led directly to meningitis, "the legacy of an attack of tertiary syphilis," as Ross said.

But the matter is not at all clear. Ellmann takes Ross's word for it, and there is a letter from Reginald Turner to Robert Sherard on the same lines. But there are studies by competent medical people such as Terence Cawthorne and McDonald Critchly that tell a different story, that the cause of death was indeed a disease of the middle ear, complicated by an abscess in the left lobe. There was also cerebral meningitis. But I am persuaded, in this instance, by Hyde rather than by Ellmann: "It is practically certain that neurosyphilis was in no way responsible for [Wilde's] terminal illness."

These are details. But to a biographer God is in the details; larger matters can often be left to issue from local episodes. Still, sometimes, as in the case of this biography, they need to be a little teased out. Ellmann does not raise many of the important questions. His sense of Wilde established itself, I think, at a fairly early stage of his writing, and it seemed a sufficient task to represent a personality, a distinctive presence in the world. When Ellmann does treat Wilde's ideas, he takes them more seriously than they deserve. I can't see Wilde, as a thinker, in the company of Nietzsche and Pater; his thinking was a series of flourishes, not a body of thought valuable beyond its occasion. Ellmann's claims for Wilde are excessive; and they are sustained more by the warmth of Ellmann's affection than by any irresistible arguments in their favour.

Thus Ellmann doesn't go into the important question of Wilde's neo-aristocratic pose. In *Some Versions of Pastoral,* William Empson glanced at it, remarking that the Byronism of the dandy, as in Baudelaire and Wilde, stood for the idea "that crimes are the fate of the artist merely because of his greatness, and that to commit hubris is only to admit that one is the tragic demigod." Everything depended on what the dandy appeared to be taking for granted. Empson says that "the aristocrat is essentially like the child because it is his business to make claims in advance of his immediate personal merits." The best the aristocrat can do, "if actually asked for his credentials, since it would be indecent to produce his pedigree, is to display charm and hope it will appear unconscious, like the good young girl."

But Wilde's pedigree wasn't impeccable. His father was Sir William Wilde, but the title wasn't hereditary; he was knighted for his work as a doctor, especially for his discoveries in diseases of the eye and the ear. Oscar's mother was a poet, a flamboyant personality, a Nationalist whose ardour was compatible with attendance at the Lord Lieutenant's Christmas Ball. Her verses were evidently not a threat to the empire. But she was not a fool. Indeed, her influence on Oscar was immense and, as Ellmann shows, much to his good. But her reputation wasn't serious enough to provide her son with a pedigree. Oscar was a social climber, an Irishman out to conquer London, and while it often appears that he found the conquest easy, many of his quips seem designed to intimidate, in advance, people who might indeed ask to examine his pedigree. Of course he gave a good performance, an extended run of the show he devised; but it's hard to be quite convinced by it, as Ellmann evidently was, especially if one adverts to the sense that a touch of vulgarity was never far from the declared appurtenances of a superior tone.

Wilde's version of aristocratic hauteur, as Empson puts it, "leaves a rather bad taste in the mouth because it is slavish; it has something of the naive snobbery of the high-class servant":

Whistler meant this by the most crashing of his insults—"Oscar now stands forth unveiled as his own 'gentleman' "—when Wilde took shelter from a charge of plagiarism behind the claim that a gentleman does not attend to coarse abuse.

Indeed, Whistler's dealings with Wilde were largely a matter of showing that Wilde's claim to the superior graces was a fraud.

There were other ways of engaging with Wilde. One could refuse to let him enter one's home, as Mrs. Henry Adams did when he came to Washington in January 1882, copious with introductions, on a lecture tour. "I have asked Henry James *not* to bring his friend Oscar Wilde when he comes; I must keep out thieves and noodles or else take down my sign and go West." Not that James was a friend of Wilde's; he told Mrs. Adams, after a visit to Wilde, that the fellow was (her words, admittedly, not necessarily James's) "a fatuous fool, a tenth-rate cad."

Ten years later, when Wilde was a successful dramatist and James in the process of recognizing himself as a failed one, he described the (by then, standard) way of taking Wilde. Having attended the opening night of *Lady Windermere's Fan* on February 20, 1892, and deeming the play "infantine," he reported that "the pit and gallery are so pleased at finding themselves clever enough to 'catch on' to four or five of the ingenious—too ingenious—*mots* in the dozen, that it makes them feel quite 'decadent' and *raffiné* and they enjoy the sensation as a change from the stodgy." As for "the virtuous journals" and their response to Wilde: their tone, James said, "makes me despair of our stupid humanity":

> Everything Oscar does is a deliberate trap for the literalist, and to see the literalist walk straight up to it, look straight at it, and step straight into it, makes one freshly avert a discouraged gaze from this unspeakable animal.

James is a good witness to call, not merely because he was a superb social analyst and had, as Richard Poirier has shown, a remarkable comic sense, but because the structure of his feelings would have enabled him to understand Wilde's. I refer not just to his homoerotic desires, but to his emphatic sense of the consequences, many of them rightly acceptable, of being a visible presence in the social world. James's presentation of Gabriel Nash in *The Tragic Muse* (1889–90) illustrates most of the attributes that he thought could be permitted in an aesthete. Such a person might go so far as to assert that "my only behavior is my feelings" and to regard himself as "a fine consequence." There was no harm in that, only a limitation: the price one had to pay for such lucidity. The social world was large and various enough to house an aesthete or two. But they, in turn, would have to observe the social decencies and put up with the constraints.

Much of this comes out, but more explicitly, in James's consideration of the merits of John La Farge, artist and aesthete, in *Notes of a Son and Brother* (1914). Twenty years after the imprisonment of Wilde, James thought that La Farge (certainly not Wilde, Whistler, or Beardsley) was the true "embodiment of the gospel of aesthetics." In a clear reference to Wilde, James said of the young La Farge:

> Those more resounding forms that our age was to see this gospel take on were then still to come, but I was to owe them in the later time not half the thrill that the La Farge of the prime could set in motion. He was really an artistic, an aesthetic nature of wondrous homogeneity; one was to have known in the future many an unfolding that went with a larger ease and a shrewder economy, but never to have seen a subtler mind or a more generously wasteful passion, in other words a sincerer one, addressed to the problems of the designer and painter.

James's references to homogeneity and sincerity are enough to show what form a more elaborate distinction between Wilde and La Farge as types would take. If he were writing now, he would find it harder to persuade his readers that these terms of praise are self-evident.

Trilling remarked how easy it has become to patronize sincerity, and "the sharp diminution of the authority it once exercised." He had rueful and ambiguous feelings about the displacement of sincerity in favour of authenticity, supposedly "a more exigent concept of the self and of what being true to it consists in, a wider reference to the universe and man's place in it, and a less acceptant and genial view of the social circumstances of life." And Wilde seemed to Trilling immensely important in this consideration, not merely because he could sustain comparison (as Mann claimed, too kindly) with Nietzsche, but because he anticipated so clairvoyantly the modern system of valuation by which, as Wilde said, "what people call insincerity is simply a method by which we can multiply our personalities." The method is now called the American system of role-playing. (It was denounced, to no visible avail, by Adorno in *The Jargon of Authenticity*.)

Many of Wilde's contemporaries, including Yeats, found his notion of multiplied personalities a gratifying release from prescribed axioms of sincerity. James didn't, because he regarded homogeneity as the only reliable mark of a person, the only proof that one was indeed in the presence of an achieved form of humanity. He, too, recognized the risk of vulgarity. Reading Ellmann's book, I am struck by the risks appallingly taken, and by the vulgar consequences. These arise whenever Wilde trades—slavishly indeed—for his own advantage in the very system of values he claimed to scorn.

It is wretched to find him, in Reading Gaol, petitioning the Home Secretary for his release on the grounds that such actions as those of which he was found guilty were, according to the best scientific authorities, "diseases to be cured by a physician, rather than crimes to be punished by a judge." Every sentence of the petition is a lie, starting with its reference to Max Nordau's *Degeneration* (1893), in which Wilde's public demeanour was adduced as a symptom of disease. Wilde did not believe that his homosexuality was a disease; it is disgusting that he went through the pretence. If you set yourself up as a mocker of the bourgeoisie, it is vulgar to pretend that you accept its morality and are ill in not being able to live up to it. Ariel should not tell lies, or say that Caliban is right.

Wilde's bad faith affected his plays too, except for *The Importance of Being Earnest*. The plays were supposed to achieve at large what his paradoxes accomplished in the miniature form of their sentences: to disturb the equilibrium of a system, to embarrass conventional values with their own stodginess. Wilde's sentences ("All bad poetry springs from genuine feeling") set speech upon a course of disruption. But if you restore such sentences to their standard form, replacing (in the one just quoted) "bad" by "great" or "good," you feel a fool; you can't ever again sink to rest on that particular cliché.

Wilde's plays were supposed not only to give bourgeois morality a good shaking, but to transform its terms into those of art, a much superior address. But *Lady Windermere's Fan* (1892), *A Woman of No Importance* (1893), and *An Ideal Husband* (1895) are halfhearted in this aim. They give too much credence to the moral issues (as in the cheating and blackmail plot of *An Ideal Husband*) that they claim to transform. Untransformed, untranscended, the old values remain in place at the end, and make the last-minute resolutions seem a mere sleight of hand. The plays leave an awkward residue, they are issueless and inconclusive, not because the audience insists on staying complacently middlebrow, but because Wilde hasn't shown them an image more alluring than their own.

In *The Importance of Being Earnest,* however, the awkwardness is removed. Wilde achieved his most assured artistic success not by showing that moral issues could be "sublimed away," the disgraces of a plot appearing as rough places on the way to graces and mobilities in a transfigured social scene, but by disclosing a social and linguistic utopia. It offers a world, as Ian Gregor said in an influential essay, "fit for the dandy to live in," and fit, too, for anyone with the wit to see that the dandy's way is superior to Everyman's not only in charm but in justice.

Ellmann well remarks that *The Importance of Being Earnest* is "all insouciance where *Salome* is all incrimination." The insouciance is the delighted tone in which surfaces and appearances are appreciated for what they are, without any insistence that they are merely clues to something else. "It is only shallow people who do not judge by appearances," Lord Henry tells Dorian Gray: "The true mystery of the world is the visible, not the invisible." The utopia of *The Importance of Being Earnest* is every charmed form of life that does not have to be earned: it is not a gift, but the context from which every gift flows. Like Nietzsche and Pater, Wilde believed that the Victorian age could maintain only an ironic sense of itself. To fail to maintain it was to fall into the mud of received ideas.

One could be, in any case, only a spectator of gone deeds. The question was: could a spectator take the harm out of an obviously congealed scene by cultivating his own art of seeing? It was Wilde's achievement in *The Importance of Being Earnest* to transform a predicament, a state of belatedness, into a fresh world, by declaring that he himself, with a wave of his wand, would make it all fresh. He does this by showing that appearances, trustworthy or not, may be appreciated for their beauty. The play has marriages, intrigues, and double lives: only the attributes of these states are altered. The marriages are made to seem to tremble upon a name, the intrigues upon a syllable. But these matters, the heavy stuff of morality in life as in the theatre, yield themselves in this play to aesthetic determinations. Wilde is Prospero here, and the English language is his Ariel.

To see morality yielding to art is at least a gratifying hallucination, effected most elegantly in the third act of *The Importance of Being Earnest.* There are glimpses of it in the earlier plays, as in *Lady Windermere's Fan,* when Mrs. Erlynne says to Lord Windermere: "I lost one illusion last night. I thought I had no heart. I find I have, and a heart doesn't suit me, Windermere. Somehow it doesn't go with modern dress. It makes one look old."

But the third act of *The Importance of Being Earnest* is Wilde's jewel, his greatest moment as a utopian. Cecily and Gwendolen are at the window of the morning-room at the Manor House, Jack and Algernon are in the garden. Cecily says: "They have been eating muffins. That looks like repentance" (an interpretive act that must be a comic transformation of poor, demented Ophelia's essay in the distribution of justice: "There's rosemary, that's for remembrance; pray you, love, remember. And there is pansies, that's for thoughts. . . . There's fennel for you, and columbines. There's rue for you, and here's some for me; we may call it herb of grace o' Sundays. You may wear your rue with a difference"). When Algernon flourishes a plausible excuse for having pretended to be Worthing's brother, we get this little sequence:

CECILY (to Gwendolen): That certainly seems a satisfactory explanation, does it not?

GWENDOLEN: Yes, dear, if you can believe him.

CECILY: I don't. But that does not affect the wonderful beauty of his answer.

GWENDOLEN: True. In matters of grave importance, style, not sincerity, is the vital thing. Mr. Worthing, what explanation can you offer me for pretending to have a brother? Was it in order that you might have an opportunity of coming up to town to see me as often as possible?

WORTHING: Can you doubt it, Miss Fairfax?

GWENDOLEN: I have the gravest doubts upon the subject. But I intend to crush them. This is not the moment for German skepticism.

The deflection of every prescribed relation between cause and consequence: this is Wilde's carnival. The morality of sufficient ground is elegantly mocked in the retention of an exacting syntax. And the syntax, in turn and in its turnings, mimes a moral argument, while it blithely sets aside the gravitas that such an argument would entail.

Among Wilde's several analogues for such a transformation, I mention two. In Shakespeare, he preferred the late romances to the tragedies. "Give me *A Winter's Tale,*" he said to Yeats. "What is *King Lear* but poor life staggering in the fog?" In art, he approved the Japanese forms of disconnection. "The Decay of Lying" has Vivian saying to Cyril:

I know that you are fond of Japanese things. Now, do you really imagine that the Japanese people, as they are presented to us in Art, have any existence? . . . If you set a picture by Hokusai, or Hokkei, or any of the great native painters, beside a real Japanese gentleman or lady, you will see that there is not the slightest resemblance between them. . . . In fact the whole of Japan is a pure invention.

The passage issues from a late Victorian fascination with Japanese art as an alternative to dreary realism. It is similar to Beardsley, Whistler, and other artists of Wilde's generation. It also anticipates Roland Barthes's account of Japan in *Empire of Signs.* Barthes was edified by the willingness of Japanese writing, and of Japanese society, to see itself emptied of the demands of meaning. He was exhilarated to discover "the features with which Zen, in the exemption from all meaning, writes gardens, gestures, houses, flower arrangements, faces, violence." He speaks of "an excision which removes the flourish of meaning from the object and severs from its presence, from its position in the world, any tergiversation." (I would not press the comparison of Wilde and Barthes beyond this point.)

It is one of the Japanese attributes of *The Importance of Being Earnest* that we are given everything to look at and to admire, and nothing to worry about; surfaces beneath which, with respect to their meaning, we feel no inclination to pry. We enjoy the play not by interpreting it, not by looking through its signs for a separable meaning authenticated in the end by its having come to pass, but by following the trajectory of its speech. Each character is an agreeably personified form of behaviour, a figure of speech that produces further figures in its vicinity. We attend to the play not as we would imagine persons in conflict and in confluence, but as we would participate in a vision, a joust of pure play, a masque of reason — and mercy.

From *The New Republic,* February 15, 1988.

Postscript

1. It was not a postcard, something that might be mailed; it was one of Queensberry's visiting cards, with "Marquis of Queensberry" printed on it.

2. About syphilis and the female prostitute at Oxford: this is conjecture on Ellmann's part, relying on statements by Reginald Turner and Robert Ross. The medical certificate to which Ellmann refers (p. 92n.) doesn't mention syphilis.

3. My reference to "irrefutable evidence" is misleading. At Queensberry's trial, no witnesses were called. But his detectives had worked hard. His senior counsel, Edward Carson, cross-examining Wilde, was evidently in possession of a vast amount of incriminating detail. On the third day of the trial, Wilde caved in and withdrew the prosecution. Mr. Justice Collins instructed the jury to find that it was true in substance and in fact that Wilde had indeed, as Queensberry alleged, posed as a sodomite.

4. On Wilde's later homosexual activities: these would have been criminal in Britain, but not in France.

5. Ellmann, referring to the trial of Wilde and of Alfred Taylor together, says (p. 459) that "the charges were indecency and sodomy." Wilde was never charged with sodomy: the charge was gross indecency, a far less serious offence which carried a maximum sentence of two years' hard labour. Taylor was charged with sodomy, but the charge was later reduced to gross indecency, and he got the same sentence as Wilde.

6. On the visiting card: Queensberry handed it to the hall porter, Sidney Wright. Wright looked at it, didn't understand it, and put it in an unsealed envelope to await Wilde's next visit. What Queensberry wrote on the card is still unresolved. Ellmann (p. 613n) expresses gratitude to R. E. Alton "for his study of Queensberry's handwriting, which enabled him to read for the first time correctly the message on Queensberry's card." The message, according to Alton and Ellmann, reads: "To Oscar Wilde posing Somdomite." This is wrong. Whatever else is ambiguous in the card, the first word is obviously "For," not "To." It reads: "For Oscar Wilde." Underneath these words, nearly everything is ambiguous, except for "Somdomite." In *The Trials of Oscar Wilde* (1948), H. Montgomery Hyde read the message as: "To Oscar Wilde posing as a somdomite." In

Oscar Wilde: A Biography (1976), he construed it as: "For Oscar Wilde posing as a somdomite." This version is far more persuasive than Alton's. (The card is photocopied in *Oscar Wilde: A Biography* and in the Dover Books reprint [1973] of the second edition of *The Trials of Oscar Wilde*.)

It is not known whether or not Wilde had difficulty in deciphering Queensberry's message. He was ready to find an allusion to "posing" because the word had come into the argument he had had, at the end of June 1894, when Queensberry descended upon him in his home in Tite Street. According to Wilde in court, when he said, "Lord Queensberry, do you seriously accuse your son and me of improper conduct?", the Marquis answered: "I do not say that you are it, but you look it, and you pose as it, which is just as bad." On February 28, 1894, Wilde read Queensberry's insult as "posing as a sodomite"; and since he wasn't one, the word "sodomite" sent him running to law. In court, his senior counsel, Sir Edward Clarke, used the phrase exactly in that form. The judge accepted that the phrase was the gist of the case.

The matter remains unclear. If I say that you are posing as a sodomite, my first implication is that you aren't one but that for some probably unpleasant reason you're pretending to be one, or aping the demeanour of sodomites. I might indeed be conveying a more occult meaning, that you really are a sodomite and that you're concealing the fact by making your demeanour an absurdly exaggerated mimicry. At Tite Street, Queensberry may have been saying to Wilde: "Of course I can't prove that you're a sodomite, since I can't be a fly on your bedroom walls, but your public demeanour when you're with my son in the Café Royal and such places is consistent with your aping the sodomite, and in any case it's bringing disgrace on my son." The difference between being a sodomite and posing as one wasn't raised in Queensberry's trial, mainly because Carson's cross-examination of Wilde brought forward such lurid images that the jury would have found Queensberry justified in writing any message, however dreadful.

MEREDITH'S POEMS

George Meredith (1828–1909) was never a popular writer; more often than not he had to pay the printer. But for many years he was a presence, if not a persuasive force, in the literary scene. "Meredith is not the great name he was twenty or thirty years ago," E. M. Forster told his Cambridge audience in 1927, "when much of the universe and all Cambridge trembled." But he did not indicate who trembled or why.

In *Notes of a Son and Brother* (1914) Henry James recalled the excitement with which, during a summer in Bonn in 1860, he received the periodicals his father sent him as a relief from the student's servitude to the German language. The *Cornhill* gave him Trollope and a sense of the density of "constituted English matters." *Once a Week* gave him "the prime of George Meredith and Charles Reade and J. E. Millais and George du Maurier." "I rioted," James reports, "all that season, on the supreme German classics *and* on [Meredith's] *Evan Harrington,* with Charles Reade's *A Good Fight,* the assured little prelude to *The Cloister and the Hearth,* thrown in." James recalled the time as offering happy conditions for authors and readers. The conditions of authorship, until about 1860 but not for long thereafter, were such that a given product of the press might have a situation and an aspect, a considerability, so to speak, a circumscription and an aura; room to breathe and to show in, margin for the casting of its nets.

By the end of the century, spaciousness and leisure were gone. The tenderness with which James recalls reading Meredith's novel is warmed by his sense that the book found, on its first appearance in the periodical, an audience, generously spirited if not numerous, and ready with the leisure it required. The occasion at large, as James says, was doubtless shrinking, readers were beginning to run short of time and patience. That the conditions were becoming more difficult is the theme of several of his stories, including "The Lesson of the Master," "The Death of the Lion," and "The Next Time," where James presents the creative imagination in the increasingly crippled conditions it had to meet. The situation is presented from several points of vantage, but they all amount to waste, frustration, and the wretchedness of writing for people more and more unable to bring their minds to the occasion. In "The Next Time," a novelist, Ray Limbert, tries year by year to write a popular novel but is prevented by the fineness of his imagination, until at last he yields to that beautiful imperative. "He had merely waked up one morning again," as James says, "in the country of the blue and had stayed there with a good conscience and a great idea" until he died.

Meredith, like other Victorian novelists who tried for popularity and only got fame, turned to poetry for his country of the blue. But the comparison with Ray Limbert is only an approximation. Limbert was one of those people "who can't be vulgar for trying," and, thus disabled, can only be fine. Meredith's values were not as strict. He could be vulgar, if not vulgar enough for the multitude, but when he was not vulgar it was not because he had to be fine. His country of the blue was a place in which he made free with language, but freedom was not, as it turned out, the best condition for his art; it made him garrulous, repetitive, self-indulgent. Bad as it was to have to please the populace, his art was not well served merely by electing to please itself.

James does not allow for such a disability among the predicaments he assigns to the artist; he confines his care to the highest type of the artist, and therefore to the imagination when it is the writer's best self. I do not recall any story by him in which the artist is ruined not by the conditions at large but by his own fault, an impurity of motive. James touched upon the impurity in *The Question of Our Speech* (1905) when he referred to novelists in whom the lyrical or poetical element is dominant; the reference implied that this dominance marked a limitation in their art. Balzac stood for everything that was wonderfully unlyrical, unpoetic, terrestrial, and for that reason James thought of him as the highest expression of the nature and effort of the novelist. The lyrical element, according to James,

> is considerable in that bright particular genius of our own day, George Meredith, who so strikes us as hitching winged horses to the chariot of his prose—steeds who prance and dance and caracole, who strain the traces, attempt to quit the ground, and yearn for the upper air.

The description does not take the fault out of Meredith's style: it is with a critical and denigrating intention that James points to the lyrical element, which amounts to a defect because it aspires to a degree of purity foreign to the novel. Meredith's winged horses testify to divided purposes in an artist who should have been dogged in his sense of the novel and its natural relation to stories, scenes, images of life, the states and feelings of others. You can hardly say anything worse about Meredith than that he set his style prancing and dancing to make his novels lyrical; or, nearly as bad, that he would not stay quiet or subdue his lyricism in favour of his subject.

There are many reasons for disapproving of Meredith's art, and many for disliking it, before you start liking it despite yourself. To keep on disliking it you have to apply yourself to the task. T. S. Eliot thought it important to dislike Meredith's writing, which he evidently regarded as corrupt. He disapproved of Meredith for thinking, or for engaging in what he regarded as thought; Eliot construed it as mere doodling with the tokens of the day—evolution, creation, the consanguinity of blood, brain, and spirit, caracoling with Whither and Whence. Eliot distrusted anyone who proposed to think for himself; he disliked Meredith, Hardy, Lawrence, and Yeats for the same reason, spiritual vanity. But the dislike goes further. Eliot had no time for thought unless it was a delicate organization of feeling; he despised the process of thought which issued in ideas, bright at their worst but vain in any case. To set up as a thinker, a sage, was to commit the first of the deadly sins, pride as damaging to Meredith's soul as to Chesterton's.

Most of Eliot's references to Meredith are nasty, with that excuse. But Meredith gave Eliot one of his best lines. In "Lucifer in Starlight" Meredith has the Prince daunted by evidence of God's power in the stars:

> Around the ancient track marched, rank on rank,
> The army of unalterable law.

In Eliot's "Cousin Nancy" Miss Nancy Ellicott dances undaunted by New England's stars, Arnold and Emerson:

> Upon the glazen shelves kept watch
> Matthew and Waldo, guardians of the faith,
> The army of unalterable law.

The allusion does not damage Meredith's poem, or mock the awe which is, in any case, Meredith's tribute to *Paradise Lost* as much as to *Isaiah*.

Forster picked up Meredith's phrase, probably from "Cousin Nancy," and quoted it in his Cambridge lectures, *Aspects of the Novel*, soon after his famous account of Meredith's novels. His criticism is commonly thought to have put an end to Meredith, but it merely stopped the trembling. The gist of the criticism is that Meredith's philosophy is dead, his vision of Nature has too much Surrey in it, his seriousness is strident, his social values faked, his tailors are not genuine tailors. "What with the faking," Forster says, "what with the preaching, which was never agreeable and is now said to be hollow, and what with the home counties posing as the universe, it is no wonder Meredith now lies in the trough."

But Forster still wanted to claim that Meredith was in some sense a great novelist, not only on the strength of his plots but because he had the intelligence to let plot win when it conflicted with character. This helped Forster's distinction between flat and round characters: when characters are sacrificed to plot, they are likely to be flat rather than round.

They remain in the reader's mind as unalterable for the reason that they were not changed by circumstances; they moved through circumstances, which gives them in retrospect a comforting quality and preserves them when the book that produced them may decay.

The nearest example of a flat character is the Countess de Saldar in *Evan Harrington* (1860), whom the reader recalls for the formula surrounding her, "Proud as we are of dear papa, we must conceal his memory." There is more to the Countess than that, but it is more of the same.

I have glanced at these aspects of the reception of Meredith mainly to indicate the depth of his trough. It cannot be expected that he will ever be popular: no change of taste will raise him from the trough. It is edifying that Phyllis B. Bartlett was willing to devote many years to a definitive edition of Meredith's poems; and very sad to think that she died while the volumes were still in the press. On the whole the good poems are the ones we have always known to be good, though John Bayley recently pointed to a relatively obscure poem, "Aimée," which is superb.

The edition is welcome for several reasons: it prints many unpublished poems, early drafts of published poems, material from two notebooks in the Beinecke Library at Yale, variant readings, changes from periodical to book publication. A few textual questions still arise. In "The Three Singers to Young Blood" I assume that "Dearer dying that all sweets" should read "Dearer dying than all sweets." The last line of "Grace and Love" sounds odd. In "A Faith on Trial" I deduce that "fresh," at line 544, should be "flesh." Editorial notes are not lavish; a reader interested in sources, for instance, must do most of the work for himself. But the main reason why the edition is welcome is that, despite everything said against him, Meredith refuses to be uninteresting.

Generally, readers of Meredith seem to begin with *The Egoist, Diana of the Crossways,* or *The Ordeal of Richard Feverel,* but *Evan Harrington* is more engaging than any of these, for autobiographical reasons. Meredith, like Evan, was the son of a tailor, so he had to decide whether and how he should raise himself out of his class. *Evan Harrington* bears upon that question just as interestingly as his poem *Modern Love* bears upon the circumstances in which Meredith's first wife ran off with her lover Henry Wallis. The relation between fact and the compensations of fiction is as moving in the novel as in the poem. It is reasonable to think that Meredith's styles, in fiction and verse, were designed to enable a tailor's son to move into superior life and talk to the best people, minor aristocrats, literary editors, and such respected figures as John Morley and G. M. Trevelyan.

Evan Harrington explores the issue of social climbing and transposes it into social comedy. The "papa" whose memory the Countess de Saldar wants to conceal was the leading tailor of Lymport; this must not be known if her brother Evan is to make his way in the grand world. The Countess shows how absurd you become if you go too far to repudiate your class, but the advantage of making her define the limit is that you can justify yourself so long as you stay on one side of it; some degree of repudiation is all right so long as you don't make an ass of yourself. The comedy shows that Meredith is in control of the situation, and therefore in control of his own: stability comes to mean a judicious move out of your class—but you must not do it precipitately or hide your origin. Such moves are supposed to be fairly easy in English society if you're prepared to be sensible about them.

The interesting thing is that Meredith, in his poems, tries to avoid the issue of class by appealing to attitudes and feelings deemed to be universal. His first poetic themes were general invocations to human fellowship, "sweet sympathies for human kind." "The Wild Rose and the Snowdrop" speaks of each flower "fulfilling nature's law," mortality is made to seem natural and beautiful. The poem was published in 1851 when it was still easy, following Gray and Wordsworth, to derive a fairly sanguine moral from meditation on flowers, the seasons, the wind, and mountains. Perfection is identified with being, and removed from the qualification you would have to impose if you let being take its chances with time and death.

Meredith's early poems locate their country of the blue outside time, as if only space were the true dimension and perfect things were perfect forever. In *The Egoist*, written in 1879, Meredith invokes the Spirit of Comedy to exert pressure upon the ways of the world: the spirit is not at all spiritual, but worldly, directed upon psychological habits and foibles which stay funny while you have them in your sights. There is a late poem which celebrates this Spirit of Comedy in much the same terms as in Meredith's essay on comedy and his prelude to *The Egoist*. But in the early poems the genius of the place is the Spirit of Pity, which reconciles the perfection of being to the more pressing natural law of time and decay. The Spirit of Pity works upon daily events by abstracting and mystifying them, drawing them into a deeper blue, the colour of promise and prophecy:

> *From the snowdrop learn;*
> *Not in her pale life lives she,*
> *But in her blushing prophecy.*
> *Thus be thy hopes,*

> *living but to yearn*
> *Upwards to the hidden copes;—*
> *Even within the urn*
> *Let them burn!*

When this mood prevails, Pity becomes Romance, as in "Pictures of the Rhine," where the spirit of Romance assures us that "there glows / Above dead things a thing that cannot die." The magnificence to which the poems aspire is the endlessness of communication between man and nature, change and rebirth, time and eternity. Clearly the novels could not accommodate this chorale, even if Meredith's lyricism let his narratives yearn for the upper air. The cosmic ambition of the poetry rises from claims made for the grandeur of human feeling, universal and classless: the scene at hand merely provokes this feeling and receives it.

It follows that Meredith's descriptive poems are more conceptual than sensory, the language serves not the eye but the mind's eye, the spirit's yearning and exaltation. In "South-West Wind in the Woodland," one of Meredith's many additions to Shelley, the comparison of the wind to a horseman on a fiery steed is entirely conceptual, what is represented is "the union of our earth and skies / Renewed," and the horseman is the emblem of that renewal:

> *He comes upon the neck of night,*
> *Like one that leaps a fiery steed*
> *Whose keen black haunches quivering shine*
> *With eagerness and haste, that needs*
> *No spur to make the dark leagues fly!*

This is acceptable because it is sustained by a tradition of romantic figures which do much the same work, but Meredith is not always as secure either in his relation to a tradition or in the possession of his own feelings. When he writes badly, he makes us think he's trying to hide something or get away with a crime. Often he didn't know how much feeling the situation warranted; and he set up a flurry on all sides of it, as if he wanted to avoid being held accountable for its claims. In 1870, during the Franco-Prussian War, he wrote a long Ode to France in which the zeal of propaganda is absurd enough to please the Countess de Saldar:

She sees what seed long sown, ripened of late,
Bears this fierce crop; and she discerns her fate
From origin to agony, and on
As far as the wave washes long and wan
Off one disastrous impulse: for of waves
Our life is, and our deeds are pregnant graves
Blown rolling to the sunset from the dawn.

It's hard to find a feasible rhyme for "waves" which won't get you into Meredith's trouble with "graves." The pregnancy doesn't help, especially when it grossly becomes the blown and rolling figures of the last line; getting graves to roll is an empty achievement. Throughout the poem, Meredith forgets the lesson he teaches, if only in theory, in his fiction, that if you can only express a feeling by exceeding every reasonable limit of it, the feeling itself is probably vain. Forster spoke of the bullying element in Meredith's seriousness, but I detect more insecurity than bullying, as if his feeling and his mind were estranged. Even in the novels, where he knew so much, he never knew when to stop. Here is a passage from *The Egoist,* where Meredith is presenting the relation between the conceited Sir Willoughby Patterne and poor, adoring Laetitia:

A clear approach to felicity had long been the portion of Sir Willoughby Patterne in his relations with Laetitia Dale. She belonged to him; he was quite unshackled by her. She was everything that is good in a parasite, nothing that is bad. His dedicated critic she was, reviewing him with a favour equal to perfect efficiency in her office; and whatever the world might say of him, to her the happy gentleman could constantly turn for his refreshing balsamic bath. She flew to the soul in him, pleasingly arousing sensations of that inhabitant; and he allowed her the right to fly, in the manner of kings, as we have heard, consenting to the privileges acted on by cats. These may not address their Majesties, but they may stare; nor will it be contested that the attentive circular eyes of the humble domestic creatures are an embellishment to Royal pomp and grandeur, such truly as should one day gain for them an inweaving and figurement— in the place of bees, ermine tufts, and their various present decorations —upon the august great robes back-flowing and foaming over the gaspy page-boys.

A cat may look at a king, said Alice; but she did not encourage anyone to think that a cat may simultaneously fly and stare. If Meredith had stopped before the balsamic bath, he would have saved himself from the nonsense of souls, cats, and robes. He was always at risk when left entirely to his own judgement: he needed to be held, at least in some measure, to a situation he had not invented. He could permit himself to yearn for the upper air only if he had one foot on the ground.

Meredith's best poems are "Love in the Valley," *Modern Love*, "Lucifer in Starlight," "Dirge in Woods," and now, thanks to Bayley's attention, "Aimée." On April 14, 1894, Robert Louis Stevenson wrote to Yeats, recalling "Love in the Valley," presumably the revised version published in *Poems and Lyrics of the Joy of Earth* (1883). "Some ten years ago," he wrote, "a spell was cast upon me by Meredith's 'Love in the Valley'; the stanzas beginning 'When her mother tends her' haunted me and made me drunk like wine; and I remember waking with them all the echoes of the hills about Hyères." Here is the beginning of the passage:

> *When her mother tends her before the laughing mirror,*
> *Tying up her laces, looping up her hair,*
> *Often she thinks, were this wild thing wedded,*
> *More love should I have, and much less care.*
> *When her mother tends her before the lighted mirror,*
> *Loosening her laces, combing down her curls,*
> *Often she thinks, were this wild thing wedded,*
> *I should miss but one for many boys and girls.*

Phyllis Bartlett said that Meredith got the trochaic meter of this poem from George Darley's "Serenade of a Loyal Martyr" (1836). If so, Meredith distinguished his poem from its source by quickening the tempo and getting rid of the tearful note which makes Darley kin to, say, Tom Moore. In any event the metrical problem was demanding enough to curb Meredith's facility; it served instead of quotidian fact. "Dirge in Woods" has been compared to Goethe's *"Über allen Gipfeln,"* the second of the *"Wandrers Nachtlieder,"* and the resemblance is striking; it is not a translation but an imitation or an allusion. I quote it entire:

> *A wind sways the pines,*
> *And below*

> *Not a breath of wild air;*
> *Still as the mosses that glow*
> *On the flooring and over the lines*
> *Of the roots here and there.*
> *The pine-tree drops its dead;*
> *They are quiet, as under the sea.*
> *Overhead, overhead*
> *Rushes life in a race,*
> *As the clouds the clouds chase;*
> *And we go,*
> *And we drop like the fruits of the tree,*
>   *Even we,*
>   *Even so.*

Without the last two lines the comparison between our lives and the pine cones would be lugubrious, mortality too obviously underlined. The last lines turn the poem to music, prevent it from dropping into itself completely. The feeling is stabilized. Goethe's poem uses a quite different range of tones, sounding between *"Ruh"* and *"Hauch"*:

> *Über allen Gipfeln*
> *Ist Ruh,*
> *In allen Wipfeln*
> *Spürest du*
> *Kaum einen Hauch;*
> *Die Vögelein schweigen im Walde.*
> *Warte nur, balde*
> *Ruhest du auch.*

But Meredith's poem survives the comparison by virtue of its poise: it is perfectly phrased and composed.

 Modern Love is extraordinary. It was right and honest of Meredith to make the situation not a triangle but a quadrilateral. When his wife left him, he did not, so far as we know, take up with another woman, but the poem would have been cast too much in his favour if he had presented himself as the faithful, wounded husband. In the poem the other woman has the effect of restraining the husband's self-pity and letting the poem extend its range of feeling: recrimination, mainly, but tenderness, too, as well as envy, rage, and a sense of the price he pays for his superiority.

John Hollander mentioned recently the kinship between Meredith and Robert Frost, with Emerson as a common possession. The point is well taken. There are several passages in *Modern Love* which sound like Frost's grim narratives; including one passage that Frost often quoted:

> 'Tis morning: but no morning can restore
> What we have forfeited. I see no sin:
> The wrong is mixed. In tragic life, God wot,
> No villain need be! Passions spin the plot:
> We are betrayed by what is false within.

Can't you hear Frost reciting those lines and making them sound like a poem by Frost, to whom all wrongs were mixed?

It would be a pleasure to go through *Modern Love,* quoting: it is one of the few poems of 800 lines (fifty near-sonnets, each sixteen lines) I've ever wished longer. Meredith's best novel? Yes, in the sense that he never again wrote a story as forceful and as controlled. Reading many of his poems, I find myself thinking of other poets who would have done them better; Hardy, in many cases, sometimes A. E. Housman. Reading *Modern Love,* I think of other poets who wrote, or might have written, this sort of thing, but without doing it better: Tennyson, in one respect, Frost in another, E. A. Robinson yet another. Of the fifty sonnets, my anthology would include numbers 15, 17, 25, 34, 35, 36, 47, and if I had to choose only one, I'd take the last. Meredith was not always strong in his endings: like Donne, he often started best and wavered thereafter. But the last poem of *Modern Love* is masterly. The erring wife has killed herself:

> Thus piteously Love closed what he begat:
> The union of this ever-diverse pair!
> These two were rapid falcons in a snare,
> Condemned to do the flitting of the bat.
> Lovers beneath the singing sky of May,
> They wandered once; clear as the dew on flowers:
> But they fed not on the advancing hours;
> Their hearts held cravings for the buried day.
> Then each applied to each that fatal knife,

Deep questioning, which probes to endless dole.
Ah, what a dusty answer gets the soul
When hot for certainties in this our life!—
In tragic hints here see what evermore
Moves dark as yonder midnight ocean's force,
Thundering like ramping hosts of warrior horse,
To throw that faint thin line upon the shore!

The problem here was to end the poem in terms which manage to accommodate everything that has happened, in gist and essence and not merely in summary.

There must be a final sense of the range of feeling through which the poem has passed, from colloquial moments ("a dusty answer") and flashes of mockery ("hot for certainties") to a decently grand note stopping well short of taking pleasure in its grandeur. The genre implied by the images (falcon, bat, dew, the surgeon's knife, the ocean's horses) must be Jacobean rather than Shakespearean, because the experience must find in magniloquence a certain relief but not the final relief of certainty. The warrior horse of the ocean enforce a sense of disproportion between the flurry of events and the values to be derived from them. We are certainly not to feel, as in Shakespearean tragedy, that the cost of the experience is somehow just. Jacobean melodrama provides the decorum the situation needs, if we can somehow take melodrama as a genre not at all shamed by a comparison with tragedy. Tragedy and melodrama are each adequate to the feelings in the case: only the feelings are different. Meredith speaks of "tragic hints," presumably to disclaim any ambition to present his story as a complete tragic action. The gaps between one hint and the next, like the gaps between one sonnet and the next, point to the things in experience which we have to leap across or take for granted or feign or forget or ignore, if we are to sustain ourselves at all on the advancing hours.

Some readers, like Frost and Joyce, value Meredith for a phrase, a line or two, a stanza. In *Ulysses* the telegram Stephen Dedalus sends Mulligan is a sentence inaccurately recalled from *The Ordeal of Richard Feverel*:

The sentimentalist is he who would enjoy without incurring the immense debtorship for a thing done.

It speaks well for Meredith that he could be quoted as a rebuke against the mocking Mulligan. I imagine that Frost respected Meredith for the tone, independent if not defiant, in which the poet may negotiate his experience. Robert Lowell's reading of Meredith seems to have had a more urgent cause. When he was writing "The Mills of the Kavanaughs" he took from *Modern Love* ("The first marriage-torture, marriage-strife poem," he called it) not only the sixteen-line stanza but the technique of diverting a personal wrangle into ostensibly objective form; holding back as much of the marital detail as he could, short of keeping it secret. Lowell added the dream of the rape of Persephone and many other bits of mythology, which extend and obscure the personal situation from which the poem began. These seem designed to estrange the poem from its origin rather than to claim for it some enormous universal bearing. But Meredith showed Lowell what might be done, and the Jacobean rhetoric which would give the occasion the lurid decorum it needed.

Review of *The Poems of George Meredith,* edited by Phyllis B. Bartlett. From *The New York Review of Books,* February 22, 1979.

THE GOOD SOLDIER

egin at the beginning. Let us suppose that we are reading the book for the first time, starting with the title page which has Ford's name, the title *The Good Soldier,* the subtitle *A Tale of Passion,* and in quotation marks the words "Beati Immaculati." Let us assume that we recognize the Latin as the first words of the Vulgate version of Psalm 119, in the Authorized Version, "Blessed are the undefiled in the way, who walk in the law of the Lord." The meaning of these several phrases is merely virtual at this stage; they promise to mean something, but only in the future and therefore in retrospect. We do not yet know who the soldier is, or what is the form of his merit. *A Tale of Passion* is another promissory note, nothing more. The allusion to Psalm 119 is as distant as Latin from any local reference. These phrases will signify, but not yet. So we turn the page and find a "dedicatory letter" to Stella Ford, signed F.M.F. and dated New York, January 9, 1927. We are reading not the first edition (1915) but a text warmed by Ford's affection: "I have always regarded this as my best book." The letter tells us that Ford sat down to write the book on his fortieth birthday, December 17, 1913, and that he wanted to do for the English novel what Maupassant had done for the French in *Fort comme la mort.* We are also told that Ford originally called the book *The Saddest Story* and that he changed the title only because the publisher found its reference to sadness inopportune, sadness being already universal in 1915. *Ford comme la mort?* In any case we have come to the end of the letter and are ready for Part I:

> This is the saddest story I have ever heard. We had known the Ashburnhams for nine seasons of the town of Nauheim with an extreme intimacy—or, rather, with an acquaintanceship as loose and easy and yet as close as a good glove's with your hand. My wife and I knew Captain and Mrs. Ashburnham as well as it was possible to know anybody, and yet, in another sense, we knew nothing at all about them. This is, I believe, a state of things only possible with English people of whom, till today, when I sit down to puzzle out what I know of this sad affair, I knew nothing whatever. Six months ago I had never been to England, and, certainly, I had never sounded the depths of an English heart. I had known the shallows.
>
> I don't mean to say . . .

And so on.

A first reading of that paragraph would pick up such things as the following: a story, to be told by a voice peremptory about its role if a little helpless about its knowledge: a tone which commands attention even while it confesses itself bewildered. Not "the saddest case I have ever known" but "the saddest story I have ever heard"; as if the narrator were telling you a story he had heard from someone else; a story, then, as such, to be told for its interest. But it is odd that the narrator is already making such a fuss about the insecurity of knowledge: he knows something, presumably, but insists that he does not know it securely. On a first reading we hardly stop to count the number of occasions on which the verb *"to know"* is invoked—seven, in fact, high frequency for a short paragraph—but we register the narrator's nervousness in the presence of knowledge. He says something, and then he qualifies the saying, as if the words pushed him further than he cared to be pushed, his scruple being what it is. "Or, rather . . . And yet, in another sense . . ." The business of England and the English is also odd. The kind of knowledge in question is based upon social meetings, society's seasons rather than nature's, but the narrator has adverted to another kind, the depths of an English heart to be sounded. Depths, distinguished from the shallows, if not further plumbed. We do not measure those depths; we do not know how deep the narrator thinks they are. For all we know, the depths of an English heart may be a contradiction in terms: no heart, no depth. Already we have caught the narrator's misgiving: the relation between words and what they claim to know seems confused. It is not that the words cannot rise to a real knowledge, but that they presume upon it. They are premature, pretending to know in advance what the narrator cannot even claim to know in hindsight. The sentences seem explicit, but what they explicate is far darker than their syntax implies, and so the narrator must confound their lucidity, intervene on behalf of truthfulness. Truthfulness, rather than truth, since truth refers to the facts of the case and truthfulness to the spirit in which they are to be declared; his truthfulness, the narrator's.

The experience of a first reading is more telling than criticism has recognized. When we write a critical essay on a text, we read the text over and over and look at it every which way in the hope of seeing something aslant that we could not see directly. Every further reading has to deal with our previous readings: we write, then, from impressions which are already a palimpsest. We assume that the latest reading is best, richest, issuing from a greater experience of the text. I do in part believe it. Every book asks to be read. Johnson: "That book is good in vain which the reader throws away." Most books are content to be read once, they do not claim to be worth reading twice. Literature claims to be worth reading twice. If you can bear to read a detective story twice, it is because the book has aesthetic interest over and beyond its detective interest. Even so; a first reading has at least this privilege, that we can ask ourselves what keeps us turning the pages. With later readings, that question cannot arise; we keep turning the pages to verify or qualify what we recall from earlier readings.

What am I talking about? Only this: the privilege of a first reading not because it is likely to be better than any subsequent reading—there is no evidence for this—but simply because it is first, like our first meeting with someone who becomes a friend. Ideally, a critical essay would be written directly after the first reading of a text, to gain all the advantages of firstness, ignorance, contingency. Later readings should issue in marginalia, addenda, perhaps corrigenda, but should not suppress the first report. I recall one of William Troy's essays on Virginia Woolf which produced his several accounts of the same body of fiction, accounts written at different times over a period of many years. I do not recall that the earliest account was based upon a first reading, but I hope it was. I mention the matter now mainly because its merits are impossible. I wish I could report upon my first reading of *The Good Soldier,* but I cannot; it is lost in a mass or mess of several readings. My account of a pretended first reading of the first paragraph is merely formal, a conceit devised from regret that the real first reading is gone from me. What follows is drawn from the welter.

In the first paragraph, beginning with "This is the saddest story I have ever heard," the narrator presents himself as a storyteller, though he appears to take little pleasure in that role. He tells the story because he is the only one left to tell it or with an interest in telling it. Edward and Florence are dead, Nancy is mad, and Leonora is pursuing her new life by putting the old one behind her. The narrator, Dowell, is fated to tell the story, and he tells it with an air of fatality. But his genre is necessarily talk, garrulous enough to roam and digress, raise hares, engage in speculation and surmise. Ford is writing a book by pretending that Dowell is telling a story to a silent listener:

> So I shall just imagine myself for a fortnight or so at one side of the fireplace of a country cottage, with a sympathetic soul opposite me. And I shall go on talking . . .

The pretence is insistently oral. "But I guess I have made it hard for you, O silent listener, to get that impression," he says at one point, one of many. The terminology of print and paper is voided. In Part 3, Dowell describes his wife as "a personality of paper," in the sense that "she represented a real human being with a heart, with feelings, with sympathies, and with emotions only as a bank note represents a certain quantity of gold." The true element is air, breath: the story is given not as so many pages of print but as a mouthful of air. The pretence is maintained until twenty pages from the end. At the beginning of the fifth chapter of Part 4, Dowell gives up all pretence of storytelling and insists upon the work as writing. "I am writing this, now, I should say, a full eighteen months after the words that end my last chapter. Since writing the words 'until my arrival,' which I see end that paragraph, I have seen again," and so on. The reason is that Nancy, who is with him ("sitting in the hall, forty paces from where I am now writing"), is gone far beyond dialogue. No conceit, no romantic fancy, could allow Dowell to think of her any longer as his "dear listener"; she is "not there." So he gives up the pretence of speech and hands over the ending of his story to loneliness and print. And, worse still, he makes his written words turn upon Nancy, accusing her of cruelty comparable with Leonora's, a sinister conspiracy of the two women against Edward. Till that point, Dowell had taken the dear listener as a surrogate for the still dearer Nancy. Now that the pretence has to be dropped, Nancy is replaced by the severity of the written word, and punished for her absence; she is beyond speech, beyond hearing.

Going back to the first paragraph for a second, third, or fourth reading: Dowell's gestures are now familiar to us, especially his trope of correction and his trope of ignorance. For the first, we hear with now greater emphasis his revisions, when he says something and then backs away from its commitment. In the first paragraph, having said that the Dowells knew the Ashburnhams "with an extreme intimacy," he immediately qualifies the saying: "or, rather, with an acquaintanceship as loose and easy and yet as close as a good glove's with your hand." Intimacy seems to be vetoed by acquaintanceship, but the acquaintanceship is then warmed, like fingers in a good glove. A few pages later Dowell has a grandiloquent passage about the intimacy of the two couples as a minuet, and he leads the dance for half a page only to wave it away: "No, by God, it is false! It was not a minuet that we stepped; it was a prison." Much later he says, "And yet I do believe that for every man there comes at last a woman . . . ," and he changes the form of his belief even before the sentence is complete: "or, no, that is the wrong way of formulating it." When he says something, the saying makes it feel wrong, too much more often than not enough. A paragraph ends, "So, perhaps, it was with Edward Ashburnham," and the next paragraph begins, "Or, perhaps, it wasn't. No, I rather think it wasn't. It is difficult to figure out."

As for Dowell's trope of ignorance, I would not blame a reader who finds tedious his constant insistence that he knows nothing, that nothing can be known. "I know nothing—nothing in the world—of the hearts of men." "Who knows?" resounds through the book. Questions are posed, two alternative answers offered, but neither of them is an answer, and the whole episode is voided with an "I don't know" or "It is all a darkness" or "Perhaps you can make head or tail of it; it is beyond me." Facts are recited as if they were significant, but then the official significance attached to them is prised away, first with revisions and modifications, then with a gesture of ignorance. Why?

Think again of Dowell as narrator, or rather as storyteller. The question of reliable and unreliable narrators has often been raised in reference to him, but it is not the real question. Reliable or not, he is the only narrator we have, and we must make the best of him even when he makes the worst of himself. The real question is: what remains, now that nearly all the ostensible significance of the facts has been drained from them by Dowell's scepticism? And the answer is: Dowell himself remains. If you are listening to a storyteller, and he is telling the story subject to constant interruptions, his backward glances, revisions, corrections, and protestations of his own ignorance; these interrogations may damage the confidence with which you receive the story, but not the zest with which you attend upon the storyteller. The more he disputes the significance of the facts he recites, the more indisputable he becomes. We accept him precisely because he is evidently more scrupulous than we would be, in the same circumstances. Accepting him does not mean that we think him infallible but that we think him honest: he may still be obtuse, slow to sense the drift of things. No matter; we listen to his voice. Nothing in *The Good Soldier* is allowed to escape from Dowell's voice, until in the end he disowns voice itself and goes over to the cold fixity of print. It does not matter what he says, as distinct from the saying, which matters all the time. The force of the story, whether it is maintained, deflected, or subverted, returns intact to the teller. It is here that the story is performed; the unity of the tale is in the teller, not in the facts he recites. With Dowell, the tropes of correction and ignorance which seem to warrant our discounting in advance nearly everything he reports, or at any rate our subtracting from its authority, have an entirely different effect; they keep him immune to his subject, or superior to it. The gestures by which he answers contingency make him immune to it. No wonder he survives its attack.

Dowell cannot defeat contingency in its own terms. He survives not only because, as the narrator, he must, but because he converts everything that happens into his own gestures, which are all the better for being his trademarks. Let me explain. Fredric Jameson argues in *Fables of Aggression* that Anglo-American modernism has been dominated by an impressionistic aesthetic rather than by Wyndham Lewis's externalizing and mechanical expressionism. The most influential formal impulses of modernism, he continues, "have been strategies of inwardness, which set out to reappropriate an alienated universe by transforming it into personal styles and private languages." Such wills to style now seem "to reconfirm the very privatization and fragmentation of social life against which they were meant to protest."[1] Jameson does not discuss these strategies of inwardness in detail, but I assume he means, mostly, the impulses common to Joyce's early fiction and Eliot's early poems. Call those strategies Stephen Prufrock, for want of an official name. Is it not clear that Dowell's way of dealing with crass contingency is by transforming it into a personal style and private language? His apparently obsessive themes (heart; Catholicism; good people; knowledge; service) should be construed, like Prufrock's fancies and Stephen's murmurs, as his poetic diction, a specialized vocabulary significant only in relation to him; his private language to which he resorts not only when he has nothing else to do but when a strategy of such inwardness is the only device he can practise. The chief attribute of such a diction is that it is self-propelling; that is (so far as the disinterested reader receives it), repetitive. A diction is that in our language which seeks to establish itself by repetition; it acts in a poem or a novel as a cell acts in politics, a clique, a party of like-minded people. In a poetic diction the words are not the same but similar in their origins, affiliations, let us say in the ideology they sponsor. What, besides the narrator, is John Dowell? He is an ideologist who deals with a flagrantly alienated universe by forcing it towards the inwardness of his diction. We say the diction is obsessive, but we really mean that it has established itself in advance of any contingency that might threaten to overwhelm it. Dowell, not a strong character in other terms, has the strength of the voice he is given, the strength to draw every event towards himself. If his voice remains unanswered, it also remains unanswerable; his style is answerable to contingency by virtue of being, in Jameson's sense, private.

Impressionism is as good a word as any to describe this device. Dowell is like Ford in this respect: the truth of an event is always the accuracy of his impression of it. He despaired of ever achieving an autonomous truth, independent of his sense of it; and he converted despair into scruple. The words he needs and uses are those which, with maximum resource and accuracy, convey his impression of a fact or situation, and they release themselves from further obligation. So the direction of force in *The Good Soldier* is always from the outer event to the inwardness which receives and transforms it. Tropes of correction and ignorance arise from Dowell's sense that the event and his impression of it do not necessarily coincide; but this is a misgiving congenital to idealists. Meanwhile his speech is an exercise of the only power he commands, the power to draw every event into himself and convert it into privacy and inwardness.

Why do we speak? The question is reasonable when asked of a Dowell, who has nothing but speech. We speak to exercise the faculty and power of speech. Again we speak from need, the need to recognize our need, including especially our sense of the inadequacy of speech. We speak to be completed and fulfilled; meanwhile to be appeased. In *The Good Soldier,* Dowell's speech is the only power he commands, and what speech commands is mostly the space of its presence, its resonance. Dowell's voice has every power in the world except the power to change anything or forestall it: it can do all things, provided that they are all the one thing, the conversion to inwardness by repetition. So there is no contradiction in referring to the power of Dowell's voice and recognizing that, for himself, he insists only upon helplessness. Up to the end and more especially at the end, Dowell insists that he is feeble, effete, a mere shadow of greater men: specifically, he insists, "I have only followed, faintly, and in my unconscious desires, Edward Ashburnham." As Prufrock says, "No! I am not Prince Hamlet, nor was meant to be"; a Polonius, perhaps. But voice, in Dowell, is more powerful than anything he knows in himself: in his mere person he has nothing to match it.

That is to say: the power is in the role of storyteller. It does not matter that he is obtuse, if he is obtuse; slow to grasp what Leonora knows when she rushes from the room at M— and speaks of "accepting the situation"; and naïve generally about Ashburnham and Florence. No matter; the beauty of the book arises from the ironic relation between two factors—the primacy of Dowell's voice, if for no other reason than that it is the only voice we really hear; and his persistent effort to direct all our attention and nearly all our sympathy towards Edward, who has wronged him in every way that seems at first to matter but finally does not matter, since Florence was already bogus. The book draws every event or fact towards Dowell; while he insists that, by comparison with Ashburnham, he is nothing, a shadow at best of a greater self.

Much of our understanding of storytelling is due to two studies, Albert B. Lord's *The Singer of Tales*[2] and Walter Benjamin's "The Storyteller," in *Illuminations,*[3] a collection of his essays edited by Hannah Arendt. *The Singer of Tales* is a study of oral narrative, the epic construed as an oral art. Particularly we note the formulaic element in epic narrative, phrases which make a breathing space for the singer and establish the provenance of epic poetry as such: they correspond to Dowell's recurrent themes or motifs, which otherwise look like nervous tics and allow some readers to refer, too casually, to obsession. *The Singer of Tales* also supports, only less specifically, the notion of our attention, as listeners, being drawn always to the singer, the storyteller. The narrative always remains a mouthful of air, enacting not only ostensible events in a world at large but the proximity of the singer to his voice. Benjamin's essay mainly distinguishes between novel and tale; between fiction as a function of the printing press and fiction as story, oral narrative. The novel is meant to be read in solitude, and it features an elaborately detailed psychology. The tale is meant to be heard in common, it is a function of speech and, equally, of listening; its psychology is general rather than specific, more interested in the sort of thing people do than in any particular thing a particular person has done. In the tale, the explanation of the events is left loose, open-meshed; in the novel, the explanation is inscribed. We are discouraged from offering our own reasons to account for what people have done or failed to do. The events narrated in a novel generally proceed in accord with the linear, sequential form sponsored by pages and print: in the tale, the storyteller is free with the circuit of his story; he delivers things in the order in which he forms impressions of them, he remembers and forgets, he adverts to the slack of his narrative and stops to take it up. *The Good Soldier* has often been read as a precociously modern novel that anticipates many of the procedures of more recent French fiction in the fractures of its narrative. A simpler explanation is that it is what its subtitle says it is, a tale told by an amateur storyteller who does the best he can and takes every latitude offered by that genre.

Northrop Frye has pointed out in *Anatomy of Criticism* that a genre tends to be mixed rather than simple, and that fictions tend to result from mixtures of generic elements.[4] Very few fictions are single-minded instances of their genres. So it is not an embarrassment to say that *The Good Soldier* is a mixture of novel and tale; though I would maintain that it is a tale incorporating, often with only a show of interest, some elements from the novel. The novel tends to place its events in society; its art is politics so far as its themes are evident; it concerns itself with the human relations provoked by a given society. These elements are active in *The Good*

Soldier, but not as active as a list of its ostensible themes would suggest. We hear a good deal about property, travel, love affairs, the season at Nauheim and other places, but the social atmosphere is notably thin: we are not encouraged to sense, beyond the four chief characters and the various women whom Edward loved, a social world densely wrought, going about its business. The social atmosphere is thin for a book that seems to present itself as an account of such things. But the explanation is that in its scheme of organization and judgement, *The Good Soldier* is only nominally a novel. The novel supplies only its decor, not its judgements. The judgements issue far more directly from the tale, in which characters are more types than individuals and psychological explanations are felt to be beside the point. Why does Edward do the things he does? Because he is the type to do them: that is Dowell's pervasive implication. His actions are not explained, as a novel would offer to explain them, by reference to his early circumstances, and so forth. Again: where blame must be laid, Dowell does not lay it upon society, but upon Fate. The ordinances of society are not invoked. The main conflict is not between self and society but between type and morality, and finally the blame is laid upon Fate, the force of nature that ordained the type in the first place. In Dowell's account of Edward and the Kilsyte girl, only Edward's nature is blamed, and thereafter the God of his nature. "There is no priest that has the right to tell me that I must not ask pity for him, from you, silent listener beyond the hearthstone, from the world, or from the God who created in him those desires, those madnesses." The same page has a rather Conradian passage about "that inscrutable and blind justice" which punishes you "for following your natural but ill-timed inclinations." A few pages later we hear of "the shadow of an eternal wrath"; later still, of "the ingenious torments that fate prepares for us" and our drifting down "the stream of destiny." Bad coincidences are attributed to "a merciless trick of the devil that pays attention to this sweltering hell of ours." And so forth. Dowell's accusations become more extreme as the story goes on, and in the end Fate becomes a neo-Darwinian mutation by which vivid organisms are suppressed so that ordinary, normal, prudent organisms may survive.

Since this development brings the major judgement of the book, I should round it out. The crucial passage comes at the beginning of Part 4, Chapter 5, where Dowell, thinking of Edward and Nancy and Leonora, says that events worked out "in the extinction of two very splendid personalities—for Edward and the girl *were* splendid personalities, in order that a third personality, more normal, should have, after a long period of trouble, a quiet, comfortable, good time." That last phrase, which refers to the married life of Leonora and Rodney Bayham, is enough to show what Dowell feels about the dispositions of Fate which have issued in a good time for such trivial people; and about the cost to other people. He reverts to the point a few pages later:

> Conventions and traditions I suppose work blindly but surely for the preservation of the normal type; for the extinction of proud, resolute, and unusual individuals.

And again, later, mocking the happy disposition of blessings and punishments:

> Well, that is the end of the story. And, when I come to look at it, I see that it is a happy ending with wedding bells and all. The villains—for obviously Edward and the girl were villains—have been punished by suicide and madness. The heroine—the perfectly normal, virtuous, and slightly deceitful heroine—has become the happy wife of a perfectly normal, virtuous, and slightly deceitful husband. She will shortly become a mother of a perfectly normal, virtuous, slightly deceitful son or daughter. A happy ending, that is what it works out at.

Indeed, he cannot leave the point alone. On the next page he refers to the sinister conspiracy of Fate and Society:

> Mind, I am not preaching anything contrary to accepted morality. I am not advocating free love in this or any other case. Society must go on, I suppose, and society can only exist if the normal, if the virtuous, and the slightly deceitful flourish, and if the passionate, the headstrong, and the too-truthful are condemned to suicide and to madness. But I guess that I myself, in my fainter way, come into the category of the passionate, of the headstrong, and the too-truthful. For I can't conceal from myself the fact that I loved Edward Ashburnham—and that I love him because he was just myself.

The Byronism of these passages is of course odd, except that it is a Byronism of desire and not of deed. Society has nothing to fear from such desire, unless it forces itself into action and calls itself Edward Ashburnham. *The Good Soldier* is not "a novel without a hero," it is what it claims to be, a tale of passion in which passion is found in Edward and only its desire in Dowell. And since the ground of Edward's passion is his nature, the force that destroys it and destroys him can only be called Fate. If the force were contingent or conventional and not categorical, it could be called Society. But the book is a tale because its conflicts are social only betimes and by the way; the true conflict is aboriginal, it has to do with natures and principles. Fate is what we call Nature when its dealings with us are sinister not by chance but by design and malice. Society is a cultural term, and it arises in *The Good Soldier* only at the last moment and, even then, misleadingly; it is nothing more than the visible form of Fate, Fate's conspirator on the daily surface of life. The chief irony of the book is that these warring principles are narrated and invoked by a storyteller who knows them only in shadow and by the intermittent knowledge of his own desire. "I don't know why I should always be selected to be serviceable," he muses at one point. He seems born to be in attendance; diversely upon Florence, Edward, Leonora, and Nancy, but more fundamentally upon passions that he cannot feel in himself but only through others, especially through Edward. If he is superior to the events by being immune to them, he gains this immunity by being fated to know only indirectly and at several removes the passions that made the events. No wonder we recall him as rueful and sedentary, when his own feelings are present; and as rising only to the occasions provoked by others.

There is no contradiction in thinking of Dowell as Byronic in desire and again, in the way he thought of himself, as a nurse if not a poodle; because his Byronism is a value asserted in the modern world but known, and known well enough by him, to be archaic and belated there. It is precisely because the value is archaic that it has to be asserted, and may be. Dowell's Byronism remains nostalgic so long as it is doomed in practice and archaic in every form of itself short of practice. If it had the slightest chance of being embodied successfully and at large, it could be invoked and would not need to be asserted. So it stands for all those "lost values known to be lost" which R. P. Blackmur has ascribed to Ford's novels as the substance of their unmoored sensibility. "Each of these books," Blackmur remarks, "has something to do with the glory of an arbitrary prestige resting on values asserted but not found in the actual world: values which when felt critically deform rather than enlighten action in that world, so that the action ends in the destruction of the values themselves."[5] In Edward Ashburnham the destruction of Byronism is complete; it survives only as a pale shadow of itself, and only as a virtual value, in Dowell, where it never reaches further than mockery. Who are mocked? The "beati immaculati" who walk in perfectly normal, virtuous, and slightly deceitful ways which they appropriate as the way and the law of the Lord. But the mockery, valid enough in the usual anti-bourgeois tone of modern literature, is itself mocked by being ascribed to a man whose criticism of life is, in every limiting sense of the phrase, merely verbal. Dowell says of Edward and Nancy at the end:

> So those splendid and tumultuous creatures with their magnetism and their passions—those two that I really loved—have gone from this earth.

What does Dowell know, we may well ask, of tumult and magnetism, except as his own unconscious desire, carefully suppressed from the field of action and belatedly incited into words? For him, and not for him alone, the words become a substitute for the action that cannot otherwise be taken. If we forgive him, it is because he has not quite forgiven himself.

We return to our starting point: Dowell as narrator, reciting the deeds of others and the suffering which in part he shares with them. His reliability is not the problem. He is central to the story because he is the storyteller. The pathos of the book is that the passion to which Dowell appeals has no continuing place in the world. In many senses, we have approved its loss; in a residual sense, our approval is itself compromised. We do not want Byronism back, but we cannot be sanguine about the ease with which we have repudiated all such desires.

NOTES

1. Fredric Jameson, *Fables of Aggression* (Berkeley: University of California Press, 1979), p. 2.
2. Albert B. Lord, *The Singer of Tales* (Cambridge: Harvard University Press, 1960).
3. Walter Benjamin, *Illuminations* (New York: Schocken Books, 1969).

4. Northrop Frye, *Anatomy of Criticism* (Princeton: Princeton University Press, 1957).
5. R. P. Blackmur, "The King over the Water: Notes on the Novels of F. M. Hueffer": *Princeton University Library Chronicle*, 9 (3); reprinted in *Modern British Fiction: Essays in Criticism*, ed. Mark Schorer (Oxford: Oxford University Press, 1961), p. 141.

From *The Sewanee Review*, Vol. LXXXVIII (Fall 1980).

Postscript: In Reply to Frank Kermode

It is common knowledge that Frank Kermode is engaged in a major study of fiction and the theory of fiction. I assume that "Novels: Recognition and Deception" in the first number of *Critical Inquiry* is part of that adventure, and that it should be read in association with other essays on cognate themes which he has published in the last two or three years. This may account for my impression that the *Critical Inquiry* essay is not independently convincing. There are splendid things in the essay, perceptions so definitively phrased that I cannot promise not to steal them. My copy of the journal is heavily marked on Kermode's pages, invariably on passages I dearly wish I had had the wit to write, notably his remark of certain fictions by Henry James that "they create gaps that cannot be closed, only gloried in; they solicit mutually contradictory types of attention and close only on a problem of closure." But these perceptions are like indelible events in the diction of a poem which, as a whole, does not seem to cohere. Let me try to account for this impression.

Kermode's theme in this essay is plurality of interpretation, and he encourages us to rise to such occasions when we meet them in novels. The object is "productive reading," and we are to assume that the reader's share in the experience of the novel is considerable; we do not merely consume the work, we should respond in our own way to the "treatment" embodied in the text. I am inclined to say of Kermode what James said of Conrad, that he is "a votary of the way to do a thing that shall make it undergo most doing." As for the doing, he illustrates what he has in view by commenting in detail upon the first paragraph of *The Good Soldier*. I shall return to the commentary after remarking that Kermode offers it as sustaining his reference to "the *deceptions,* the *multiple* voices, the absence of a simple complicity, of a truth vouched-for and certainly known." "We are in a world of which it needs to be said *not* that plural readings are possible (for this is true of all narrative) but that *the illusion of the single right reading is possible no longer.*"

My first point is that this last assertion, whatever its merits as a general proposition, is not verified by *The Good Soldier* or by Kermode's commentary. Ford's novel strikes a bargain with the reader in the terms given by the narrator John Dowell in Part 4, Chapter 1: "You have the facts for the trouble of finding them." Dowell has one story to tell; he is at once the narrator and the victim of the events narrated. As narrator, he is strikingly unreliable. Many of his judgements are morally obtuse, he has a touch of the Prufrocks, his limitations are not charming. "And this, and so much more." Worse still, he gets things wrong. As Kermode mentions, Dowell has Nancy Rufford dead twice when she's still babbling about the omnipotence of God. It's just possible, incidentally, that on the first occasion Dowell is referring to Mrs. Maidan and on the second to Florence; possible, but I don't believe it. However, the main point is that there is only one story, and the reader is provoked into finding it, piecing it together with the doubtful aid of a narrator who, having survived the events, has time on his hands. There may be trouble in finding out precisely what happened, but Ford is determined that the reader will take this trouble. Novels generally proceed by giving genuine information but not enough of it at any moment, so you stay with the book until you are satisfied. Satisfaction is usually at once a moral and a formal fulfilment. *The Good Soldier* proceeds by keeping you doubtful about the status of what you're getting, and you stay with it to have your doubts removed. They are removed, eventually and by and large, though there are a few unexplained things at the end. This is only another way of saying that the novel puts Dowell under pressure and interrogation; the reader is meant to be suspicious and only gradually to be convinced that he has in fact heard a genuine story. But the novel does not require us to believe that "the illusion of the single right reading is possible no longer." The facts are there, we have only to find them.

Kermode's commentary supports my case rather than his. It takes each sentence as it comes, interprets the evidence, broods over questions of tone, and assumes throughout that there is one story but the narrator has an odd way of telling it. The whole enterprise is in keeping with the first mode of interpretation which Derrida describes in a passage which Kermode quotes from *L'écriture et la différence:*

> There are two interpretations of interpretation, of structure, of the sign and play. One seeks to decipher, dreams of deciphering a reality or an origin which evades the game and the order of signs, and lives like an exile the necessity of interpretation. The other . . .

Kermode's commentary on the first page of *The Good Soldier* is singular rather than plural; it addresses itself to the difficulty of deciphering the evidence and finding the story, but it does not undermine the validity of the search. So there is a disjunction between his commentary on the only text he examines and the later paragraphs sponsoring plurality of interpretation.

Perhaps I am merely saying that *The Good Soldier* was not a good illustration for Kermode's argument. The most helpful critical work on Ford's novels is based on the assumption that there is in each case a story to be told, however complicated the telling or the teller. I'm thinking of something as straightforward (for once) as Blackmur's "The King over the Water," which studies Ford's novels as dramatizations of men and women devoted to "lost causes known to be lost." (Blackmur's little essay is more readily available in Mark Schorer's *Modern British Fiction: Essays in Criticism* [1961] than in its first printing, *Princeton University Library Chronicle,* 9:3.) Doesn't this phrase, even apart from the other perceptions which flesh it in Blackmur's treatment, throw a genuine light upon the relation between Dowell and Ashburnham; Dowell and Florence; Leonora and Ashburnham; Leonora and her own life, including not least her weird version of Catholicism? And what about these sentences as offering an effective entry to *The Good Soldier,* though Blackmur's use of them had Ford more generally in view:

> He dealt with loyalty and the conflict of loyalties like Conrad, he dealt with fine consciences and hideously brooded sensualities like James. But all the loyalty he did not find heightened by Conrad was obstinacy, and all the conscience and sensuality he did not find created by James were priggery and moral suicide. Adding this to what has already been said of the chief novels makes a terrible simplification: it says that Ford supplied only the excesses of his

characters' vices and virtues, and only the excesses of their situations; and it suggests that his sensibility was unmoored, or was moored only in the sense that a sensibility may be moored to lost causes known to be lost.

The real question about *The Good Soldier* is how a story gets told, and how these excesses are represented without loss of their exacerbation, through a narrative victim who seems to consist of nothing but his limitations. So we have to come back again to what we have never really left, a question of style.

May I make a few marginal glosses upon Kermode's commentary, based upon my assumption that in this novel we do not fall into error, at least not necessarily, if we read upon the illusion of a single right reading?

1. "This is the saddest story I have ever heard." Kermode says that "*saddest* is a bit lame, perhaps, and certainly misleading . . . and *heard* is strikingly peculiar." But *saddest* is all right, because Dowell is presented as the kind of man to whom *mezzo forte* terms of description come naturally; even his superlatives sound like comparatives. And *heard* is all right, because the events have become for him, as for any other survivor, a story to be told as though they made a story he has heard. The point is to keep the events in a middle distance.

2. KERMODE: "The word *know* in different forms occurs in this second sentence, three times in the third, twice in the fourth. In the second it is intensified—'with an extreme intimacy'—but that qualification is at once withdrawn: 'or, rather, with an acquaintanceship . . .'" Yes, and this is the first hearing of what I might call Dowell's cadence of revision, the chief characteristic of his style. He is always saying, "It was X. No, it was not X, it was Y. No, by God, it was really Z." "Upon my word, yes, our intimacy was like a minuet . . . no, by God, it is false! It wasn't a minuet . . . it was a prison. . . . And yet . . . it was true sunshine; the true music; the true splash of the fountains from the mouth of stone dolphins." Later: "I suppose, therefore, that her eyes had made a favourable answer. Or, perhaps, it wasn't a favourable answer." These cadences often die away in a "Who knows?" or an "It is all a darkness." I take this cadence of ostensible revision as one of the ways in which Ford exerts pressure upon Dowell; showing Dowell as a man who dribbles from one

moral position to another because he cannot register, with passion or conviction, any difference between them.

3. Ford's second sentence: "We had known the Ashburnhams for nine seasons of the town of Nauheim with an extreme intimacy—or, rather, with an acquaintanceship as loose and easy and yet as close as a good glove's with your hand." KERMODE: ". . . the simile of the glove, which professes closeness and warmth but betrays itself as the index of a trivial relationship dependent on a peculiar social usage of the word 'good.' " Not quite, I think. Our sense of the relationship is first alerted by "seasons," which draws a social circle within which the phrase "extreme intimacy" is given a correspondingly limited scale of values. Then the cadence of revision begins: "or, rather . . ." But the descent from "intimacy" to "acquaintance-ship" is not as dramatic as Kermode makes it seem. And I think Kermode's remark about the glove a bit rough. The glove does not betray anything, the reader is not encouraged to wince at the "trivial" relationship. Of course there is, as Kermode says, "a great deal of textual whispering about *know*," and nearly as much about *good*, as in "good people"; but the whispering about good hasn't started yet, and the qualities of a good glove are still immune to irony, except insofar as everything in this second sentence is placed within the circle inscribed by "seasons."

I would enjoy a bit of wrestling with Kermode's prose at any time. He is one of the few critics who please while instructing. But it is unnecessary to keep on glossing him in this way. I only wanted to make the point that his commentary, like my glossing, is propelled by the assumption that there is a story to be received for the labour of putting the pieces together. Nothing in his commentary, or in my gloss, is consistent with the second interpretation described by Derrida:

> The other, which is no longer oriented towards the origin, affirms the game and tries to pass beyond man and humanism, the name of man being the name of that being who, throughout the history of metaphysics and ontotheology—that is, throughout his history—has dreamed of full presence, of the reassuring referential basis, the beginning and the end of the game.

Kermode quotes this, but it really has little bearing upon his essay, it does not describe his own practice as a critic. He has not tried to pass beyond man and humanism, he is tender to origins, and I think he is less interested in game theory than in using every available means of making sense of our experience.

I don't deny, of course, that there are fictions which call for new ways of reading, as invoked diversely by Barthes, Derrida, and other critics. Not all of these fictions are to be found on the shelves marked *Nouveau Roman.* Conventional ways of reading haven't had much success with *A Tale of a Tub.* But I find it odd that Kermode, always alert and sensitive, offers as proof of the necessity of new ways in reading fiction *The Good Soldier,* a novel which seems to me to thrive upon the old ways, if we use them for all they are worth.

From *Critical Inquiry,* Vol. I, No. 2 (December 1974).

D. H. LAWRENCE IN HIS LETTERS

O ne of the risks incurred by a reader who takes an interest in Lawrence is that such an interest is likely to become omnivorous. It is hardly possible to place *The Rainbow* and *Women in Love* in the centre of that interest without engrossing, as one moves toward the circumference, pretty nearly everything else in the canon. In theory, it is possible to discount Lawrence's metaphysic, and to assume that his recourse to the idiom of Father, Son, and Holy Ghost is merely vulgar, a minor essay in blasphemy. Some readers consider themselves free, when Lawrence's poems are offered, to take them or leave them. As for the argumentative Lawrence, T. S. Eliot was not alone in concluding that Lawrence had no talent for sustained thought: a glazed look descends upon such readers when he stops describing things and takes to the high horse of doctrine. There is always an implication in such readers that Lawrence wrote the major novels by default, and that if he had acted more characteristically he would have made a mess of them. According to these reservations, he was an untutored genius who developed, by sheer determination, a late and wilfully declared vocation for thought. The simplicity of this argument has a certain charm, it is pleasant to dispose of a writer by saying that he did not know enough and that he was ill-advised to go to the trouble of knowing anything. But it will not do. If you want to get rid of Lawrence you must do so with a certain majesty by ignoring him, or by setting up as the coordinates of modern literature those lines of force which exclude him; as Hugh Kenner did in *The Pound Era,* taking possession of the early twentieth century on behalf of Pound, Eliot, Wyndham Lewis, Joyce, and Yeats, with James in the shadows nodding assent. But if you admit Lawrence at all, you are likely to make the admission complete, retaining everything merely because he wrote it. I have no fault to find with this attitude, I do not think idolatry a necessary consequence. If Lawrence is received as a major presence in modern literature, we ought to have his rough with his smooth. So I am not daunted to hear that hefty batches of letters are turning up day by day, and that the big edition now being prepared will run to several volumes. When James received a selection from Hawthorne's French and Italian notebooks, he raised the question of the proper limits of curiosity, while recognizing that its actual limits would be fixed only by a total exhaustion of matter. But James had particularly in mind his sense of Hawthorne's retiring nature, and he thought the collection of his jottings made excessively liberal excisions "from the privacy of so reserved and shade-seeking a genius." Hawthorne was someone to whom James felt a particular obligation to be tender. It is unnecessary to feel such an obligation to Lawrence. He did not seek the shade, he thrust himself forward into the life of his time as into the life of his fiction and poetry; one feels no obligation to cherish him, or to protect him from the heat of the sun. So our attitude to the accumulation of letters must be: the more, the better.

This is not to confess to an appetite merely gross. Lawrence's letters are objects of independent interest, they are not mere messages delivered to make up for the absence of a telephone. The interest they incur is consistent with a still greater interest in the art of his fiction: the letters are continuous with the fiction, they punctuate a life which is embodied in the novels and stories. It is hardly too much to say that they are more intimately related to his art than to the daily events upon which they appear to feed. If you want to know what Lawrence was doing on Friday, May 5, 1916, you will find one part of the answer in a letter, the following Thursday, from Katherine Mansfield to S. S. Koteliansky: i.e., Lawrence was engaged in an appalling row with Frieda, which started from a remark of Frieda's about Shelley's "To a Skylark." Lawrence screamed at her and, according to Katherine Mansfield, ended up beating her and pulling her hair. Another part of the answer is that Lawrence was meditating on the Easter Rising, Yeats's theme and Ireland's blood sacrifice, the war, the end of democracy: he was reading Kitty O'Shea's *Life of Parnell:* he was at work on "my novel," evidently the first draft of *Women in Love*. The row with Frieda does not appear, so far as I know, in Lawrence's letters. Katherine Mansfield's version is confirmed, as we would expect, in Middleton Murry's *Between Two Worlds,* but the most concentrated reading between the lines of Lawrence's correspondence does not yield as much information as one would expect about the imperfection of the life, set off against a possible perfection of the work. Six months later, the violence of May 5 has been assimilated. "Frieda and I have finished the long and bloody fight at last, and are at one," he wrote to Murry on October 11. So the *Collected Letters* does not make an auto-biography, any more than an autobiography makes a life: in both cases, we have to reckon with the diverse interventions of evasion, silence, form, and art. Reading the letters is a strenuous exercise because the reader cannot take them at face value, he must understand them as subject to many of the same forces which are at work in the fiction; he must interpret them, even when they appear to be merely offering themselves as vehicles of information. On April 15, 1908, Lawrence wrote to Blanche Jennings: "and to be sure I am very young—though twenty two; I have never left my mother, you see." What Blanche saw is of little account: what the reader sees is what he makes of the sentence, how he disposes its several notes, *naïf, faux-naïf,* ingenuous, disingenuous, coy, and so forth. It is never enough if the reader merely takes the correspondence as a neutral context for the fiction, with an assumption that the correspon-dence is simple even when the fiction is complex. The simplicity is merely ostensible, as anyone can see who compares *Sons and Lovers* with Lawrence's several accounts of it in letters to Edward Garnett. The reader has to enter into a relation with the letters comparable, for tension and interrogation, with his relation to "The Crown," the "Study of Thomas Hardy," and the novels themselves. He cannot take the letters as they appear to come, straight from the shoulder or the heart: their origin is more obscure than that. They are to be read, like Keats's letters, with a sense of their belonging to the creative work, even if there is a sense, too, that at a certain point a distinction between them and that work must be made. In both enterprises, the same forces are engaged; feeling, imagination, rhetoric, style, the symbolic act of language. What distinguishes the fiction from the correspondence is the more imperious vocation of form to which the fiction responds; what the correspondence responds to, in respect of form, is a relatively minor demand.

It is generally agreed, however, that Lawrence's letters are among the most achieved letters in English literature: that they are regularly compared with Keats's letters is sufficient testimony. But there is at least a marginal case to be made against them, at least in normal terms, and it is well to consider it sooner rather than later. Bluntly, it amounts to this; that too many of the letters are essays in self-pity, that some of them disclose a mean spirit, even though "many a true word is spoken in spite," that they are good for nothing but intensity. Some of the harm can be taken out of these charges by reducing them to such a formula as the following, from Kenneth Burke's novel *Towards a Better Life:* "When people are both discerning and unhappy, they tend to believe that their unhappiness is derived from their discernment." Generally, and especially in the early adult years, the declared form of Lawrence's unhappiness was poverty. He was poor because he insisted on living by his pen, he would not go back to teaching. But Frieda had some money, friends were generous with their houses, gradually the novels began making a good deal of money, and after 1920 the Lawrences were reasonably comfortable, with Mabel Luhan as their chief benefactress. Lawrence protested his poverty too much. The latitude of his spite is a more serious matter. Of Gordon Campbell: "He lies in the mud and murmurs about his dream-soul, and says that *action* is irrelevant. Meanwhile he earns diligently in munitions." Of Hugh Walpole: "Is he anybody? Could I wring three ha'porth of help out of his bloody neck?" Heinemann was regularly described as "his Jewship," Murry as a stench, "a little muck-spout." Katherine Mansfield, demonstrably ill, was on the Riviera "doing the last-gasp touch, in order to impose on people." Philip Heseltine and his wife were "such abject shits it is a pity they can't be flushed down a sewer." Perhaps we should call it spleen rather than spite, a momentary rage rather than a settled habit. In rage, Lawrence seized the first available object to attack, mostly a friend: sometimes the spleen was exhausted by its expression. But he was niggardly in praise of other artists, unless they were dead. He was generous to Mark Gertler on the strength of his *Merry-Go-Round,* but generally he defined himself in relation to his contemporaries by denouncing them. He was often right, as in denouncing Bertrand Russell's Cambridge.

These and other charges can be documented from the letters. Some parts of the correspondence are so obnoxious, at least on first appearance, that one is astonished to find them issuing from a writer so zealous in defence of his reputation. Surely, we say, he must have known that these things would be brought to public light one day, and that they would not easily be forgiven. A writer who determined, as James said of Emerson, "to limit and define the ground of his appeal to fame" would have schooled himself to hold his tongue, or would at least have withheld the most ferocious letters from the mailbox until his wrath had subsided. A cannier man would have done so. But the fascination of Lawrence's letters consists precisely in the relation between the rough and the smooth: we respond to their authenticity, warts and all. But there is another reason which makes forgiveness easy once it makes it possible. "Of course I say all sorts of things—you yourself know perfectly well the things I say about people—but they aren't malicious and *méchant* things, just momentary. People who *repeat* things are really wicked—because they *always* pour in vitriol of their own." This was offered to Juliette Huxley on April 26, 1928, when Lawrence had got himself into a tangle because of something he was reported as saying about Catherine Carswell. Another version of the same defence was given to Mabel Luhan, on October 17, 1923: "As for reviling you, when I am angry, I say what I feel. I hope you do the same." I find the defence acceptable. Lawrence could forgive anything, so long as it came as a manifestation of energy: a momentary explosion of rage or resentment was true to its occasion, it was a form of energy, so it was not a sin. But he did not always consult this criterion. When Aldous Huxley sent him a copy of *Proper Studies,* Lawrence thanked him with a rigmarole of teasing comment (? November 14, 1927) ending in praise: "very sane and sound and good." But his true opinion was reserved for Koteliansky, a week later: "Huxley's *Proper Studies* is a bore!" I concede that such duplicity is exceptional. Generally, Lawrence told the truth even when it would have been easier to tell a white lie; when he refused to write for Murry's *Adelphi,* or when he told Aldington to stop presenting himself as a pillar of society: "I never knew a man who seemed more to me to be living from a character not his own, than you. What is it that you are afraid of?—*ultimately?*—is it death? or pain? or just fear of the negative infinite of all things? What ails thee, lad?" (May 24, 1927). But he could also be wonderfully tactful and generous. He wrote to Rachel Annand Taylor, a minor poet (? November 15, 1910): "All I meant was that some of the poems in *Rose and Vine* seemed made to fit experiences which you have hidden in yourself and then dreamed different, so that the verses seemed fingered by art into a grace the experience does not warrant." Shortly after meeting Katherine Mansfield and Middleton Murry in 1913, Lawrence trounced Murry for refusing to take Katherine's money: "Make her certain—don't pander to her—stick to *yourself*—do what you *want* to do—don't *consider* her—she hates and loathes being considered. You insult her in saying you wouldn't take her money." Lawrence was right, as Murry eventually acknowledged. He was right again when he told Murry, after the dreadful months together in Cornwall: "Till the fight is finished, it is only honourable to fight," while adding: "But, oh dear, it is very horrible and agonizing" (October 11, 1916). And I love Lawrence for the strong tenderness with which he wrote to poor Caresse Crosby, after her husband had killed himself and his mistress: "I hope time is passing not too heavily for you—time is the best healer, when it isn't a killer" (February 14, 1930).

I have said that Lawrence was niggardly in praise. That is true; but he could praise, when his temper allowed him. Or, better still, he could rise to an occasion and genuinely enter into a relation with other writers. With Wells, for instance, whose strength he admired; or Whitman, Synge, Swinburne, Shelley, Melville, Balzac, Hardy. He made inordinate demands upon literature, as upon life; a writer touched by Lawrence's attention was never the same again, for better or worse. Who, before Lawrence, could have read Fenimore Cooper as Lawrence read him: who can read him now without feeling Lawrence's presence in the reading? It was the same with Lawrence's friendships. Lady Glenavy has a passage in *To-day We Will Only Gossip* in which she reflects somewhat harshly upon Lawrence's talent for friendship, comparing him unfavourably with Koteliansky in that respect. Koteliansky was, by normal standards, a more amiable man than Lawrence, and a more reliable friend, but on the other hand he approached friendship in a much less demanding spirit. Prepare a list of Lawrence's major friendships, beginning with Frieda in 1912, Katherine Mansfield and Middleton Murry in 1913, Koteliansky, Hilda Doolittle, Aldington, and Gertler in 1914, Lady Ottoline Morrell, Aldous Huxley, Heseltine, and Bertrand Russell in 1915. Some of these people lived to curse the day they met Lawrence, but not one of them passed through the relationship without bearing an indelible mark. The evidence is in Lawrence's letters, and in their own testaments. What

Lawrence demanded of friendship was tension, energy, desire. "God in me is my desire." The nature of a friendship is the flow of feeling, going both ways, and energy is the sign of value. In love, "I go to a woman to know myself, and knowing myself, to go further, to explore into the unknown, which is the woman, venture in upon the coasts of the unknown, and open my discovery to all humanity" (February 2, 1915).

This is only another way of describing Lawrence's sensibility, by recourse to his congenial idiom. A frail man, he loved strength, he loved to invoke the source of vitality and power. "I want to write live things, if crude and half formed, rather than beautiful dying decadent things with sad odours" (January 20, 1909). This is not the whole story, but it marks its direction. "Writing should come from a strong root of life: like a battle song after a battle" (December 22, 1913). So he hated the mere ego or the mere will as a malignant force setting itself against "the real genuine sacred life." The famous letter (June 5, 1914) in which Lawrence warned Garnett that he must not look in *The Rainbow* for "the old stable *ego*—of the character" is not as clear to me as it is, apparently, to other readers. "There is another *ego,* according to whose action the individual is unrecognizable, and passes through, as it were, allotropic states which it needs a deeper sense than any we've been used to exercise, to discover are states of the same single radically unchanged element." He then talks of diamonds, coal, and carbon. Now the dictionary says that allotropy means the variation of physical properties, without change of substance, to which certain elementary bodies are liable. Presumably the substance, in Lawrence's sentence, is human feeling, it can hardly be anything else, but it may be supposed, under his persuasion, to change its properties, changing especially the tendency to gather its energies together in a tight, self-protective form: in that form we insist on becoming "independent little gods, referred nowhere and to nothing, little mortal Absolutes, secure from question" (August 16, 1915). Against this, Lawrence urged another attitude: "Let us be easy and impersonal, not for ever fingering over our own souls, and the souls of our acquaintances, but trying to create a new life, a new common life, a new complete tree of life from the roots that are within us. I am weary to death of these dead, dry leaves of personalities which flap in every wind" (December 12, 1915). This is about as much as I can make of Lawrence's argument, and I find it difficult to see how he can speak of the happier condition as that of "another *ego.* " He told us to take life easy, not to insist upon our separateness, but to see ourselves as parts of "the whole." I am not sure that the argument amounts to much more than that. Still, it is clear enough to explain why Lawrence, immediately after *Sons and Lovers*, moved away from the conventional idea of a novel as an arrangement of characters and scenes. He is not now interested in characters as statuesque figures cut out from their backgrounds: after 1914 we do not find him praising writers, as he praised Garnett in 1912, for getting characters to "stand off from one another so distinctly." "I don't care much more about accumulating objects in the powerful light of emotion, and making a scene of them," he explains to Garnett (January 29, 1914). He calls his new procedure "the exhaustive method," as distinct from that of "pure object and story," and he warns Garnett that the new style "may not be sufficiently incorporated to please you." That means, I suppose, sufficient to the development of separate characters in action. "I prefer the permeating beauty," he says. It is hard to say how much of this argument is merely an attempt to answer the war with a corresponding gesture of distaste for individual people; and how much is genuinely achieved vision. "I find people ultimately boring: and you can't have fiction without people. So fiction does not, at the bottom, interest me any more. I am weary of humanity and human things. One is happy in the thoughts only that transcend humanity" (May 23, 1917). The war, the suppression of *The Rainbow*, the lapse of friends: only a brave reader would presume to disentangle these threads of outrage from the fabric of Lawrence's aesthetic or his metaphysic. Francis Fergusson gives Lawrence's attitude in a somewhat milder version when he says that Lawrence's characters interest their author far less than the emotional states they share. Suppose a number of congenial people were to come together in a common purpose, holding their separate personalities in abeyance or sinking them in a good cause. Presumably this is the kind of thing Lawrence had in mind. There is a crucial letter to Gordon Campbell in which he attacks those writers who "see only the symbol as a subjective expression." Lawrence thought Yeats guilty in this respect, so that even when he invoked the ancient symbols his invocation was sickly, merely an expression of himself. True symbolism, in Lawrence's terms, "avoids the I and puts aside the egotist": it is that whole in which, if we are in the right spirit, we can take "our decent place" (? December 19, 1914). "That was how man built the cathedrals. He didn't say 'out of my breast springs this cathedral!' But 'in this vast whole I am a small part, I move and live and have my being.'"

I am still in doubt about the theory. Perhaps it only means that people are no good by themselves: by themselves, they are nothing but self-delighting, self-devouring egos. They are good only when they are stirred to share a common life. Ursula is no good by herself. Birkin, by himself, is a menace. Together, they are as good as the vitality they engender, the energy of their relation. Readers of *Women in Love* are likely to say that Fergusson is right, Lawrence is less interested in Ursula and Birkin than in the magnetic field between them, and the nature of the feeling transacted there. This feeling is compatible with Lawrence's reverence for precognitive states of being, presumably allotropic states before the mind has broken the substance, once for all, into separate elements. In theory, transcendence has a similar advantage, except that it must be understood as coming after the human event, not before: it has every merit, except a future. So it begins to appear that Lawrence is outraged by society, by the governing institutions, by his discovery that feeling is humiliated in the public forms offered for its reception. Perhaps this explains why he always speaks of institutions as if they were bad minds, evil forms of mentality which have already imposed themselves upon human feeling. In a good relationship, according to this argument, a space is cleared and the domination of institutions is broken. In such spaces, there you feel free.

When Lawrence dreamed of a new society, a colony for a common purpose, he called it Rananim, taking the name from one of Koteliansky's Jewish hymns. When he formed a friendship, he sprang to the conviction that now at last it would be possible to make a new Eden, inhabited by aristocrats of feeling. At one time or another he issued invitations to W. E. Hopkin, Lady Ottoline, Murry of course, Gordon and Beatrice Campbell, Lady Cynthia Asquith, the Huxleys: they must set off together to Florida, or New Mexico, or wherever, "California or the South Seas," and "we can be a little community, a monastery, a school—a little Hesperides of the soul and body" (January 8, 1917). To Lady Ottoline he explained his plan:

I want you to form the nucleus of a new community which shall start a new life amongst us—a life in which the only riches is integrity of character. . . . I hold this the most sacred duty—the gathering together of a number of people who shall so agree to live by the *best* they know, that they shall be *free* to live by the best they know. The ideal, the religion, must now be *lived, practised.* . . . curse the Strachey who asks for a new religion—the greedy dog. He wants another juicy bone for his soul, does he? Let him start to fulfil what religion we have.

The gospel of this Rananim would not be "Follow me," but rather "Behold" (February 1, 1915). Some of Lawrence's most touching letters are draft Constitutions for his dream: they cannot be set aside as merely the latest version of pastoral, Lawrence's Brook Farm with a better climate. Of course it never came to anything: the nominated members shied away from an Eden already occupied by Lawrence and Frieda. With that beginning, there was no need of a serpent. But Lawrence kept coming back to the theme, even after the war, when things began to look up a little of their own accord. His friends, those few who had survived the initiation ceremonies, constituted the Remnant: "we must still be the chosen few," he told Cecil Gray, "who smear our doorposts with hyssop and blood" (Summer 1917). Sometimes the chosen few were to live as if in *Under the Greenwood Tree* or *The Deserted Village,* their only obligation a matter of getting the Morris dances right. Sometimes the new life must take an Indian or Etruscan form, compounded of ancestral intuition and snake dances. In autumn 1917 Lawrence came to the apocalyptic stage, longing for another Deluge and a Noah's Ark suitably small, just big enough for the remnant, the few, the best. Life must begin again; history must be abolished, since it is merely a heap of broken promises, the only sanctioned tenses are present and future.

On these scores, Lawrence was never entirely free of misgiving. Denouncing ego and will, he was still required to find a place for individual feeling. Society was a miserable affair, but he was still left with "my primeval societal instinct," which he thought "much deeper than sex instinct" (July 13, 1927). The correspondence with Trigant Burrow brought Lawrence yet again to this acknowledgement, though he insisted that the present moment, August 1927, was like "the time between Good Friday and Easter" (August 3, 1927). "One has no real human relations—that is so devastating." Humanity is still the bad egg it was in 1917.

It is indisputable that Lawrence, in the last years, turned away from people and looked to the earth itself for the only genuine values. In fiction after *The Plumed Serpent,* and in the corresponding letters, there is a new recognition of the plenitude of the natural world, with a new distrust, deeper than ever, of man's interventions. "Inhuman" becomes a term of praise. Mexico "is so lovely, the sky is perfect, blue and hot every day, and flowers rapidly following flowers. They are cutting the sugar cane, and hauling it in in the old ox-wagons, slowly. But the grass-slopes are already dry and fawn-coloured, the unventured hills are already like an illusion, standing round inhuman" (November 15, 1924). Lawrence was ready to argue that the relation between men and the earth was more profound, because more fundamental, than their relation to others of their kind. "There is a *principle* in the universe, towards which man turns religiously—a *life* of the universe itself" (July 31, 1927). In May 1929 he wrote to the Huxleys, describing a trip to Chopin's Valdemosa. The description registers the beauty and splendour of the place with an art which corresponds to the fiction in its sense of the "quickness" of life; then the atmosphere, the "queer stillness where the Moors have been, like ghosts." Everything is strong and vivid, except the people: "the people seem to me rather dead, and they are ugly, and they have those non-existent bodies that English people often have, which I thought was impossible on the Mediterranean." Before the letter is finished, the ugly Majorcans have become humanity itself, everybody is ugly. Conclusion: "the world is lovely if one avoids man—so why not avoid him! Why not! Why not! I am tired of humanity." He stayed tired till the end. "When the morning comes, and the sea runs silvery and the distant islands are delicate and clear, then I feel again, only man is vile" (October 4, 1929). It is the idiom of *St. Mawr*, with Lou Witt heading for the freedom of the desert. So Lawrence, too, ran from one place to another. Usually there was a pragmatic reason for packing up and moving on: the climate was hard on his health, someone offered him the loan of a house, a disciple wrote from afar to say that the grass was green, the sea incredibly blue, the welcome so warm that it must not be refused. "One's *ambiente* matters awfully," Lawrence told Earl Brewster. It mattered so much because of the demands Lawrence placed upon it: it must make up for the gruesomeness of the time, the people, the war, his health. It is my impression that Lawrence wanted the earth to do for him what his friends had failed to do, and that he moved from one place to the next partly because the first place, like a friend, had let him down, and partly because he craved diversity in places as in friends. When he was pleased with Majorca, he loved the "stretches of wild coast, and little uninhabited bays on this island, really lovely, like the first day of time" (May 17, 1929). That was the note he wanted; the earth to begin again, the first day, and now the entrance qualifications would be more stringent than in the historical world. The place of good hope was always the South. Reading the letters, one is struck by Lawrence's determination to keep going South, when it came to a change, not only for the warmth but because he associated the South with the place of ancestral wisdom, home of the old gods. "I prefer the pagan many gods, and the animistic vision," he told Rolf Gardiner (July 4, 1924). On those mornings in Mexico it was easy to fill the open spaces with gods of one's own devising, and to ascribe to them the grandeur of one's passion: easy, and better for Lawrence's purposes than the "Pale-face and Hebraic monotheistic insistence." Let the dark gods thrive, propitiated by the dancing Indians. Lawrence needed the gods for several reasons, but mostly to certify his belief in "blood-consciousness," the great dark half of life, denied by the other half, the mind, the nerves.

I hope I have not given the impression that Lawrence made himself a "citizen of the world," as if in preference to the complex fate of being an Englishman. He was hardly a citizen at all, at least in the sense of acknowledging social and moral obligations to his nation. But he was always an Englishman at heart, if not on principle. England irritated him beyond endurance, but it also made him what he was. Lawrence acknowledged his fate: "I am English, and my Englishness is my very vision" (October 21, 1915). We might be listening to Blake. "If England goes," Lawrence said during the war, "then Europe goes." His sense of the decay of old England is often like Forster's in *Howards End*. "So much beauty and pathos of old things passing away," Lawrence was not ashamed to find himself saying of the view from Lady Ottoline's Garsington. As late as December 1926, writing to Gardiner, he went back in his mind's eye to Hucknall Torkard and Newstead Abbey, Annesley and Felley Mill: "that's the country of my heart." Even when he felt himself insulted by England, it was an English form of insult he registered: when he persuaded himself that America was the only hope, it was because he thought America had already gone all the way in corruption, with England lagging behind, and that the new seed must spring from total decay.

Finally, of course, he trusted nothing but his genius. As early as 1913, when evidence was still thin on the ground, he told Garnett "I *know* I can write bigger stuff than any man in England." He never doubted it: indeed there is a sense of impersonal truth in his certainty. Perhaps this gives us a clue to that "other ego," which still troubles me as a working theory.

Genius is at once personal and impersonal; the writer's own nature, and yet the god he serves. If he claims genius, he claims nothing for himself, it is a gift, his ego has not demanded it. Genius is therefore "the whole" in which the mere man, the mere ego, finds his decent place. So Lawrence made every experience grist for his mill. Even when he detested a new experience, in another sense he welcomed it, and held it forever in his memory. He detested Ceylon: "not wild horses would drag me back." But wild horses could not have dislodged the memory, the images, sights, sounds, and smells, which he retained for their force, while hating them for other qualities. Everything was a blessing, however dreadfully disguised; a blessing to the artist, if a misery to the man. The artist hid every experience in himself, and then dreamed it different. It comes back to the question of energy. Lawrence always thought of himself as a fighter. "I am essentially a fighter—to wish me peace is bad luck—except the fighter's peace" (July 4, 1924). "All truth—and real living is the only truth—has in it the elements of battle and repudiation" (August 30, 1926). This explains why he distrusted Gordon Campbell's cult of ecstasy, in which conflicts are transcended. "All vital truth contains the memory of all that for which it is not true" (? December 19, 1914), an aphorism endlessly responsive to meditation. Even his rows with Frieda: Katherine Mansfield thought them merely appalling and obscene, but it is probable that Lawrence engaged in them in a warrior's spirit. He had Keats's feeling, that a quarrel may be a fine thing, if genuine energies are engaged. What Lawrence could not bear was what he called friction, "the sort of mental and nervous friction and destructiveness" which he ascribed to the Huxleys. Hating the war, he insisted that it was merely friction on a grotesque scale. It was not heroic; or at least it did not answer to Lawrence's sense of the heroic. It was mechanical, obsolete, and therefore hideous. "I know that, for me, the war is wrong. I know that if the Germans wanted my little house, I would rather give it them than fight for it: because my little house is not important enough to me. To fight for possessions, goods, is what my soul *will not* do. Therefore it will not fight for the neighbour who fights for his own goods. One is too raw, one fights too hard already, for the real integrity of one's being" (July 9, 1916). It is hard to know what to say about this. If someone were to accuse Lawrence of being a coward, of hiding his cowardice in the safety of words while better men were shot to hell at the Somme, I would not be able to produce a ready answer. He hated the war; so did everyone.

What more is there to say? I do not agree that his attitude was cowardly, or that a debate on it would necessarily use the idiom of Quakers or conscientious objectors who turn the other cheek. Lawrence was not indifferent: his letters in the years of war are desolate. But I think he judged the war by reference not to the fate of Europe or even the fate of the world but by reference to the laws of his own sensibility, his own genius. He could not live by any other criterion. His genius, propelled by intimations of life as energy, purpose, "blood-consciousness," was outraged by the mechanical perversions which traded under their names from 1914 to 1918. There is nothing as galling to the propounder of a personal text as the public apocrypha which usurp its place. So I have no difficulty in finding Lawrence's wartime letters poignant, because beneath every cry of rage there is a cry of pity, present even when least audible. We are too ready to assume that words mean what they say, and only that. When reading Lawrence's letters, I often recall that passage in Machado's *Juan de Mairena* where Mairena, the greatest of teachers, tells Martinez, a student, to go to the blackboard and write: "The olden blades of a glorious day ..." Martinez complies. Then Mairena asks him: "To what day do you think the poet is alluding?" Martinez, finest of pupils, answers: "The day in which the blades no longer were olden." Martinez would be the best reader of Lawrence's letters, because he would listen to the silence between the words, and sense the pity which surrounds the rage. When Rupert Brooke was killed, Lawrence wrote to Lady Ottoline: "The death of Rupert Brooke fills me more and more with the sense of the fatuity of it all. He was slain by bright Phoebus's shaft—it was in keeping with his general sunniness—it was the real climax of his pose. I first heard of him as a Greek god under a Japanese sunshade, reading poetry in his pyjamas, at Grantchester,—at Grantchester upon the lawns where the river goes. Bright Phoebus smote him down. It is all in the saga. O God, O God, it is all too much of a piece: it is like madness" (April 30, 1915). I find it remarkable that Lawrence's sense of the pity of it all has survived, in that passage, the apparent severity of "pose." That Lawrence's assessment of Brooke as an artist would be a limiting critique, there is every reason to believe; but there is also, competing with that severity, a sense of Brooke's beauty which includes the charm as well as the narcissism of that pose. It is all in the saga, but only if Brooke is felt as bright Phoebus himself, as well as the appropriate victim of his shaft; his death in some measure a case of suicide. Even in letters of a less elegiac note, there is often the equivalent of this tact, the gentleness. Often in a most hostile and bitter letter, when the venom has expelled itself, Lawrence ends with a paragraph not of apology but of recognition; as if to say that beneath the flow of violence and rage there is another, of consanguinity and peace.

It is beautiful, especially towards the end. Readers of the letters probably agree with Lady Glenavy, who spoke of Lawrence as overwhelmed by Frieda: Frieda "whose over-vital and noisy presence usually reduced him to a gentle, bearded shadow." Lawrence saw the fun of that, too, as well as its figurative truth. When he and Frieda combined in a letter, he said that Frieda's hand sprawled só large over the page that he had to squeeze himself small, and he added: "I am very contractible" (April 18, 1913). Frieda's "God Almightiness" was always to be taken into account: she was a German *Hausfrau,* and she wanted a *Haus,* not Lawrence's next Paradise. She stayed large: Lawrence, consumed with illness, wasted away, he weighed six stone at the end. A few days before he died he had visits from Wells, a disappointment; from the Aga Khan, in whose fat face he discerned "a bit of real religion": from the Huxleys, their play running its last week. He died on March 2, 1930, in Vence.

From Stephen Spender (ed.), *D. H. Lawrence: Novelist, Poet, Prophet* (London: Weidenfeld and Nicolson, 1973).

WYNDHAM LEWIS

Wyndham Lewis is surely the least read and most unfamiliar of all the great modernists of his generation," Fredric Jameson remarks, "a generation that included the names of Pound and Eliot, Joyce, Lawrence and Yeats; nor can it be said that his painting has been assimilated any more successfully into the visual canon." Lewis's work is normally reckoned less than the sum of its many parts: novelist, painter, poet, polemicist, critic, but in the end nearly a dead letter. His repute might now be higher if he had written less and painted more: if he had written only *Tarr* (1918, 1928), *Time and Western Man* (1927), *The Revenge for Love* (1937), and *Self Condemned* (1954), and otherwise kept his brushes active and his mouth shut.

Lewis was born on November 18, 1882, aboard his father's yacht, then moored at Amherst, Nova Scotia. Christened in Montreal, he retained Canadian nationality for the rest of his life. In 1888 the family moved to England, and lived comfortably on the Isle of Wight till Lewis's father ran off with one of the housemaids. There was still enough money to send Lewis to decent schools, including Rugby, and later to let him study art at the Slade, but gradually the checks arrived later than expected, and the amounts inscribed were not enough to support an artist who liked restaurants and champagne. Lewis earned little; he lived mostly by borrowing money, which he neglected to pay back.

Jeffrey Meyers's biography is richly informative, fair, lively, and in every good sense disinterested. He is sympathetic to Lewis, but not besotted with him. He gives Lewis's many causes their due, and he elucidates every fuss, but he does not demand that the reader beat all those antique drums. He doesn't fudge the political issues. Lewis's reputation never recovered from some extraordinarily foolish articles he wrote about Hitler and gathered into a book peremptorily called *Hitler* (1931). He tried to undo the damage with *The Hitler Cult* (1939), but it was too late. Most of his contemporaries thought him, on every political question, an idiot. Auden and MacNeice in their "Last Will and Testament" (*Letters from Iceland,* 1937) wrote:

> *We leave the Martyr's Stake at Abergwilly*
> *To Wyndham Lewis with a box of soldiers (blonde)*
> *Regretting one so bright should be so silly.*

On September 2, 1939, the day before England declared war on Germany, Lewis sailed for Canada. He lived out the war in Toronto, miserably poor and hating his life. In 1946 he went back to London as art critic for *The Listener,* a post he held with honour. But he started going blind in 1951, and had to give it up. He died on March 7, 1957.

Jeffrey Meyers doesn't hedge the fact that Lewis was one of the most obnoxious men of his time. Only Bertolt Brecht and Evelyn Waugh are in the same league when it comes to nastiness. In sexual achievement, anything Augustus John could do, Lewis determined to do better and more. He treated his women abominably: got them pregnant and then cleared off. In financial dealings, he was a sponger. He never forgave anyone who helped him, especially if the help came in the form of money. His strongest instinct was to find persecution and mischief where they did not exist: he felt wounded so often that he must have taken pleasure in the feeling.

John says in his autobiography that Lewis, living the bohemian life in Montparnasse, played the part of an incarnate Loki, bearing the news and sowing discord with it. "Sarcasm, with daring touches of scurrility, was his strong card." I think what he mostly felt was disgust that he couldn't entirely transform his appetites into ideas: many of them remained in the deplorable environment of discarded mistresses, creditors, patrons he despised, and venereal diseases he regarded as proof of his virility. His methods were "a whisper here, a dark suggestion there." It is true that his women cared for him, and stayed in his vicinity even when he had replaced them in bed. It is also true that some of his peers admired him, notably Yeats, Pound, and Eliot, who thought him "the most fascinating personality of our time" for reasons not stated.

Proof of Lewis's genius seems to me clearer in his paintings than in his writings. Despising "the Impressionist fuss," the fuss over the lazy felicities of Nature, he made his art an art of line: his paintings emphasize lines, outlines, setting limits for the moment upon whatever he deems to be the case. An effect of the macabre is gained by applying to ostensibly human occasions shapes drawn from animal, vegetable, and mineral sources. The paintings seem to have issued from another planet, a place governed by rules not necessarily superior to ours but evidently different. *The Surrender of Barcelona* (1936) is a painting that removes Barcelona from Spain as assiduously as it removes every other expectation aroused by its title. The drawings for *Timon of Athens* are extraordinary, though they might with equal cogency be attached to any work of notable virulence. As for the portraits: the 1938 portrait of Pound is more genial than the first Eliot portrait of 1938 or the portrait of Edith Sitwell (1923–34), but they all seem to minister to the painter's desire to hasten his sitters to their deaths or, while they survive, to their fated prisons.

The power of Lewis's fiction, and the limits of that power, issue from his theory of comedy. "The root of the Comic is to be sought," he writes, "in the sensations resulting from the observation of a *thing* behaving like a person. But from that point of view all men are necessarily comic; for they are all *things,* or physical bodies, behaving as persons." The imagination that construes people in this way is associated with the eye, Lewis's favorite sense. "Dogmatically, then," he says, "I am for the *Great Without,* for the method of *external* approach, for the wisdom of the eye, rather than that of the ear."

In writing, he continues, the only thing that interests him is the shell, the actions and appearances of people, not their internality. "The ossature is my favourite part of a living animal organism, not its intestines." Of course the ossature is just as internal as the intestines, but Lewis's novels, like his paintings, proceed as if this were not so. In the portraits the skin seems to be stretched, like a bank robber's stocking mask, over bones which do not share accommodations with veins, gut, and blood.

In *Time and Western Man, Paleface, The Art of Being Ruled, Men Without Art, The Roaring Queen,* and *The Writer and the Absolute,* Lewis attacks virtually every manifestation of modern literature and philosophy for presenting life as if from the inside: this is what the seemingly diverse attacks upon Proust, Joyce, Hemingway, Lawrence, Pound, Bergson, Woolf, and Sartre come to, Lewis's contempt for inwardness, and especially for the philosophies of Time that allow us to distinguish between mechanical time, mere *chronos,* and some deeper, private time made available to intuition, memory, and chance.

To write Lewis's kind of fiction, it would be necessary to assume that when two people look at each other, each regards the other with such suspicion that the look turns him into an object, hostile in principle and, if it moves, a dire contraption. Sentences that mime the experience of looking have as their first obligation the elimination of anything that might betoken affection or sympathy. Lewis's aesthetic is a function of his disgust, so he joins one sentence to another not according to any principle a reader would recognize as natural or otherwise privileged but on the assumption that every appeal to the natural is impertinent.

In both versions of *Tarr,* the memorable chapters are those in which the characters, puppets one and all, find themselves engaged in social rituals. Otto Kreisler and the widow Mrs. Bevelage, dancing in the Bonnington Club, are limbs running amok. The fact that Mrs. B. is whirled into something resembling rapture accounts for Lewis's recourse to a diction ready-made to deal with such vulgarity:

The widow had come somewhat under the sudden fascination of Kreisler's mood: she was really his woman, the goods, had he known it: she felt deliciously rapt in the midst of a simoom—she had two connected thoughts. All her worldly Victorian grace and good management of her fat had vanished: her face had become coarsened in those few breathless minutes. But she buzzed back again into the dance, and began a second mad, but this time nearly circular, career.

The vision of a puppet in abrupt contact with an emotion is always enough to disgust Lewis. At such times his glance dismembers the object it lights upon. The entire mechanism is disassociated into fragments until whatever coherence they have had seems a sordid function of chance. Here is a passage from *The Childermass* (1928):

> A longshoreman fidgets at the movements of the small observer, finally thrusting first one long-booted leg and then another into his bark, a giant clog whose peaked toe wavers as he enters its shell, he walks off wagging his buttocks as he churns the rudder-paddle upon the rusty tide, an offended aquatic creature. A stone's-throw out he stops, faces the shore, studying sombrely in perspective the man-sparrow, who multiplies precise movements, an organism which in place of speech has evolved a peripatetic system of response to a dead environment. It has wandered beside this Styx, a lost automaton rather than a lost soul. It has taken the measure of its universe: man is the measure: it rears itself up, steadily confronts and moves along these shadows.

Fredric Jameson, quoting from this passage, says that it arises as a proto-narrative form from the situation of the portraitist before his model, a relation organized in Lewis's case into "two mechanisms squaring off against each other, each quasi-automatically readjusting itself to the automatic movements and tremors of its opposite number." The relation between the model and the eye that takes its inventory might be congenial in another writer, but in Lewis it becomes a "reciprocal interaction of tics and twitches ordered into an obligatory circuit, a reflex of vasomotor action and reaction which provides the spectacle of a ceaseless exchange of sparks between any two existents felt as contrary or opposing poles."

Jameson's reading of Lewis is based upon the notion that the most influential formal impulses of modernism—he has in view Yeats, Joyce, Eliot, and Pound—have been "strategies of inwardness, which set out to reappropriate an alienated universe by transforming it into personal styles and private languages." Lewis's strategy has been different. While his peers, Impressionists to a man, kept faith with the illusions of subjectivity, he produced a form of Expressionism which, as Jameson argues, "marks those illusions with the stamp of their own spuriousness, keeping the place of the Real warm by deforming its caricatural substitutes in the realm of the sheerly phenomenal." The official modernists, according to Jameson, invested in "the valorization of myth and symbol, temporality, organic form and the concrete universal, the identity of the subject and the continuity of linguistic expression." Lewis should be read, however, as a postmodernist and poststructuralist writer, stressing "discontinuity, allegory, the mechanical, the gap between signifier and signified, the lapse in meaning, the syncope in the experience of the subject." Jameson would persuade us that Lewis's style, "the only true English futurism," should be approached as the political sign of a postindividualist age. He makes him sound like Jacques Derrida.

The question is: what is a nice Marxist like Jameson doing promoting Wyndham Lewis? Lewis hated Marxism, despised everything proletarian, and stayed longer than any of his colleagues with the glamour of Hitler. The explanation is that Lewis's enemies were also Marx's enemies. Lewis attacked liberal humanism, bourgeois subjectivity, and the strategists of inwardness far more effectively than any Marxist critic did. Compare him with Christopher Caudwell, the best that English Marxism could produce in his time, but inept. Lewis's friends are not Jameson's, but they have the same enemies. So it is not surprising that Jameson is thrilled by Lewis's futurism, which, he says, "projects the symbolic value of an antitranscendental, essentially democratic option—the machine as against the luxury furnishings of the great estates, with their ideology of natural beauty, the sheer production of sentences as against the mysteries of poetic creation and the organic primacy of the beautiful or the masterpiece."

What Jameson admires in Lewis is his satirical collage, which "draws heavily and centrally on the warehouse of cultural and mass cultural cliché, on the junk materials of industrial capitalism, with its degraded commodity art, its mechanical reproduceability, its serial alienation of language." Lewis uses the cliché against itself, not to achieve homogeneity of tone—such an impression would hold out the possibility of the unification of subjectivity—but "a kind of perceptual freshness reinvented out of the unexpectedly virulent interaction of stale and faded substances."

Finally, Jameson proposes an entirely unconvincing comparison between Lewis and Lawrence: on the strength of the famous letter in which Lawrence repudiates "the old stable *ego* of the character" in favour of a deeper, more elemental sense of life, Jameson finds "remarkable affinities" with Lewis's satirical program, "by which Lewis meant to underscore the nonethical, purely external mode of his new representation as cubist-caricatural, its materialist techniques affirming their kinship with the visual, rather than the temporal, arts, with space rather than time, and knowing a symbolic mission to discredit the shapeless warm organic *durée* of the inner monologue and of a psychology-oriented subjectivism." This seems to me far more confused than Lewis's account of Lawrence in *Paleface;* Lewis at least recognized that he and Lawrence were alien to each other, and that they could not make common ground against their colleagues.

But the really peculiar part of Jameson's argument turns on the question of the "Strong Personality." Having argued that Lewis is post-individualist and committed to the dispersal of subjectivity, he has the problem of explaining how Lewis could insist on making an exception in favour of himself: worse still, how he could turn that exception into a cult of the fascist personality. Jameson is clear that the ideal of the Strong Personality is

> the central organizational category of Lewis's mature ideology, and the primary "value" from which are generated all those more pro-vocative, yet structurally derivative ideological motifs and obsessions of racism and sexism, the attack on the Youth Cult, the disgust with parliamentary democracy, the satiric aesthetic of Otherness, the violent polemic and moral stance of the didactic works, the momen-tary infatuation with Nazism as well as the implacable repudiation of Marxism.

But he offers to explain Lewis's commitment to this ideal by saying that ideology is "not a coherent system of ideas, but rather the desperate response to a contradictory situation." The situation, as Jameson then describes it, isn't in fact at all contradictory, it is perfectly straightforward. Jameson identifies Lewis's situation with that of the petty bourgeois subject, terrified of being overwhelmed, crowded out of his already cramped space, by the "anonymous and faceless multitude." It begins to appear that Lewis's satire has far more to do with money, his own ungenteel poverty, his dependence upon patrons, and such factors, than upon any grander or more disinterested motives.

Socialism or communism is fantasized in Lewis, according to Jameson, "as the completion of this process of levelling, and as the definitive loss of even this embattled and precarious, historically threatened status to which the petty bourgeois subject desperately clings." If you add a conspiracy theory, and imagine an evil genius in the guise of the Bailiff in *The Human Age,* Lewis's fiction then becomes "the unmasking of a vast cosmological plot by the *Zeitgeist* to reduce strong personalities to the level of the mediocre and the mindlessly standardized." The only answer to such a conspiracy is a still stronger personality capable of bringing the mob to heel.

It is edifying that a Marxist can find so much worth bothering about in Wyndham Lewis. Admittedly, Jameson is more interested in Lewis as symptom than as genius: but that is only to say that his supreme concern is to produce, from evidence that threatens to postpone the production indefinitely, a Marxist apocalyptic vision. By calling Lewis a political novelist, Jameson can deal with the symptomatic aspects of the work without too much ado. Naturally, he is angrier with the degraded world that provoked Lewis than with anything in Lewis himself. But I don't see how Jameson's account of the degraded world of commodity values takes the harm out of Lewis's response to it; or removes Lewis's motives, by recourse to a situational politics, from psychological consideration which suggests that they are understandable but mean.

Jameson has not convinced me that Lewis was clearheaded where Joyce, Eliot, Yeats, and Pound were bewildered; or that he mastered a *Zeitgeist* rotten with subjectivity while they lay victims to it. "The approach of a postindividualistic age argues powerfully for the discovery of Lewis's kinship with us," Jameson says. The assertion is premature on every count. The approach of such an age is not clear to me, and I suspect it is a mirage in the eye of the Marxist beholder. "Lewis's kinship with us" is very odd. People used to scold Lionel Trilling for that "us," and demand to know whom he meant. There can't be many people in the category that includes Fredric Jameson. Then again I wonder what he means by referring to "kinship": it seems a singularly inappropriate word, given the particular force and bias of Lewis's work.

In any case, I can't see how Lewis's politics gives Jameson any comfort. It is probably true, as Alfred Kazin has been maintaining, that the sense of self and freedom in contemporary fiction is extremely feeble. This argument doesn't contradict Christopher Lasch's position in *The Culture of Narcissism:* clearly, if we were secure in our sense of self, we wouldn't feel the need to cultivate it or shore it up. Jameson takes pleasure in a vision of the dispersed self, presumably because such a predicament would find a Marxist answer as the only hope. Lewis would help the work of dispersal, but his politics thereafter would give not only Jameson but many others a rough time.

Review of *The Enemy: A Biography of Wyndham Lewis,* by Jeffrey Meyers, and *Fables of Aggression: Wyndham Lewis, the Modernist as Fascist,* by Fredric Jameson. From *The New York Review of Books,* April 29, 1982.

EMPSON'S "ARACHNE"

The poem first:

Twixt devil and deep sea, man hacks his caves;
Birth, death; one, many; what is true, and seems;
Earth's vast hot iron, cold space's empty waves:

King spider, walks the velvet roof of streams:
Must bird and fish, must god and beast avoid:
Dance, like nine angels, on pin-point extremes.

His gleaming bubble between void and void,
Tribe-membrane, that by mutual tension stands,
Earth's surface film, is at a breath destroyed.

Bubbles gleam brightest with least depth of lands
But two is least can with full tension strain,
Two molecules; one, and the film disbands.

We two suffice. But oh beware, whose vain
Hydroptic soap my meagre water saves.
Male spiders must not be too early slain.[1]

Two of Empson's notes bear on the poem, and may as well be given together. On "Arachne":

> The caves of cavemen are thought of as by the sea to escape the savage creatures inland. "Man lives between the contradictory absolutes of philosophy, the one and the many, etc. As king spider man walks delicately between two elements, avoiding the enemies which live in both. Man must dance, etc. Human society is placed in this matter like individual men, the atoms who make up its bubble." The spider's legs push down the unbroken surface of the water like a soft carpet, which brings in the surface-tension idea. The bubble surface is called land, the thin fertile surface of the earth, because the bubble is the globe of the world. The water saves the soap because the soap alone couldn't make a bubble. Arachne was a queen spider and disastrously proud.[2]

On a line from "Bacchus"—"Arachne sailing her own rope of cloud"—he commented: "Arachne who out of pride against the pride of Juno hanged herself in her own web and became a spider is here a gossamer spider, who can fly on it."[3]

The commonest version of the story is in Ovid, *Metamorphoses,* Book VI: her skill in weaving leads her to challenge Athena; when Athena, defeated, tears up Arachne's weave, Arachne hangs herself but is changed by Athena into a spider.

In an interview, Empson told Christopher Ricks why he had kept "Arachne" out of the LP of his poetry: "I left it out because I'd come to think that it was in rather bad taste. It's boy being afraid of girl, as usual, but it's boy being too rude to girl. I thought it had rather a nasty feeling, that's why I left it out."[4]

The poem uses only two bits of the story, the girl's being disastrously proud, and her being changed into a spider, making the boy a king spider and therefore doomed. The weaving doesn't come into it, or the challenge to Athena, but there is a touch of "Who do you think you are, anyway?"

It starts off frigidly; the metaphysical pronouncements are ponderous, but they seem to indicate the labour of maintaining some better self at a distance from his local resentment. He says these weightily true things in the hope of staving off the more pressing truths he'll probably have leisure to regret saying. Many of Empson's poems make similarly grand pronouncements not because he believes them or thinks them adequate but because even pseudo-statements, which bracket the question of true or false, are good enough in practice to "keep a steady hold on the controls." One's virtuosity, Empson seems to say, is probably absurd, but it's at worst a show of bravery, like trapeze work without a net, as in "Sea Voyage":

> *Pillowed on gulfs between exiguous bobbins*
> *The Son of Spiders, crucified to lace,*
> *Suspends a red rag to a thousand dobbins*
> *And sails so powered to a better place.*
> *All his gained ports, thought's inter-reached trapeze,*
> *Map-sail, transport him towards Hercules,*
> *Earth-bound* . . . [5]

So the first suggestion of "king spider" is heroic, the grandeur of the perhaps ridiculous poise.

Everything depends on the tone. When Pope wants to wipe out a writer's vanity, as in the poem to Arbuthnot, he emphasizes the nastiness of his self-conceit:

> *Who shames a Scribbler? break one cobweb through,*
> *He spins the slight, self-pleasing thread anew:*
> *Destroy his fib or sophistry, in vain,*
> *The creature's at his dirty work again,*
> *Throned in the centre of his thin designs,*
> *Proud of a vast extent of flimsy lines!*

The mockery in "throned" carries over into the sneer of "designs" and the implacably rhyming "lines." But he can look at the spiders differently, as in the first Epistle of the *Essay on Man*:

> *The spider's touch, how exquisitely fine!*
> *Feels at each thread, and lives along the line.*

—where "touch," "fine," and "feels" are given the right to expand into the comprehensiveness of "lives."

Empson, too, holds open the two possibilities: the spider is absurd, but also splendid: it is as much worthwhile in morality as in virtuosity to be willing to turn out to be futile.

Up to this point, the poem has distanced itself to the outer limit of generalization: man. But the personal application is anticipated in "mutual" and "at a breath"; the one betokening a desperate need as well as a possibility; the other, mostly the caprice of blowing something out, a candle, a dandelion, a life. "Two" holds the personal application further off; if two is least, the tension might be among three or four or hundreds, like a daisy chain or ring-a-ring-a-rosy. But "one" makes it appalling.

"We two suffice." Following the grand pronouncements, this succinctness is astounding. After "man," the "we" is a revelation, "suffice" makes a show of being judicious, refusing to overstate the case. Suffice for what? To be sufficient to each other; to maintain mutuality; to sustain each other against the terrors of the deep? It is at once a claim for them together, and a threat if she keeps them apart; he waves a stick at her. "But oh beware . . ."

The inversion of subject and object in "whose vain / Hydroptic soap my meagre water saves" makes the stick-waves more dreadful still, because more vindictive. In Browning's "Grammarian's Funeral" we have

> He, soul-hydroptic with a sacred thirst,
> Sucked at the flagon . . .

but I suppose Christopher Ricks is right in alluding to Donne's "A Nocturnall upon S. Lucies Day" —

> The generall balme th' hydroptic earth hath drunk,
> Whither, as to the beds-feet, life is shrunke,
> Dead and enterr'd.

Helen Gardner comments, in her edition of Donne's *Elegies and Songs and Sonnets,* that "the dropsical man, though swollen with water, is afflicted with raging thirst: the sodden earth of midwinter has drunk down the life-giving force of all things." Empson's "vain" pushes the reference towards the girl's perverse selfishness: she can't gain from it in the end. She'll still need him, as the swollen soap needs water, however meagre. Of course she doesn't need him in particular; any man, any water, would do, but the man can't let that thought weaken the threat. "Saves" is an enormous claim, unless there have been grounds for it. Ricks has a perceptive comment on the last lines, though he doesn't seem to find them as vindictive as I do. Thinking that most of Empson's poems are about fatherhood and engendering and the misgiving that properly attends such a possibility, he says that the last line of "Arachne" enters "upon a different dimension of threat and fear: that a woman can be so predatorily proud as not just to destroy life but to preclude it." "Male spiders must not be too early slain." The movement back to generalization, fleeing the dreadful violences at hand, tries to retain the threat and make it impersonal. The poem, Ricks says, "includes its own plea for something other than pride all round."[6] But it includes it only as if by a peacemaking accommodation which the poem doesn't specifically make. I agree that if anything further were to be said, in the embittered and embittering silence after the threat, it should only be such a plea as "Let's stop, both of us, being stiff."

The business with the spiders would make this plea either fairly feasible or quite impossible. At some point, boy might have been able to say to girl: "Look, by any sensible criteria, we're neither of us very important, so we must stop this strutting." But by insisting on queen spider and what happens to male spiders, boy has probably gone too far, he has been too rude, as Empson says.

The problem is one that Empson often comes back to, in *Seven Types of Ambiguity* and the later books: the fact that he shared it with I. A. Richards doesn't much matter. "The object of life, after all," Empson says in *Ambiguity*, "is not to understand things, but to maintain one's defences and equilibrium and live as well as one can; it is not only maiden aunts who are placed like this."[7] If, too, as he says a page or two earlier, "it does not even satisfy the understanding to stop living in order to understand,"[8] you have to do the best you can by a decently pragmatic way of life, the *ambulando* method of conducting your relations. Muriel Bradbrook caught this note superbly when she said that the casual tone of Empson's poems "serves as a means of defence, and is part of his recognition of the latent hostility in any relationship."[9]

How then, in the spirit of "Arachne," can one be intelligent, decently vulnerable, and yet not abjectly prepared to be walked on? This seems to me to indicate the tone of the poems. If so, their method and their inspired dependence upon Donne in one respect become clearer. "Arachne"

starts as a metaphysical conceit—man as spider—and works out the consequences to the point where the conceit, outstripping itself, falls upon
desires and fears which conceits are helpless to remedy. The merit of such a
procedure is a matter of learning how to cope. Again in *Ambiguity* Empson
says that "many works of art give their public a sort of relief and strength,
because they are independent of the moral code which their public accepts
and is dependent on; relief, by fantasy gratification; strength, because it
gives you a sort of equilibrium within your boundaries to have been taken
outside them, however secretly, because you know your own boundaries
better when you have seen them from both sides."[10] Works of art do this,
but Empson also says that in any case it was the best way of getting to
know something. In a review of E. A. Burtt's *The Metaphysical Foundations
of Modern Science* he scolded Burtt for trying to explain discovery in
terms of a man's intellectual preconceptions: "the act of discovery is precisely that of stepping outside preconceptions."[11] Metaphysical poetry
was good because it practised this stepping-outside even at the risk of
appearing absurd: it was noble of Donne to be willing to seem daft.

The whole idea of having a boundary and stepping outside it has to
do with breaking up, at least experimentally, the configurations and
associations which have established your boundary in the first place.
Kenneth Burke's version of it, in his *Permanence and Change,* is called
"perspective by incongruity," a technique to free yourself from the
boundary by juxtaposing incongruities fatal to its coherence. Metaphor is
one of its means. Whatever method is adopted, it is a way of dealing with
the unthought linkages I described in earlier comments on the association
of ideas.

Empson's favourite way of taking himself outside his boundaries has
been, in the poems, to think of stars, planets, galaxies. The essay "Donne
the Space Man" (*Kenyon Review,* Summer 1957) is his most extended space
flight, but he was always keen on the notion that Donne dragged
Copernicus into the love poems so that he could make "the idea of the
inhabited planet a symbol of the lovers' independence from the world."[12]
The risk in this planetary business is that it is equally plausible to see the
lovers stationed each on a separate planet; a predicament most powerfully
imagined in John Crowe Ransom's "The Equilibrists":

> *And rigid as two painful stars, and twirled*
> *About the clustered night their prison world,*

They burned with fierce love always to come near,
But honor beat them back and kept them clear.[13]

A point Empson doesn't pronounce on is whether the aim is to keep the boundary intact by testing it from an alien viewpoint or to devise a new and better boundary. The whole question of equilibrium, in Empson as in Richards, remains contentious: is it a case of any port in a storm, or a neo-American Pragmatism by which we make sure that our insistence on the true and the best doesn't drive out the likely and the next-best good? Hugh Kenner once scolded Empson on this point:

An equilibrium has been discovered; it consists in contemplating the way your peripheral emotions get entangled with the absurd.[14]

It doesn't seem to me a vain contemplation, especially if it prevents us from indulging ourselves in otherwise unexamined certitudes. The real moral risk is that, having taken myself outside my boundaries, I return to them and vent upon other people the perhaps shrill discovery I have made. Boy, having turned himself into king spider, returns to threaten girl with a fate the sinister felicity of which he has just discovered.

NOTES

1. William Empson, *Collected Poems* (London: Chatto & Windus, 1955), p. 23.
2. *Ibid.*, pp. 100–1.
3. *Ibid.*, pp. 109–10.
4. *The Review*, Nos. 6 and 7 (1963), p. 27. Quoted in Christopher Ricks, *The Force of Poetry* (Oxford: Clarendon Press, 1984), p. 232.
5. *Collected Poems*, p. 12.
6. Ricks, *The Force of Poetry*, pp. 231, 232.
7. William Empson, *Seven Types of Ambiguity* (3rd ed.; London: Chatto & Windus, 1953), p. 247.
8. *Ibid.*, p. 245.
9. Muriel Bradbrook, "The Ambiguity of William Empson," in Roma Gill (ed.), *William Empson: The Man and His Work* (London: Routledge & Kegan Paul, 1974), p. 6.
10. Empson, *Seven Types of Ambiguity*, p. 246.
11. *The Criterion*, X, No. 38 (October 1930), 169.
12. William Empson, "Still the Strange Necessity," *The Sewanee Review*, LXIII, No. 3 (Summer 1955), 477.
13. John Crowe Ransom, *Selected Poems* (New York: Alfred A. Knopf, 1964), p. 84.
14. Hugh Kenner, *Gnomon* (New York: McDowell, Obolensky, 1958), p. 258.

NINETEEN EIGHTY-FOUR: POLITICS AND FABLE

When we are speaking casually, we call *Nineteen Eighty-Four* a novel, but in a more exacting context we call it a political fable; political because it appears to deal with human life in society. This account of it is not refuted by the fact that we recall the book as preoccupied with an individual, Winston Smith, who suffers from a varicose ulcer, and that it takes account of other individuals, including Julia, Mr. Charrington, Mrs. Parsons, Syme, and O'Brien. These figures claim our attention, but they exist mainly in their relation to the political system that determines them. It would indeed be possible to think of them as figures in a novel, though in that case they would have to be imagined in a far more diverse set of relations. They would no longer inhabit or sustain a fable, because a fable is a narrative relieved of much contingent detail so that it may stand forth in an unusual degree of clarity and simplicity. What a fable says is that the world is essentially like this image of it, even though it has many other qualities which the image ignores. The fabulist's sense of life may be as responsive as anyone else's to contingency, the clash of chances and choices, but for the sake of his fable he sacrifices this sense to another one, his presentation of life chiefly as a *type* of life. A fable is a typology, a structure of types, each of them deliberately simplified lest a sense of difference and heterogeneity reduce the force of the typical. The claim a fabulist makes is that his narrative is essentially true; that the narrative truly represents the form and destiny of the world. Let us say, then, that *Nineteen Eighty-Four* is a political fable, projected into a near future in a mood variously to be described as one of threat, warning, despair, or rage, and incorporating historical references mainly to document a cancelled past.

If a fable is predicated upon a typology, it is likely to be written as if from a certain distance. We recognize a type of person by abstracting certain features from many people, different in other respects, who share them. But we can't retain that sense of similarity while we immerse ourselves in detail and differentiation. A fable, in this respect, asks to be compared to a caricature, not to a photograph. It follows that in a political fable there is bound to be some tension between a political sense, which deals in the multiplicity of social and personal life, and a sense of fable, which is committed to simplicity of form and feature. If the political sense were to prevail, the narrative would be drawn away from fable into the novel, at some cost to its simplicity. If the sense of fable were to prevail, the fabulist would station himself at such a distance from any imaginary conditions in the case that his narrative would appear unmediated, free or bereft of conditions. The risk in that procedure would be considerable: a reader might feel that the fabulist has lost interest in the variety of human life and fallen back upon an unconditioned sense of its types, that he has become less interested in lives than in a particular idea of life. The risk is greater still if the fabulist projects his narrative into the future: the reader can't question it by appealing to the conditions of life he already knows. He is asked to believe that the future, too, like the past in *The Go-Between,* is another country, and that in all probability they do things differently there. In a powerful fable the reader's feeling is likely to be mostly fear: he is afraid that the fabulist's vision of any life that is likely to arise may be accurate and will be verified in the event. The fabulist's feeling may be more various. Such a fable as *Nineteen Eighty-Four* might arise from disgust, despair, or world-weariness induced by evidence that nothing, despite one's best efforts, has changed and that it is too late to hope for the change one wants.

It is fairly generally agreed that Orwell's sense of the political fable as a genre was influenced, in various ways, by at least five examples of it:

these, in chronological order, are *Gulliver's Travels* (1726), Jack London's *The Iron Heel* (1908), Yevgeny Zamyatin's *We* (written in 1920 and published in English translation in 1924), Huxley's *Brave New World* (1930), and Koestler's *Darkness at Noon* (1940). It is also agreed, but less generally, that *Nineteen Eighty-Four* was more immediately influenced by James Burnham's books, especially by *The Managerial Revolution,* which was published in England in May 1942. Burnham's books are discursive, not fictional; they are concerned to say how the world will be, not to show it in that character. But in any case the books I have listed are so different from one another that in bringing them together as political fables we have to take care not to sink their differences.

At the same time, the books have certain preoccupations in common. Each imagines a form of life ordained so completely in accordance with a particular set or model that the perfection of its character is monstrous. Any principle, enforced with impeccable logic, is monstrous, as Orwell recognized in *Nineteen Eighty-Four* by showing the good principle of communication carried to the mad pedantry of its conclusion, the vetoing of privacy. In each of these books, human beings who have come to value their uniqueness, their differences one from another, are forced to relinquish that conviction and to lapse into an undifferentiated state of being. In each book, history is shown as having ended by coinciding once for all with an imperative declaration of its meaning: existence has removed itself from historical process and culminated in an irresistible essence, withdrawing from every attribute but its official meaning.

Perfection, in the sense in which it is featured in these books, means the state of being complete, fully in accordance with the terms prescribed for it; as a proposition in logic might be faultless, or a theorem in mathematics. The terms of the prescription might be those of biology and genetic engineering, as in *Brave New World;* or of mathematics and mechanical engineering, as in *We;* or of the technology of omnivorous communication, as in *Nineteen Eighty-Four.* Perfection, in any form, would be especially repugnant to Orwell, an English socialist who wanted for political life not a fixed principle but a decently mixed economy.

The plot of such a book would then suggest itself along a fairly obvious line. Suppose the perfection of a political system were endangered by some residual sentiments in one of its citizens; or, worse still, in two, who might be drawn together to make a little rival world. The perfection of the system would either be spoiled, or it would have to be enforced upon the deviant citizens. In the major political fables the plot shows the deviants perfectly assimilated to the system at the end. But there are many cosier fables, including a TV series some years ago called *The Prisoner,* in which a determined and ingenious citizen maintains his selfhood and ties the system in knots.

Of the books I have mentioned, those which seem to have meant most to Orwell, whether he accepted their images or not, are *We* and *The Managerial Revolution.* So far as I know, Isaac Deutscher was the first to establish the bearing of *We* upon *Nineteen Eighty-Four,* and to show that Orwell's book to some extent draws upon Zamyatin's for its plot. In *We* the narrator, known only as D-503, works as an engineer in a society called The One State, a marvel in the engineering of glass. All goes perfectly until D-503 is roused to imperfection by a woman known as E-330. In the end, the system wins: D-503 is carried off to Auditorium 112, where he undergoes an operation and is reconciled to the perfection of rationality.[1] Orwell read the book in a French translation in February 1944: he started working on *Nineteen Eighty-Four* in 1945: he published a review of *We* in *Tribune* on January 4, 1946.[2] He finished *Nineteen Eighty-Four* in 1948. In the review he made the point that *Brave New World* was clearly based upon *We.* His own debt to *We* is mainly a matter of several affinities: Orwell's "Thought Police" are close to Zamyatin's "Guardians," his "Big Brother" is like Zamyatin's "Benefactor," and the particular form of imperfection is a love affair. But the crucial consideration is that Zamyatin's book showed Orwell how he might move beyond the allegory of *Animal Farm.* In the review Orwell said that "what Zamyatin seems to be aiming at is not any particular country but the implied aims of industrial civilisation." To avoid repeating *Animal Farm,* Orwell had to find a larger or, better still, universal system of reference. Zamyatin showed him how it might be done, and how features of "the novel" could be drawn into "the fable." Many details in *Nineteen Eighty-Four* clearly refer to Russia. Big Brother has the ruggedly handsome face of Stalin, given not only historical but mythological status. Emmanuel Goldstein is clearly Trotsky. But the drabness of Oceania, the rationing of chocolate, the pervasive dreariness of the place testify to Orwell's dispirited sense of English life before, during, and immediately after the war. Much of this sentiment is drawn from the experience attributed to George Bowling in *Coming Up for Air,* the colourlessness of English working-class life despite whatever good could be said of it, and the guilt

English intellectuals should bear for letting the workers sink into such drugged apathy. This part of *Nineteen Eighty-Four* also issues from the failure of Attlee's government to give English society any real vitality. More particularly, the Ministry of Truth, where Winston Smith works, comes from Orwell's experience of the British Ministry of Information during the war, and the lies purveyed in the evening news by the BBC's assurance, following bombing raids on German cities, that "all our aircraft returned home safely." The shifting alliances between the three powers, Oceania, Eurasia, and Eastasia, are based in the first instance on those between Russia and Germany, and, I think, on the postwar arrangements between the great powers as recorded in a famous photograph of Stalin, Roosevelt, and Churchill at Yalta.

Zamyatin's book showed Orwell that he could go beyond *Animal Farm* by moving freely between local reference and wider, more diffuse implication: the ideal form would be a series of short, brittle chapters illustrating various aspects of the system while discounting any possibility of a development within it. Each chapter would be an illustration, controlled by the idea governing the whole book. The form, like the system, would be entirely closed. Oceania lives only by repeating itself. The same applies, indeed, to any corporation—hence the fear provoked by a collectivity. Much of the power of *Nineteen Eighty-Four* arises from the reader's sense of a system which perpetuates itself without human intervention.

In practice, most political theorists have distinguished between three entities: the individual person, the society in which he lives, and the state. It is also normal to begin with the individual person and then to consider society as the embodiment of his nature as a social being, the relations he makes, his participation in personal and social experience. The state would then be a more distant entity, engaged in such matters as legislation, taxation, foreign relations, alliances, war, and peace. But suppose this division of purposes were to be perverted: suppose the state were to become an oligarchy so omnivorous that it swallowed up society and made the individual person a mere function of itself. That supposition is Orwell's vision, but it came to him nearly ready-made, complete in every respect except a fictional form, from Burnham's books, and from three in particular, *The Managerial Revolution*, *The Machiavellians*, and *The Struggle for the World*.

Burnham changed his mind on points of detail, large and small, between one book and the next, mainly because—as Orwell pointed out—he thought that what was happening at each moment was decisive and that it would persist. But his general sense of the form political and administrative power would take didn't move far from the version of it he gave in *The Managerial Revolution.* In that book he predicted that the weakness of capitalism would continue to show itself; mainly because capitalism couldn't cope with mass unemployment, couldn't deal with public debts, or resuscitate a dying agriculture, couldn't handle its own resources, or do anything with an impotent bourgeois ideology. However, the downfall of capitalism would not mean the victory of the proletariat or any Marxist paradise. Capitalism would not be replaced by any form of socialism: autocracy was even more extreme in Stalin's Russia than in Hitler's Germany. This would not mean that states nominally socialist would revert to capitalism: instead, they would move toward a managerial form. Burnham's idea of managers was simple: they are the people who direct the process of production. A managerial state is based upon state ownership of the major instruments of production; more and more government control of the economy. Such a state would be the "property" not of rich men or capitalists but of managers: the managers would be the ruling class.

Burnham argued that the countries which had already gone furthest toward the managerial revolution were in fact the totalitarian dictatorships. What distinguished totalitarian dictatorship was "the number of facets of life subject to the impact of the dictatorial rule":

> It is not merely political actions, in the narrower sense, that are involved; nearly every side of life, business and art and science and education and religion and recreation and morality are not merely influenced by but directly subjected to the totalitarian regime.[3]

But the managerial state, Burnham supposed, would be an oligarchy in possession of an exploiting economy. Managers would control the instruments of production in their own corporate favour: sovereignty would be located in various administrative bureaus which would displace parliament and issue decrees. An economy of state ownership would provide the basis for domination and exploitation "by a ruling class of an extremity and absoluteness never before known." The masses would be curbed or constantly diverted so that they would, as we say, go along with the managerial arrangements.

Zamyatin envisaged one world-state, but Burnham allowed for three. Three super-states would divide the world between them and would enter into shifting alliances with one another. In 1941 Burnham thought the three would be the United States, Europe (meaning Germany, the Netherlands, Belgium, northern France, and England), and "the Japanese islands together with parts of eastern China." The superpowers would wage war over marginal territory. "Ostensibly," Burnham said, "these wars will be directed from each base for conquest of the other bases. But it does not seem possible for any one of these to conquer the others; and even two of them in coalition could not win a decisive and lasting victory over the third." Or, as Orwell wrote in *Nineteen Eighty-Four*, "None of the three super-states could be definitively conquered even by the other two in combination."

Orwell published two important essays on Burnham in May 1946 and March 1947.[4] In the first, he gave a severe account of *The Managerial Revolution* and *The Machiavellians,* partly because several of Burnham's predictions had already been disproved. But Orwell was also irritated by Burnham's habit of thinking that because something was the case, it must continue to be the case. Orwell argued that "the real question is not whether the people who wipe their boots on us during the next fifty years are to be called managers, bureaucrats, or politicians: the question is whether capitalism, now obviously doomed, is to give way to oligarchy or to true democracy." He also maintained that Burnham, while attacking totalitarianism in all its forms and especially in its Russian form, was infatuated by its images: he was fascinated by the power he attacked and despised the democracy he should have defended. Indeed, Orwell accused Burnham of voicing the secret desire of the English intelligentsia, the desire "to destroy the old, equalitarian version of Socialism and usher in a hierarchical society where the intellectual can at last get his hands on the whip." At the end of the essay, Orwell offered his own prediction:

If I had to make a prophecy, I should say that a continuation of the Russian policies of the last fifteen years ... can only lead to a war conducted with atomic bombs, which will make Hitler's invasion look like a tea-party. But at any rate, the Russian regime will either democratise itself, or it will perish. The huge, invincible, everlasting slave empire of which Burnham appears to dream will not be established, or, if established, will not endure, because slavery is no longer a stable basis for human society.

Nonetheless, in May 1946, Orwell found Burnham's general thesis of a managerial revolution plausible. A few months later he reviewed *The Struggle for the World:* by March 1947 America, but not Russia, had the atomic bomb. Burnham now took the view that the three superpowers envisaged in *The Managerial Revolution* were not, after all, morally much of a muchness. There were now, in any event, only two such powers, and one of them, the United States, was morally vastly superior to the other. Logic would suggest a preventive war against Russia, since Russia was clearly preparing to destroy the Western democracies. At the very least, the United States should immediately draw Britain and as much of Europe as possible into an anti-Communist crusade.

Orwell's response to Burnham's arguments was fairly mild. He thought an anti-Communist crusade would probably come about, but he hoped that it might be possible to establish democratic socialism over an area of the globe as large as, say, western Europe and Africa. "If one could somewhere present the spectacle of economic security without concentration camps, the pretext for the Russian dictatorship would disappear and Communism would lose much of its appeal." If that were out of the question, then only two possibilities would remain. Russia might become more liberal and less dangerous over a period of a generation or so, if war could be avoided in the meantime. The other possibility, Orwell said, "is that the great powers will be simply too frightened of the effects of atomic weapons ever to make use of them." In either case, Orwell cheered himself up by thinking that history would not be as melodramatic as Burnham's predictions.

But it is clear that while Orwell rejected many of Burnham's arguments, he found the plot and indeed some of the imagery of *The Managerial Revolution* highly persuasive. The book was a good description, he said in 1947, of "what is actually happening in various parts of the world, i.e. the growth of societies neither capitalist nor Socialist, and organised more or less on the lines of a caste system." He couldn't refute Burnham's arguments; all he could do was find them distastefully extreme and hope for a political future somewhat quieter and more tolerant than anything Burnham envisaged. He wanted a world in which states would indeed exist, but in which decent societies would be allowed to thrive. The source of his most acute anxiety in *Nineteen Eighty-Four* is the fate of self, individuality, and mind in a system that reduces them to mere repetitions of the same. What he most fears in the technology of communication is the loss of privacy, the fact that O'Brien knows what Winston Smith is thinking even before Smith has articulated it for himself. "They can't get inside you," Julia said. "But they could get inside you," Winston learns. Orwell rebuked Burnham for not asking himself what power is for: power to do what? But in *Nineteen Eighty-Four* power is for the sake of power. Winston and Julia are forced to betray each other because the Party wants to exercise its power.

Nineteen Eighty-Four doesn't even try to refute Burnham on his own terms: it doesn't offer the world a more accommodating destiny. But it shifts the terms of discourse to discourse itself: the fate of the world is to be represented by analogy with the fate of language, and specifically of the English language. The main reason for this shift is that while it is reasonable to feel that the English language is being corrupted, it is also reasonable to feel—what few of us can claim in politics—that we can still take action to save it.

I have mentioned Orwell's experience of the BBC and the Ministry of Information during the war. I think he felt misgiving, at least, about the daily work of propaganda, even in a cause he believed to be just. In an essay, "Writers and Leviathan," which he wrote in March 1948, he distinguished between the citizen and the writer: when they are one and the same person, the citizen should do nearly any work for his political party, but he should not write for it or engage in propaganda in its behalf. A man's work for a cause should be the rough-and-ready thing it usually is, but his writings should always be "the product of the saner self that stands aside, records the things that are done and admits their necessity, but refuses to be deceived as to their true nature." I think Orwell also felt that this saner self was particularly available to an Englishman because of the splendour of the English language. He felt that English, if we treat it decently, is an instrument of unique capacity. Indeed, he shared this sentiment with men as different in other respects as Herbert Read, Robert Graves, and—his colleague in wartime propaganda—William Empson. Empson has an early essay in which he maintains that a decent English style "gives great resilience to the thinker, never blurs a point by too wide a focus, is itself a confession of how much always must be left undealt with, and is beautifully free from verbiage. To an enemy it looks like sheer cheating." Empson's *The Structure of Complex Words,* Herbert Read's *English Prose Style,* and Graves's book, written with Alan Hodge, *The Reader Over Your Shoulder* issue from much the same experience as Orwell's essay "Politics and the English Language."

"Politics and the English Language" is closer to the interests of *Nineteen Eighty-Four* than to anything else Orwell wrote: it is the essay to read when the theme is his ideology of "the plain style" and the political attitudes it supports. Orwell's sense of language could not have been simpler. He was indifferent to philosophical issues, and most of all to issues in the philosophy of language. He would certainly have despised our current preoccupation with questions of indeterminacy, logocentrism, and the like. He regarded a language—the English language, for instance—as an instrument in the furtherance of thought. If the instrument is in good order, the mind can work well with it: if it is blunt, sloppy, or otherwise decayed, the mind is disabled. The English language, he said, "becomes ugly and inaccurate because our thoughts are foolish, but the slovenliness of our language makes it easier for us to have foolish thoughts." If thought corrupts language, "language can also corrupt thought." A writer writes well when he picks out words for the sake of their meaning and invents images to make his meaning clearer. Orwell also assumed that we can do our thinking without recourse to words, and that we go to words only to convey our meaning: he didn't advert to the notion that our thinking is already inscribed in the language native to us, and may be partly determined by its syntax.

The passage in "Politics and the English Language"[5] which makes Orwell's position entirely clear is this one:

What is above all needed is to let the meaning choose the word, and not the other way about. In prose, the worst thing one can do with words is to surrender to them. When you think of a concrete object, you think wordlessly, and then, if you want to describe the thing you have been visualising, you probably hunt about till you find the exact words that seem to fit it. When you think of something abstract you are more inclined to use words from the start, and unless you make a conscious effort to prevent it, the existing dialect will come rushing in and do the job for you, at the expense of blurring or even changing your meaning. Probably it is better to

put off using words as long as possible and get one's meaning as clear
as one can through pictures or sensations. Afterwards one can choose
—not simply accept—the phrases that will best cover the meaning,
and then switch round and decide what impression one's words are
likely to make on another person.

Virtually every sentence in that passage is questionable: but that doesn't
mean that it's demonstrably wrong. Most philosophers of language would
maintain that the relation between mind and language is far more complex than Orwell implies. To what extent wordless thinking is possible is
also a contentious matter. It is not clear what would be entailed in
"letting the meaning choose the words": the phrase is culpably vague,
since the meaning doesn't choose anything, it is the mind that chooses.
Orwell's linguistics doesn't amount to more than the assertion that a
pudding is a pudding, and that good plain cooking is the best.

But the aspect of the passage I want to look at more closely is its
assumption that good plain writing is an ethical choice. Orwell believed
that a writer who tries to write well takes the language—the English
language, if that is the case—as the custodian of his best and sanest self.
Part of the writer's concern is to rid himself of dying metaphors, pretentious diction, meaningless expressions. Another part is his effort to think
of vivid images to make his meaning clearer. Now these concerns
correspond, I think, to a writer's scruple: a good sentence issues from
one's best self and from a language responsive to ethical choices. The
effort of writing well is the writer's version of conscientiousness: a decent
English prose is decent in an ethical sense, too, and not because it observes
any official form of decorum.

Orwell doesn't say precisely how a language exerts this ethical
authority. It doesn't, indeed, unless we let it. But *Nineteen Eighty-Four*
makes it clear that the ethical authority of a language comes not only
from the fact that we can say of some sentences that they are decent and
of other sentences that they are corrupt: it comes more specifically,
I think, from the history of the words in a language and from our respect
for that history. The sense of the past is most acute in Orwell when it
appears as respect for the associations of words; not casual or impressionistic
associations but those which tell of all they have come through, their
historical weight and density. Newspeak is the linguistic form of brainwashing. It is worth mentioning, too, that Empson's *The Structure of*

Complex Words is based on the assumption that most of our feeling and sentiment is located in certain rich adhering words. Newspeak nullifies this accretion of feeling by disengaging words from their history; it is mostly a matter of abbreviating them. As Orwell says in the appendix to *Nineteen Eighty-Four,* "It was perceived that in thus abbreviating a name one narrowed and subtly altered its meaning, by cutting out most of the associations that would otherwise cling to it."[6] The words "Communist International," for instance, "call up a composite picture of universal human brotherhood, red flags, barricades, Karl Marx, and the Paris Commune." But the word "Comintern" "suggests merely a tightly knit organization and a well-defined body of doctrine." "Comintern" "is a word that can be uttered almost without taking thought, whereas Communist International is a phrase over which one is obliged to linger at least momentarily." What Orwell means by that lingering is one's response not only to the immediate meaning of a word but to the historical and moral experience it enacts. Newspeak, incidentally, may also have issued from Orwell's misgiving about such artifices as Esperanto and the Basic English of C. K. Ogden and I. A. Richards—products of good intention but, like "universal education," a far poorer thing in event and consequence than in anticipation.

It follows that two major concerns in *Nineteen Eighty-Four* are so close as to be nearly one: the mutability of history and the elimination, in Newspeak, of heretical words and the sentiments they embody. Orwell's understanding of history is nearly as unquestioning as his sense of language. He did not confront, as in our own time, the widespread disaffection from history, and scepticism about historical knowledge. Orwell took it for granted that historical events were recoverable and that a decent, scrupulous mind, by taking thought, could make sense of them and offer that sense as their meaning. The mutability of history, in *Nineteen Eighty-Four,* is an outrage to Orwell because it mocks the efforts men have made to produce from historical events a privileged meaning; privileged in the sense of being self-evidently cogent and persuasive. In Oceania, the past, too, can be brainwashed.

I have been maintaining that Orwell's distinctive intervention in the tradition of the political fable was his representation of systematic cruelty and intimidation by analogy with the deliberate degradation of language. The fact that politics and language are both systems made the analogy available. But the most questionable aspect of the analogy is Orwell's implication, in both *Nineteen Eighty-Four* and "Politics and the English Language," that a decent style, specifically his own plain style, is directly sanctioned by nature. He doesn't acknowledge that writing in a plain style is just as much a rhetorical act as writing in, say, the style of Walter Pater or Sir Thomas Browne. No style arrives with the authority of nature. Orwell's plain style is not independent of rhetoric: indeed, only by a strikingly elaborate rhetoric was it possible to imply a "natural" kinship between his plain style, the truth of common sense, a politics of decency, and a notion of historical truth as self-evident. Orwell contrived to enforce the assumption that his intimacy with these values was a matter of sound instincts and that rival values were merely forms of decadence issuing from a perverse intelligentsia. Such decadence was available to intellectuals because they weren't required to carry their notions into social and political practice.

The main problem in reading *Nineteen Eighty-Four* in 1984 is that the book has so often been compromised: it has rarely been read in a disinterested spirit or, as we say, as a work of literature. Like *Animal Farm,* it has been received by readers on the political right as irrefutable evidence that they have been accurate from the start in their judgement of Communism. The evidence has been particularly welcome, coming from a man who had good reason to know the character of Communism: he had seen such men, after all, in Spain. So *Nineteen Eighty-Four* has had far greater political reverberation than, say, Constantine Fitzgibbon's *When the Kissing Had to Stop,* because Fitzgibbon was never anything but a man of the right. *Animal Farm* and *Nineteen Eighty-Four* have been read as tracts for the times, especially by readers who practise a rhetoric of the Cold War, McCarthyism, or the version of those sentiments which is in some vogue again.

Readers whose political attitudes coincide with liberal democracy—or whose attitudes have changed to that position—have welcomed the book as a truthful indictment of totalitarianism. I am thinking of Philip Rahv, Irving Howe, and—in his general sense of Orwell's achievement—Lionel Trilling. Trilling's essay on *Homage to Catalonia* has been extremely influential in maintaining the impression that Orwell, by being a virtuous man, was what an evil time most urgently needed. Trilling's sense of Orwell is totally free from the triumphalism of the right—he doesn't produce Orwell's evidence with a flourish as if to say, "I told you so." But his essay has had one regrettable effect: it has established too firmly the kinship between Orwell's being a virtuous man and his endorsement of a certain set of attitudes. As a result, readers on the left have reacted, more strongly than they might otherwise have done, against the identification of virtue with the opinions Orwell held.

I am thinking of two such reactions. Isaac Deutscher's essay—which I have already mentioned—accused Orwell of indulging himself in the mysticism of cruelty. Having lost confidence in the power of intelligence, Orwell "increasingly viewed reality through the dark glasses of a quasi-mystical pessimism." Deutscher's charge against Orwell is the same as Orwell's against Burnham; that in the end, finding that plain open-air thinking hadn't transformed the world, he abandoned it in favor of fanaticism and hysteria. *Nineteen Eighty-Four,* according to Deutscher, has frightened millions of people, "but it has not helped them to see more clearly the issues with which the world is grappling . . . it has only increased and intensified the waves of panic and hate that run through the world and obfuscate innocent minds."[7]

The second critic on the left I want to invoke is Raymond Williams. A socialist with occasional connections of discourse with Communists, Williams has often written about Orwell, sometimes with reluctant sympathy and respect, as in his "Modern Masters" book on him. But he now finds Orwell's books intolerable. In *Politics and Letters* (1979) he discussed Orwell with the editors of the *New Left Review,* who were hostile to Orwell in every particular. They asserted that: (1) Orwell didn't produce any new theoretical knowledge about society or history, and "1984 will be a curio in 1984"; (2) his novels "range from the mediocre to the weak"; (3) his social reporting, as in *The Road to Wigan Pier,* is vitiated by suppression and manipulation of the evidence; (4) in the creation of a character called "Orwell," he indulged himself in masquerade "in the sense that under the guise of frankness and directness the writing posture is more than usually dominative." Williams didn't disagree with these views. In fact, he attacked the Orwell of *Nineteen Eighty-Four* in far more extreme terms. "The recruitment of very private feelings against socialism becomes intolerable," he said, "by *Nineteen Eighty-Four*":

> It is profoundly offensive to state as a general truth, as Orwell does, that people will always betray each other. If human beings are like that, what could be the meaning of a democratic socialism? . . . *Animal Farm,* for all its weaknesses, still makes a point about how power can

be lost and how people can be misled: it is defeatist, but it makes certain pointed observations on the procedures of deception. As for *Nineteen Eighty-Four*, its projections of ugliness and hatred, often quite arbitrarily and inconsequentially, onto the difficulties of revolution or political change seem to introduce a period of really decadent bourgeois writing in which the whole status of human beings is reduced.[8]

Williams accuses Orwell of capturing the role of the "frank, disinterested observer who is simply telling the truth," and then of producing as the truth a report entirely defeatist. I don't agree with Williams in this charge, but I understand his irritation—not to represent it as more than that—when he is asked, by Trilling, Howe, Kazin, and many other liberal writers, to revere Orwell as a virtuous and truth-telling man. It's like being asked to take Gandhi as a saint. In private life, Orwell seems to have been a decent man, but there is evidence of shoddy sentiments, and intermittently of cruel behaviour to rather vulnerable people. The answer to this is that he deeply regretted his offences and, when they were public acts, confessed them, as in *Burmese Days*. But I don't think he was, in fact, a particularly nice man or that a halo sits well on his head. I'm sure he tried to tell the truth as he saw it and worried a great deal when he didn't tell it. But so do most people, even when in retrospect it emerges that they deceived themselves or fell into bewilderments they could have avoided.

But Williams's account of *Nineteen Eighty-Four* is not valid. The book doesn't say that people will always betray each other: you could derive that grim moral from it only if you claimed that you, for instance, would hold out for ever against the most appalling torture; or that you, unlike hundreds of tortured people, could never be brainwashed. Again, Williams is inaccurate when he refers to Orwell's "extreme distaste for humanity of every kind, especially concentrated in figures of the working class." The only incident I can think of, in *Nineteen Eighty-Four*, as at all supporting that charge is the appalling fight of the two prole women over the saucepan—in many ways the most dreadful episode in the book. But in *Nineteen Eighty-Four* as a whole the proles get a better showing than anyone else; it is not their fault that they are kept in cultural sedation, like the English working class, kept inert on drink, gambling, and the popular newspapers. But no such argument would satisfy Williams, short of representing the working class as ready and determined to fulfil the redemptive destiny Marx prescribed for them. Orwell's relation to the working class was indeed ambivalent: his sympathy was too much an act of goodwill to be really convincing. But he wasn't, after all, a member of the working class, so it is hardly surprising or scandalous that, while making every effort to like workers, he found them extremely limited in their interests and values.

A valid reading of *Nineteen Eighty-Four* would entail several recognitions. The book is not a documentary account of any regime; it is a fable, written in fear by a writer beset with his own illness and the illness of the world. I think Orwell was English in the sense we associate with Hardy and Elgar: the idyllic episode in *Nineteen Eighty-Four* evokes the English countryside in those terms. Experience of war and time of war—Barcelona and London—exasperated Orwell's sensibility to the point of making him, intermittently, conspire with what he feared and hated. He lent his imagination, I believe, to images and visions which did not endorse his discursive habit. Indeed, I think well of G. S. Fraser's view, outlined in a letter to *Critical Quarterly* in 1959, that *Nineteen Eighty-Four* is horrible because Orwell started to write it to say "this *may* happen," but his imagination turned that moral impulse into one of morose delectation, as if to say "this *must* happen." I think *Nineteen Eighty-Four* should be read much as the fourth book of *Gulliver's Travels* is read, though Orwell's imagination is of a much inferior power to Swift's. Both books have many local references, political allusions which only the elect recognize, but beyond these allusions both are universalist in their ambition, exempting no one from their strictures. What *Nineteen Eighty-Four* describes is a system. Orwell does not explain how the system came into being, unless we are to suppose one dreadful cause, the failure and treason of intellectuals. As it stands, the system is there; it is what it is; it corresponds to the exercise of power for the sake of power. René Girard has complained that the book does not show the connection between individual desire and the collective structure: "we sometimes get the impression from Orwell's books that the 'system' has been imposed from the outside on the innocent masses."[9] But that impression is consistent with the managerial character of the system; it is an oligarchy, and it has separated its activities from the proles. But I would make more than Girard does of the doubleness he speaks of in the totalitarian structure; especially as it is given in the relation between Winston Smith and O'Brien —which is not adequately thought of as one between a victim and his assailant. What is peculiarly insistent is the degree to which Winston feels himself drawn to speak to O'Brien and enters into extraordinary complicity with him: so far as the reader's access to it is in question, it is the most telling relation in the book. It is also the relation which underlines most compellingly the character and force of a system; its appalling capacity to operate independently of the people who compose it.

NOTES

1. Yevgeny Zamyatin, *We,* trans. Bernard Guilbert Guerney (Harmondsworth: Penguin Books, 1972).
2. Sonia Orwell and Ian Angus (eds.), *The Collected Essays, Journalism and Letters of George Orwell,* 4 vols. (London: Secker and Warburg, 1968), IV, 75.
3. James Burnham, *The Managerial Revolution: Or What Is Happening in the World Now* (London: Putnam, 1942), p. 145.
4. Both essays are reprinted in Vol. IV of *The Collected Essays: In Front of Your Nose,* pp. 160–81 and 313–25.
5. *Ibid.,* pp. 127–39.
6. George Orwell, *Nineteen Eighty-Four* (Harmondsworth: Penguin Books, 1983), p. 264.
7. Isaac Deutscher, "*Nineteen Eighty-Four:* The Mysticism of Cruelty," in *Heretics and Renegades* (London: Hamish Hamilton, 1956); reprinted in Raymond Williams (ed.), *George Orwell: A Collection of Critical Essays* (Englewood Cliffs, N.J.: Prentice-Hall, 1974), p. 132.
8. Raymond Williams, *Politics and Letters* (London: NLB, 1979), pp. 384–92.
9. René Girard, *Deceit, Desire, and the Novel,* trans. Yvonne Freccero (Baltimore and London: Johns Hopkins University Press, 1965), p. 226.

From *George Orwell and Nineteen Eighty-Four* (Washington, D.C.: Library of Congress, 1985).

GRAHAM GREENE, AUTOBIOGRAPHER

"H ere at last is the long-awaited sequel to the autobiography of
Graham Greene," according to the publisher. The offer is
misleading. *Ways of Escape* is a sequel to *A Sort of Life* (1971),
but neither of them is an autobiography. Greene has been
rigidly unforthcoming about his private life. The only information he
gives in *Ways of Escape* about the breakdown of his marriage is that
apart from "the separation of war and my own infidelities" he was on
Benzedrine for most of the crucial weeks. There is a brief reference to
"my mistress." Also to "a difficult decision in my private life" which had
something to do with Greene's decision to leave England and settle in
France in 1966. We gather that his religious belief has waned. The
Catholicism to which he converted in 1926 has lost his allegiance, for
reasons not disclosed, unless his "small belief in the doctrine of eternal
punishment" is a reason. Readers who have been awaiting revelation on
such matters are free to persist, but the odds are against it. Greene has
been playing Garbo for so long that he would be wretchedly capitulating
if he gave up the performance now.

Not an autobiography, then, but a memoir. In an autobiography,
even the most external events are so narrated as to shine upon the

narrator. External and internal motives are deemed to be continuous. But a memoir works in favour of the event narrated; it supposes that private life and public life are discontinuous; it allows the narrator to sequester his private life, on the grounds that it is not a matter of general interest, it concerns only himself and a few friends. It is true that *A Sort of Life* describes Greene's childhood in Berkhamsted, his school, his games, fear of boredom, his taste for minor writers, Oxford in 1926, Greene's doomed passion for a governess, and what it was like to be a drunken undergraduate. But these experiences are narrated as if their interest were somehow intrinsic, and not necessarily germane to Greene's later life. Even the famous essay on Russian roulette, Greene's derring-do with the derringer, available in "The Saturday Book," *The Lost Childhood,* and yet again in *A Sort of Life,* is treated as a spectacle, and is not supposed to adhere permanently to its narrator.

A Sort of Life dealt with Greene's life, selected fragments of it, from childhood till 1931, when he was twenty-seven years old. The new book is a sequel in the technical sense that it takes up the story in 1931 and brings it, more or less, up to date. Most of it consists of the introductions Greene wrote for the uniform edition of his novels, stories, and plays, starting with *The Man Within* and ending, for the moment, with *The Human Factor;* glancing at the plays and screenplays from *The Third Man* to *Carving a Statue.* Occasionally, we are given a few affectionate pages about one of Greene's friends: Nordahl Grieg, Herbert Read, Robert Scott, Evelyn Waugh, Carol Reed, Alexander Korda. The introductions are extremely interesting; they set out the circumstances in which each book was written, the difficulties, the technical problems of, say, first-person narration. The rest of the book is an account of Greene's travels in Liberia, Malaya, Hanoi, Saigon, Dien Bien Phu, Kenya, Warsaw, Havana, the Belgian Congo, Haiti, Israel, and Paraguay. The relation between Greene's imagination and the places that stimulated it is described from time to time, but briefly and unfussily.

Ways of Escape makes one feel, yet again, how much a writer of the thirties Greene is. The work he did in that decade, from *Stamboul Train* (1932), *England Made Me* (1935), *A Gun for Sale* (1936) to *Brighton Rock* (1938), *The Lawless Roads* (1939), and *The Power and the Glory* (1940), is not his best; much of it is overwritten, besotted with a rhetorical extravagance taken over from Conrad's *The Arrow of Gold.* But if not his best work, it is his most typical, producing his major themes, situations, and images.

Greene's mind, like Auden's during the same decade, was appeased mainly by lurid occasions. The imagery common to Greene, Auden, Isherwood, MacNeice, and Spender is of frontiers, maps, passports, an atmosphere not of death, Juliet's tomb, but of terror, mostly sought for its *frisson.* In *Ways of Escape* Greene says that he went to troubled places "not to seek material for novels but to regain the sense of insecurity which I had enjoyed in the three blitzes on London." The enjoyment of insecurity, fear, and terror, sought as an escape from boredom and depression, is one of Greene's themes in *Ways of Escape.* When we accept the force of it in him, we find ourselves revising our sense of Auden and his friends; reading *Look, Stranger!* and *Letters from Iceland* as rituals against boredom, not merely against the public nightmare, dread, and war.

Greene's themes in *Ways of Escape* are also retained from the thirties. Betrayal, it is true, is perennial, but Greene's sense of it issues from a set of circumstances, conventions, and assumptions peculiar to the English thirties; and shared by many bright young men who entered upon their careers with a view of life largely provided by their experience in such institutions as Berkhamsted and Balliol. Such men had their first experience of betrayal in school; a friendship spurned, a secret disclosed. Greene derived his title, *The Lost Childhood,* from George Russell's poem "Germinal":

> *In the lost boyhood of Judas*
> *Christ was betrayed.*

The epigraph to *The Human Factor,* taken from Conrad, is a lesson that could be learned just as painfully at school as in any other dangerous place:

> I only know that he who forms a tie is lost. The germ of corruption has entered into his soul.

Or, as Dr. Plarr says in *The Honorary Consul,* "caring is the only dangerous thing."

I want to press the matter. Wouldn't it be convenient, as compensation for the pain of betrayal, to brood upon a morality in which one state merges in another? You could then evade the otherwise stark choice between good and evil, right and wrong. Thomas Hardy wrote, in a passage Greene chose as the epigraph to *The Honorary Consul,* that "all things merge in one another—good into evil, generosity into justice, religion into politics." And in *A Sort of Life* Greene chose as epigraph for all his novels a passage from Browning's "Bishop Blougram's Apology":

> *Our interest's on the dangerous edge of things.*
> *The honest thief, the tender murderer,*
> *The superstitious atheist.*

With Browning, Greene said, "I lived in a region of adulteries, of assignations at dark street corners, of lascivious priests and hasty dagger thrusts, and of sexual passion far more heady than romantic love." Browning found such motifs not only in Shelley but in Jacobean melodrama. Greene found them not only in Browning but in school, classroom, dormitory, playing field, and the neo-Jacobean fiction most compellingly exemplified in Marjorie Bowen's *The Viper of Milan.* It is a short distance from that world to Greene's notion of the novelist as spy, playing a game at once seedy and heroic.

My argument is that Greene, coming of age in the thirties, defined his art mainly in melodramatic terms, with corresponding themes of betrayal and equivocation. After *The Power and the Glory,* he put his talent on a thin diet, got rid of Conrad, and took his themes more casually. *The Heart of the Matter* (1948) and *The End of the Affair* (1951) are just as serious as the earlier novels, but they don't proceed upon an assumption of universal menace. And they have moments in which the ironies of *The Comedians* (1966) and *Travels with My Aunt* (1969) are anticipated. But they are still derived from gestures which were already habitual to Greene in the thirties. It has always been the habit of Greene's intelligence to seek menacing occasions; of his morality to lure temptation; of his body to seek danger; and of his convictions to long to be undermined. Even in his later years, his exploits have often retained a trace of adolescence. In *Ways of Escape* his account of being deported from Puerto Rico has every sign of being a prank on his part, and, worse still, a Balliol prank. Many of his travels, which could have been serious, sound like mere escapades. Why did he go to Havana?

I came there ("in search of pleasure for my punishment," Wilfred Scawen Blunt wrote) for the sake of the Floridita restaurant (famous for daiquiris and Morro crabs), for the brothel life, the roulette in every hotel, the fruit machines spilling out jackpots of silver dollars, the Shanghai Theatre, where for one dollar and twenty-five cents one could see a nude cabaret of extreme obscenity with the bluest of blue films in the intervals.

Greene doesn't strike me as the sort of man who could treat these joys as lightly as they deserve: even in books which seem particularly accomplished, his style broods upon matters which a mind of a different cast would brush aside. But the brooding has little moral force, it calls attention to a merely picturesque array of experiences which Greene reports in much the same spirit as a schoolboy produces his clutch of nudes. Greene may feel that his relation to experience is, and should always be, experimental: something useful may turn up if you give yourself a chance of finding it. But he doesn't distinguish between an experiment that is justified by its results and an ostensibly experimental habit which has no difficulty accommodating itself to sleaziness. The alternative to Greene's procedure is not that a novelist should stay at home and, when he travels, confine his attention to museums, but that he should judge his experiences and discriminate between the qualities they entail. The sentence I have quoted has not been required to judge anything.

One of the many interests of *Ways of Escape* is the question of character. Greene has always been more concerned with character than with action or plot. He has referred to "the abiding temptation to tell a good story," and has often yielded to it, but only to give a character room to move. In the same spirit, he remarked in *The Lost Childhood* that "we are saved or damned by our thoughts, not by our actions." The distinction between thoughts and actions is not as easy as Greene makes it sound. Never mind. It is good enough to show that he has maintained a corresponding distinction between what a person is and what he has done; and he has taken a more committed interest in the former than in the latter. *In Search of a Character* (1961) describes how Greene came to write *A Burnt-Out Case* (also 1961), a book that started from the notion that a man turned up one day in a leper colony. "The novel is an unknown man," Greene said, "and I have to find him."

In all his novels, Greene's procedure, he tells us, is to begin with a hunch, an intuition of a person, a character. The book then goes in search of him. The object is to achieve virtually complete knowledge of this character. Greene explains in *Ways of Escape* that few of his characters were based upon people he knew; the reason being that, even in the case of an old friend, he knew him only well enough to realize that complete knowledge of him was impossible. With an invented character, complete knowledge is, at least in theory, possible. When he imagined the sinister Doctor Percival in *The Human Factor,* he knew that such a man would admire Ben Nicholson's paintings. When he imagined Colonel Daintry for the same book, he knew that the Colonel would open a tin of sardines on his return from the funeral of his colleague.

Greene's assumption of complete knowledge of his invented characters may explain, incidentally, one irritating feature of his novels, his relation to a character called God. Greene has often written as if he had complete knowledge of God, knew what he would forgive, and so forth; since God is by definition an invented or imaginary character, the assumption doesn't seem preposterous, though its reiteration is tiresome. Anyway, when the novelist has achieved complete knowledge of his character, he is in a position to lavish his sympathy upon him, even if to more disinterested eyes he seems, like Kim Philby, a liar and a scoundrel. In an essay on Henry James, Greene wrote that "it is in the final justice of his pity, the completeness of an analysis which enabled him to pity the most shabby, the most corrupt, of his human actors, that he ranks with the greatest of creative writers."

Greene would not now use these terms; in *Ways of Escape* he refers to "the disastrous effect on human beings of pity as distinct from compassion." Complete knowledge makes possible complete compassion. The purpose of the novel, I infer from Greene's account of more immediate issues, is to enable the novelist and his readers to practise complete compassion, an impossible task in real life, since we can never know enough. In *The Heart of the Matter* Scobie, referring to West Africa, says, "Here you could love human beings nearly as God loved them, knowing the worst."

But even if a novelist knows the worst and the best and everything in between, he is not obliged to make his disclosures as full as his compassion. There is more to Colonel Daintry than sardines. Greene's way is to seek complete knowledge of a character, and then to disclose enough about him to keep his secret, while convincing the reader that the character has one. Opening a tin of sardines implies all the other things Greene knows of Colonel Daintry: it is the novelist's privilege to keep most of them to himself. A novelist's style depends on the relation he maintains between disclosure and secrecy. In *The Genesis of Secrecy* Frank Kermode proposes a distinction between carnal and spiritual readings of a novel: the carnal reading is what everybody agrees on, but spiritual readings are all different. There is no dispute about what the novelist gives us; there is nothing but dispute about what each reader divines thereafter. A carnal reading of *The Human Factor* opens the tin of sardines, an act unlikely to be opaque. Spiritual readings differ because each reader divines differently the relation between the tin of sardines and all the other things that together would constitute the complete knowledge of Daintry which Greene alone has in his keeping.

A character begins to form when the novelist senses that he is being solicited by a person, a figment as yet, a phantasm. For the reader of *Ways of Escape* and *A Sort of Life,* the character is one Graham Greene. There is reason to suppose that the novelist Greene was solicited by the character eventually named Greene. The novelist has a novelist's interest in this person. He seeks complete knowledge of him, and sends him into several remote corners of the world partly to try him out, make him disclose himself: more exploits, more knowledge. The process is one by which a something vague becomes a something more definite, comes from mere potentiality into being. Or comes from one phase or mode of existence into another. A type becomes a character.

It seems feasible to think that the novelist Graham Greene saw himself as a type, to begin with, and that the particular type was the spy, the confidential agent so congenial to the English thirties. Notoriously, he has defended the type, especially when one of them has been caught. I recall being incensed upon some such occasion: didn't Greene publicly lift his glass in honour of Philby, or was it Burgess, or Maclean? But it's clear that, like any schoolboy worth his class's approval, he was defending himself; or rather, the role, the type common to Greene and his friends. The fact that Philby, Burgess, Maclean, and now Blunt have turned their types into "character parts" and continued to play them after Greene has given his farewell performance is merely a matter of history. Nonsense, of course, but entirely compatible with the Balliol thirties.

The purpose of *Ways of Escape,* as of *A Sort of Life,* is to transform a type, the spy, into a character continuous with the type, the novelist as spy. Greene's travels become secret missions, carried out ostensibly for *The Sunday Times* but in truth for himself, to acquire complete knowledge of himself. Haiti differs from Cuba in many respects, but mostly—so far as the narrative is in question—in the different relations each place offered its visitor, Graham Greene.

But Greene is also real, if a distinction is allowed to persist between the real and the imaginary. He is real, and he is also imaginary; a function of some other imagination, God's, for instance, as much as a function of his own. I interpret Greene's secretiveness in this way. Of course he has kept quiet about many things lest he hurt people dear to him. But he has also used *Ways of Escape, A Sort of Life,* and a few other essays to maintain, in relation to himself, the distinction between the real and the imaginary. In these personal writings, he could have gone the whole way and turned himself into a character. But he has retained a scruple about doing so; there is a real person, too, not his invention. The comparison with Garbo is only partially correct: she has gone further than Greene in turning herself into a character, a fiction. The problem is given back to the reader. The bearing of Greene's secrecy upon his disclosures must be apprehended with whatever consequences, in the act of reading. Beyond a certain point, the novelist can't prescribe the form these spiritual readings are to take: that is what makes them spiritual. Each reader does his own work of divination. The agent, after all, may be a double agent; the novelist is telling an uncertain mixture of lies and truths.

Ways of Escape ends with a bizarre Epilogue called "The Other," about another man called Graham Greene, or at least a man who has been using various names, including John Skinner, Meredith de Varg, and Graham Greene. Our man in Antibes, our Graham Greene, proposed to *Picture Post* that they send him to find and interview the other joker, then in jail, apparently, in Assam. The plan didn't work out, because the Other had by then jumped bail, and there was a risk that our man might be arrested in his place. The story has more plot than novels by Graham Greene tend to have; and the characterization is thinner than usual. I take "The Other" as Greene's version of Conrad's "The Secret Sharer." And I do in part believe it.

The book, then, is interesting, enjoyable, and informative. But it does little to remove one's misgivings about Greene's entire work, misgivings which I have suggested by describing him as very much a novelist of the English thirties. My implication is that he settled for themes all too congenial to that decade, and for a melodramatic assumption of their significance. The later novels toned down the portentousness and assimilated their style to a more accomplished urbanity, but they did not question, in any radical way, the melodramatic privilege. Greene's fiction is, at the very least, memorable: to advert to the novels is to recall scenes, characters, atmospheres, and to renew one's sense of having felt their force, mostly as incrimination and conspiracy. But I find a residual feeling in myself of dissatisfaction, reflecting an achievement on Greene's part limited to the possibilities indicated by my reference to melodrama. His novels have always had an insecure sense of how seriously they should take themselves; an insecurity not at all stabilized by Greene's tactical division of his fiction into "novels" and "entertainments."

A case in point: several pages of *Ways of Escape* deal with Greene's experience of smoking opium in Hanoi. These pages are related to Fowler's opium smoking in *The Quiet American*. But neither in the novel nor in the memoir is there an indication of what the experience comes to, or what value the reader is invited to give it. Does it stand for the *"luxe et volupté"* to which Greene refers in *Ways of Escape,* with a claim for significance lodged by further reference to Baudelaire's *"L'Invitation au voyage"*? Or is it to be read as merely exotic, part of the wisdom of the Orient which the reader is not required to receive? In the novel, as in the memoir, it seems to veer between triviality and ominousness. In the memoir, these pages have an air of significance, but only the air is conveyed, not the significance. Greene's novels, too, leave it open to question whether, in his relation to his perceptions, he is a native or a tourist.

_____

Review of *Ways of Escape,* by Graham Greene. From *The New York Review of Books,* February 19, 1981.

LEAVIS ON ELIOT

We are reading Eliot's poetry, and we have also in view, for a certain enrichment of our context, his critical essays and plays. We do not ascribe the same degree of significance to all these things, but taken together, they enliven our sense of a body of work, a crucial presence in modern literature, to speak of it for the moment merely in these terms. We are reading Eliot's work, and the quality of our reading is what matters, since it determines the degree to which the work indeed becomes a presence, becomes present to us in our lives. We are also reading Leavis on Eliot, and we have in mind that his critical writings on Eliot are crucial interventions in the rhetoric of modern literature, in literature considered as power and transaction. Reading constitutes this power and engages in the transaction by transposing the language of poetry into the language of discourse. The poem remains unchanged, but the act of reading it gives it a further life in the form of discourse. The heresy of paraphrase does not arise: it would arise only if we were naïve enough to think the paraphrase in some sense equivalent to the poem.

Critical discourse gives the poem a life other than its own but cognate to its own. The power we ascribe to the poem is answered by another power, that of a reading adequate to it in principle and by intention, if inadequate in the event. I don't know what the power of a poem means unless it means the degree to which it demands from the reader a response similar in kind if less and dissimilar in every other respect. The correlation of Eliot and Leavis has the merit of indicating what I mean by the power of a poem and the power of reading it. If you think the correlation arbitrary, or that the poet could with equal point be associated with another critic, I answer not by claiming that Leavis was the greatest modern critic, but that he was the greatest critic who took the experience of reading Eliot as the representative type of a serious engagement with modern literature. It was Leavis, rather than Blackmur, Ransom, Burke, Frye, or any other critic, who felt called upon to respond to Eliot's poetry over a period of fifty years on the assumption that nothing else in modern poetry would prove equally exacting to the reader's intellectual and moral life. Leavis did not, in fact, regard Eliot as the greatest modern writer: the demand so urgently made in that phrase was fulfilled for Leavis not in Eliot but in Lawrence. But the particular challenge offered by Eliot's poems was of a special kind, issuing in an irregular mixture of recognition and rejection, qualification, outrage, and delight. If a true criticism means discrimination, it was Eliot, even more than Lawrence, who offered Leavis the most testing as well as the most telling occasion.

We are reading Eliot and Leavis with a sense not only of their context but of our own. Reading has become—what it has not always been—a question. We are in a self-conscious phase of criticism, asking ourselves not "How can we become better readers?" but "What precisely are we doing, so far as we are readers?" Do we, by reading, rise to our authentic selves, or do we merely extend our daily selves, authentic or not? The notion of authenticity, once associated with the rhetoric of Existentialism, has returned in the hope of plaguing us: the axioms and principles which govern our reading are again under interrogation, like political or ethical attitudes. Much of the interrogation is displaced from poet to reader: the intention of plucking out the heart of the poet's mystery while leaving it residually there in the vocabulary of genius and inspiration is now turned upon the reader. It appears that, having removed the mystery from the poet to the language in which he is implicated as in the air he lives by breathing, we feel obliged now to retain the mystery—or at least the air of mystery—if only by ascribing it to ourselves.

This is not the occasion to say much on that score, but what we understand by reading is very much to the point of our understanding Leavis and Eliot. When we read Leavis's several essays on Eliot, from the early work in *Scrutiny* and *New Bearings in English Poetry* (1932) to the later interrogations in *Lectures in America* (1969), *English Literature in Our Time and the University* (1969), and the culminating analysis of *Four Quartets* in *The Living Principle* (1975), we find that his sense of Eliot changed and that the change was provoked not only by Eliot's later poetry but by a newly acknowledged sense of what reading amounts to and the nature of the response it exacts. Indeed, to refer to response and analysis is to be content for the moment with approximations.

Leavis has reported that he came upon Eliot's name for the first time in 1920, when by some accident he bought a copy of *The Sacred Wood*. For the next few years, he says, "I read it through several times a year, pencil in hand." The book showed him "what the disinterested and effective application of intelligence to literature looks like, what is the nature of purity of interest, and what is meant by the principle (as Mr. Eliot himself states it) that 'when you judge poetry it is as poetry you must judge it, and not as another thing.'" I should remark, not at all parenthetically, that Eliot's principle of judging poetry as poetry and not as another thing seems to me unclear except in instances so extreme as to be, for more complicated occasions, quite useless. For one thing, the principle implies that in considering poetry you can say with certainty where the poetry begins and ends, and where precisely your attitudes and responses step beyond the presumed boundary of poetry and walk into some other terrain. In practice such a boundary cannot be defined. Purity of interest sounds virtuous, but I cannot find that it is ever sustained in any practice worth invoking, or indeed in Leavis's own reading of the later Eliot. In a reading as arresting and relentless as Leavis's reading of Eliot, where the questions engaged are not only matters of life and death but of rival understandings of life, considerations in favour of purity of interest have not prevented Leavis from driving his argument as far as his critical and discursive powers enable it to go.

But the point to emphasize to begin with is that Leavis's early experience of Eliot's poems, and specifically of *Poems* 1909–1925, conformed to a definition of reading as the responsible elucidation of meanings, directions, and significances. It was not exactly Practical Criticism, the

Basic English of a literary education. Indeed, Leavis was not content with the purpose achieved in I. A. Richards's early books. Richards was chiefly concerned with the transmission and reception of meaning, and he thought of reading according to a fairly simple theory of communication. The theory supposes that a poem is a message which the poet wants to deliver to someone. The message is complex, therefore it is a poem rather than a newspaper article; so the poet wants to have it delivered intact, with all its constituents precisely in place and relation. It is up to the qualified reader to receive it in that form and to protect it from misunderstanding. *Practical Criticism* was Richards's contribution to safe delivery and good keeping. But his critical interest ended with the reception of the message. What happened to it thereafter, and what happened to the reader who received it, were questions for another day's work, to be pursued mainly in psychological rather than linguistic terms.

Practical Criticism seemed to Leavis a worthy but inert activity; he wanted a more challenging relation between poem and reader; he was not persuaded by a theory of messages and communication. In practice—as *New Bearings* makes clear—Leavis's early commentaries on Eliot's poems were mostly acts of testimony bearing upon Eliot's distinctive way with the English language, his sense of possibilities among the words which were also and correspondingly possibilities among the relevant feelings and intuitions. When Leavis praised Eliot's "Portrait of a Lady," he pointed to its "audacities of transition and psychological notation"— audacities that demonstrated that Eliot had released himself from the conventional habits of poetic association which Leavis thought of as disablingly Victorian, Tennysonian, and Swinburnian. The poems he especially praised were the "Portrait," "Gerontion," "Ash Wednesday," and "Marina." His account of *The Waste Land* emphasized that "the unity the poem aims at is that of an inclusive consciousness," an aim approached by Eliot's allusive procedures which attain "a compression approaching simultaneity—the co-presence in the mind of a number of different orientations, fundamental attitudes, orders of experience." The power of an inclusive consciousness, I assume, is that it holds itself immune to solicitation from any of its constituent attitudes. I shall argue later that an inclusive consciousness is something to be approached rather than achieved or possessed; indeed that it has nothing to do with possession of certitude and exists only as a heuristic desire, a hypothetical possibility which is a merit only so long as it remains a virtual impossibility. If it were to be achieved, the achievement would at any moment be premature, a fall into a complacent possession. (But I anticipate.)

Leavis's praise of Eliot's early poems testified to his sense of Eliot's importance as one who indicated certain possibilities in relation to modern society. Leavis identified the modern world as the Machine Age, and thought it exemplified mostly "breach of continuity and the uprooting of life." He believed that it would never again be possible for a distinguished mind to be formed "on the rhythms, sanctioned by nature and time, of rural culture": "uprooted" had its meaning in that belief. The anthropological theme in *The Waste Land* was Eliot's way of recognizing that the breach in continuity had already happened; it was precisely as an act of creative power that Eliot, "a mind fully alive in the age," compelled a poetic triumph out of the peculiar difficulties facing a poet in our time. Leavis represented the difficulties as manifesting the dominance of "the technologico-Benthamite society," a phrase he reiterated so compulsively that I cannot believe it was based upon evidence continuously reconsidered: it goes along with his characterization of contemporary society by reference to packaged holidays, fish and chips eaten in Majorca, and transistor radios in public parks. But the explanation is clear enough. Leavis shared the assumption, common in the thirties, that scientists and technologists represented forces shamelessly destructive. John Crowe Ransom's *The World's Body* is typical of this attitude: the scientific stance is deemed to be aggressive, the outward sign of a predatory relation to the world, while the poetic attitude is offered as courteous, contemplative, ungrasping. Leavis continued to feel that technologico-Benthamite forces had divided people into two unequal groups: the unthinking, victimized mass, fated to be consumers, their desires fraudulently stimulated, and the second group, the educated minority, a group hardly exemplifiable in practice but sustained chiefly by an evident need that it should exist. Hence the importance of the university—"conceived as a creative centre of civilization" —and of literature and criticism in their bearing upon "the effort to re-establish an educated, well-informed, responsible and influential public." Such poems as "Gerontion" and "Marina" showed what might still be done to sustain an educated public in conditions almost entirely unpropitious but not yet absolutely lethal.

When Leavis considers what such poems meant for Eliot himself, as an achievement at once personal and civic, he defines their achievement in relation to sincerity. Sincerity is the criterion, not of course solely in regard to Eliot. In *Lectures in America* Leavis argued that Yeats's "extra-poetic habits," the habits to be diagnosed by pointing to *A Vision,* often got in the way of poetic success, poetic success here meaning "a kind of convincingness and inevitability that comes of, that *is,* a complete sincerity—the sincerity that is of the whole being, and not merely a matter of conscious intention." Leavis speaks of "Ash Wednesday" as embodying "a process of self-scrutiny, or self-exploration," and says that Eliot's poetic problem is at every point a spiritual problem, "a problem in the attainment of a difficult sincerity." Clearly there is a direct relation between Eliot's compelling a poetic triumph out of the peculiar difficulties facing a poet in our time and, viewed more intimately, his compelling a spiritual triumph out of the peculiar difficulties facing his own sincerity. I propose to hover upon this theme because the attainment of a difficult sincerity is the main criterion by which Leavis judges Eliot's poetry from beginning to end.

Our first question must be: what does it mean to present sincerity as something difficult to achieve rather than as something commonly taken, as we ordinarily take the goodwill of our friends, for granted? Lionel Trilling has argued in *Sincerity and Authenticity* that modern society places a low value upon sincerity, not because it does not approve the concord of feelings and avowals—and this is what he takes sincerity to mean—but because it demands "a more strenuous moral experience" than anything fulfilled in "sincerity," "a more exigent conception of the self and of what being true to it consists in, a wider reference to the universe and man's place in it, and a less acceptant and genial view of the social circumstances of life." To praise a work of literature by calling it sincere, Trilling says, "is now at best a way of saying that although it need be given no aesthetic or intellectual admiration, it was at least conceived in innocence of heart." In the next sentence he adduces as a case in point our probable response to Leavis's use of sincerity as a criterion. "When F. R. Leavis in all seriousness distinguishes between those aspects of T. S. Eliot's work which are sincere and those which are not, we are inclined to note the distinction as an example of the engagingly archaic quality of Dr. Leavis's seriousness."

In fact, Leavis does not make the distinction in the form Trilling has ascribed to him. The distinction he enforces is between those moments in Eliot's work in which a difficult sincerity is indeed achieved, the achievement being at once linguistic, poetic, moral, and spiritual—the quality of sincerity being indicated by its difficulty; and those moments in which an illusion of sincerity is the result of Eliot's having taken sincerity for granted as one of his personal and well-attested merits. It is true that sincerity is a quality Leavis has not defined, and that without the renewed force such a definition would give, the word no longer carries the moral virtue it had for him. If he were writing today, he might choose to replace "sincerity" by "authenticity." But on balance I think he would retain "sincerity" as his criterion and take the imputed relaxation out of it by adding the adjective "difficult." In any case, "sincerity" as he used the word marks a spiritual progress and not an established attribute. He makes this clear by insisting that for the poet "technique" acquires a serious meaning only when it is identified with the problem of sincerity and the difficult form in which it is worth seeking. In "Ash Wednesday," for instance, Eliot "had to achieve a paradoxical precision-in-vagueness; to persuade the elusive intuition to define itself, without any forcing, among the equivocations of 'the dreamcrossed twilight.'" The poetry is "an effort at resolving diverse impulsions, recognitions, and needs." A few sentences later Leavis speaks of "the subtle treasons, the refinements, of egotism that beset the quest of sincerity in these regions": the regions in view are those occupied by "the pride of humility."

When we give these hints their full value, we find that sincerity, as the difficult quality in question, is the moral equivalent of the inclusive consciousness to which *The Waste Land* powerfully and conscientiously aspires. Such a consciousness would mediate between diverse impulses, discriminating between the genuine and the specious; it would resolve these diverse impulses, needs, and recognitions. Sincerity as a moral force would do no less. But I have to repeat that an inclusive consciousness and a complete sincerity are the words we ascribe to an ideal, impossible in anyone's practice and therefore that to which desire and conscientiousness aspire. "For us there is only the trying."

I feel justified in proposing this correlation between the attainment of a difficult sincerity and the attainment of an inclusive consciousness because of a passage in *Lectures in America* where Leavis, reflecting severely upon Eliot's resort to "the supernatural" or a continuous suggestion of the supernatural in *The Cocktail Party,* says that such resort is indefensible and betraying: "it reveals in Eliot an inner pressure towards the worst kind of insincerity, that which is unconscious." I take this to mean that insincerity is the wilful putting of consciousness in abeyance, and the corresponding relaxation upon an assumed righteousness.

Now we have to ask another question: assuming that sincerity is difficult for anyone to achieve, was it—according to Leavis—peculiarly difficult for Eliot? The question is important because it marks the transition in Leavis between a criticism of Eliot mainly appreciative and a criticism mainly diagnostic. It is in his account of Eliot's achievement of sincerity and the special impediments to its achievement in his case, as well as the particularly acute temptation to leave it unattained by taking it for granted and relapsing into the more genially accepting merits, that Leavis becomes a different kind of reader and takes the risk of a flagrant impurity of interest. His general argument in the later essays is that Eliot suffered from an appalling self-division; he was, Leavis says in *The Living Principle,* "a major poet who had disabling inner contradictions to struggle against." What precisely those contradictions were Leavis does not specify. To give a discursive account of them would entail removing from them the qualifications that Leavis brings to bear, each in its own place: the diagnosis does not allow for paraphrase. At the same time, to avoid suggesting the nature of Eliot's alleged disability would mean indulgence in mystification.

It would be absurdly simple to regard Leavis as saying that Eliot's early poems are a technique for sincerity, a technique for the attainment of a difficult sincerity, and that the later poems give up the struggle and settle for the minor amenities. If that were the asserted case, the later poems would not call for Leavis's incessant reading and the incessant wrestling that constitutes the reading. But the sentence may stand as a cartoon of Leavis's argument. His indictment, because it amounts to nothing less, is not in itself especially original: much of the comment elicited from other critics by *The Cocktail Party* took the same direction. What distinguishes Leavis's engagement with the later poems is that his essays are themselves a technique for sincerity, and that the relation between assertion and qualification, dismissal and appreciation, is such that the "case" of Eliot, as Leavis approaches it, emerges as far more elusive than any account of the mere gist of it can imply.

Leavis's argument is that the force engaged in Eliot's work, "the great drive behind his creativity," is desperation. The desperation is a revulsion from life, an obsessive sense of "the unreality, the unlivingness, of life in time." Leavis goes on to say, using a phrase no other critic would risk using, that "the ultimate really real that Eliot seeks in *Four Quartets* is eternal reality, and *that* he can do little, directly, to characterize." Eliot can't even believe that his own creative power has representative validity, that it guarantees a distinctively human power available at large. What he feels, rather, is that each of us is in a prison of self, a condition formally described in philosophic terms by F. H. Bradley's *Appearance and Reality*. Eliot's assertion of human abjectness and nullity—I am still using Leavis's terms—made it impossible for him to have more than a limited awareness of other people, or to conceive of any possibilities which might be exemplified by human love. As a dismal result, he could represent human value only as involving the transcendence of time; just as he could represent consciousness only in opposition to flesh, spirit only in opposition to body. In the most extreme form of these obsessions an apparent failure of courage was involved; and also, as a poet, a failure to understand, as Blake understood, that a poet gains his strength from the language, which is not his own creation but a great collaborative venture of generations. Of course there is the individual talent, if for no other reason—though there is other reason—than that "human life lives only in individuals." But the English language is more than an instrument; it is the living form of the relation between the poet and everyone who has preceded him in a common enterprise. Eliot's failure to understand his participation in this venture Leavis attributed to his being an American, a disability just as grave as the other relevant disability—from which Yeats and Joyce suffered—that of being an Irishman. Eliot was "a fellow-countryman of Ezra Pound, and shared the American blankness, the inability to recognize the evidence—the fact—of the kind of human world that has vanished." In his later work, so Leavis's argument runs, Eliot intermittently maintained the effort to attain a difficult sincerity, but just as often he settled upon the easy acceptability of a merely public and social world to which his later plays offer wretchedly servile deference.

I shall postpone the question of the justice of Leavis's mainly diagnostic judgement of the later Eliot. If there is one "moment" in Eliot's development which, more than another, marks the crisis in Leavis's account of it, it comes with "Burnt Norton" (1935) and the interval between that poem and its ramifications both in *The Family Reunion* (1939) and the three later Quartets: "East Coker" (March 1940), "The Dry Salvages" (February 1941), and "Little Gidding" (October 1942). The feeling of nullity and pointlessness, of guilt Original and Actual, took possession not only of Harry Monchensey in the play, but of Eliot himself in the composition of the play and the later Quartets. Between *The Family Reunion* and *The Cocktail Party* he participated in a social world on terms that could not have satisfied the author of "Gerontion" and "Marina." In the Quartets, the effort to achieve a difficult sincerity seemed intermittently the only effort worth making, and at other moments, too arduous to be faced. *Four Quartets* calls, therefore, for a kind of reading in which, moment by moment, the emphasis must fall upon appreciation or dismissal, delighted recognition or the disappointment attendant upon the spectacle of courage having lapsed. I shall give an example of each.

Leavis quotes, in his account of "East Coker," the passage about the light falling over the field:

> *Now the light falls*
> *Across the open field, leaving the deep lane*
> *Shuttered with branches, dark in the afternoon,*
> *Where you lean against a bank while a van passes,*
> *And the deep lane insists on the direction*
> *Into the village, in the electric heat*
> *Hypnotised.*

Then he comments:

> The major quality of the poet is manifest in the vivid completeness of the immediacy. This, we can't fail to recognise, is a creative master of the English language; only poetic genius could do this with words. The critical recognition is spontaneous; it is an essential element in the recreative response—that which pays one's proper tribute to the compelling felicity. We feel the rhythmic livingness as, in the particular rightnesses, inseparable from the felicities of evoked concreteness and actuality. So in

> > *leaving the deep lane*
> > *Shuttered with branches, dark in the afternoon,*

> the "shuttered" takes inevitably the right emphasis, and the ensuing phrase leaves the lane shuttered (as if it were an airless room) in contrast to the open field across which the light falls—the "deep lane" which

> *insists on the direction*
> *Into the village, in the electric heat*
> *Hypnotised.*

We recognise immediately that "insists" does more than tell us that the lane winds. "Electric heat" recalls the "autumn heat" and the "vibrant air" of the rose-garden, but the suggested imminence is different. What we get is indeed a transition from the "now" of present actuality, but it is not to the eternal or transcendent, but to the evocation of an imagined actuality now long dead ...

I have quoted that passage mainly to show that Leavis's rejection of the later Eliot, if we have to call it that, goes along with a reading so sustained and, in much of its detail, so appreciative, that while speaking of rejection we know the word is inadequate. We are also keeping in mind the fact that Leavis's method, that of comparison and contrast from which relative judgements are to ensue, is quite different from the neutral receptivities and communications favoured by the Richards of *Practical Criticism.* Leavis pays a high price for comparative judgement: it often appears that he can praise one writer only by depreciating another. The best has the drastic duty of displacing the good. When he mentions Hardy and Yeats, it is invariably to say that Eliot is greater than either. In *For Continuity* the Joyce of *Work in Progress* is rebuked by the example of Lawrence. In *New Bearings* Eliot is the central modern poet, a far greater writer than Hopkins or Pound, the only other poets given sustained consideration. In the later books Eliot is largely displaced or, as Leavis tended to say, "placed" by comparison with Blake and Lawrence. In *Anna Karenina and Other Essays* Lawrence is placed, far more severely than a reader of Leavis would have expected, by comparison with Tolstoy.

When Eliot is in question, Leavis's recourse to Blake and Lawrence is a critical shorthand; the reader soon learns what these names signify and the values they enforce. It is also to the point that during the years in which Leavis was renewing his early sense of Lawrence's greatness, he was also convicting Eliot of a complete incapacity to read Lawrence, an incapacity demonstrated in *After Strange Gods* and *Revelation,* where Eliot had the effrontery to contrast Lawrence with Irving Babbitt, to Babbitt's advantage as "by nature an educated man." Again it is Lawrence who is always available to Leavis when he has to point to a disability in Eliot's criticism. In *The*

Common Pursuit, Leavis says that "Lawrence stood for life, and shows, in his criticism, tossed off as it was, for the most part, in the most marginal way, an extraordinarily quick and sure sense for the difference between that which makes for life and that which makes against it." For Leavis, Lawrence is always present to characterize Eliot's deep recoil against life, just as Blake is called upon to exert the same critical pressure against Swift. It is particularly the Lawrence of *Studies in Classic American Literature* and the *Study of Thomas Hardy* who directs Leavis to the discriminations and rejections he brings to bear, in *The Living Principle,* on *Four Quartets.* The climax of that tendentious relation is represented by Leavis's saying: "My own tribute to Eliot's genius must be a profoundly convinced 'No.' "

It is time to ask whether the reading that issues in the "No" is a fair reading or one vitiated by an impurity of interest. When Leavis says, in *The Living Principle,* that "the ultimate really real that Eliot seeks in *Four Quartets* is eternal reality, and *that* he can do little, directly, to characterize," isn't it reasonable to focus upon that "directly" and protest that of course eternal reality can't be directly characterized? The object of such a desire can't be represented: analogies and figures can only point in its presumed direction. Eternal reality is by definition that which can't be characterized, least of all "directly," and indirectly only by representing the desire for it and never its fulfilment. Hasn't Eliot done much, in *Four Quartets,* to characterize not indeed eternal reality but the search for it, and the feeling of absence and desolation which provokes the desire and keeps it always unappeased? We believe in it, after all, on the strength and power of the seeking rather than on some produced evidence, even if such could be offered, of its possession. Leavis's argument smacks of the humanist challenge to the religious believer requiring him to show cause, visibly inescapable evidence, so that faith may be admitted only when it is rendered indistinguishable from sensory recognition. Again, when Leavis maintains that Eliot "insists on the unreality, the unlivingness, of life in time," it is fair to ask: isn't the possibility of redeeming the time a constant preoccupation of Eliot's poetry from "Ash Wednesday" to "Little Gidding"? One might point for evidence to the third movement of "Little Gidding," the invocation to memory, and the presentation of history as both servitude and freedom. It is true that disgust, and especially self-disgust, is a powerful force in Eliot's poetry, but even this, alienating as it strikes us as being, has its meaning only in relation to the facile amenities and complacencies which it opposes in Eliot as in other people. It is a counterstatement rather than a statement.

There is a passage in Eliot's essay on Pascal which bears upon these issues:

> It is recognised in Christian theology—and indeed on a lower plane it is recognised by all men in affairs of daily life—that free-will of the natural effort and ability of the individual man and also supernatural *grace,* a gift accorded we know not quite how, are both required, in co-operation, for salvation. Though numerous theologians have set their wits at the problem, it ends in a mystery which we can perceive but not finally decipher. At least, it is obvious that, like any doctrine, a slight excess or deviation to one side or the other will precipitate a heresy. The Pelagians, who were refuted by St. Augustine, emphasized the efficacy of human effort and belittled the importance of supernatural grace. The Calvinists emphasized the degradation of man through Original Sin, and considered mankind so corrupt that the will was of no avail; and thus fell into the doctrine of predestination.

Eliot then remarks that "heresies are never antiquated, because they forever assume new forms":

> For instance, the insistence upon good works and "service" which is preached from many quarters, or the simple faith that anyone who lives a good and useful life need have no "morbid" anxieties about salvation, is a form of Pelagianism.

You can see that I am proposing, with whatever risk of outrage, to place Leavis and Eliot in this context, and to understand the dispute between them in these terms. Eliot goes on to say:

> A moment of Jansenism may naturally take place, and take place rightly, in the individual; particularly in the life of a man of great and intense intellectual powers, who cannot avoid seeing through human beings and observing the vanity of their thoughts and of their avocations, their dishonesty and self-deception, the insincerity of their emotions, their cowardice, the pettiness of their real ambitions. Actually, considering that much greater maturity is required for

these qualities than for any mathematical or scientific greatness, how easily (Pascal's) brooding on *the misery of man without God* might have encouraged in him the sin of spiritual pride, the *concupiscence de l'esprit:* and how fast a hold he has of humility!

It is clear that Eliot in those sentences is touching upon issues at least as close to his own intellectual and spiritual temper as to Pascal's: the passage has little of the character of a disinterested summary turned upon an object at every point separate from the speaker. We have also Leavis's word "sincerity" through its opposite, "the insincerity of their emotions," and we have Eliot's word of culminative force in the Quartets, "humility." I suggest that we have, too, the real ground of the dispute: the misery of man without God. Eliot believes that human misery is categorical, an irrefutable consequence of man's being without God. Leavis believes that human misery, or such misery as actually exists, is a consequence of man's having removed himself from his own powers and creative possibilities, a removal the more desperate when its motive is wilfulness or a recoil from life itself. Leavis also believes that the removal is commonly effected by forces at large in society, forces which therefore have to be countered and defeated, having first been named: the act of critical intelligence which engages in this effort is the same as the force of discrimination, in the act of reading, by which a poet's vanities, equivocations, and revulsions are recognized for what they are.

The last passage I have to quote from the essay on Pascal bears even more directly upon the dispute:

> Capital, for instance, is (Pascal's) analysis of the *three orders:* the order of nature, the order of mind, and the order of charity. These three are *discontinuous;* the higher is not implicit in the lower as in an evolutionary doctrine it would be.

Leavis's, this is the time to say, is precisely an evolutionary doctrine, as he makes explicit in his commentary on "The Dry Salvages" in *The Living Principle.* The commentary defends the axioms of development and evolution against Eliot's dismissal of them in the poem, and it calls upon the philosophers Alexander, Whitehead, Polanyi, and Collingwood to endorse the position. Leavis's attitude is, although he does not use either Pascal's terms or Eliot's, that since the order of nature developed into the order of mind, it is an insult to posit discontinuity between them; and it is a further insult to deny continuity of development between the order of mind and the order of charity. He refuses to concede to Eliot sole possession of the vocabulary of religion. He says that "unless it has a religious quality, the sense of human responsibility can't be adequate to the plight of the world that so desperately needs it—won't, in fact, be what is needed." But you'll notice that the reference to "a religious quality," a quality of reach and development, is, from the point of view of a convinced religious believer, merely the claim to enlightenment a humanist regularly makes; it does not require him to believe in anything but his own powers.

It would not be fair to either party in the dispute to say that Eliot's temper is Jansenist and Leavis's Pelagianist, but it would be reasonable to indicate, by reference to these names and tempers, the tendency dominant in each case. The fact that the tendency, again in each case, is at least intermittently qualified by scruples developed within its own conscientiousness complicates the argument but does not refute it. If it is true, even in its mere tendency, the question now arises: is there any point, given such a case as Leavis's, in alluding to purity of interest in the reader, or in saying that when we judge poetry it is as poetry we must judge it and not as another thing? The dispute between the two men is, to put it directly, a dispute about values and belief. It is no use saying that poet and reader meet on the ground of language, the particular use of language in the particular poem, and that only a fanatic would drive the question of language as far as Leavis has driven it in his account of *Four Quartets*. There is no official limit; no consideration of decorum tells a reader where, in such a transaction, it behooves him to stop. But it is odd, in fact, that Leavis's account of, say, "Little Gidding" does not examine the use of language in that poem, finding it disabled. In his commentary on the first section he is so affronted by Eliot's reference to "pentecostal fire" that he directs his affront upon Eliot's metaphorical procedure, that of transferring evoked finite splendour "to the postulated transcendental apprehension," the transference being, he says, "nothing more than mere assertion." It is impossible to reconcile Leavis's procedure in this instance with a definition of literary criticism which would prescribe limits upon its range of reference or indicate that at some point such a criticism has become something else.

What Leavis objects to in Eliot's later poetry is represented by the use of the word "pattern" in "Burnt Norton," a word not at all redeemed in that use by being accompanied by the word "form" and the elaborate presentation of the Chinese jar which "still / Moves perpetually in its stillness." The word "pattern" is offensive to Leavis because it makes a claim upon finality; it indicates a value upon which conviction may rest. The same consideration in Leavis's account of Hopkins's poetry is deemed to be a comparable scandal: his concern with pattern in the poems Leavis takes to be related to "a certain restriction in the nourishing interests" behind the poetry. But it is for once an enjoyable irony that it is Eliot whom Leavis calls upon to indicate that a poetry may be religious without incurring the limiting judgement of being called devotional. It is deemed a disability rather than a merit that "for Hopkins the truths are *there,* simply and irresistibly demanding allegiance." Hopkins's habit, therefore, is "utterly remote from Eliot's extreme discipline of continence in respect of affirmation—the discipline involving that constructive avoidance of the conceptual currency which has its exposition in 'Burnt Norton.' " These sentences appeared in an essay on Hopkins—it is reprinted in *The Common Pursuit*—dated 1944, when the four Quartets were already in print: evidently Leavis's sense of them, in this crucial respect, had not yet committed itself to finding that in them the extreme discipline of continence in respect of affirmation had been at least partly abandoned.

We may offer a general comment at this point. Leavis's mind, invariably alert, was provoked to diagnostic action whenever in reading it came upon a word that proclaimed a conviction already formed or a truth already accepted, especially if the conviction, once challenged, were to offer as evidence a doctrine, a dogma, or any other impersonal form of certitude. Recall, for instance, with what limiting force Leavis refers to "ritual," "apparatus," and "order" in the essay on Milton's verse in *Revaluation,* or the dismissive references to Yeats's ostensibly philosophic system or his "addiction," as indicated by *A Vision* and "Phases of the Moon" (the strictures appear most sharply in *Lectures in America*). Leavis's relation to Marxism is sufficiently rendered by the dismissive references, in *The Common Pursuit,* to the thirties as "the Marxizing decade." And since I have associated him with a position ultimately indistinguishable from Humanism, it is only fair to recall the force with which he repudiated both Humanism and Enlightenment. In *Revaluation* he refers to "the kind of intellectual bent that produces Humanism—that takes satisfaction in inertly orthodox generalities." The case is simple:

Leavis repudiates any claim that offers to provide certitude or to entice the reader into the security of its satisfaction.

We can now begin to understand the peculiarly personal animus which Leavis directs not indeed upon Eliot himself or even upon the author of *Four Quartets,* but upon the motives in Eliot which make him content, at least for the moment, with convictions represented by "form" and "pattern." These words are taken to mean not that the search for a difficult sincerity has been successful but that it has failed, and that the poet is content to mistake his failure for a desperately won success. But it is fair to ask: wouldn't any declared conviction on Eliot's part be, by definition, premature; and wouldn't its prematurity mean that the search for it was always and already compromised? When Eliot, with Pascal in mind, appeals to an order of grace beyond the orders available to people through their innate faculties, and when he asserts that the higher order is not implicit in the lower orders or continuous with them, Leavis takes the assertion as an insult, and points to Blake to show the enormity of the scandal.

But Blake, heroic as he is to Leavis, is not enough. Or rather, in one aspect he is too much. Leavis reveres virtually everything in Blake except his Jerusalem, his preoccupation with a final cause. There is a powerful paragraph in the Introduction to *Nor Shall My Sword* in which Leavis says that while Blake could represent "human creativity in the fallen human condition as working creatively though unpossessed of the vision of any justifying ultimate end," he could not, "with the Bible, Swedenborg, Boehme and Milton behind him, help feeling that he must himself aspire to a certitude and clarity of such vision." This, he continues, "is the aspect of Blake to which Lawrence's sharp comment applies: Blake is committed to knowing where knowing is impossible."

Clearly, in Lawrence as in Leavis, we are dealing not with purity of interest but with a criticism in every emphasis diagnostic. But we can now qualify our argument. Many of Leavis's strategies are indeed those of Humanist rhetoric, but the sensibility at work in him is that of a great Nonconformist. It is against Eliot's Anglicanism, finally, and against the poetry in its Anglican mode of conviction that Leavis directs his Nonconformist fury. We come back to that sentence: "My own tribute to Eliot's genius must be a profoundly convinced 'No.'" There is no official name for the kind of criticism or the kind of reading which issues almost inevitably in such a sentence; its fervour arises from passions that dominated English life for the first time in the seventeenth century. There is deep appropriateness in the fact that Leavis's imagination, like Eliot's, was first provoked by the literature of the seventeenth century—Pascal's century as much as Donne's—and that Leavis never gave up the sense, as vigorous in Eliot as in Whitehead, that everything since that century has been a footnote to its text. When Leavis presents the issue of modern literature as a struggle between Lawrence and Eliot, the fury in his words has its provenance not in modern criticism but in the seventeenth-century controversies about belief and atheism, natural reason, and revelation.

It is no contradiction to say, then, that there were feelings and motives in Leavis himself which could be dealt with only by diagnosing them in Eliot, and that correspondingly Lawrence meant to Leavis a peculiarly personal and creative possibility. Leavis's engagement with these writers was such as to remind us of Henry James's remark about Flaubert, that "he felt of his vocation almost nothing but the difficulty." Leavis sometimes found it possible to be easy and mischievous, especially when he was disputing with a distinguished scholar, Dr. Tillyard or Sir Herbert Grierson. But the issues he faced in Eliot and Lawrence did not allow for a light touch: nothing less than his own creative life was at stake.

Finally we have to ask: why was Leavis's relation to certitude—the critic himself spending his entire life enforcing his own forms of it—so hostile? Or rather: why, as a reader, does he find the search for certitude a reliable sign of seriousness in a writer, and yet find the slightest claim to its possession a scandal? He approves the search only upon the promise that it must fail.

There is a passage in Italo Svevo's novel *Confessions of Zeno* where Zeno, thinking himself in love with Ada, wants to learn whether or not she is lost to him:

> If I learned, and I could only learn it from Giovanni, that Ada was definitely lost to me, at least I should no longer have to contend with time, which would then flow peacefully on without my having to urge it forward. Something settled is always calm because it is dissociated from time.

Doesn't this bear upon Leavis's relation to certitude? If certitude is calm because it is dissociated from time, the language which lays a claim upon certitude must aspire to transcend not only time but its own temporal, historical, and evolutionary character. Such a language would insist upon poetic access, when Eliot is in question, to a Christian paradise, more remote from time than Blake's Jerusalem. Leavis's own language, it is worthwhile saying, is equally determined to remain within the dimension of time; his syntax, which many readers have hastily mistaken for a vehicle of bad writing, is determined to prevent the reader from escaping into any form of transcendence. Leavis's language is impassioned in its advocacy of time, process, and development. The challenge he feels in the later Eliot is that of relegating such a language to the merely provisional. Leavis is content only with those dissociations from time which are, in fact, temporal; memory is the power which gives us access to them. But he resents the visionary ambition which would direct us beyond time altogether, for the possession of any certitude worth having.

From *Raritan,* Vol. I, No. I (Summer 1981).

RAYMOND WILLIAMS

I'll talk mostly about *Towards* 2000, so I should give a brief account of *Writing in Society* and *Radical Earnestness* to begin with. *Radical Earnestness* is a brisk survey of a "tradition of thought," a "mode of feeling," which Fred Inglis identifies as English and, in a vague sense, socialist. The tradition is characterized by "a habit of recourse to concrete examples in argument, a calm refusal of formal metaphysics, an unexamined criticism of 'over-abstraction' (which means other people's abstractions), and a general preference for non-systematised or pluralist theories of political life." The writers Inglis presents under this rubric are William Morris, T. H. Green, John Maynard Keynes, R. G. Collingwood, F. R. Leavis, George Orwell, Adrian Stokes, Tony Crosland—as he calls him— Richard Titmuss, Richard Hoggart, Raymond Williams, John Berger, E. P. Thompson, and Isaiah Berlin. If you need a stereotype of the English socialist, you may as well take this one as any other, though it's hard to do any worthwhile thinking so long as you burden yourself with such a thing. I infer from Inglis's reference to "the chic notation of the Parisian deconstructionists" and from a footnote citing Jacques Derrida's *Grammatology* that radical earnestness is what he claims for the Englishness of his English socialist tradition, a quality of mind or character consistent with a national commitment to roast beef.

In the chapter on Hoggart, Williams, and the *New Left Review,* Inglis nominates Williams as "a plausible candidate" for "a little decorous hero-worship," "for leading hero of the years in which the forward march of consumer individualist values halted itself at the cliff edge, and the call for different, new, vastly more mutual, altruistic, and less destructive values-with-practices became paramount." Who called, and how the call became paramount, Inglis doesn't say. In the event, he presents Williams as a stout-hearted man, as decent as they come, but politically naïve. On occasions, he says, Williams "seems to flinch from acknowledging the deadly and disgusting things done in the names of both Marxism and Communism, the hateful guilt borne by some socialist intellectuals, including heroes such as Liebknecht and Rosa Luxemburg, Benjamin and Brecht, for their lying and distortions wittingly performed in the names of freedom and the masses." I have curtailed the quotation, but the gist of it is that if you can believe in "actually existing socialism," you can swallow anything. Inglis ends the account of Williams with the obligatory applause, but I'm left feeling that if he called me a hero I'd say: "Thanks, I suppose."

Writing in Society is a selection of the essays, lectures, and occasional interventions Williams has published over the past decade or so; a few pieces go back much further, one of them a piece of verse he didn't choose to publish twenty-seven years ago. Some of them are worked up from university courses, mostly courses in drama. The sturdiest are continuous with the books in which Williams has turned mid-nineteenth-century English fiction, the novels arising from the experience of industrial life, into an academic genre. Three lectures reflect upon "Cambridge English" and its vicissitudes. Then there are larger meditations on region and class in the English novel. The essay I like best is a dogged effort to make sense of *Hard Times* and of the "two incompatible ideological positions" it articulates: "first, that environment influences and in some sense determines character; second, that some virtues and vices are original and both triumph over and in some cases can change any environment." Williams argues that the incompatibility, which could easily lapse into muddle, is resolved not in the novel but in the reader, in "the production of a general reader who is also a generalised response." I'm not sure how a particular reader can become, in Williams's sense, a general reader, though I think an adequate theory of the imagination would allow for the production of sympathies and recognitions which would hold rival attitudes simultaneously in the mind. A theory of the imagination is not, I know, Williams's business; he would regard such a theory as playing into the hands of idealists, his chosen enemies in the fight for "cultural materialism."

Towards 2000 is the second attempt he has made to review his *The Long Revolution* (1961) and refine its arguments. The first was *Politics and Letters* (1979), a big book of specific questions posed by Perry Anderson, Anthony Barnett, and Francis Mulhern, members of the editorial committee of the *New Left Review;* and of answers, rarely as specific or pointed, offered by Williams. The second section of *Politics and Letters* includes detailed criticism of *The Long Revolution* and Williams's response to the various points made. In *Towards* 2000 he reprints the third part of *The Long Revolution,* the chapter called "Britain in the 1960s," silently deleting, so far as I have noted, only one passage—two long sentences about the Tory victory in the 1959 election. The rest of *Towards* 2000 is a reconsideration of "Britain in the 1960s," in the light, if that is what it is, of the past twenty years.

The main difference between *Politics and Letters* and *Towards* 2000 is that Williams was far more dashing and radical in 1979 than he is now. Age? Hardly. There isn't much difference between fifty-eight and sixty-two, I hope. I think there's a simpler reason—that Williams, under some pressure from those young Turks of NLR, wanted to show them that he was as tough a man as ever was. In any case, his positions on race, the nullity of Parliament, nationalism in Wales and Scotland, and several other questions, were far more truculent and radical than anything in *Towards* 2000. For instance: the lesson he learned from the Labour government that came to office in 1966, he told the *NLR* trio, was "the end of the notion of parliament as the principal, central agency for social change." There's nothing like that lesson on view in *Towards* 2000, though there are several proposals for change in the system of elections. In the same *NLR* conversation Williams told his friends that the notion of parliamentary representation "now seems to me in its common ideological form fundamentally hostile to democracy." He had said much the same thing in *Keywords* (1976), in the entry on Democracy, distinguishing between the socialist and the liberal traditions and concluding that these two conceptions—democracy as popular power, a state in which the interests of the majority are paramount and are controlled by the majority, and democracy as a system featuring openness of election and free argument— "in their extreme forms, now confront each other as enemies." The theme is taken up again in *Towards* 2000, where there is an elaborate account of "representation," leading to a discrimination between "bourgeois democracy" and "socialist democracy." But the account is far more muted than the one in *Politics and Letters.* Arguing with himself, Williams is a mild disputant.

But the main difficulty with *Towards* 2000, among many difficulties nearly equal, is that Williams doesn't know where to stand: the book is the tragedy of a man who can't any longer make up his mind. His relation to Marxism is heretical, except for the sentiment that keeps him to some degree in the fold. He doesn't even accept the Marxist vocabulary of base and superstructure, and while he makes the standard comments on "the confusions of late-bourgeois subjectivism," his own sentences feature, by appeal to "experience," a structure of feeling not clearly different from subjectivism. He seems to think, in his *NLR* moments, that there is some necessary contradiction between private and social experience, or that a respect for privacy sends you straight to "the Me Generation" and "solipsism." But at other times he speaks in terms which a bourgeois liberal would find entirely acceptable.

The same confusion arises at nearly every fundamental point. Is the system of "late capitalism" omnivorous or not? When Williams gets worked up on "the coercive power of the capitalist state," it seems that nothing, no act or purpose, can elude the capitalist determination. But in more subdued moments he thinks that "when people are living under a dominant system, you both get alternative sources of social experience in other modes which have survived from the past or are in active opposition to the system, and you seem to get other impulses which have not been produced by the known calculus of forces." I have never doubted the possibility of those "other impulses," and while I'm delighted to find Williams acknowledging them and the fact that the known calculus of forces doesn't account for them, I think the concession makes nonsense of the cultural materialism he avows. I don't see any evidence, though, that Williams has questioned the adequacy of materialism in its bearing—or rather, the bearing he gives it—upon the acts and processes which constitute cultural life. "Material" is just as much a mystification as "spiritual" is, if a claim to account for, say, a work of art is in question. But "spiritual" doesn't make this claim; "material" does, and the claim is specious.

It is also a contradiction that in *Marxism and Literature* Williams interprets the Saussurian distinction between *langue* and *parole* as yet another instance of the ubiquitous bourgeois opposition between society and the individual. Nothing in Saussure warrants this conclusion. Saussure knew as clearly as Williams does that a language is the result of—I quote Williams's version in *Politics and Letters*—"the activities of real people in social relationships, including individuals not simply as products of the society but in a precise dialectical relation both producing and being produced by it." Has anyone ever doubted this, or denied it? It is perfectly compatible with Saussure's account of *langue* and *parole* and of the synchronic and the diachronic aspects of language.

But why does Williams want to turn these straightforward matters into a continuous horror show? *Towards* 2000 is constantly talking about community, settlement, and—Williams's favourite sentiment—bonding, but the book feeds upon hostility. Williams is indeed a kind, unwounding man, but his writing seems to crave the dynamics of antagonism. *Towards* 2000 doesn't attack anyone by name, but it disposes its entire discourse by setting up anonymous forces in full fighting kit. The fact that the forces are invariably abstract doesn't alter the fact that Williams's setting them up for combat is itself an act of violence. I'm reminded of an essay in which Emmanuel Levinas says that Hegel's praise of the sense of sight for fostering an ungrasping sense of life is specious: because sight, in Hegel's account of it, is the mere abstraction of seeing. The solitude of a mute glance upon the object, while it can be represented as the fine withholding of desire and possessiveness, is an act of violence because it doesn't respect the Other sufficiently to acknowledge its face. Williams's writing is, in this rather occult respect, violent. In *Writing in Society* he criticizes Shaw's challenging style, in the Preface to *Back to Methuselah,* on the grounds that it "comes not only to harden into a party trick, but takes over, as a whole way of experiencing others and the world, in which people and objects shrink to fixed appearances, and nothing is left but, playing entertainingly over them, a single confident voice."

Now nobody has ever accused Williams of sending his mind to play over its own evidence, or of maintaining a single confident voice: but I find it dismal that he is so ready to turn people into forces, and forces into monsters. Discrimination can't survive the automatic form of attention. To give an example: I don't spend much time defending the virtue of the International Monetary Fund or the World Bank, but it is absurd and undiscriminating for Williams to say, in *Towards* 2000, that "many of the most effective international forms—not only the multinational corporations but also the World Bank and the International Monetary Fund—are in effect wholly irresponsible to any full actual societies; indeed it is often their specific business to override them." If Williams can square that charge with the IMF's recent dealings with Brazil and Mexico, he can square anything with anything. I'm afraid it's at least as true of him as of Shaw that in his style "people and objects shrink to fixed appearances."

The argument of *Towards* 2000 hasn't developed far beyond *The Long Revolution.* In the earlier book Williams favoured general planning, elections every two years and on fixed dates, and more participation in the processes of government. Capitalism was the only enemy. He also warned his readers against "technological determinism" and "cultural pessimism." In *Towards* 2000 he renews his commitment to these values, and emphasizes the necessity of developing "new kinds of communal, co-operative and collective institutions." The three minimum conditions "for Britain to become a modern parliamentary democracy," he says, are "the transfer of legal sovereignty to the people or to their elected parliament"; "abolition of the second chamber now based on heredity and patronage, and its replacement by a differently constituted body, based on election"; and the "adoption of an electoral system which would determine the composition of an elected parliament in terms of the actual distribution of popular votes." I don't think he proposes to get rid of the Monarchy.

The most sustained arguments in *Towards* 2000 favour "the recovery of control of our own production" and "first limiting and then breaking the arbitrary power of capital: increasingly, in practice, of international capital." Small is beautiful, especially in the form of "popular self-management." As in *Politics and Letters,* Williams thinks that you could start with the kind of democracy "previously imagined only for very small communities," and then use the new electronic technologies of communication in administering larger communities. He seems to envisage legislation by some kind of phone-in TV. The object in view is "the direct exercise of popular power."

What these suggestions have to do with keeping people alive till 2000 A.D. is not clear. Williams asks us to think in a wider context, but he has kept his own extraordinarily narrow. He has turned his eyes away from the fact that the lives of people living in a valley in Wales are affected not only by the National Coal Board and the Tory Government but by decisions taken in Brussels, Washington, Moscow, Zurich, and—it has happened, and can happen again—at a meeting of OPEC in some London hotel. I have never thought of Williams as a Little Englander or even a Little Welsher, but his concerns in *Towards* 2000 are extraordinarily parochial. Elections every two years on fixed dates? We'll be lucky if the question even arises.

If it arises—assuming we survive to use those technological marvels to effect legislation—it will not be because of thinking as abstract as Williams's. I can't imagine how Fred Inglis can include Williams in a tradition characterized by "a habit of recourse to concrete examples in argument." *Towards* 2000 is the most unconcrete, unspecific, undocumented book I have read in years. Let me give two examples. One: in the chapter "Culture and Technology" Williams writes about "the two faces of 'modernism,'" but he doesn't put a name on either of them. He refers to "those innovative forms which destabilised the fixed forms of an earlier period of bourgeois society, but which were then in their turn stabilised as the most reductive versions of human existence in the whole of cultural history." This sentence is like the assertions university teachers set as examination questions, except that those are usually followed by the instruction: "Discuss, giving examples to clarify your argument." Williams doesn't refer to a single work, either of the innovative or the debased form. I assume he means, for the innovative, Joyce, Eliot, maybe Beckett, Schönberg, Picasso: but why doesn't he say what works he has in view? One generalization leads to another. "Apparently simple kinds of adventure and mystery have been transformed and newly marketed in highly specific representations of crime, espionage, intrigue and dislocation, mediating the deep assumptions of habitual competitive violence, deception, and role-playing, loss of identity, and relationships as temporary and destructive." Such as what? *To Russia with Love, The Sweeney,* the several *Godfather*s, 2001, *Looking for Mr. Goodbar*?

Two: in a chapter called "War: The Last Enemy" Williams distinguishes between deterrence as a military strategy—which he accepts—and deterrence as ideology, which he repudiates. But the only example he gives of deterrence as ideology is American anti-Communism. He doesn't even mention the Russian recourse to deterrence as ideology. Does he seriously think that the Russian buildup of its nuclear arsenal since the ABM treaty of 1972, and the Russian BMD programme—two to three times larger than the American one—has been purely for defensive purposes? As for unilateral disarmament, he doesn't think Britain should "go it alone"—

indeed he is severe on "the relatively unfocused demand for 'unilateral renunciation.' " "Thus in Europe," he says, "we should consistently advance European rather than British unilateralist arguments and objectives." But he opposes—he wrote this chapter, I assume, a year or so ago—the siting of cruise missiles in Britain and the buying of Trident. Fine. But there is not a word of detail, no comment on Germany's position on nuclear defence, nothing on NATO or the Warsaw Pact situation. He blesses the peace movement, the ecology movement, feminism, "an oppositional culture": but again, there is nothing specific. E. P. Thompson has been quoted in the United States recently as saying that the peace movement must be supported even if it fails to press Russia for disarmament, that disarmament of the West is enough. Assuming that Thompson said anything as specific as that, does Williams agree? The last chapter of the book is called "Resources for a Journey of Hope." Williams concedes that the capitalist social order, as he calls it, has done "its main job of implanting a deep assent to capitalism even in a period of its most evident economic failures." Three things are now, from his standpoint, necessary: "First, we have to begin, wherever we can, the long and difficult movement beyond a market economy. Second, we have to begin to shift production towards new governing standards of durability, quality and economy in the use of non-renewable resources. Third, and as a condition of either of the former, we have to move towards new kinds of monetary institutions, placing capital at the service of these new ends." These recommendations seem to me to correspond to unilateral disarmament: they don't take any account of international conditions, or of the fact that Britain is no longer her own master. To call this chapter "Resources for a Journey of Hope" is to disclose how meagre the named resources are, and how implausible, in the terms Williams proposes, the journey is.

Review of *Towards 2000*, by Raymond Williams; *Writing in Society*, by Raymond Williams; and *Radical Earnestness: English Social Theory, 1880–1980*, by Fred Inglis. From *The London Review of Books*, February 15, 1984.

CHATTERTON

Peter Ackroyd has written a superb novel—I call it a novel for want of a better word—about the poet Thomas Chatterton.

According to the standard accounts, Chatterton was born in Bristol on November 20, 1752, three months after his father's death. Educated at Colston's Charity-School, he occupied his mind with history, especially the history of the Church of St. Mary Redcliffe, where his father had worked as a chorister. When his mother gave him a few scraps of manuscript found in the muniment room of the church, he started writing poems about the history and lore of Bristol. When he was fifteen or sixteen, he invented a fifteenth-century poet, Thomas Rowley, and a poetic style archaic enough to pass for Rowley's. At the age of seventeen, Chatterton went to London to seek his fortune. He wrote lyrics, elegies, lampoons, and satires, but he could not make a living. Broken by poverty and neglect, he killed himself by swallowing arsenic on August 24, 1770.

No collection of Chatterton's poems was published while he lived. In 1777 Thomas Tyrwhitt edited *Poems, Supposed to have been Written at Bristol by Thomas Rowley and Others*. A second edition followed in the same year, but a third, published in 1778, included "an Appendix, containing some Observations upon the Language of these Poems; Tending to Prove that They were Written not by any Ancient Author but entirely by Thomas Chatterton." Thereafter, Chatterton's short and wretched life was turned into a Romantic emblem of the fate of genius. Keats wrote a sonnet to Chatterton—"Dear child of sorrow—son of misery"—and in "Sleep and Poetry" alluded clearly enough to Chatterton as one of those "lone spirits who could proudly sing / Their youth away, and die." In "Resolution and Independence" Wordsworth invoked the lives of Chatterton and Robert Burns to prove that

> We Poets in our youth begin in gladness;
> But thereof come in the end despondency and madness.

The emblem remained in force throughout the nineteenth century. Oscar Wilde's last lecture, in March 1888, was on Chatterton: "He had the artist's yearning to represent, and if perfect representation seemed to him to demand forgery, he needs must forge: still, this forgery came from the desire of artistic self-effacement."

Like Wilde, Peter Ackroyd has been much taken with Chatterton. In his novel *The Last Testament of Oscar Wilde,* he has Wilde writing:

I was fascinated in those days also by Chatterton, Poe, Baudelaire and by the horror of their fate—when you are young, you play with the fire which you do not understand. The death of Chatterton still brings tears to my eyes—with scarcely bread to feed himself but charged with the knowledge of fame to come, a strange, slight boy who was so prodigal of his genius that he attached the names of others to it.

Like Wilde and Chatterton, too, Mr. Ackroyd is preoccupied with the double or multiple life. In 1979 he published *Dressing Up: Transvestism and Drag, the History of an Obsession.* The fifth chapter deals with "Transvestism as Performance," and the whole book is an attempt to understand the desires, compulsions, and gratifications involved in impersonation. Why do some men dress up as women? Is it necessary that the pretence of being another self be incompletely realized; that is, that it remain recognizable as a pretence? In literature, when Wilde, Yeats, and T. S. Eliot take upon themselves a mask, or several masks, is it necessary that the self-effacement be complete?

Given these interests, Mr. Ackroyd cannot be content to write historical novels, even though many of the events he narrates have indeed happened. He is not interested in discovering "how it was," or even in provoking a sense of historical periods and scenes. In this respect he differs from the Irish novelist John Banville, whose novels *Kepler* and *Doctor Copernicus* give the impression that if we knew more about Kepler and Copernicus, our knowledge would coincide with Banville's imagining. Mr. Ackroyd's novels are historical romances, because they refuse to discriminate between the life a character apparently lived and the other lives he or she performed. Mr. Ackroyd seems to reject the implication, in the historical novel, that people coincide with themselves and settle for the one life which the decorum of historical narration gives them.

In all his books, the people who interest Mr. Ackroyd are those who do not consent to coincide with their official lineaments. In *The Last Testament of Oscar Wilde* he gives more privilege to the experiences which Wilde imagined and proclaimed than to those he merely happened upon and suffered. In *T. S. Eliot: A Life* he makes much of Eliot the impersonator, the ventriloquist, the poet who preserved his voice by pretending that he didn't have one, who kept himself concealed behind the masks of Prufrock and Gerontion. In *Chatterton* the hero is allowed to strut through many roles:

> Of course these [Satires] I composed willingly enough, for I hold that Man in contempt who cannot write to Measure: for the Town and Country I wrote political Satires against all Parties, Whig or Tory, Papist or Methodist; for the Political Register I compos'd meer Squibs, which they took up gladly tho' they did not know the true Range of my Shot; and, knowing my own Skill in the Art of Personation, for the Court and City I set myself to write the memoirs of a sad dog (a gentleman pursewed by Bailiffs), of a malefactor chain'd in Newgate, of an old Relict thirsting for a Man, and of a young ripe Girl about to be pluck'd. And these I related in their own Voices, naturally, as if they were authentick Histories: so that tho' I was young Thomas Chatterton to those I met, I was a very Proteus to those who read my Works.

In *Hawksmoor* (1985) the historically verifiable acts and monuments of the early eighteenth-century architect Hawksmoor are ascribed to one Nicholas Dyer, who then takes on a secret life unknown to history. In the second part of that novel, Hawksmoor is a Scotland Yard detective beset with murders committed near the several churches built by the historical Hawksmoor.

Mr. Ackroyd's procedures differ from those of the dramatic monologue or the historical novel because he links events, real or imagined, by likeness and not by chronology. He sets aside the official privilege of sequence, cause and effect, and produces a simultaneous concatenation of likenesses and differences, regardless of temporal impediments. Wilde is allowed to quote Eliot, without acknowledgement, of course. Simile and metaphor exert their authority over and-then-and-then-and-then. The passive form of similitude is coincidence, gratefully received or imagined; the active form is impersonation, by which a different life is appropriated to one's own.

But we are not accosted with mere ingenuities. Mr. Ackroyd is not interested in conceits. His new novel has itself a multiple life or, to be more precise, four lives at the cost of one. In different ways, it is easy to care about them all. Perhaps one of them, the story of Charles Wychwood —I hear an allusion to Wishwood, the scene of Eliot's play *The Family Reunion,* another tale of double lives—needs our care most urgently. The modern hero of Mr. Ackroyd's novel is a failed, doomed poet, engrossed in a portrait which may be of Chatterton: dated 1802 and signed George Stead, it may or may not be genuine. If it is genuine, it raises the possibility that Chatterton may not have died in 1770 after all. Wychwood bears some resemblance to Eliot in the early years of vulnerability and bad nerves, but the resemblance goes no further. He has a precocious son and a splendid wife named, like Eliot's first wife, Vivien, but unlike that woman in virtually every respect. The second life is Harriet Scrope's: she is an aging popular novelist, an amiably caustic fake, a plagiarist, trying to write her memoirs. Her friend Sarah Tilt is an art historian trying to write a study of death paintings. These two have dealings with a mysterious painting which may or may not be genuine.

The third tale is true. In 1856 Henry Wallis completed his "Death of Chatterton," now one of the most perused paintings in the Tate. His model for the painting was the poet George Meredith, with whose wife Wallis was soon to be illicitly engaged. Mrs. Meredith ran off with Wallis, who abandoned her when she became pregnant. In "Chatterton" Meredith is to be found miming death in a Holborn garret sometime before he writes "Modern Love," a sequence of sonnets on his destroyed marriage.

And finally there is Chatterton, present by way of an autobiographical document which has come into Charles Wychwood's hand; he is present, too, as an unnamed young man who appears to Charles, in a moment of the latter's collapse, and restores him to health.

These four tales are elaborately interlinked. Ingenuity is exerted in ways that leave us free, while the reading lasts, to be unaware of it. Plausibility is not an issue: by disconnecting the orthodoxy of sequence and causation, Mr. Ackroyd makes it seem natural that any event should summon its kin. I have been wondering why Charles Wychwood's story is the one I care most about, and I think it is because he is the only one of the principal characters who can't in the end live a double or a multiple life. Chatterton, a very Proteus to himself as to his readers, has his Rowley. Meredith, abused as we know him to be, has his playacting, his modelling, his Chatterton. Wallis, directing him, says: "No, you look as if you are about to fall asleep. Allow yourself the luxury of death. Go on." "I can endure death," Meredith answers. "It is the representation of death I cannot bear." But he learns to bear it. Harriet Scrope, too, has a double life: engaging in neo-Wildean asperities lavished upon Ms. Tilt, a ready opponent, she appropriates a verbal life quite separate from the mundane chores otherwise her fate. Poor Charles is alone in having only one life to live, one interest to be pursued by.

Chatterton is a wonderfully vivid book, continuously at home to its many lives. Mr. Ackroyd has relaxed a little from the constantly directed pressure of *Hawksmoor*, but there is no loss of vitality. The several styles of the book are most persuasively managed, and even if the memorable bits of dialogue are neo-Wildean flourishes, they are lively enough to live in Wilde's vicinity. An art dealer says to Stew Merk, a forger of his master's paintings: "We will buy your paintings. We will go on with your story, but only on condition that nothing happens next." I balked only once: when Mr. Ackroyd has the same art dealer quote Ackroyd. Examining a fake picture, he remarks: "And the hair is quite wrong. Men's hair was the greatest tragedy of the eighteenth century, with the possible exception of George Stubbs's animal paintings." It was better the first time, in *The Last Testament of Oscar Wilde*. A few sentences are a bit arch, I suppose: "Crocodile tears and crocodile shoes are matching accessories." Elsewhere: "A wig can cover a multitude of gins." But I'm not quarrelling. The book is superb.

From *The New York Times Book Review*, January 17, 1988.

PERMISSIONS ACKNOWLEDGEMENTS

Some essays in this work were originally published in the following publications: *The New York Review of Books, The New York Times Book Review, The Sewanee Review,* and *The New Republic.*

"Raymond Williams" and Shelley's Way" were originally published in *The London Review of Books.*
"Shakespeare in the Sonnets," and "Leavis on Eliot," were originally published in *Raritan.*
"D. H. Lawrence in His Letters" was originally published in *D. H. Lawrence: Novelist, Poet, Prophet* edited by Stephen Spender. Published in 1973 by Weidenfeld & Nicolson, London.

Grateful acknowledgement is made to the following for permission to reprint previously published material:

Harvard University Press: "Emily Brontë: On the Latitude of Interpretation" from *The Interpretation of Narrative: Theory and Practice,* edited by Morton W. Bloomfield. Reprinted by permission.

Kent State University Press: "Sterne, Our Contemporary" from *The Winged Skull: Bicentenary Conference Papers on Laurence Sterne,* edited by Arthur H. Cash and John M. Stedmond, from pages 42–58. Published by The Kent State University Press, Kent, Ohio 44242, 1971. Reprinted by permission.

The New York Times Company: "One Life Was Not Enough" was originally published in *The New York Times Book Review,* January 17, 1988. Copyright © 1988 by *The New York Times Company.* Reprinted by permission.

Routledge & Kegan Paul: "A View of *Mansfield Park*" from *Critical Essays on Jane Austen,* edited by B. C. Southam. Reprinted by permission of Routledge & Kegan Paul, London.

The Sewanee Review: "The Values of Moll Flanders" was originally published in *The Sewanee Review* 71 (Spring 1963). Copyright © 1963 by the University of the South. Reprinted by permission of the editor.

Studies: An Irish Quarterly Journal: "Shakespeare's Rhetoric" from *Studies,* Winter 1958 issue. Reprinted by permission.

The Times Literary Supplement: "Arnold as Critic" from *The Times Literary Supplement,* August 28, 1981 issue. Reprinted by permission.

The University of California Press: "The English Dickens and *Dombey and Son*" from *Dickens Centennial Essays,* edited by Ada Nisbet and Blake Nevius. Copyright © 1971 by The Regents of the University of California. Reprinted by permission.

The University of Chicago Press: "A Reply to Frank Kermode" from *Critical Inquiry,* Vol. 1 (1974): 447–52. Copyright © 1974 by The University of Chicago Press. All rights reserved. Reprinted by permission.

A NOTE ON THE TYPE

The text of this book was set in film in a typeface called Griffo, a camera version of Bembo, the well-known Monotype face. The original cutting of Bembo was made by Francesco Griffo of Bologna only a few years after Columbus discovered America. It was named for Pietro Bembo, the celebrated Renaissance writer and humanist scholar who was made a cardinal and served as secretary to Pope Leo X. Sturdy, well-balanced, and finely proportioned, Bembo is a face of rare beauty. It is, at the same time, extremely legible in all of its sizes.

Composition by Superior Type, Champaign, Illinois

Printed and bound by The Maple-Vail Book Manufacturing Group, Binghamton, New York

Based on a design by Tasha Hall